the secrets of
dance music production

Contents

Chapter one:
Drums and beats
- Tone, transients and tuning
- The kick drum
- The snare drum
- Hats
- Percussion and cymbals
- The theory of rhythm
- Swing and groove
- Drum synthesis
- Layering drums

Chapter three:
Bass and basslines
- Bassline archetypes
- Bass synthesis
- Sub bass
- Mixing bass
- D&B basslines
- Deep house organs and 'cut and paste' bass

Chapter five:
Theory crash course
- Keys and chords
- Chord development
- Chord progressions
- Voicings and inversions
- More chords and progressions
- Melodies and toplines
- Syncopation

Chapter two:
Synthesis and sound design
- Subtractive synthesis
- Other forms of synthesis
- Leads and arps
- Pads and soundscapes
- FX
- Keys
- EDM synths

Chapter four:
Using samples
- Genesis of the sampler
- The old-school vibe
- Stretch and pitch
- Creative sampling
- The art of multi-sampling
- Amen to that: the last word on breaks
- Mixing samples
- Sampling and the law

Chapter six:
Vocals
- Types of vocals
- Recording vocals
- Pre-production
- Production
- Processing different vocal elements
- Vocal FX

Chapter seven:
The studio and its tools

- Acoustic space and ergonomics
- Studio essentials and beyond
- Processors and effects routing
- EQ and tonal enhancers
- Compression and other processing
- Advanced compression
- Modulation effects
- Reverb
- Delay and echo
- Stereo effects
- Saturation, overdrive, distortion and bit-crushing
- Lo-fi production
- Other effects

Chapter eight:
Mixing and mastering

- What makes a great mix?
- The golden rules of mixing
- Arrangement
- Structure
- Transitions and transition FX
- Mixdown approaches and prep
- Initial balance
- Loudness
- Compression in the mix
- EQ in the mix
- Mixing kick and bass
- Ambient effects in the mix
- Ear candy and automation
- Common mix problems and how to fix them
- Mastering: the theory
- Mastering: the process
- Mastering: final duties

>>
Appendices

- 1: Bpm to tempo (ms) chart
- 2: Note to frequency chart: what goes where

>>
Index

Credits

WRITERS
David Felton, Greg Scarth and Chris Barker

ADDITIONAL CONTENT
Oliver Curry, Marc Adamo, Steve Young, Bruce Aisher, Richard Salmon, Israel Medina, Ronan Macdonald, Joe Rossiter, Tim Cant, Declan McGlynn and Paul White

EDITOR
David Felton

DESIGN
Chapman Design

PRINT
Latitude Press

PUBLISHED IN THE UK BY ATTACK MAGAZINE UNDER LICENSE FROM JAKE ISLAND LTD
books@attackmagazine.com
jake.island@gmail.com

Attack Magazine, 8 Prospect House,
Frean St, London, SE16 4AE

WWW.ATTACKMAGAZINE.COM

Seventh edition (revised), June 2020
Sixth edition (revised), November 2019
Fifth edition, August 2019
Fourth edition, May 2018
Third edition (revised), October 2017
Second edition (revised), January 2017
First edition, November 2016

ISBN: 978-0-9564460-3-9

All content © 2020. All rights reserved. No part of this book may be used or reproduced in any manner without the written permission of the publisher.

All musical samples offered for download are © Jake Island Ltd and Attack Magazine, expect those credited to Sample Magic, which are © Sample Magic Ltd. All samples are provided for illustrative purposes only. They may not be used in original compositions without express written permission from the publishers.

ACKNOWLEDGEMENTS
Special thanks to Team Attack, Marc Adamo and Chris Barker for taking this book to the finish line. Shout out too to Cormac from the Electric Piano forum.

PRINTING
This book is printed in China on FSC®certified paper, using wood sourced from well managed forests and other controlled sources.

Getting around

DOWNLOAD WALKTHROUGH ASSETS
www.attackmagazine.com/sod

You can use this book in a number of ways.

On first reading, we recommend taking it old school... start at the beginning and work through to the end. Later chapters refer back to earlier ones and by the time you reach **Chapter eight, Mixdown and mastering**, the collected knowledge from earlier in the book will help you get the most from the final – and most important – chapter.

But we understand that real-life studio sessions rarely allow the luxury of a full sitting.

On these occasions, the book has been written to make dipping in easy. So if you're working on beats, simply head to **Chapter one, Drums and beats**. If you're synthesising your own drum sounds you might supplement that with **Chapter two, Synthesis and sound design**. And when it comes to mixing the beat into a track add **Chapter eight, Mixing and mastering** to your reading list.

You will find occasional overlaps in the book. This is both intentional and inescapable – compression, for example, is given a detailed overview in **Chapter seven: The studio and its tools**, while practical techniques for its application can be found in pretty much every other chapter. In an art form that is so all-encompassing, these overlaps are the nature of the beast.

Unlike its predecessor, this book is genre blind and you'll find pages, beats, sounds, arrangements and techniques dedicated to styles from house to D&B, chillwave to breaks, techno to trance.

Instead of penning each genre and subgenre into its own chapter though, we've scattered references to all genres throughout the book. It felt more natural this way; in the real world genres aren't neatly defined, and some of the best DJ sets encompass music from myriad traditions. And while you'll find references to and walkthroughs for specific genres where applicable, the core techniques for making dance music are almost all genre independent.

A note on DAWs and plugins. You can make release-quality dance music using any mainstream DAW. DAW-wars are boring. And there's a fine line between being a gearslut and having all the gear and no idea. Many of the world's best producers make tracks using little more than a DAW, a laptop and a few soft synths. Technique and talent will take you further than any number of new toys.

So where a walkthrough references a particular plugin or DAW, simply replicate what's happening in your own gear. If you don't know if your DAW offers a particular feature, do a quick online search.

All mp3s and other files related to the walkthroughs can be found on the big URL above. Grab the zip file to bring them to life.

If you have any questions about or suggestions for future updates of this book, you can contact the team on books@attackmagazine.com. We are always pleased to hear from readers.

Introduction

Eight years ago we published *The Secrets of House Music Production.*

It became the go-to resource for a generation of house music producers and a mainstay in studios worldwide.

Ever since then producers of other forms of dance music – from D&B to techno, EDM to chillout – have requested a version for themselves; a more expansive book that covers more dance genres.

Our answer was to launch Attack, a magazine packed with insight and production knowledge. It was a success from day one.

But still the calls for a book continued; this time from Attack readers. *We want the best of Attack distilled into a beautiful manual that we can keep at hand in the studio,* they said. *And we want more; more beats, more technique; more breadth, more depth.*

This is the result of those requests: 300+ pages of essential insight from some of the finest producers and writers working in dance music today.

Not only have we brought on board Attack's award-winning writing and production team, we've also garnered dozens of pro tips from the artists that inspire us, from Justice to Huxley; Tricky to Sigur Rós; Kenny 'Dope' Gonzalez to Breach.

Although Attack regulars may recognise a few walkthroughs, the vast majority of *The Secrets of Dance Music Production* is exclusive new content, with thousands of fresh tips and deep-level chapters on beats, synthesis and mixing.

As such this is a guide not only for those making their first steps into the world of dance music production, but also a worthy companion for studio stalwarts – because there are always new tricks to learn. To showcase the knowledge you'll find close to 100 walkthroughs – all of them accompanied by media to guide your way.

Secrets of Dance has been a labour of love. It's given us an excuse to fine-tune our own studio chops and has brought together a wealth of talent to share the ongoing journey of dance music production. We've always believed in sharing that knowledge to empower those who come next.

Enjoy.

We'll listen for the results in the worldwide dance charts.

Dave Felton
Editor

Chapter one
Drums and beats

Chapter one
Drums and beats

Drums form the DNA strands of dance music.

Aside from the occasional beatless ambient track or DJ tool, it's virtually impossible to find examples of dance tracks that don't lean heavily on drums. The kick drum is to dance music what the electric guitar is to rock and roll: *the* defining sound – a signal of intent.

At this point, most music production books take a well-trod approach to discussing drums. When making rock and guitar-led pop, the standard challenges are fairly straightforward: correct mic placement around a drum kit, tuning of individual drums, maybe the use of click tracks and a bit of amateur psychology to get a good performance out of the drummer.

Dance music is different.

While live recordings of acoustic drums have their place in certain styles of dance – notably disco and chillout (although even here recorded drums are heavily processed) – it's far more common to hear programmed drums, created using a combination of synthesised electronic sounds, one-shot samples and loops.

When crafting beats the options are almost limitless.

Firstly there's the decision over **how to program them** (*page 30*). You can create an entire drum pattern with a single **drum machine** using its **built-in sequencer**. You can meticulously program **MIDI patterns** in a **DAW** (*page 32*). Or you can use **drum pads** or **triggers** to play beats by hand with a more human feel.

There are additional choices when it comes to **choosing the sounds** themselves. You can **synthesise** drums from scratch (*page 46*) or **sample** them – either from old records or commercial sample packs. These raw sounds are then edited and often **layered** (*page 50*) to create unique hybrids. Most powerfully of all, you can embrace all of these techniques – within a single production if you wish.

This chapter examines the plethora of options available to the dance producer and explains some of the principles and techniques which produce the most effective drum sounds and patterns.

There are no strict rules, but there are guidelines and conventions that can help deliver quality results more easily. Don't worry that some seem contradictory. For every rigidly quantised, meticulously processed beat there's an infectiously sloppy groove with lo-fi production values.

It's these aesthetic choices that define the sound of so many dance tracks.

ELEMENTS OF A DRUM KIT

While a drummer has to buy physical drums and cymbals to build their kit, the dance producer's kit is almost always virtual – even though it follows the paradigm of a real kit.

The modern drum kit has been recognisably standardised for the best part of a century: bass drum, snare, one or more tom toms, hi-hat and a selection of cymbals.

Some drummers add more to their kit, but there's a reason the simple setup has endured for so long and through so many stylistic upheavals: *it works*, filling the frequency spectrum and deploying a range of **tones** (*page 10*) that together can be used to create countless grooves.

The mighty **kick drum** (aka the bass drum – *page 14*) occupies the lowest frequency space of all drums. It delivers a punchy sound heavy on low-end energy and has a short, fast attack time with a clicky **transient** (*page 10*) at its start. The kick provides the rhythmic backbone for nearly all dance tracks – the driving pulse upon which all other elements rest.

In some styles of dance music, kick drums play rigid 'four-to-the-floor' patterns (a kick drum at the start of each bar). While sloppy kick drum timing may sound like it could loosen a groove, in practice it rarely works.

HUXLEY

"If you pick the right sounds in the first place you don't have to spend ages layering.

"I don't necessarily like layering sounds. If anything it takes time from making a better track. In certain scenes people are more worried about how technical something is than how the song is.

"I used to be a bit like that but as I've grown up I've mellowed."

Chapter one
Drums and beats

The **clap** and/or **snare** (*page 16*) fulfil similar roles in most dance tracks, providing mid-range contrast to the low thud of the kick. The range of tones and tunings is extensive, from entirely organic samples of real snare drums and human claps to unrealistic but immediately recognisable synthesised sounds from the likes of the Roland TR-808 and 909. Producers with a taste for the unique often **layer** claps and snares together in order to produce hybrid sounds (*page 52*) sculpted to their track.

Hi-hats, or 'hats' (*page 18*), are the most commonly used sounds from the cymbal family, typically propelling the beat forward with a series of regular hits over the course of a bar or upping the groove on the **off-beat** (*page 27*). A real hi-hat has a pedal used to adjust the tightness of the two cymbals. Synth and sampled drums mimic the effect by offering 'closed' and 'open' hats, the latter with a longer decay tail. **Choke** or **mute groups** (*page 19*) are used to model a real hi-hat's mechanics, only allowing one sound (open or closed) to play at any one time. Some drum machines also offer a 'pedal' hat sound, which imitates the sound of the pedal being closed.

The **ride cymbal** (*page 24*) has a more obviously **tuned** sound with a longer decay. It is typically used in a similar way to hi-hats. Other cymbals such as the **crash** and **splash** are used more sparingly, generally at the start or end of a bar to smooth transitions.

Drums such as **toms**, **bongos** and **congas** (the latter two are hand-drums) occupy higher frequencies than the kick drum and have clearly defined pitches. As with snares, you can either use a real sampled sound or a synthetic take on the real thing, with many drum machines offering toms and bongos (*page 22*). They're useful for adding character to a beat and can be tuned to the key of the track to play in harmony with other elements. Down-pitched and envelope-tweaked toms are sometimes used in place of kick drums.

Percussion (*page 22*) is the catch-all term for a range of other sounds, including everything from **claves**, **wood blocks** and **cowbells** to **shakers**, **tambourines** and **maracas**. These add character to a beat, often interacting with the hi-hats to create rhythmic patterns that emphasise the groove. **Finger clicks** and **rim shots** can also be included in this category as similarly short, percussive hits used to embellish a beat.

Synthesised drums of the type found in genres such as retro disco and '80s-influenced electro – **zaps**, **lasers** and **synth toms** – form a category in their own right. Even the best attempts at mimicking real drum sounds are likely to be unsuccessful with limited synth architecture, giving synthetic drums sounds a character of their own. They add colour, personality and genre authenticity to a beat.

SIX OF THE BEST...
Drum machines

DSI TEMPEST (2011) 🎧
The collaboration between Roger Linn (inventor of the Akai MPC) and Dave Smith (legendary synth designer) was always destined for greatness. It redefines the limits of a drum machine, from its ribbon controllers and deep sound design options through to its built-in distortion and compressor.

ROLAND TR-808 (1980)
The inimitable source of *that* mighty sub-shaking kick, it's almost easier to list dance producers who *haven't* used the 808 than those who have. The history of hip hop and dance music would be very different without Roland's compact and colourful 'rhythm composer'.

ROLAND TR-909 (1983)
If the 808 was the rhythmic godfather of hip hop, then the 909 is the same to techno, trance and a slice of tougher-edged house. When techno and house pioneers got their hands on the machine, its analogue sounds kick-started a generation of 909-heavy rhythm tracks.

ELEKTRON ANALOG RYTM (2014)
Elektron's cult favourite Machinedrum redefined the hardware drum machine for the modern era, but has now been replaced by the Analog Rytm, which takes a very different approach. With the ability to combine analogue synthesis and samples, it's a unique machine with a lot of character.

ROLAND AIRA TR-8 (2014)
The modern digital reincarnation of the 808 and 909 also includes TR-707 and 727 sound expansion packs. A favourite in the studio and on stage, the AIRA TR-8 offers value for money alongside an easier to use interface than that found on the first generation of Roland drum machines.

LINN ELECTRONICS LINNDRUM (1982)
Unlike Roland's TR machines, the LinnDrum used samples of real acoustic drums rendered at 28-35kHz, making it nothing short of revolutionary. Linn's machines found fans among electronic musicians and also a large number of drummerless bands who didn't want the synthetic sounds of the 808 or 909.

KORG VOLCA BEATS (2013)
At a street price of under £120 the Volca Beats ranks as one of the cheapest analogue drum machines ever produced. Don't be fooled into thinking it's a toy; this tiny, battery-powered unit rubs sonic shoulders with the best of them.

Chapter one
Drums and beats

Read this first: tone, transients and tuning

Before going any further in this chapter, it's important to understand three key qualities that define any drum or percussive hit. These terms recur throughout the book:

▶▶ **1: Tone (or timbre)**. The inherent *character of a sound* – the unique cycle of waves that together give a drum its unique sonic fingerprint, be that the trademark snap of an 808 snare or the solid thump of a live kick drum. A drum's tone can be altered using any number of processing tools, from EQ to distortion – although if you need to radically change it you're usually better off picking a different sound.

▶▶ **2: Transients**. Drums are short, highly dynamic sounds, moving from silence to full volume in the space of a few wave cycles. A huge amount of sound energy arrives in the first few milliseconds of a drum hit in the opening transients of its waveform. Because drums form the DNA of dance music, these transients are critically important. Changing them can radically alter the character of an individual drum sound and the wider beat. Transients can be shaped using compression, ADSR envelopes and/or transient shapers.

▶▶ **3: Tuning**. Almost all drums are tuned instruments. Pitching a kick or snare up or down a few notches can transform its contribution to the mix. Tuning is changed using a synth or sampler's pitch controls.

TONE

"If you pick the right sounds in the first place you don't have to spend ages layering." So says Huxley in his Pro Tip a page back. His point relates to tone; pick drums with the right tone or timbre – for a track or a beat – and you've made the first step in crafting an effective groove.

Sometimes picking the right sound for a drum is easy; you can't go far wrong using a 909 kick in a trance track. Here the genre influences the drum. At other times the drum influences the track – a beater-heavy live kick drum may steer a track into indie dance territory. Sometimes the choice is harder; you may have a song idea with melodic parts sketched out in search of the right drum to pin down the rhythm section. In each case the tone/timbre of the raw hit is what makes the drum 'fit'.

TIP Need drum direction? Study the drum tones and timbres producers use in tracks you like. Listen to drum-only sections and use your ears and visualisation tools such as a DAW's spectral analyser to identify the characteristics of the sounds you find most appealing. Which frequencies are

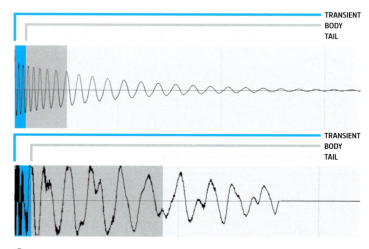

Fig 1: Two different kick drum waveforms showing the balance of the initial transients, the body and the outgoing tail. The top waveform shows a raw 909 kick drum, the bottom a heavily layered EDM-style kick.

SEE ALSO
 TUNED TOMS PAGE 12
 TUNING A KICK AND BASS PAGE 12
 TUNING AND EQ TWEAKS FOR BETTER DRUMS PAGE 13
MIXING KICK AND BASS PAGE 262

prominent? How are the transients spread? How are different drums paired?

TRANSIENTS

After tone, transients rule. In some melodic mix elements, like gentle vocals and pads, transients don't much matter. But in drums they are critical. To hear how important they are try a quick test. Load an 808 snare drum into a sampler. Play it straight and listen to the lively snap at the front end of the sound. Now lengthen its attack envelope and listen to the obvious change in impact. Gone is the snap, replaced by a gentler ramped attack, more suited to a lower tempo, less raucous rhythmic workout.

Understanding the impact of transients is a springboard to better beats. Not only can transient control give more definition, clarity and power to sounds, it can also help you

Chapter one
Drums and beats

craft intelligently layered composite hits where not all transients hit at the same time.

It is not just the opening transients that matter. Each drum sound is made up of the initial **transients** before the **body** of the sound arrives and then its **tail** fades the sound to silence (*Fig 1, left*). Tweaking the contribution of a drum sound's body plays an important role in beat sound design, giving a weak clap, for example, more bulk in a busy mix. The shape of the tail matters too – cutting tails short is one way of keeping beats tight (*page 293*).

Transient control is able to solve a variety of beat production issues. Hi-hat lost in the mix? Increase its attack transient. Snare overpowering a kick? Shift weight to its body. Bass overpowering the kick? Give the kick more front-end bite and shift the bassline's core energy back to its body. For better beats *listen for and zoom in on the transients of drum hits.* Knowing their contributions will allow you to shape them for cleverer, clearer beats.

TIP While transients can be shaped in a number of ways, including using envelopes and compression – *of which more on page 14* – the best tool is often a dedicated **transient shaper.** This has the benefit over a compressor of altering the attack (or sustain) portion of a sound without also changing the tone of the sound and its wider transient make-up.

PITCH – AND DRUM TUNING

Real-world drums are tuned instruments. Sometimes, in the case of hand drums like congas, their tuning is obvious. Conga virtuoso Poncho Sanchez is known for tuning his congas E-G-C to give the drums harmonic coherence. With other drums – like the snare or a clap – tuning is less obvious, and while some drummers go to extreme lengths to harmonise every tom and cymbal in their kit – and to tune their kit to the song they are playing on – most take a more relaxed approach, ensuring drum heads are tight and that the kit generally sounds unified and punchy.

Dance producers tend to take one of three approaches to drum tuning:

▸ **The 'Prince' full-tune**. In electronic music the bar was set to a large extent by Prince who routinely tuned each hit of his Linn Drum LM-1 to the key of the song. If you choose this approach the kick is usually tuned to the root note of the key of the track – D if the track is in D major (*page 144*) – while other sounds are either tuned to the root or notes that harmonise with it – typically thirds and fifths.

TIP To ensure a kick drum is in tune with the key of your track, *see the walkthrough overleaf,* or download any number of sample packs featuring 'tuned kick drums', which have become popular in recent years.

PRO TIPS

SCUBA

Although picking drum sounds that work tonally together will help ensure a unified beat, there are times when you deliberately want to create jarring textures.

Says Scuba: "[The track 'PCP'] was the one I was least sure about as despite the atmosphere and percussion being quite contemporary, the distorted tom riff that comes in around two minutes is definitely not, and when I've played it out there's definitely been a few confused faces on the dancefloor… although when the beat comes back in it seems to make sense to people again.

"This was the first track where I played around with re-recording parts through a guitar amp in my bathroom."

TIP If a sample has to be pitched up or down more than a few semitones and starts to sound unnatural, the easiest solution is usually to find a replacement sound.

▸ **The part-tune**. In which the kick is tuned to the track – either its root or a related interval – and sometimes the snare. Other hits are left untouched.

TIP Some drum sounds are more obviously tuned than others. The 808 kick drum has a clear pitch, to the extent that it can provide the bassline to a track. Other kicks, like the 909 (synthesised using an ultra-fast pitch descent) have a less obvious pitch and require trial and error tuning.

▸ **The 'blind' tune**. There are also plenty of producers who tune 'blind' – which is to say they don't look to create harmonic relationships when they tune; they simply find a drum sound they like, import it into the track then try pitching it up or down a few semitones before fine-tuning it. When it sounds right in the context of the beat and the wider track the tuning is left there.

The last word on tuning? Beats succeed due to thousands of interactions. Tuning is just one of them. Rigidly tuned kits often don't deliver the strongest overall sound – indeed you'd be hard pressed to find drummers who obsess to the extent Prince did. Usually tuning the main hits until they gel with the track and each other is enough.

// WALKTHROUGHS

Tuned toms

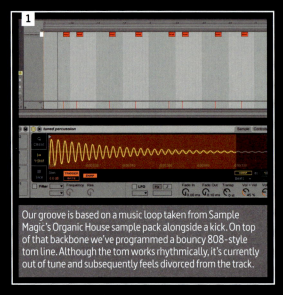

1 Our groove is based on a music loop taken from Sample Magic's Organic House sample pack alongside a kick. On top of that backbone we've programmed a bouncy 808-style tom line. Although the tom works rhythmically, it's currently out of tune and subsequently feels divorced from the track.

2 To bring the tom into tune with the music the first step is to use a tuner to identify its pitch. Transposed down an octave the tuner is able to pick up the pitch better. The raw pitch of the tom is sharp of C so we've detuned it in the Drum Rack by -46 cents so that it has a reliable C pitch.

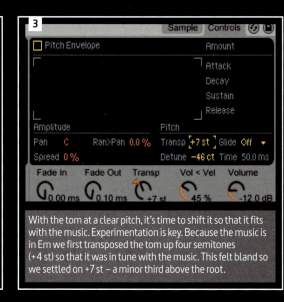

3 With the tom at a clear pitch, it's time to shift it so that it fits with the music. Experimentation is key. Because the music is in Em we first transposed the tom up four semitones (+4 st) so that it was in tune with the music. This felt bland so we settled on +7 st – a minor third above the root.

Tuning a kick and bass

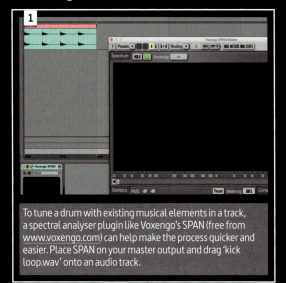

1 To tune a drum with existing musical elements in a track, a spectral analyser plugin like Voxengo's SPAN (free from www.voxengo.com) can help make the process quicker and easier. Place SPAN on your master output and drag 'kick loop.wav' onto an audio track.

2 Play the kick loop while holding Cmd/Ctrl and drag across SPAN's spectral analyser. This band-passes the signal around the drag point to help identify the kick's fundamental frequency. The big bump on the left side shows a fundamental (the thump) at 58Hz, the equivalent of A#1.

3 Drag 'bass loop.wav' onto another audio track. The bass plays a C note, which sounds slightly off when played with the kick. However, if you tune the bass loop down two semitones, it plays A#, now in tune with the A# kick. As a result it sits with the kick much more satisfyingly.

Tuning and EQ tweaks for better drums

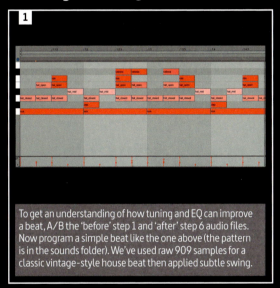

1 To get an understanding of how tuning and EQ can improve a beat, A/B the 'before' step 1 and 'after' step 6 audio files. Now program a simple beat like the one above (the pattern is in the sounds folder). We've used raw 909 samples for a classic vintage-style house beat then applied subtle swing.

2 You can use a tuner (*Tuned toms, opposite*) to repitch the kick against other elements or simply try retuning up/down up to three steps (more and the kick loses its identity) to see if you get a stronger sound – we've tuned it up one step for a livelier thump, then added saturation.

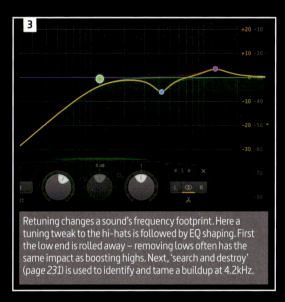

3 Retuning changes a sound's frequency footprint. Here a tuning tweak to the hi-hats is followed by EQ shaping. First the low end is rolled away – removing lows often has the same impact as boosting highs. Next, 'search and destroy' (*page 231*) is used to identify and tame a buildup at 4.2kHz.

4 Loops layered onto a drum beat frequently gel better after retuning. Here a tambourine loop is shifted down three steps so that it fits more naturally with the beat and doesn't interfere with the hats, which share the same frequency range. EQ is used to reinforce the pitch shift.

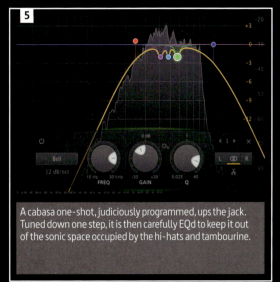

5 A cabasa one-shot, judiciously programmed, ups the jack. Tuned down one step, it is then carefully EQd to keep it out of the sonic space occupied by the hi-hats and tambourine.

6 With all beat elements playing final tweaks are made in the context of the drum group. The clap is down-tuned slightly for a better fit. Next we turn to the drum bus, adding saturation (5–10% wet) for punch before focussed EQ cuts shape the beat's tone and rein in over-strident frequencies.

Chapter one
Drums and beats

The kick drum

In dance music, kick is king. Across virtually all genres and tempos, the kick drum – and its bassline partner – lay down the foundations upon which all other beat and mix elements are built.

THE 'PERFECT' KICK DRUM: ALL ABOUT CONTEXT

Short and tight; deep and subby; raw and overdriven... When it comes to picking a kick drum for a track, the producer has a near limitless number of choices, with sounds sourced from samples, drum machines, synths, even studio recordings, all of which can be tweaked and refined to make the 'perfect' kick drum.

Stories abound of producers who spend days in the studio painstakingly crafting 'the perfect kick'. We're sceptical about this approach; however much you enjoy sound design, a single drum sound should demand no more than an hour or so's work.

Besides, what makes a kick drum 'perfect' is context. Kick drums don't stand alone. Instead in the low end the kick forms a symbiotic relationship with the bass. It's this relationship that provides the track's foundation. Higher up the frequency spectrum the crucial role the kick plays in the wider beat and its interplay with other drum elements, most notably the snare and/or clap, defines both a track's groove and its tonal aesthetic. Which means the kick drum must work seamlessly with both the bass and drum mix. *Only when it does both can it be considered perfect.*

KICK AND BASS

When choosing kick drum and bass sounds, opposites attract. As we explain in *Chapter 8: Mixing and mastering,* when mixing the lower frequencies *separation is paramount*. That separation starts with the choice of sounds. Partnering a subby 808 kick with a low sine wave bass is a recipe for disaster. Not only is such an approach courting low-end excess and asking for headroom trouble, neither the kick or bass will be clearly heard or felt in the mix.

The most effective mixes twin complementary – 'opposite' – kick and bass sounds; a subby 808 kick with a midrange-weighted stacked sawtooth bass. Or a lively Linn-style kick with a deeper bassline.

We'll say it again: *the kick and bass stand and fall together. They cannot and should not be treated in isolation.*

COMPRESSION

Compression not only allows you to alter the tonal characteristics of a kick drum, it offers a powerful means to control and change the overall shape of the drum, tightening or loosening the opening **transients** and shaping its **body**.

To easily hear what effect a compressor is having dial in a medium ratio (5:1) and set it up so that around 6dB of signal is reduced each time the kick hits. Then start tweaking...

For a smoother kick: Set a fast attack and medium release. This subdues the clicky opening transient at the start of the waveform to give a sound with more weight and body.

For a punchier kick: Dial in a medium attack and release. This allows the kick's opening transient to pass through unprocessed before the compressor sucks in the body making the sound tighter – useful not only for adding more click but also for reducing fat/mud in a saggy kick.

When the compressed sound has the qualities you want, pull back on the ratio/signal reduction as required.

NOTE Be careful not to do more harm than good when compressing. If the release is too fast, you can lose control of a kick's tail and end up with flabby results. If it's too slow you can end up hitting the compressor with a new kick before it has a chance to reset. Meanwhile, if the attack is too fast you can end up removing front-end bite.

KING OF THE...
Kick drums

TR-909
The house and techno kick drum standard, with an endlessly desirable combination of low frequency energy and mid frequency noise.

TR-808
The king of sub-heavy, boomy bass drums.

LINN DRUM
Live-style punch and presence.

TIP If all you want to do is alter the attack and/or release transient of a kick drum without impacting on its tonality or body, opt for a **transient designer** instead, increasing the attack or release time to taste. If a compressor has been used, you can add the transient designer next in line to add a spike lift at the start of the kick. Equally, if the kick has too much bite, a transient designer can be used to ease back on the front end.

TIP Transient Designers work best in moderation. You can easily get overly spiky results by pushing them too far.

EQ

The kick drum can be usefully broken down into three distinct frequency regions, each of which may need attention:

The low end (20–120Hz): The bottom end of a kick contains both subsonic frequencies that make club rigs tremble and girthy lows that ensure a solid foundation. For weight and warmth add a dB or two in the 60–80 Hz area. For punch, increase the 100–120 zone. At the lower end of the range be careful with boosts and use a frequency analyser to aid tweaks: very few project studios and/or monitors are able to faithfully reproduce these frequencies. If an analyser reveals excess headroom-munching signal in the subs, roll away extreme lows at 20–30Hz.

The mid-range (120Hz–1kHz): Knock, thump, crack and bang are the orders of the day in this wide frequency range. To help the kick cut through a busy mix, boost 200–800Hz (to find the right area use **search and destroy** (*page 231*) to pinpoint the place where the signal sounds best). For added weight, body and clout notch up the lower part of the area. When adding gain, be judicious: any more than 2–3dB is likely to overbake a kick drum. More likely you'll be cutting in this range to carve out space for the bassline – *see page 116*. An alternative to EQ boosting is to increase the kick drum's attack transient.

The high end (1–18kHz): Think kick drums are all about the lows? Not so. Almost all kick drums – especially if layered using samples that include vinyl noise and hi-hats – have information stretching up the frequency spectrum. These frequencies contain the crunch, bite and definition of the sound; if reduced you can destabilise the rhythm section and divorce the kick. To soften a kick, use a shelving EQ to roll away from around 5kHz. If boosting, go wide and gentle. To add beater 'click' try a notched boost at 1.5kHz.

TIP Remember, especially when tweaking the low and mid range, that you're operating on frequencies shared by the bassline. See *pages 282–285* for approaches to making the most of both kick and bass, and for avoiding conflicts.

Kicks in different genres

Techno
Synthesised drums prevail, either from drum machines (favourites include the TR-808, Vermona DRM1 and MFB Tanzbar), soft synths or modular systems. Subby kick drums are often paired with bass noise or low-tuned percussive sounds for a rolling bottom end.

House
Tone and type varies hugely depending on subgenre. Classic house, paying homage to its Chicago roots, makes use of 909 and disco hits, often layered, while the techier end of the spectrum makes greater use of 808 kicks. Raw, jackin' beats typically use layered hits with heavy live sample usage.

Nu disco
The modern twist on disco adds punch with drum machine kicks from the likes of the DMX, LinnDrum and TR-707. Heavier tracks thicken things up with 909-style layered kicks and tuned kicks with house-style production.

Electro
'80s inspiration rules. Think chunky E-MU Drumulator and tight 'live' LinnDrum sounds. In each case sub reinforcement is used to anchor the sound, filling in the 'missing bottom'. Other options include 808 kicks layered with disco or electronic hi-hats and raw indie/rock/funk/disco kicks sourced from vinyl, again, underlaid with a low-level sub kick.

Prog and trance
909 kicks dominate trance drum production. For crossover and prog house 909 hits may be layered with subs for a chunkier low end. Alternatively, try a layered 808/Linn-style hybrid for a gut-punch and girth double whammy.

D&B
In a genre where breaks reign, the kick has to work alongside both the often-busy sampled break (likely to already have kicks in it) and a super-sized bassline. Typically the lows of the break are EQ-bracketed to make space for the kick, which is often clicky and punchy, allowing the bassline to dominate the subs (*see pages 68–69*).

Chillout
Anything goes in this widest of genres, with stark 808s and sampled live hits common. Avoid overly punchy kick sounds like those from the 909 or Linn Drum. Soften transients to reduce aggression.

Chapter one
Drums and beats

The snare drum

The snare is the second drum in the programmer's arsenal, the *bap* to the kick drum's *boom* that provides a rhythm section's snap, crackle and pop. Its main role is to serve as a mid-tone counterweight to the kick, typically hitting on beats 2 and 4. Sometimes the snare's place is taken by a clap. At other times, both are used in a single or staggered layered hit.

Tonally a typical snare delivers the bulk of its energy in a broad frequency range above the kick and below the hi-hats, starting at around 90Hz and topping out around 10kHz. Live samples generate most energy lower down the spectrum (120–250Hz) while synthetic drums like the TR-808 punch its trademark 'thwat' at around 1–1.5kHz (depending on its tuning).

COMPRESSION

As with the kick drum, compression can be used to either subty or radically alter the **transient** shape of a snare.

Fatten a snare by using a medium attack (5–20ms) and fast release combination. This retains the snare's opening snap and thickens its body.

Smooth a snare by twinning a fast attack (<1ms) with a slower release. Here the opening transients are smashed to give a softer, deeper, more 'gluey' sound.

When working with layered snare/clap combos, send all constituent sounds to a bus then **glue compress** using a medium (5–20ms) attack and slow (100ms) release.

EQ

The snare can be broken down into four main frequency zones:

The low end (50–350Hz): The critical area here is the all-important 'body' between 120–350Hz. This contains the weight and gut-punch of a snare. To increase that weight add 1–2dB using a parametric EQ sweep (*page 231*) to identify the punch frequencies. Below around 90Hz the sound is often made up of unwanted noise and rumble that muddies a mix and interferes with the kick. Use a shelving low-cut filter to roll away below 70–100Hz. Exactly where will depend on the drum. Cut higher up the spectrum (220–250Hz) for thinner, crisper snares.

The mid-range (350–800Hz): The lower (350–500Hz) part of this area can be boxy and often benefits from a slight cut.

The upper mid-range (1–4.5kHz): Here lies the crack – the sharp attack sound that gives a snare its definition. Avoid significant boosts; cut to reduce harshness.

The high end (4.5kHz up): Presence dominates the lower part of this region, air at around 10kHz. Concentrate more energy here if you need a snare to cut through a top-heavy mix – but tread carefully, too much mid/high end on a snare can *hurt*.

LAYERING SNARES

Snares are probably the most frequently layered sounds in dance music, whether as single 'vanilla' layers featuring drum machine hits overlaid with a live sample or staggered combinations in which two or more snare layers trigger alongside a clap that hits before or after the snare.

Staggered layers (*pages 52–53*) are particularly prevalent in EDM, deep house and disco-influenced genres. The technique is inspired by classic disco workouts where a live clap occurred either before or after the beat to add a funky offset groove. You can either get this effect by dragging sounds on the MIDI grid or by using DAW delay to push a hit back a few ms. The longer the delay, the more defined the delayed hit.

KICK AND SNARE SEPARATION

Because the kick drum is the dominant rhythmic element in so many dance mixes, it can be easy for the snare to become lost in the mix, masked by the louder and often frequency-rich kick drum. Several techniques can help retain its identity:

THREE OF THE BEST...
Snares

TR-808 🎧
The snappy 'thwat' of the 808 snare drum combines a sharp attack transient made using noise twinned with a low triangle wave.

TR-909 🎧
A more complex synthesis engine.

E-MU DRUMULATOR 🎧
For full-bodied live-style snares. Tasty claps too.

Chapter one
Drums and beats

▶▶ 1: Use EQ to **roll away unwanted lows** in the snare. This reduces low-end overlap, giving a clearer identity to both the kick and snare. To find an appropriate cut point, set up a sloping filter to cut at around 80Hz then slowly raise it until you start to hear an obvious weakening in the snare's low end energy. At that point back down by 5-10Hz. Many snares benefit from a sloping cut at around 100-125Hz. Go higher when the snare is twinned with a dominant, frequency-rich kick drum.

▶▶ 2: Identify where the snare delivers the bulk of its energy (the 120-350Hz body zone detailed above) then dial in a 2-3dB **notch EQ cut in the kick** at that spot. This allows the snare to 'poke through' even the most dominant kick.

▶▶ 3: Shift the timing of the snare drum. As we note when discussing layering (*page 50*), one way to diffuse overlaps is by using EQ. The second is by shifting overlapping samples in time. If both kick and snare hit at exactly the same time, there's a lot of transient information arriving at once. To temper that united blow, ease the snare backwards (or forwards) by a few ms so that the two sounds, and their critical transients, arrive seperately. Even the briefest time difference is enough to help the ear identify the two sounds as distinct.

▶▶ 4: Alter the transients of either the kick, the snare or both. Because so much energy is contained in the opening 'hit' transients of a drum, emphasising or dampening them can alter the sound's definition in the mix. So if your kick is laden with explosive front-end energy, twin it with a smoother entry snare, and vice versa. Use a transient designer or compressor to give the snare a distinct treatment that works to complement the kick.

Of course, a clearly defined snare drum may not be what you want. In some tracks the snare is meant to do nothing more than blend in, almost subliminally, to the kicks on beats 2 and 4. If that's the case the above approaches can be reversed to create a homogenous kick/snare layer. Send both sounds to the same bus for added sonic glue.

▶▶ 5: Widen snare layers. Although using a stereo spreader or similar (*page 225*) to widen a snare should be avoided if you want a solid, weighty snare punch (widening diffuses energy across the stereo field), it can usefully aid separation in snare layers. In such cases, one snare is usually left in mono in the centre of the mix with a second, often crisper snare, receiving additional width.

TIP Struggling to naturally pair a snare and kick? Start with a pre-twinned combo, like samples from a Linn Drum or TR-909, then layer your own samples on top of them.

Snare reverb and ambience

While it's rare to add reverb to a kick drum – the ambience blurs the sacred low-end – almost all snares and claps benefit from some kind of reverb.

▶▶ To give an **obvious treatment** to a snare, use a hall or plate setting and tweak the tail length to fit with the tempo of the track. See the ms/tempo chart (*Appendix 1*) for exact times.

▶▶ To add width and a **sense of space** without compromising the up-front quality of a snare, choose a reverb with early reflections (ERs) (*page 223*) then increase the ERs and bypass the tail. Sometimes this is all you need to give a snare or clap sparkle and liveliness.

▶▶ The in-your-face reverb wash of the **'80s snare** is achieved by using a gate after a lush reverb that closes down the verb after a set period of time (usually related to the tempo of the track). Set it up by adding a plate reverb with high diffusion then following it with a noise gate set to close after, say, 200ms. Tweak the hold and release values to taste.

▶▶ Uncontrolled reverb tails clog mixes. Keep tails tidy by inserting a low-cut filter after the reverb to roll away the lows and keep the murk away from the kick and bass.

▶▶ If a reverb tail follows immediately after the snare's attack transients, the snare can lose definition. To maintain a sense of separation, use **reverb pre-delay** to push the ambient build back and away from the critical snare strike.

▶▶ In a sparse track, **make reverb tails more characterful** by feeding the reverb into a modulation effect (chorus, flange, phaser) to keep the tail changing in character.

▶▶ Delays can be used to generate ghost-style rhythms, dropping low-level echoes into the mix at defined intervals. Experiment with 1/8th note, triplet and swung values. Automate the delay on and off for irregular patterns. Filter the delay return to roll away lows and highs to avoid 'delay clashes' with the original sound.

▶▶ For an ambient effect somewhere between reverb and delay try a model of the **Roland RE-201 Space Echo**. The classic dub machine can manage everything from smeary reverb to woozy delays. Automate the repeat rate in real-time for a trippy, ever-shifting vibe. A masterclass in the use of dubby delays comes from Paul Woolford's Special Request VIP remix of Tessela's 'Hackney Parrot'.

Hi-hats

Hi-hats supply the rhythmic glue that bind kick, snare and other beat elements together. typically playing 16ths and/or off-beat eighths.

A traditional drum kit generates various distinct sounds from the same hi-hats: a tight 't' when the **closed** hats are struck with a drumstick; a looser 'ch' when the hats are closed using the **pedal**; and a sustained 'tssss' when the top hat is struck while the pedal is half **open**. These three sounds – closed, pedal and open – can be found on virtually all drum machines.

Hi-hats are either sourced from drum machines, samples or live kits. They can also be synthesised using envelopes to shape a noise or FM source *(page 49)*.

TIP If you are using closed, pedal *and* open hats in a groove and want them to share the same tonal characteristics, use grouped samples either from the same drum machine or single drum kit.

SCULPTING HI-HATS

In some tracks, hats are mixed loud at the front of the mix. Classic house workouts like Marshall Jefferson's 'Move Your Body' and trance tracks like Tiesto's take on 'Adagio For Strings' (3.00) both feature obvious hi-hats filling the rhythmic gaps between kicks. In other productions – Deadmau5 & Kaskade's 'I Remember' as an example – the hats are mixed so low as to be bordering on subliminal; beat elements whose absense is noticed only when they are muted.

How prominent you want the hi-hats to be will dictate both your choice of sounds and their subsequent processing.

Once you've found the right sound, sculpting it to fit the mix involves using the sound-shaping techniques outlined over the previous pages:

▶▶ Use a **transient designer** or similar envelope plugin. Increase the attack for added definition and bite. Decrease it to smooth out the opening transients and tuck the hat back in the mix.

▶▶ Use a **compressor** to do the same job. Read the tips for compressing snares and kicks above. The attack time is critical: the shorter it is, the less impact the opening transient will have.

▶▶ A **sampler's amp envelope** offers a third means to shape hi-hats. You might, for example, reduce decay and release to transform an open hi-hat into a closed one.

TIP When shaping hats, it's easy to concentrate on the attack portion and

JAY SHEPHEARD

"I love the LinnDrum hi-hat. It cuts through the mix so nicely at club volume and almost takes on a kind of cowbell edge on the attack."

forget decay and release. 'Note offs' are as important as note-ons when crafting a groove. Cutting a hi-hat's decay can tighten a groove while increasing it can be used, for example, to control the duration of an open hat, allowing it to precisely fill the space between kick and snare hits.

EQ

EQing hi-hats typically involves balancing clarity and sheen in the top end while reducing harshness in the mids and ensuring the hi-hats don't overpower other elements resident in the upper frequencies of the mix.

Start by using a shelving low cut filter to remove unwanted murk and mud (use a spectrum analyser if you can't hear any – hi-hats often cloak suprising amounts of bass energy). Cut at around 250Hz, higher with toppier hats.

Some producers also use bracketing EQ *(page 211)* to rein in high end energy. Do this by setting up a high-cut filter and then reducing the cutoff frequency until you get a more mellow result. This is particularly useful when you've got other parts – shakers, upper octave synths, vocals – that need to shine in the top end. Saturation plugins give a more natural result.

TIP A de-esser can be used to notch out overly harsh frequencies instead of EQ. Use the de-esser's audition function to hone in on the offending frequencies – usually in the 5–6kHz region – then reduce to taste.

TIP Hi-hats and shakers/tambourines occupy the same frequency zone. If you are using both, the most effective way of avoiding overlaps is by programming complementary patterns for each part. If they require further separation, give each a different EQ and ambient treatment.

TIP While using an exciter may feel like a natural choice for hi-hats, better results are almost always achieved using a broad EQ lift in the 6–12kHz area; even controlled use of an exciter can give brutal results.

MORE HI-HAT TIPS

TIP Hi-hats are commonly panned either centrally or slightly off-centre. Another option is to use random stereo panning – a choice that adds movement and interest to even the most mundane part.

TIP Try feeding hats through a delay on a 16th or dubby eighth-note triplet setting to add movement to a groove. Roll away highs on the return to keep things subtle.

TIP If a hi-hat nearly but not qute fits a groove, try retuning it. Also try automating an open hat's pitch gently over time for a constantly shifting sound.

TIP Linear hi-hats can be given movement by feeding them through a flanger or phaser with LFO set to sweep across an eight or 16 bar section. Adjust the wet/dry balance to keep things subtle.

TIP Hats lacking bite? For chunkier hi-hats feed them through a bit-crusher and reduce the sample rate. For more body lower the bit rate as well. 12-bit settings replicate classic beat boxes. An alternative is to use overdrive or distortion, using the tone control to shape the frequency make-up.

TIP Finally... Dance mixes don't always need hi-hats. Shakers can be used to perform a similar, if not identical, role.

Mute groups and polyphony

In the real world, drums are monophonic instruments – if you strike a drum or cymbal while it is still reverberating from a previous hit, the decaying tail of the previous sound is immediately cut off by the new impact.

When using plugins, drum machines and samplers, you can break this rule, allowing the tails of drum hits to continue ringing out even when you trigger the same drum again. In practice, however, allowing individual drums to play polyphonically tends to sound unnatural and soon clutters a beat.

Most drum machines and dedicated drum plugins solve this problem by defaulting to a monophonic setting, with analogue drum machines typically using monophonic synth circuits for each sound. If you're creating your own drum sounds with a synth or sampler, selecting monophonic mode has the same result

But what if you have multiple sounds that you want to treat as though they are a single monophonic entity? The obvious example is the hi-hat.

On a real drum kit, the decay of the open hat is cut off the moment the drummer presses down on the pedal to close it. But if you have two samples loaded into a drum sampler plugin – one closed and one open – the decay tails of the open hats will carry on alongside the closed hat sounds.

The solution is to use **mute groups** (aka **voice** or **choke groups**), which link sounds together so that they behave as a single monophonic instrument. With both the closed and open hat assigned to the same mute group, the tail of each open hat is cut off as soon as a closed hat is triggered (and vice versa).

Each sampler or plugin has a slightly different approach to setting up mute groups – see walkthroughs, overleaf.

TIP While hi-hats are obvious candidates for mute grouping, other drums can benefit from the same treatment. If you're using two kick drum samples, for example, try assigning both to the same mute group. Percussive drums like congas and bongos – which often feature multiple sounds for different hand strikes – can also be grouped for a more realistic result.

TIP You can use mute groups for more creative effects too, such as assigning unrelated sounds and short ambient effects to the same group in order to cut off decay tails in an unnatural but rhythmically interesting way.

// WALKTHROUGHS

Voice groups in Battery

1 Load up Battery in your DAW and drag 'Closed hat.wav' and 'Open hat.wav' from the Walkthroughs folder onto pads A1 and A2 respectively. If you play the closed hat while the open hat's tail is still playing, you'll hear both sounds at once.

2 This is unrealistic because a real world hi-hat is monophonic and can only be in a closed or open position. To model this behaviour allocate both pads to the same mute (Battery calls it 'Voice') group. Click the Setup tab at the bottom of Battery's interface.

3 Open the drop-down menu on the left side of the Voice Groups panel. This determines which voice group the pad is part of. Set both pads to voice group '1 – <untitled>'. Now when you play the closed hat pad, the open hat sound will be silenced.

Choke groups in Ableton

1 Start by clicking the Instrument button in Live's Browser, then drag the Drum Racks instrument onto a MIDI track. In the Walkthroughs folder you'll find a couple of hi-hat samples. Drag 'Closed hat.wav' onto the C1 slot and 'Open hat.wav' onto the C#1 slot.

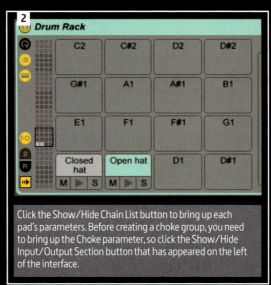
2 Click the Show/Hide Chain List button to bring up each pad's parameters. Before creating a choke group, you need to bring up the Choke parameter, so click the Show/Hide Input/Output Section button that has appeared on the left of the interface.

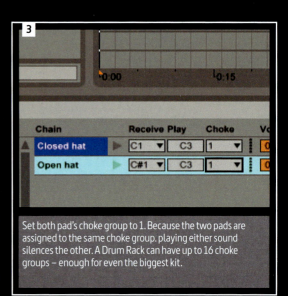
3 Set both pad's choke group to 1. Because the two pads are assigned to the same choke group, playing either sound silences the other. A Drum Rack can have up to 16 choke groups – enough for even the biggest kit.

Programming 'live' hi-hats

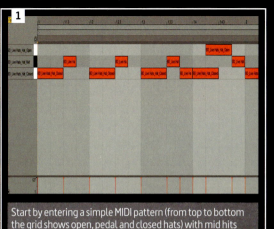

1 Start by entering a simple MIDI pattern (from top to bottom the grid shows open, pedal and closed hats) with mid hits on the off-beat in classic disco style. A couple of closed hat 16ths add momentum to the pattern and an open hat pulls the groove into the turnaround.

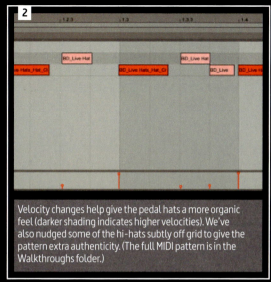

2 Velocity changes help give the pedal hats a more organic feel (darker shading indicates higher velocities). We've also nudged some of the hi-hats subtly off grid to give the pattern extra authenticity. (The full MIDI pattern is in the Walkthroughs folder.)

3 To add further detail, automate the attack time of the closed and mid hats. To do so set up two automation lanes, one for each sample.

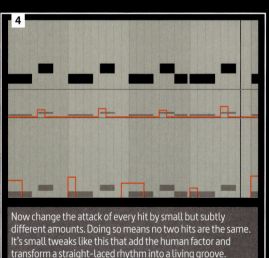

4 Now change the attack of every hit by small but subtly different amounts. Doing so means no two hits are the same. It's small tweaks like this that add the human factor and transform a straight-laced rhythm into a living groove.

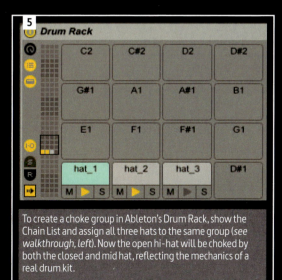

5 To create a choke group in Ableton's Drum Rack, show the Chain List and assign all three hats to the same group (see walkthrough, left). Now the open hi-hat will be choked by both the closed and mid hat, reflecting the mechanics of a real drum kit.

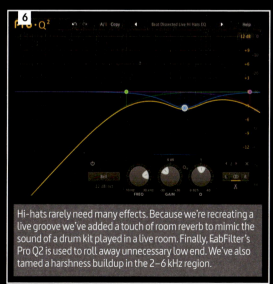

6 Hi-hats rarely need many effects. Because we're recreating a live groove we've added a touch of room reverb to mimic the sound of a drum kit played in a live room. Finally, FabFilter's Pro Q2 is used to roll away unnecessary low end. We've also tamed a harshness buildup in the 2–6 kHz region.

Chapter one
Drums and beats

Percussion and cymbals

For the sake of simplicity we're grouping all sounds that are not kicks, snares, claps and hi-hats into a single 'percussion' family. Although some of the sounds might fit the term only loosely, it's a useful enough catch-all, describing the wide array of 'other sounds' that contribute to a dance groove, from tom-toms through bongos and shakers to claves and triangles – as well as their synthetic equivalents.

Note that grouping this wide and disparate collection of sounds together doesn't diminish their contribution to dance music: these sounds not only flesh out beats, bringing characterful tones to even the most pedestrian workout, they frequently deliver rhythmic killer blows and sonic motifs: think the relentless drive of a cleverly programmed stick groove or a judiciously timed tom fill.

PERCUSSION BREAKDOWN

Although the number of potential percussive instruments a producer can draw on runs into the hundreds of thousands (almost every culture has its own unique set of drums), for most of the time you'll be using a handful of frequently used sounds.

▸▸ **Tom-toms** (or simply 'toms'): A typical acoustic drum kits features two or more toms, tuned side drums commonly played during drum fills. Most drum machines offer toms.

TIP Transpose toms low enough and they can be used to supply a track's bassline – a common technique in techno and house. *See Basic house tom walkthrough, page 49.*

▸▸ **Congas**: Tall Cuban drum with African origins played in sets of two or three. Each drum can be played using a variety of hand strikes including open, slap and touch.

▸▸ **Bongos**: Smaller paired drums from Africa played by striking skins with fingers and palms. Bongos produce lighter and higher pitches than congas. Not represented on any of the classic drum machines – *see below*.

Fig 2: Which has what? Drum machines old and new, and which percussion sounds they feature.

▸▸ **Claves**: Pair of (traditionally) wooden sticks from Cuba that when struck together produce a bright clicking tone. The 808 clave has a legion of fans.

▸▸ **Rim shot**: Technically a style of snare drum impact, where the drummer hits the rim (side) of the snare drum rather than its resonant skin for a sharper, clickier sound.

▸▸ **Shakers**: Maracas, cabasas and rainsticks are all forms of shakers – plastic or wooden containers filled with small, loose objects such as dried peas or beads. Can be tilted, shaken, swung or struck to produce a range of sounds. Typically used to reinforce (often swung) movement on 16ths or eighths. Can be used in place of hi-hats – listen to Deadmau5 & Kaskade's 'I Remember' as an example. Many sample sets offer multiple variations on a single sound, including tight and looser hits.

▸▸ **Tambourines**: Wood or plastic frame, usually circular, whose rim holds metal 'zils' that ring together when the frame is shaken or struck. Can be used like a shaker, to reinforce an eighth or 16th groove, or in place of a hi-hat.

▸▸ **Cowbell**: Named after the traditional bell worn by cattle to tell shepherds their

	Toms	Congas	Tamb	Clave	Rim shot	Shaker	Cowbell
TR-909	● Low, Mid, Hi				●		
TR-808	● Low, Mid, Hi	● Low, Mid, Hi		●	●	● Maraca	●
Linn LM-1	●	●	●	●		● Cabasa	
Drumulator	● Low, Mid, Hi			●			●
Volka Beats	● Low, Hi			●			● (Agogo)

whereabouts, metal cowbells are struck with a stick. The TR-808 cowbell sounds nothing like a real cowbell.

TIP When programming realistic ethnic percussion loops, use mute groups (*see Percussion beats walkthroughs, overleaf*) to limit polyphony when only one or two strikes can sound at once. The number will depend on the drum and how it's played, but in most cases limiting each drum to single-note mute groups will be the most realistic. (For paired drums like congas, different strikes for each drum should be sent to a single group.)

OTHER OPTIONS

Although dance producers have an almost limitless number of real-world percussive sounds that can be shoehorned into a mix, there are many other options:

▶▶ **Synth percussion**: Nearly all of the sounds outlined above can be and have been synthesised. From classic '80s electronic toms to the infamous 808 cowbell sound, some synthesised versions of traditional percussion instruments have overshadowed the real thing. *See pages 46–49 for synthesis of kick drum, snare drum, tom and hi-hat.*

▶▶ **Found sound percussion**: Any sound can be percussive. That is to say, if shaped and placed so that it contributes to the ebb and flow of the groove anything from a footstep or burst of ambient noise to the striking of a tree can be dropped into a rhythmic workout. *See Techno beat using field recordings, page 229.*

USING PERCUSSION

Where **spot sounds** are used sparingly in a track they can be added to a MIDI pattern or dropped into the arrange window.

In fuller percussive lines where a sound **plays throughout a bar** – in the case of a shaker or conga loop – the sequence can either be programmed or a commercial loop used.

Note that authentic percussion loops *are notoriously difficult to program*. Even a simple single head drum like a djembe offers a near limitless palette of tones depending on where and how hard its skin is struck and the placement of either or both hands. Trying to replicate this in MIDI is nigh on impossible – although we give it a good shot with our live bongo loop *overleaf*.

if you want a *truly* realistic percussion line you're best off getting out a microphone and recording a decent player or seeking a sample of the real thing – simply find a loop that fits the bill tonally, then use any number of sample editing techniques (*Chapter 4: Using samples*) to shape the groove to your requirements.

Percussion in different genres

Techno
Various techno subgenres layer found-sound percussion with rolling synth tom basslines. The emphasis is on finding a unique selection of sounds that replace the role of traditional percussion to lock grooves together with hi-hats and/or shakers.

House
Some house subgenres depend for their identity on percussion. Where would disco house be without bongos and congas? Or latin house? Or deep house without real or synth toms?

Nu disco
Percussion use here nods to the past with a tight, modern twist. Use syncopated congas, sticks, agogos and cowbell hits alongside wide claps and clap fills sourced from classic drums machines.

Electro
Retro 808 and 909 percussion sounds such as claves, cowbells and synth zaps are found in early electro. The percussion palette has widened to include an array of synthetic percussive noises as the genre has developed.

D&B
The classic pitched-up breaks that spawned the genre often included fragments of percussion. While tambourines and shakers form common high-end layers on these sampled grooves, the busy breaks and ghosted snare patterns leave little space for additional programmed percussion.

Chillout
From traditional acoustic sounds through all manner of exotic tribal drums to found sound and synthesised beeps and clicks, chillout embraces the widest spectrum of percussion. And with slower tempos, there's more room in the groove for percussive sounds – either subtle or centre stage – to establish an identity.

Dubstep
Complex percussion patterns and clever use of pitched tambourine, shaker and hi-hat samples keep the groove interesting without clogging it, leaving room for kicks and heavy claps and snares. See *Mystik dubstep beat dissected, page 69*.

Trance
Some trance subgenres make heavy use of ethnic percussion with busy conga, bongo and djembe grooves – often recorded live – a key part of the psy-trance DNA.

That said, there can be good reasons for programming your own percussive loops: you get full control over the rhythm and the raw sound; you can craft unique organic/synthetic hybrids; and finally, it's a great sound design challenge…

MIXING PERCUSSION

The usual production task when adding percussion to a beat is fitting it into the established groove so that it supplies movement and depth without dominating or overlapping other elements. **EQ bracketing** (*page 211*) is used to trim percussive elements to size, particularly in the upper reaches of a mix where both tambourine and shaker sounds share the same natural habitat as the hi-hat. Lower down the spectrum toms and congas can both stray into kick drum territory.

The majority of frequency overlaps are best solved by **programming**. There is little point in a hi-hat and shaker line playing the same pattern. Instead you might choose to place hats on off-beat eighths and use shakers to work the 16ths.

Where overlaps are impossible to program away, **pan** overlapping sounds to different sides of the stereo spectrum and use **EQ** to make complementary cuts and (gentle) boosts in overlapping signals so that the energy of each contrasts rather than conflicts.

As a matter of course, use low cut EQ to roll away unnecessary low end from top-heavy percussive parts (shakers, tambourines etc). With toms and other low pitched instruments, don't cut too high or you'll lose body, weight and punch.

TIP To diffuse a shaker or other percussive loop's energy away from the all-important kick and snare use a **stereo spreader**. Not only do you get instantly wide percussion, you also keep the bulk of the beat's energy where it should be: in the centre.

TIP **Be sparing with reverb** on busy percussive parts. Room or short chamber settings are usually fine to give a sound liveliness without blurring the mix. In general, the busier the part, the less reverb you'll need. This rule can and should be broken when you're dealing with **single percussive impacts** in found sound beats (*page 229*) or FX bombs (*page 254*).

TIP **When using tom drums as kicks** detune the tom to the pitch you want then tweak its envelope settings to sculpt its transient make-up – compare the waveform with a kick if useful. Next, compress and EQ it as you would a regular kick drum. For rolling tech-style kick lines, use two differently pitched instances of the same tom sent to a single-note mute group and program the two to bounce off each other. Experiment with their relative pitches until they roll as unidentical twins.

Cymbals

Crash cymbals
Crash cymbals supply bursts of sonic energy to lift grooves or to ease transitions at the start of 16 or 32 bar sections.

▸▸ Precede a transition crash with a reversed version of itself for the **classic reverse crash effect**. To do so, copy the crash, reverse it, then place the reversed version before the on-the-beat crash so the suck ends as the new beat starts, or better, slightly before it. Timestretch the reversed crash so that it slowly eases into the mix across a four or eight bar section.

▸▸ **Supersize crashes** by feeding them through a stereo widener followed by cavernous hall or plate reverb and delay/s. Route the reverb/delay tails into a pump compressor so that they fade pumping against the kick.

▸▸ Supersized crashes can be given added stereo interest by using an **auto-panner** to throw tails around the stereo field. Slow morphing between left and right channels can be particularly effective.

Ride
The acoustic ride cymbal has two distinct sounds depending on where the cymbal is struck. Hitting the edge gives a smooth, jazzy sound while tapping the central bell produces a shorter metallic 'klang'. A number of analogue drum machines offer ride sounds modelled on one or other of these sounds.

When programming, rides can be used in place of hi-hats, typically playing eighth or 16th note patterns. The results are smoother grooves – ideal if you're after a flowing sound.

▸▸ Experiment with **different velocities** and map velocity to filter cutoff and/or attack and decay times for more realistic programming. Swung rides can also sound great.

▸▸ Try twinning a sustained crash or ride sound playing a simple eighth note off-beat pattern with heavy kick-triggered **sidechain compression** for rhythmic sucking effects. Mix loud for big pumping effects or way back in the mix for low-level 'breathing'. *See Jack Ü-style EDM beat dissected, page 65.*

▸▸ Both ride and crash cymbals can be effectively modelled using **synthesis** – with white noise offering an ideal starting waveform.

// beats dissected 🎧

Realistic bongos. Tempo: 110–135bpm. Swing: 50-65%. Sounds: Real bongo samples (from the same sample set).

Tuning

> Bongos are paired drums, with one pitched higher than the other (*page 22*). So when programming you need at least two samples. For more realism, adding a third sample to the mix – usually a muted palm sound – will extend the programming options. Tuning the drums is a matter of taste. A good starting point with two drums is to tune them around a fourth apart. In this example we're cheating a bit by using bongo samples in a conga-style three drum setup to give us a wider palette.

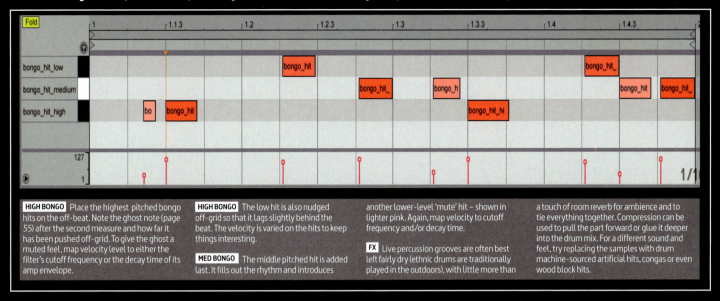

HIGH BONGO Place the highest pitched bongo hits on the off-beat. Note the ghost note (page 55) after the second measure and how far it has been pushed off-grid. To give the ghost a muted feel, map velocity level to either the filter's cutoff frequency or the decay time of its amp envelope.

HIGH BONGO The low hit is also nudged off-grid so that it lags slightly behind the beat. The velocity is varied on the hits to keep things interesting.

MED BONGO The middle pitched hit is added last. It fills out the rhythm and introduces another lower-level 'mute' hit – shown in lighter pink. Again, map velocity to cutoff frequency and/or decay time.

FX Live percussion grooves are often best left fairly dry (ethnic drums are traditionally played in the outdoors), with little more than a touch of room reverb for ambience and to tie everything together. Compression can be used to pull the part forward or glue it deeper into the drum mix. For a different sound and feel, try replacing the samples with drum machine-sourced artificial hits, congas or even wood block hits.

Organic shaker. Tempo: 110-140bpm. Swing: 50-80%. Sounds: Real (related) shaker samples.

Dynamics

> The main ingredient in a realistic shaker line is dynamic variation – you won't get a groove going unless there's clear contrast between louder and softer hits. When setting up the sampler, route velocity to volume. For even more contrast set the sample's attack envelope to respond to velocity as well.

LOW SHAKER Program a two bar 16th-note rhythm pattern, adjusting the velocities as pictured (darker red means louder hits). The louder hits fall on the off-beats.

HIT PLACEMENT Real percussionists don't play to a quantise grid. Introduce realism by shifting the hits slightly off-grid so the pattern loses its rigidity. Alter some of the note lengths to bestow a further taste of imperfect humanity. Note the relationship between the hit position and its velocity: each has an intrinsic impact on the other and on surrounding hits too. As a consequence, it's not unusual to lose an hour or so in a tweak frenzy before you get something that grooves right. Anaylse a real life shaker loop for inspiration.

HIGH SHAKER Add a second shaker sample to the sequence. We've chosen a slightly higher pitched variation of the first sample and placed it on the off-beat to reinforce the swing, the different pitch adding energy and variation.

FX Process as you would a real shaker loop, adding a touch of reverb or dash of (rhythmic) delay. To widen the image try panning the low sample a little left and the high to the right.

Chapter one
Drums and beats

The theory of rhythm

THE BEAT

The word 'rhythm' roughly translates from Greek as 'regular recurring motion'. We can think of rhythms as **patterns of sounds punctuated by silence**. These recurring patterns are underpinned by a regular pulse – a 'beat' (as in heartbeat) – which in dance music is usually defined by the kick drum. It's this fundamental recurring beat that gets feet moving and heads nodding.

TEMPO

Tempo describes **how frequently the pulse or beat occurs**, measured in **beats per minute (bpm)**. In a 125bpm house track, 125 evenly spaced pulses occur every minute – around two per second.

Different genres have different typical tempi. Chillout, for example, covers a broad tempo range of around 75-100bpm, while trance ramps up to 130-145bpm, D&B motors along at 150-180bpm and hardcore reaches a bonkers 180bpm and beyond. *The higher the bpm, the faster the track.*

Although most dance tunes pick a bpm and stick with it for the duration, it's not unheard of for the tempo to change within a track in order either to subtly pick up or slow down the transition into a build/breakdown or to radically change the pace. Check out The Insiders' 'Renaissance' for examples of both. It starts out in full-on D&B mode then drops into house territory, after which the tempo progressively ramps up again.

NOTE A healthy human heart beats at between 60–100bpm.

ALL BAR ONE

Although the beat is the foundation of the rhythm and pulse that drives a track, the main musical division we use when structuring tracks is the **bar** or **measure**.

A bar is a unit of musical time that comprises a set number of beats. In dance music, that number is usually four – although there are exceptions, as we'll see.

The number and length of beats in a bar are defined by a track's **time signature**, in the format X/X. The first (top when notated) 'X' specifies the number of beats per bar, so 4/4 is a standard four-beat measure, 5/4 puts five beats in each bar, and 3/4 has three beats to the bar (waltz time, page 29).

The second (lower) number in a time signature describes the length of each beat, with '4' equating to a crotchet or quarter-note – so-called because it constitutes a quarter of a 4/4 bar. '8' indicates quavers

Fig 3: Different note lengths in a 4/4 beat, showing, *from top to bottom*: **Four beat semibreve lasting for a whole bar, two beat minim (multiple levels); single beat quaver (beat level), half beat (eighth note) quavers and quarter beat (16th note) semiquavers.**

	BEAT 1	BEAT 2	BEAT 3	BEAT 4
SEMIBREVE	𝅝 →→→→→→→→→→→→→→→→→→→→→→→→→→			
MINIM	𝅗𝅥 →→→→→→→→→		𝅗𝅥 →→→→→→→→→	
CROTCHET	♩	♩	♩	♩
QUAVER	♪ ♪	♪ ♪	♪ ♪	♪ ♪
SEMIQUAVER	♬♬♬♬	♬♬♬♬	♬♬♬♬	♬♬♬♬

Chapter one
Drums and beats

or eighth notes (eighths of a bar) and '16' means semiquavers or 16th notes (16ths of a bar) – see Fig 3, left. So a 6/8 time signature divides each bar into six eighth notes (see overleaf).

TIP The simplest way of thinking of time signatures is as follows:
Top number = number of beats in a bar.
Bottom number = length of each beat.

PHRASING

The time signature strongly influences the **phrasing** and natural flow of a rhythm – how you *feel* the beat.

You would count a 4/4 pulse aloud like this: "**1** + 2 + 3 + 4 +". You'd count 3/4 time "**1** + 2 + 3 +" and 6/8 as "**1**, 2, 3, **4**, 5, 6". In each case, bold indicates where the natural accent in the phrase falls and the '+' indicates the eighth notes between the main beats.

LIVING ON THE GRID

How does this all impact on the dance musician? What matters most, particularly when programming drums, is the grid and how different time signatures work within it. Here's what you need to know:

▸▸ The grid is sliced into a number of equal divisions depending on the time signature and your grid display settings. In 4/4 time, the grid is split into 16 divisions (four for each beat) across each bar. 3/4 time divides the grid into 12 (three divisions for each beat).

▸▸ **The 16 division (= 4 beats = 1 bar) grid** is found in almost all drum machines, from the 1969 Rhythm Ace to in-built sequencers in nearly every DAW. It's the *de facto* standard for step sequencing.

▸▸ In a four beat bar, **the down-beat** is the first beat. It's named after the downward

Fig 4: Notation and piano roll showing 4/4 and 3/4 time. 4/4 features four quarter-note beats to the bar while 3/4 features three.

Fig 5: The 16 step buttons at the bottom of a TR-909 drum machine. Triggering a four-to-the-floor kick involves punching in steps 1, 5, 9 and 13.

motion of an orchestral conductor's baton at the start of each bar.

▸▸ **The up-beat** is the last beat in the bar, immediately preceding the down-beat – the fourth beat in a 4/4 bar. It usually feels 'weaker' than the down-beat.

▸▸ An **off-beat** is any unaccented beat (as well as the intermediate beats between the main ones – the '+' beats in our examples here). In a standard 4/4 groove, where the down-beat (**1** + **2** + **3** + **4**) is the most heavily accented, followed by the third beat (1 + 2 + **3** + 4), the weaker beats 2 and 4 are the off-beats (1 + **2** + 3 + **4**). The up-beat, described above, also happens to be an off-beat.

▸▸ When off-beats are emphasised, they are said to be **syncopated** – see *pages 164-165*. This is a key element of reggae and ska and is used to great effect in a range of dub-influenced dance music.

Chapter one
Drums and beats

Breaking timing conventions

UNCONVENTIONAL TIMING

The majority of dance music is written in 4/4 and a very large proportion is built on a rigid four-to-the-floor kick drum pattern where the kick hits on every beat.

Those conventions are informed by decades of western musical traditions and the stylistic tropes of countless 20th century popular music genres, from blues to rock 'n' roll, disco to soul. The upshot is that 4/4 is the default time signature for nearly all contemporary dance music.

But take a listen to any number of non-western grooves from Africa to India and beyond and you'll realise that 4/4 dance rhythms are far from ubiquitous.

Using a non 4/4 signature might seem risky for the dance producer, but don't underestimate listeners' receptiveness to unusual grooves. Most clubbers aren't counting crotchets on the dancefloor and if the vibe's good, they'll dance to it, whether a groove's in 4/4 or 7/8.

For a masterclass in weaving unconventional time signatures into dance tracks, check out the work of Venetian Snares.

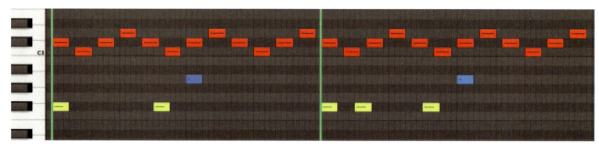

Fig 6: Polyrhythms in action, with the yellow and blue kick and snare hits playing standard 4/4 while the hi-hats (red) play triplets in 6/8. The MIDI sequencer grid is set to 1/32 resolution.

Meanwhile MGMT's 'Electric Feel' is a good example of 6/4 time and Trifonic's 'Vacuum Tree' showcases 7/4 beautifully.

NOTE If you want your odd time signatured track to be played by DJs, help them by adding play-ins and outros in 4/4.

POLYRHYTHMS

A **polyrhythm** (literally 'more than one rhythm') is the playing or programming of two or more rhythms in different time signatures at the same time. It can be used to add a layer of complexity to a beat or any melodic element in a track.

A two-part polyrhythm can be heard in Zomby's track 'Helter Skelter'. In the section starting at 0:13 the drums play a standard 4/4 beat on a 16th note grid while the sawtooth bassline plays 6/8 on a 12th note grid. The contrast creates an unexpected and engaging rhythmic tension.

While grime, hardcore and dubstep all lend themselves to complex rhythmic elements, polyrhythms can be employed just as effectively in house and techno. Listen to Disclosure's 'Tenderly' in which the timing of the claps and percussion layers contrasts with the keys, kick drum, bass and additional percussion hit coming in at 1:01, giving the piece a strong shuffle feel for the first two bars of each phrase.

When experimenting with polyrhythms, start out with relatively straightforward time signatures. In the example above (Fig 6) the kick and snare play 4/4 while the hi-hats are in 6/8. Note the interplay between the two and the breaking of rhythmic conventions.

To make programming easier, set the MIDI grid up to be as practical and useful as possible: there's no point having a grid at 1/16 note resolution if you want to punch in 6/8 quavers. Instead, set the grid up for the first rhythm (4/4, for example), program it in, then, in a new MIDI region, change the grid view to the second time signature (6/8, say). If the intertwining rhythms occur in the same MIDI sequence (which we wouldn't recommend!), you'll need to ensure the grid is at a high enough resolution to support both. In the case of *Fig 6*, which has to support both 4/4 time (16 steps) and 6/8 time (12 steps), the grid must be set to (at least) 1/32 resolution.

TIP One of the easiest ways to experiment with polyrhythms is to loop percussive sequences at odd, rather than even, beats. Try importing a 4/4 percussion loop into a 4/4 track then cutting it short so that it loops at the third, rather than fourth, beat.

TIP Once you go down the alternative rhythm rabbit hole, there can be no escaping... Tracks can switch between odd signatures, flirting with 5/4 time for one bar then 7/8 for two, then 6/8 for a few... Nothing is too wild if it engages the listener.

LINEAR DRUMMING

A drummer has two drum sticks for hitting drums and cymbals and two feet for pedalling the kick drum and hi-hats. This means up to four drums can be played at once. If the drummer chooses not to do so and only hit a single drum at any one time then they are using **linear drumming**.

Because in dance music layering and loops are commonplace, linear drumming is rare. A take on it is where the main kick/drum/percussion sounds refrain from sounding simultaneously. Check out Photek's 'ni ten ichi ryu' for an example of highly effective linear programming.

THREE'S THE MAGIC NUMBER...
3/4, 6/8 and triplet time

When dance musicians inhabit the safe world of fours life is pretty simple. But confusion abounds – often unnecessarily – when threes enter the equation.

3/4, or three time, featuring three 'full' (quarter-note) beats to the bar, is the time signature of the waltz. 'The Blue Danube' is the most famous example.

There are few examples of dance tracks written in 3/4. Apart from having virtually no contemporary pedigree, the feel of the beat is slow and rather plodding – great to soundtrack a palatial dance for the Viennese *hoi polloi*, but not what the dancefloor generally calls for. Notable exceptions include the aptly named '3 to the Floor' by S3RL (which opens and ends in 4/4 to help the DJ) and Jakatta's 'American Dream' (in 6/4).

More relevant is 6/8 time, featuring six eighth-notes rather than three quarter-notes. A halfway house between the feel of 3/4 and the flexibility of 4/4, 6/8 isn't uncommon in techno and D&B. It has also enjoyed a renaissance among EDM producers; check out David Guetta's 'Shot Me Down' for an example of a 6/8 rhythm in the lead riff – a raucous percussive groove that's hugely effective in its high-energy context.

To program 6/8 beats the sequencer grid should be set to 12 steps (three bars of four eighth-notes each).

Much more common in dance music than both 3/4 and 6/8 is the use of triplets in standard 4/4 time. These can give the

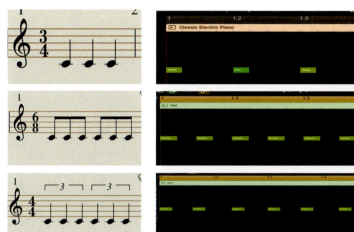

Fig 7: (*Top*) 3/4 time, (*middle*), 6/8 and (*bottom*) eighth-note triplets in 4/4 time.

impression of briefly changing time signature when in fact you're still in 4/4.

What is a triplet? In 4/4 time a single beat is divided into four equal quarter-note beats, each one normally divisible into two evenly spaced eighth notes. However, each beat can also be divided into *three* evenly spaced eighth notes – 'eighth note triplets' – collectively filling the same time as two regular eighth notes.

In dance music, there are three main uses for triplets:

Triplet songs: Although highly unusual in house, techno and other four-to-the-floor genres, it's not unusual to find heavy triplet use in D&B productions. Deadmau5's 'Right this Second' is an example of 12/8 – effectively 4/4 divided into eighth-note triplets – as is Boys Noize's 'Trooper'.

The triplet switch: Here, a track written in 4/4 transitions for a short period into triplet time to provide a rhythmic twist. Shock One's 'Polygon' is a good example; so is Noisia's 'Machine Gun', which opens in 4/4 time then transitions to triplets.

The triplet fill: While triplet switches involve a sustained use of triplets, in a triplet fill only one or two bars get the treatment. A common trick among mainroom house producers, regular 4/4 time is interrupted by a triplet fill to throw off the established groove for a short time before normality is resumed.

Chapter one
Drums and beats

Programming and sequencing drums

There are three main approaches to drum programming, each with its unique pros and cons. It's a matter of personal preference which you choose.

Almost all **drum machines** have built-in **step sequencers** (the exceptions being drum modules designed to be triggered by another piece of equipment).

Step sequencing (*see walkthrough, right*) has been popular since the first wave of programmable analogue drum machines in the late 1970s and early '80s. The most iconic version is based on the sequencers found in Roland's TR drum machines (which is why it's sometimes known as 'x0x-style' sequencing).

It's a simple approach typically based around 16 steps per bar where the user selects a drum then presses any of 16 buttons to trigger that hit. Some sequencers offer longer pattern length options.

Step sequencing may appear constraining, but it's both speedy and tactile. That's why it's included in so many modern drum machines and plugins despite the fact that they can also be programmed using seemingly more versatile approaches.

Other forms of built-in sequencer were introduced in the mid '80s as digital technology became more advanced. Early sampling sequencers such as the Akai MPC60 and Emu SP-12, for example, allow the user to program drum parts by **hitting buttons in real-time** as the track plays.

The result is a more human feel, albeit one which can be sloppy and imprecise if your timing's not up to scratch. Quantisation (*page 38*) is offered in order to correct human imprecision if required.

The first generation of these early sequencers offered only basic editing options at best, and usually very little in the way of visual feedback on recorded sequences and patterns. More recent developments of the same concept – such as those found in the current generation of Akai MPC models – have improved in both areas.

The built-in sequencer is, in many ways, like a more basic form of the **MIDI sequencing grids** found in DAWs (*see walkthrough, overleaf*). If you're working in a sequencer you have much more control over the placement and timing of individual hits. Whether you're using MIDI drum pads, playing drums in using a controller keyboard or drawing notes into a piano roll, you have near-infinite control over everything from velocities to hit placement,

◯ **Sequencing with the TR-909 is done using the 16 buttons running along the bottom.**

◯ **Drum programming using Ableton (*top*) and using audio clips directly on a channel in Logic (*below*).**

with no limitations in terms of sticking to a rigid 16 step pattern – or adhering to a grid at all.

The third and final approach is to place **audio loops and hits directly onto audio channels**, dragging them back and forth along the timeline in order to create a beat.

While there's nothing wrong with this approach, it offers less flexibility than dropping the hits into a sampler and triggering them using MIDI (which, at the very least, allow you to use different velocity settings for hits, even if you don't use any of the sampler's other features).

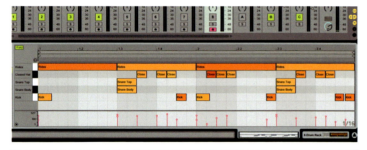

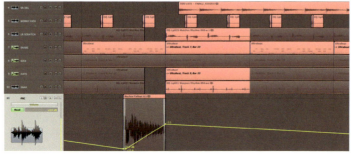

Starter for ten: step sequencing a house beat in D16's Nepheton

1

Step sequencing is *the* original way of making dance beats – and is still popular today. We're using D16's Roland TR-808 emulation Nepheton to demonstrate it. Load the instrument onto a MIDI track in your DAW and click the Patt. Write button to enable step sequencer editing.

2

Hold Cmd/Ctrl and click Clear. You'll see the cursor in the patch name flash, prompting you to enter a new name. Enter a name like 'House Beat' and press Enter. Click the Int Sync. button off so that Nepheton syncs to the DAW host tempo.

3

You'll see the Instrument Selector at the bottom of the display is set to BD - Bass Drum. Click on steps 1, 5, 9 and 13 to put a bass drum trigger on each beat of the bar. To audition the emerging four-to-the-floor groove press play on the DAW.

4

The bass drum is too long so turn down its Decay parameter in the Synthesis Module above to around 0.34. Add more drums as the beat plays back. Click the OH button in the Instrument Selector to switch to Open Hihat. Place hats on steps 3, 7, 11 and 15.

5

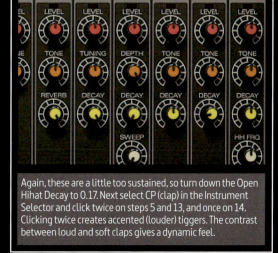

Again, these are a little too sustained, so turn down the Open Hihat Decay to 0.17. Next select CP (clap) in the Instrument Selector and click twice on steps 5 and 13, and once on 14. Clicking twice creates accented (louder) triggers. The contrast between loud and soft claps gives a dynamic feel.

6

Turn the Clap's Reverb and Level down to 0.4. Finally add more hats. Select CH for Closed Hihats then click steps 4, 6 and 12. The beat sounds more techno than house at the moment so turn the Shuffle knob up to 69% to inject a little swing.

// WALKTHROUGHS

Using a MIDI editor/piano roll to program drums

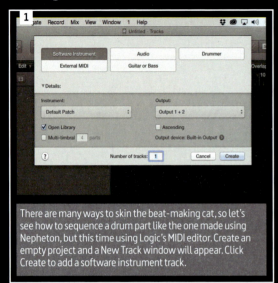

1. There are many ways to skin the beat-making cat, so let's see how to sequence a drum part like the one made using Nepheton, but this time using Logic's MIDI editor. Create an empty project and a New Track window will appear. Click Create to add a software instrument track.

2. Click the right hand side of the button that currently says E-Piano in the Inspector to bring up a list of available instruments. Select Ultrabeat (Drum Synth) > Stereo. When Ultrabeat's interface appears, click where it says Factory Default and select Drum Kits > Boutique 808.

3. Right-click the software instrument track and select Create Empty MIDI Region. Double-click the new MIDI region to bring up the MIDI editor. Drag over the ruler at the top of the editor to set the cycle range around the bar you've just created – this allows you to listen back to it on a loop.

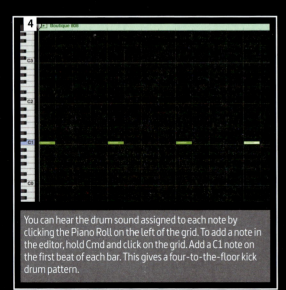

4. You can hear the drum sound assigned to each note by clicking the Piano Roll on the left of the grid. To add a note in the editor, hold Cmd and click on the grid. Add a C1 note on the first beat of each bar. This gives a four-to-the-floor kick drum pattern.

5. Place A#1 notes on the off-beats for open hats, G#1 (closed hats) on steps 4, 6 and 12 and D#1 (claps) on the second and fourth beats (steps 5 and 13). Add a clap on the 16th note after the second clap (step 14), then click the MIDI Draw button. The MIDI Draw area will appear below the grid.

6. To make step 14's clap into a more dynamic ghost note (page 55), reduce its velocity to 25 or so. Finally, apply swing. Press Cmd+A to select all notes, then in the Time Quantize panel on the left of the grid drag the horizontal Swing fader up to 89.

Adding audio to and refining a MIDI drum sequence

1 We're continuing with the MIDI sequenced house beat started opposite. Currently the different sounds don't feel like they fit seamlessly together. Tuning will help this. Double-click the centre of the button that says Ultrabeat in the Inspector to bring up the instrument's interface.

2 Click the Open HH1 tab on the left of Ultrabeat to select the open hat. The panel in the lower left corner displays the hat sample assigned to the key. The sample's start point is controlled by the velocity it's played at but as all notes triggering it are the same velocity it sounds consistent.

3 Drag the Max fader on the waveform to the right to adjust the position the sample plays from. As you move the fader further right, the shorter and more subdued the sample becomes. Set the fader about half way along the sample. You can now edit the hi-hat MIDI velocities for more interest.

4 Let's spice up the beat with some samples. Drag Perc Loop. wav from the Walkthrough files into Logic's arrangement. Click the audio track to select it, then click the Audio FX slot on the audio track's mixer channel in the Inspector to bring up a list of available effects.

5 Select Dynamics > Enveloper > Stereo from the list. Turn the vertical Gain fader on the right hand side of the Envelope's interface down to -100%. This attenuates the tail of each drum hit in the loop, giving a tighter sound. Turn the Time knob on the right up to 310ms to make it even snappier.

6 The loop feels dry and isolated. Click the Send slot on the audio track's channel strip and select Bus > Bus 1 (Small Room/0.4s Snare Chamber). The small knob on the right side of the slot controls the bus send level. Turn this to -12dB to give the percussion loop a more organic vibe.

// WALKTHROUGHS

Extracting the snare from a drum loop

1 Extracting drum sounds from loops is a great way to build a library of unique one shots. This walkthrough shows you how in Ableton Live, but the principle is similar in every DAW. Drag Drum Loop.wav – a Sample Magic break – onto an audio track in Live. Ensure the clip's warping is disabled.

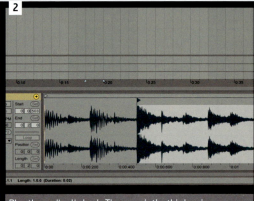

2 Play the audio clip back. The snare is the third major transient. In clip view drag the start marker to roughly the start of the snare, then drag down on the top half of the sample display to zoom in more closely to the start marker's position.

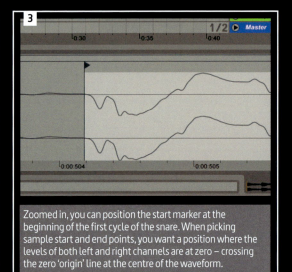

3 Zoomed in, you can position the start marker at the beginning of the first cycle of the snare. When picking sample start and end points, you want a position where the levels of both left and right channels are at zero – crossing the zero 'origin' line at the centre of the waveform.

4 Now when you play the clip back it'll start with the snare. A cymbal plays during the snare sound, but this doesn't have to be an obstacle to extracting the snare. Drag up on the top half of the sample display to zoom out then drag the end marker to the beginning of the cymbal.

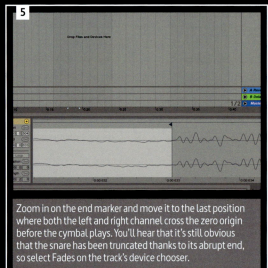

5 Zoom in on the end marker and move it to the last position where both the left and right channel cross the zero origin before the cymbal plays. You'll hear that it's still obvious that the snare has been truncated thanks to its abrupt end, so select Fades on the track's device chooser.

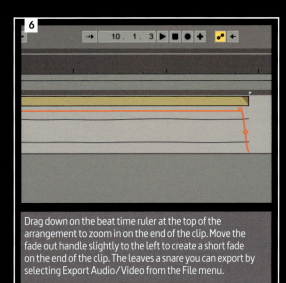

6 Drag down on the beat time ruler at the top of the arrangement to zoom in on the end of the clip. Move the fade out handle slightly to the left to create a short fade on the end of the clip. The leaves a snare you can export by selecting Export Audio/Video from the File menu.

Chapter one
Drums and beats

The fundamentals of beats

Wordsmith Samuel Coleridge famously wrote of poetry that it was "the best words in their best order".

Something similar can be said of great drum beats. *They are the right sounds in the best order*. Which is to say, **the right choice of sounds arranged into an engaging pattern**.

We've talked in length over previous pages about the raw sounds themselves. Suffice to say for now that two things matter above all; firstly, picking the right sounds to begin with; secondly, choosing sounds that *complement each other*.

What are the *best* or *right* sounds? To that question there is no single answer. *They are right according to the demands of the track, the genre and your intentions as an artist*. The decision is an aesthetic one.

The best beatsmiths have an innate understanding of which sounds will work together. For those who find it more of a challenge, trial and error (laying down a kick drum and then auditioning a snare alongside it to work out which sound/s work best with it) is usually the way to go. A shortcut for getting sounds that you know will complement each other is to use samples from drum machines. The 909 kick drum, for example, was designed from the ground up to work with the 909 snare and hi-hat, while the pairing of the LinnDrum kick and snare is about as good as it gets.

Picking a few sounds that complement each other is just the start. Next, you have to take those individual sounds and sequence them into a groove. Dozens of factors influence the effectiveness of the final beat, including:

- **velocity** of hits (how loud)
- **length** of hits (how long)
- **pitch** of hits (tuning)
- **placement** of hits (where)
- **opening (and later) transients** of hits (impact and body)
- **the amount of swing applied**, either to a single element or the whole beat (how swung).

The final beat is more than the sum of individual parts (or a literal interpretation of changes in external sound pressure level).

VELOCITY OF HITS

One of the key factors in determining the flavour of a groove is the velocity of its constituent hits.

The best way of illustrating how much difference velocity changes can make is to compare a sequence of eighth note hi-hats

Fig 8: The top grid shows eighth note hi-hats played at the same velocity while the lower grid shows the off-beats played at 50% velocity.

played with the same velocity (*Fig 8, top*) against the same sequence with varying velocities (*Fig 8, bottom*). While the first has a mechanical drum machine feel, the second has an organic, human feel to it – more characteristic of a live disco groove.

By tweaking velocities across a beat, you can generate fairly complex grooves from simple patterns. *Fig 9, top (overleaf)*, shows the same pattern but with a more detailed edit to the velocities. In this case each hit has been tweaked to shape the resulting groove – a more complex and characterful variant of the basic original version.

When a beat comprises more than a single hi-hat line it's easy to see how much can be achieved by simply tweaking velocities across a few parts, with dramatic differences fundamentally altering a rhythm's feel.

Chapter one
Drums and beats

An alternative effect can be achieved by mapping velocity to a low-pass filter. Because high frequency sounds attenuate faster than lower frequencies due to their relative energy level and the ease with which less powerful high-frequency changes are absorbed, differing high-frequency content will be perceived as coming from different depths in the sound field. *Fig 9 (bottom)* shows the same pattern but with velocity mapped to filter cutoff rather than volume.

Although trial and error is the best way of identifying velocity changes that work, there is one rule to bear in mind: while variable velocities work well for hi-hats and percussion parts, the kick drum is almost always best kept at the same velocity (particularly in straight four-to-the-floor beats; less so in two-step styles), as, to a lesser extent, is the snare/clap. Destabilising these foundations of the groove can lead to problems in the mix – and bewilderment on the dancefloor.

LENGTH OF HITS

When we hear sounds, our auditory system uses an averaging system to determine relative loudness. This averaging 'window' can last as long as a second. Tests have shown that up to this point, noise bursts of constant sound pressure level but increasing duration appear to get progressively louder.

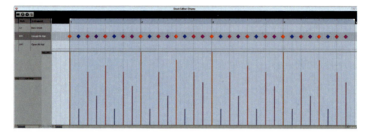

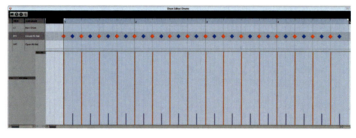

Fig 9 (*top*): A more complex hi-hat groove featuring multiple velocities. (*Bottom*): With velocity mapped to cutoff frequency, high velocities let all frequencies through, whilst lower velocities remove increasingly more top end. The effect is similar to using different velocities and can make for a more organic groove.

Which is to say, *the longer a hit – i.e. the more pronounced its body portion (page 10) – the louder it will sound than a shorter hit of the same volume*. Rhythmic material is particularly suited to making use of this psycho-acoustic effect given the short duration of all but the most bombastic orchestral percussion.

Fig 10, below, uses hi-hats again, this time with varied sample lengths. Note how the hi-hats feel organic and natural even though the sound itself doesn't change in volume. You can exploit this effect in your own productions by mapping sample length to velocity in a sampler and tweaking velocity values over time.

OPENING TRANSIENTS

A similar effect can be achieved at the start of a drum sound. Here, lengthening a drum's opening transients (*page 10*) has the effect of reducing both its impact and perceived volume. *The faster a transient peaks, the more impact it has*, a psycho-acoustic fact which is particularly pertinent to beat programming, in which sounds are heavily transient, featuring significant bursts of energy in their opening portions.

Tweaking transients allows you to reduce the contribution of an overbearing snare drum, for example, by increasing the length of its attack envelope or by using a transient designer to reduce the attack.

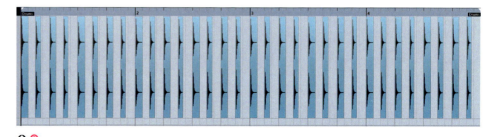

Fig 10: Using the same hits with different sample lengths to invoke the illusion of changing velocities.

Chapter one
Drums and beats

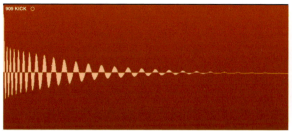
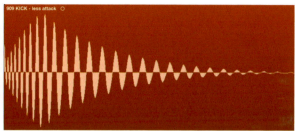

Fig 11: Rebalanced transients – The waveform on the left shows a 909 kick drum sampled straight from the machine. The right waveform shows the same sample fed through a transient designer with less aggressive attack and more body. The sound is very different, with the characteristic energy bump at the front end of the kick now heavily tempered.

Refined beatsmiths have an innate understanding of how the opening and closing transients of each sound in a beat affect the groove. They can give a beat a more laid-back feel by simply extending opening transient/s or give a groove more insistence by reducing drum tails and shortening attacks.

TIP To ease meter overload and masking or congestion caused when key sounds like kicks and snares hit at the same time, adjust the attack and release settings of each so that the initial transient builds don't coincide. Transient design plugins allow you to 'de-transient' a sound to soften its impact, allowing other sounds to punch through – as in *Fig 11*.

PLACEMENT OF HITS

We started this section by saying that the skill of the beat builder is arranging the right sounds into an engaging pattern.

That pattern is defined by the placement of hits on the grid – typically a 16th note grid in dance music – of which there are 30 in the closing pages of this chapter.

But that's only part of the story. Because while a sound's placement on the grid is important, so too is any fine-tuning to this placement – shifting a sound in time so that it falls slightly before or after a beat, or indeed somewhere entirely *off grid*.

The most common example of this technique is the shift of a snare or clap a few milliseconds before or after the beat when layering a snare/clap combo (*pages 52–53*).

By shifting one or more layers off the beat, a sound is not only given clearer definition (it's no longer masked by other sounds playing at the same time), but it also has an effect on the feel of the groove, with hits falling before the beat giving the groove a more urgent, insistent feel and hits falling after the beat giving a more relaxed, lazy vibe.

Fig 12, below, shows how even subtle shifts to a snare sound (before, after and on the grid) affect the groove.

The 'off-grid' snare technique is widely used, but it can be extended to pretty much every sound in a beat. Techno and chillout, in particular, are awash with beats composed using off-beat and off-kilter placements of interesting, often percussive, sounds.

Here it's just a case of dragging hits around the programming grid until what you hear is interesting, unique or plain funky-as-hell.

Fig 12: The same beat with the snare and clap falling on the beat (*top*), slightly before the beat (*middle*) and slightly after (*bottom*).

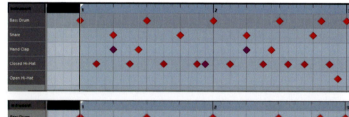

Quantisation, swing and groove

QUANTISATION

Quantisation is the process of aligning notes onto a defined grid so that a beat plays rigidly in sync.

The grid can be divided into a range of time divisions, from bars to single beats and fractions up to 128th of a beat – or beyond. The typical setting for dance music is a 16th note grid governed by a 4/4 rhythm (*page 26*) with kicks on steps 1, 5, 9 and 13.

Quantising, like step sequencing, was first introduced in sampling sequencers like the E-MU SP-12 as a mechanical way of correcting timing mistakes made when users punched-in grooves using rhythm pads.

The in-built quantise would nudge loose hits to the closest regular interval, tightening the beat and giving it a mechanically perfect feel – the trademark sound of many '80s hits (*Fig 13*).

Quantise is available in all DAWs for the same purpose. It can be turned on and off to snap out-of-time programmed beats or any other musical parts – whether MIDI or audio – onto the grid.

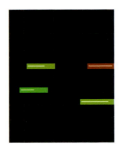

Fig 13 (*top*): Notes programmed roughly into a sequencer. (*Bottom*): The same notes with quantise applied. Note how they are now perfectly aligned to the 16th-note grid.

SWING

"If you have to ask, you'll never know." So said jazz legend Louis Armstrong when asked to define the concept of swing. And while there's an element of truth to the great man's words – understanding swing is not the same as being able to deliver it – the concept as it applies to dance music is easy enough to grasp.

The word 'swing' is one of those confusing terms that has different meanings to different people. Its jazz origins provide a useful starting point for understanding how swing works in software and electronic music hardware.

In jazz, 'swing timing' typically refers to a specific rhythm and notation convention, where the first beat of a bar is twice as long as the second, then the third beat is the same length as the first, and so on. It's effectively a variation on triplet or 6/8 time. The timing gave its name to swing music – the 1930s offshoot of jazz based on those same lopsided rhythms.

In a broader sense, *swinging* eventually came to be used to describe any rhythm with an off-kilter groove. Drummers 'swing' the beat to add a groove, introducing a slightly irregular feel to the rhythm.

It's important not to confuse swing with sloppy, imprecise timing. *Swing is not inaccuracy*. Instead, *it's the deliberate, introduction of subtle timing variations*.

The term is mainly used in reference to drumming because drummers set the groove of a band and generally play repetitive rhythmic patterns. But swing can and is applied to the timing of other instruments too.

How do we apply this idea of loose, fluid timing to electronic music?

The earliest sequencers and drum machines played using rigid timing with evenly spaced gaps between each division of the bar (*as in Fig 14, right, top line*). Using the Roland TR-808, for instance, each of the 16 steps in a programmed beat is played with perfectly straight timing.

The 'swing' function as we now know it – originally known as '**shuffle**', a term still used by some hardware manufacturers and software developers – was first introduced in Roger Linn's 1979 LM-1 Drum Computer. Linn realised that he could approximate the effect of a human drummer playing in swing timing by quantising each eighth note drum beat to the nearest step and then delaying the playback *of every other (16th) step* in the sequence.

"My implementation of swing has always been very simple," explains Linn. "I delay the second 16th note within each eighth

Chapter one
Drums and beats

note. In other words, I delay all even-numbered 16th notes within the beat (2, 4, 6, 8, etc)."

Linn's system – which forms the basis of all modern swing templates and remains virtually unchanged to this day – is illustrated in *Fig 14, above*. It uses percentages to express the amount of swing applied to every second step. Those percentages pertain to the degree that every second 16th note is positioned in relation to the eighth beat either side of it. So 50% swing refers to straight timing, where every second step is played *exactly half way between the two beats either side of it* while 70+% swing refers to a heavily swung beat with the alternative steps leaning heavily into their neighbours.

Adding swing to a beat introduces a more human feel to a pattern, but just as importantly, even the smallest amount of swing can enhance a groove in a uniquely appealing way. So ubiquitous has its use been throughout dance music that swung beats using Linn's original groove templates (later adopted by the MPC line of samplers), often just sound contextually 'right'.

NOTE A common source of confusion when getting to grips with swing is to try and apply 16th note swing to a pattern with hits that only appear on eighth notes (i.e. on-the-beat hits) and wonder why nothing happens. *When all hits land on eighth notes, you won't hear any effect when applying 16th note swing as the delayed steps (in orange above) don't have any hits on them.*

SWING IN DAWS

Although most drum machines, sequencers and DAWs handle swing in essentially the same way – delaying alternate notes by slightly different amounts – there are a number of different ways of describing the same process.

The most common approach (and the system used in the beat grids at the end of this chapter) is the one implemented by Linn back in 1979, where straight timing is referred to as 50%, meaning that the first beat of every pair of 16th notes takes up 50% of the time of those two notes (i.e. the full eighth note). At a 60% swing setting the first beat lasts 60% of that eighth note.

Fig 14: What swing looks like.

The top row shows a simple 16th note hi-hat pattern with no swing applied (50% swing or 16 Swing A in Logic terms).

Subsequent rows show increasing amounts of swing being applied, with the playback of every other 16th step (the ones in orange) being delayed by increasing amounts. (54%/16B; 58%/16C; 62%/16D; 66%/16E and 71%/16F.)

Note how far the delayed steps get pushed at more extreme settings, leaning ever closer to the on-the-beat eighth note hits. It is this delay and leaning that gives the feel we know as swing.

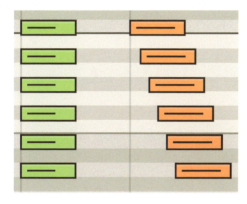

You'll still find that approach in hardware such as **Akai MPCs**, **Korg Electribes**, the **DSI Tempest** and DAWs including **Reason**.

The main swing option in **Logic** dispenses with percentages, offering a choice of six settings instead. In the case of 16th note swing, these are referred to as 16 Swing A through to 16F. The manual defines those settings by swing percentage, using the same convention (50% = straight timing) as Linn: 16A – 50%, 16B – 54%, 16C – 58%, 16D – 62%, 16E – 66% and 16F – 71%.

Note that these six swing settings are almost exactly the same as the factory settings offered on the LM-1 and other vintage drum machines including the E-MU

Drumulator, SP-12 and SP-1200, and the Oberheim DMX. Because it's difficult to hear a difference in timing from small changes in the swing setting, 4% increments work well – you can hear the difference from one setting to the next, but it's not such a dramatic change that you're constantly wanting an option between settings.

DAWs often allow you to generate swing in a few different ways. **Logic**, for example, also offers Q-Swing and Advanced Quantization settings for each region. Built-in sequencers in plugins like Ultrabeat often also include a dedicated swing knob (Ultrabeat allows you to dial in anything from 50–85% swing).

Likewise, the step sequencer in **FL Studio** offers a different approach to the groove template options in the piano roll.

Both FL Studio and **Cubase** use a subtly different numerical convention to achieve the same result as the likes of the LM-1, MPC, Logic and Reason. The manual for Cubase 7 is the best part of 1,000 pages long, but this is just about all it has to say on swing: "This parameter lets you offset every second position in the grid, creating a swing or shuffle feel." No wonder so many people struggle to understand how swing works! The simple explanation of the difference is that Cubase uses 0% to represent perfectly straight timing, while 100% equates to triplets (page 29).

PRO TIPS

ROGER LINN

"All the swing, dynamics and other tricks won't do you any good unless you come up with a good beat in the first place."

Recent versions of **Ableton** have integrated swing with the DAW's groove features and, specifically, the Groove Pool.

In the Groove Pool you'll find groove templates which recreate the sound of various third-party sequencers and drum machines. This means you'll need to understand both systems.

In the MPC folder, for example, you'll find eighth and 16th note swing options which copy the timing of the MPC, using the convention where 50% swing equals straight timing. But in the Swing folder you'll find eighth, 16th and 32nd note options which use the convention where 0% swing is straight timing (as in Cubase and FL Studio).

Ableton's groove options offer a lot of control over how the swing is applied – from the Global Groove Amount to individual Base, Quantize and Timing settings for each groove template used in a particular project.

In some DAWs you get a visual display of the effect your swing setting has on the position of the notes. In Logic and Cubase's piano rolls, for instance, applying swing quantisation shifts the notes on the grid

TOOLS OF THE TRADE
Faking the funk – virtual drummers and drum replacement

Although dance music tends to rely on programmed beats and sampled or synthesised drum hits, there are times when the sound of a live drummer is what's required. However, recording drums to a high standard is tricky and requires access to a drummer, a good kit, all the necessary mics and a suitable recording space.

One potential alternative is to use a virtual drummer plugin in your DAW. Plugins such as Toontrack's Superior Drummer or Steven Slate Drums are realistic sample-based instruments which offer a hugely versatile approach to emulating the sound of real drums. Each drum is meticulously multisampled with a range of different velocity levels and articulations and recorded through a range of microphones which can be mixed and matched to create a fully customisable virtual kit with a sound to match your track. The drums can then be triggered by MIDI (most plugins bundle in MIDI patterns) either using pads or by programming them in.

The results may not sound exactly the same as a real drummer, but it's an option worth bearing in mind, especially considering the time, effort and potential expense of recording live drums.

Drum replacement tools are also worth exploring. They automatically replace each hit of an audio recording with a sample of your choice.

So if you've recorded a kick pattern from a drum machine but you're not happy with the sound, you can use a plugin such as WaveMachine Labs' Drumagog or Massey DRT to layer a sample over each hit or replace the original audio recording entirely, retaining the same timing and velocity levels. Some DAWs have basic equivalents built in as standard.

(you can turn the swing off and the notes jump back to their original positions). In others (Ultrabeat, FL Studio's step sequencer), notes are delayed without their position on the grid changing.

Ableton falls somewhere in the middle, shifting the timing of notes without moving them on the grid unless you hit the Commit button.

The important thing to remember here is that all of these approaches ultimately achieve the same end result: *they all delay alternate steps in a sequence.*

SWING IN PRACTICE

To draw all the information about swing together, look at *Fig 15*. The top sequence shows a simple TR-909 beat with straight swing (50%, 16A), with the gaps between 16th notes equal.

The lower sequence features a 58% (16C) swing setting where every other 16th hit (coloured in blue) is slightly delayed to give the characteristic swung sound.

As we now know, the 58% figure relates to the distance between the (green) odd on-the-beat hits. Which is to say that the blue swung hits are positioned 58% of the distance between the on-the-beat green ones. *No green, on-beat hits, are affected by the swing.*

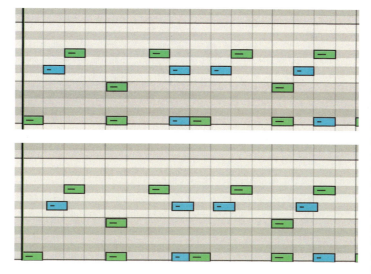

🎧 ⏺
Fig 15: A simple TR-909 drum beat using no/straight swing (*top*) and 58% (16C) swing (*bottom*).

SWINGING BOTH WAYS

Some of the most effective grooves are made when different swing settings are used across multiple parts. So while the hi-hats may be given a 16B/54% swing, a wonky percussive part might be treated to a more extreme 16E/66% setting. Although on paper this sounds like a recipe for disaster, with the right sounds the differently timed elements can work beautifully together, creating rhythms full of vibe.

Nor do different swing settings have to be limited to drum parts. A long-standing technique with its roots in disco is to twin a heavily swung bassline – and other musical elements – with a rigidly straight 4/4 beat.

Human after all

Sometimes you want a beat that sounds deliberately live or lazy.

Rejecting the rigidity of the quantise grid is a legitimate aesthetic choice – but bear in mind the point from *page 38*, that **random timing is unlikely to create a great beat**: the best beats come about due to the deliberate introduction of subtle timing variations.

For more organic grooves:

Program beats live
Close your DAW's drum grid. Tap in beats live instead using a keyboard or drum pads and your fingers. Keep quantise settings off and keep looping until you get a good take – as you would during a real recording. Major timing errors can be rectified manually against the grid.

Humanise
If you don't have access to a keyboard you can get a similar effect by programming onto the grid and then manually shifting hits by a few ms. Some DAWS offer 'humanisation' algorithms, which randomly move hits off-grid and introduce subtle velocity variants. In Logic X, select Functions > MIDI Transform > Humanize.

Pick the right sounds
Live sounding beats are based on real live drum samples. Instead of relying on stock machine 'dance' drums, splash out on a few jazz, funk or rock samples – replete with natural sounding room ambience.

Keep it real
Live drummers have a limitation on what they can play on their kit at any one time dictated by the number of limbs they have (typically four). This means programming MIDI in which: no more than four drums play at any one time; no more than two stick-struck drums play at once (snare, hat, tom etc); and only one hi-hat sounds at any given time.

Swing in Logic

1 Create an instrument track and click the right-hand side of the instrument slot in the software instrument's channel to bring up the list of available instruments. Select Ultrabeat (Drum Synth) > Stereo, then click the patch name on Ultrabeat's interface and select Drum Kits > Boutique 909.

2 Right-click on the software instrument track in the arrangement and select Create Empty MIDI Region. Double-click the region to bring up the MIDI grid editor, then hold Cmd and program in 16th notes on G#1 to create a simple closed hi-hat pattern.

3 Drag on the ruler at the top of the arrangement over the first bar to loop it and play the project back. You'll hear the lack of timing variation in the part gives it a robotic feel that might be ideal for certain types techno, but not house. Let's funk it up a bit.

4 Press Cmd+A to select all notes in the region, then in the Time Quantize (classic) panel on the left of the grid editor, gradually turn up the horizontal Swing fader. You'll see every other note move slightly further to the right and hear the hats get the flavour of a jackin' house groove.

5 Set Swing to 50 then click where it says 1/16 Note above to bring up a drop-down list of available quantisation resolutions. Select 1/16 Triplet (1/24), and you'll see the notes snap into new positions. This changes the feel of the groove entirely.

6 Swing can be applied to audio as well. Mute the instrument and drag Straight Hats.wav onto the arrangement. Select the audio region and activate Flex. In the Region Inspector set Quantize to 1/16 Note and drag up on the Q-Swing slot as you would on the MIDI grid editor's Swing fader.

Swing in Ableton

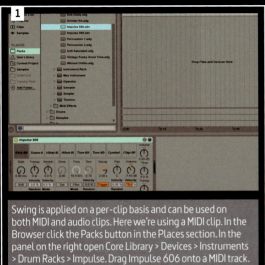

1 Swing is applied on a per-clip basis and can be used on both MIDI and audio clips. Here we're using a MIDI clip. In the Browser click the Packs button in the Places section. In the panel on the right open Core Library > Devices > Instruments > Drum Racks > Impulse. Drag Impulse 606 onto a MIDI track.

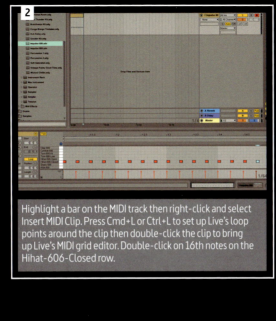

2 Highlight a bar on the MIDI track then right-click and select Insert MIDI Clip. Press Cmd+L or Ctrl+L to set up Live's loop points around the clip then double-click the clip to bring up Live's MIDI grid editor. Double-click on 16th notes on the Hihat-606-Closed row.

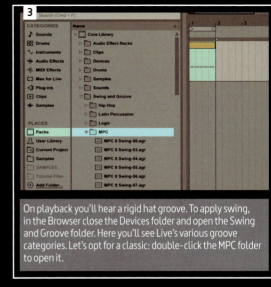

3 On playback you'll hear a rigid hat groove. To apply swing, in the Browser close the Devices folder and open the Swing and Groove folder. Here you'll see Live's various groove categories. Let's opt for a classic: double-click the MPC folder to open it.

4 Drag MPC 16 Swing-67 onto the MIDI clip. Now when the clip plays back it has the trademark swing of the MPC. You can control the swing amount by opening the Groove Pool with the wavy button on the left hand side of the interface and dragging down on the Timing fader.

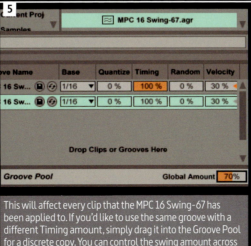

5 This will affect every clip that the MPC 16 Swing-67 has been applied to. If you'd like to use the same groove with a different Timing amount, simply drag it into the Groove Pool for a discrete copy. You can control the swing amount across a whole project using the Global Amount fader.

6 You can change which groove a clip uses by selecting it with the Clip Groove menu in Clip View. Clicking the Commit button on the Clip Groove menu 'flattens' the clip, committing the notes to their swung positions – helpful if a part requires subsequent timing edits.

Chapter one
Drums and beats

Swing and groove: Next steps

EXTRACTING MIDI GROOVES

Even though bundled libraries and online resources offers enough groove templates to keep even the most demanding beatsmith happy for months, sometimes you hear a groove – on a track or commercial loop – that you just have to add to your personal groove pool. Fortunately all major DAWs offer means of extracting grooves from loops and translating them into MIDI or audio groove templates and storing them with your project or in your quantize menu for later use.

When choosing audio to extract a groove from, listen through the complete song to find the most appropriate loop. An ideal candidate has clean transients, ideally on every 16th note. If you're extracting a drum groove aim for a section where the beat plays alone. To make the extraction process as reliable as possible:

▸▸ **Prepare the audio so that it loops seamlessly** – cut precisely and audition it alone and in the context of a mix,

▸▸ **Ensure the loop starts and ends on zero-crossing points** to avoid clicks and pops. Insert inaudible (2–3 ms) fades at the start and end of the loop to 'force' zero crossings if you need to, and

▸▸ **Check the groove markers.** You may need to manually tweak the markers to match the transients exactly – especially for less prominent or quieter hits in the audio.

TIP Grooves aren't just for beats. Tighten up rhythm guitar or percussive parts in audio or apply the same MIDI groove from a programmed soft-synth to an acoustic bassline.

TIP Duplicate a signal, pan the two instances left and right then use two subtly different groove settings to create the illusion of double-tracking. The technique is particularly effective on synths and rhythm guitars, but try it on percussion too.

TIP Try extracting grooves from audio parts that aren't drum or percussion patterns like FX or busy full-track loops. Although experimental, this can produce unique results.

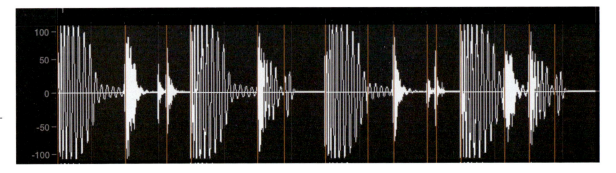

🎧 🔴
A well prepared loop for extracting a groove. Note zero crossings at the loop start and end and manually tweaked markers that accurately fall at the start of almost every transient. It's worth experimenting with transient placements. In this example we deliberately deleted a double transient that had been automatically generated around the first percussive shuffled hit in the fourth beat to get a better result. The shuffle is obvious on the image: look how far away the third and sixth (orange) transient markers are from the (light grey) beat divisions.

TIP Many samplers let you stack multiple samples on the same MIDI note and set velocity ranges that trigger each different sample. Use this to create more realistic drums by, for example, programming higher velocities to trigger snappier, brighter snare drums and lower velocities to trigger softer, duller snare sounds. Trigger entirely different samples at different velocities for quasi-random beat making mayhem.

TIP Although it's normal (and good) practice to trim drum one-shot start times to the opening transient, extending the silence before the transient hits adds micro delays that can give extra character to a beat.

TIP Track delay can be useful for triggering parts slightly off-grid. In Logic you can sit layered claps slightly ahead of or behind the snare by using the delay option in the region panel and using the +/- ticks. The audio won't move on the arrange page but any audio on the delayed track will be played earlier or later.

Extracting a groove: Logic 🎧

1 Open Logic and select Empty Project. When the New Track window appears, click Audio > Create. In the Walkthrough files folder locate the drum loop 'Disco.wav'. Drag this onto the audio track and double-click it to bring up the audio waveform. Click the Flex button to activate Flex mode.

2 In the Region Inspector, click the Quantize value (set to 'off' by default) and select Make Groove Template. Logic creates a new groove template instantly from the disco beat. Now when you click Quantize again you'll see a new groove template, 'Disco', is available at the bottom of the list.

3 You need to keep the source region used to create the groove template in a project to use it. If you delete it, the template will remain visible in the Quantize menu but selecting it won't have any effect. To permanently add a groove template you need to save the MIDI track into the Autoload project.

Extracting a groove: Ableton 🎧

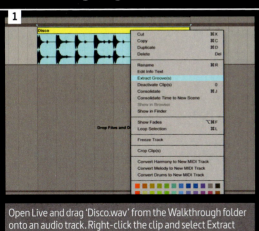

1 Open Live and drag 'Disco.wav' from the Walkthrough folder onto an audio track. Right-click the clip and select Extract Groove(s) from the menu. A progress bar will appear as Live analyses the audio and creates a groove. This process should only take a few seconds.

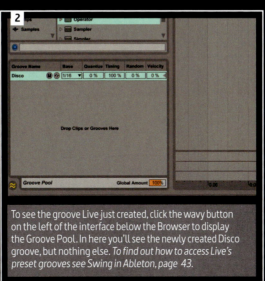

2 To see the groove Live just created, click the wavy button on the left of the interface below the Browser to display the Groove Pool. In here you'll see the newly created Disco groove, but nothing else. *To find out how to access Live's preset grooves see Swing in Ableton, page 43.*

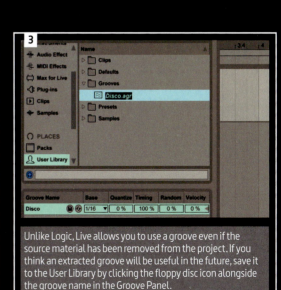

3 Unlike Logic, Live allows you to use a groove even if the source material has been removed from the project. If you think an extracted groove will be useful in the future, save it to the User Library by clicking the floppy disc icon alongside the groove name in the Groove Panel.

Chapter one
Drums and beats

Synthesising drum sounds

There are an enormous number of drum sample libraries, drum machine plugins, drum synths, virtual drummer instruments and of course dedicated hardware available to help you make the best beats possible. This begs the question: why bother with learning about drum synthesis at all?

The answer is threefold:
▶▶ 1. **Flexibility**. Synthesising a drum sound allows you to give it the perfect shape and tone for a track.
▶▶ 2. It's a great way to **improve your sound design skills**. Although some drum synthesis can be demanding, it's easy enough to make a quality kick drum – as the walkthrough opposite shows – giving synthesis newbies plenty to learn and inspire.
▶▶ 3. It's **fun**.

THE BASICS

Using some pretty simple **frequency modulation** and **subtractive synthesis** techniques (page 72) it's possible to create a wide range of drum sounds.

At their core, most drums are fairly basic instruments – they are, after all, the oldest known instrument in the world, clocking in at more than 6000 years of age. A typical drum is based around a membrane stretched over a hollow body. When the membrane is struck it vibrates, with the hollow body amplifying the sound. This can be replicated in synthesis using a **simple oscillator** and **amplifier** combination.

ENVELOPES

Drum sounds are defined by their shape, which means envelopes play a critical role. Drums rarely require a sustain stage – just a tweaked decay and moderate release will usually do the job – while a fast attack gives a drum its up-front transient impact. But pitch envelopes and filter envelopes are also crucial for sculpting drum sounds. As the walkthrough on the right demonstrates, envelopes that allow you to create curves offer far more sound design flexibility.

KICK DRUMS

Making your own kick is simple: a sine tone with a linear drop in pitch gives a basic facsimile of the real thing. The pitch drop gives the percussive feel. By tweaking its envelope shape you can change the kick's character from tight tech-house bass drum to full-on trance belter.

However, this alone isn't enough to really satisfy the ears, and it's only when you create a more interesting attack phase (for example, by creating a more involved pitch movement using FM synthesis or a non-linear pitch modulation envelope) that a synthetic kick starts to excite.

TIP An alternative to using an oscillator and sine wave for kicks is to sweep the cutoff frequency of a self-oscillating resonant filter. Combine both approaches for interesting effects.

TIP Try applying the same pitch modulation envelope to bass or lead sounds to make them more percussive.

SNARES AND TOMS

Once you've nailed the basics of synthesising kick drums, snares and tom sounds follow a similar template. Introduce a noise oscillator to add snap to a snare and use filters to sculp the tone.

CYMBALS

Cymbals are more complex to recreate because of the inharmonics they create. Many producers 'cheat' and use filtered and carefully shaped white noise for a deliberately artificial sound. Because it's crammed full of harmonics, white noise works well for short hi-hat sounds.

TIP Check out dedicated drum synths such as Logic's Ultrabeat, SonicCharge's MicroTonic, Audio Damage's Tattoo and Sample Magic's Stacker.

PRO TIPS

MAELSTROM

"Before buying an analogue oscillator-based drum machine, I often struggled to find interesting drum sounds.

"Most of the samples you'll find are either samples of classic Roland drum machines, or boring and generic drum hits aimed at specific music styles.

"So I progressively started learning how to design my own drums, using both hardware and software synths.

"All you need is an oscillator, a noise generator, an ADSR and a resonant filter. I ended up with a large collection of drum hits that I started using in my own productions."

Analogue kick drum

1 Most synths can create analogue-style kicks, but some are better suited to the job. The ideal candidate must provide flexible control of the envelope curves. Start with a sine wave oscillator and set the amp to last around 300ms with zero attack and a short release to smooth out the tail.

2 The fun starts with the pitch envelope, which we're using to define the transient attack, the thump of the body and the power of the sub. The key of the track is E, so set the start point to E4 (329.6 Hz) and the end to E1 (41.2 Hz). With a straight envelope it's a simple kick, and a good starting point.

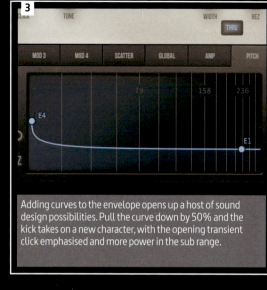

3 Adding curves to the envelope opens up a host of sound design possibilities. Pull the curve down by 50% and the kick takes on a new character, with the opening transient click emphasised and more power in the sub range.

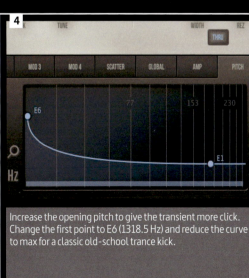

4 Increase the opening pitch to give the transient more click. Change the first point to E6 (1318.5 Hz) and reduce the curve to max for a classic old-school trance kick.

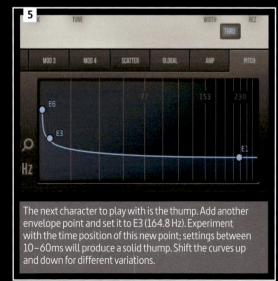

5 The next character to play with is the thump. Add another envelope point and set it to E3 (164.8 Hz). Experiment with the time position of this new point; settings between 10–60ms will produce a solid thump. Shift the curves up and down for different variations.

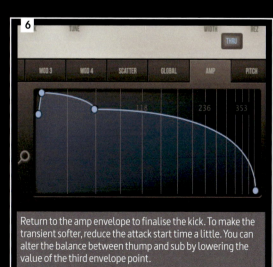

6 Return to the amp envelope to finalise the kick. To make the transient softer, reduce the attack start time a little. You can alter the balance between thump and sub by lowering the value of the third envelope point.

// WALKTHROUGHS

Analogue snare

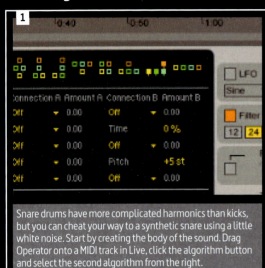

1 Snare drums have more complicated harmonics than kicks, but you can cheat your way to a synthetic snare using a little white noise. Start by creating the body of the sound. Drag Operator onto a MIDI track in Live, click the algorithm button and select the second algorithm from the right.

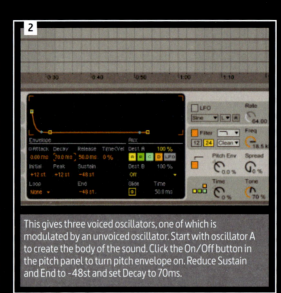

2 This gives three voiced oscillators, one of which is modulated by an unvoiced oscillator. Start with oscillator A to create the body of the sound. Click the On/Off button in the pitch panel to turn pitch envelope on. Reduce Sustain and End to -48st and set Decay to 70ms.

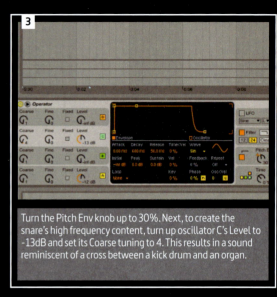

3 Turn the Pitch Env knob up to 30%. Next, to create the snare's high frequency content, turn up oscillator C's Level to -13dB and set its Coarse tuning to 4. This results in a sound reminiscent of a cross between a kick drum and an organ.

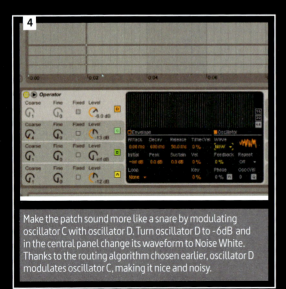

4 Make the patch sound more like a snare by modulating oscillator C with oscillator D. Turn oscillator D to -6dB and in the central panel change its waveform to Noise White. Thanks to the routing algorithm chosen earlier, oscillator D modulates oscillator C, making it nice and noisy.

5 Click oscillator C's panel again, and set its Sustain to -infdB and Decay to 130ms. This gives the snare a punchy, percussive top end. Set oscillator A's Sustain to -infdB, Release to 100ms and Decay to 500ms, making it more percussive too.

6 Finally, add an instance of EQ Eight after Operator and set the first filter band to high pass. Use it to take out the snare's lowest frequencies then hollow out the mids for a more natural sound. Because the snare can be played chromatically, the exact cut will depend on the track key.

White noise hi-hat

1 You can synthesise hi-hats in a few moments using nothing more than a noise oscillator and filter. In this example we're using Logic's ES2 synth. Load the synth on a software instrument track and set oscillator 3's waveform knob to Noise.

2 Drag the pointer in the Oscillator Mix Triangle to 100% 3 so that all you hear is the noise. Drag Env 3's Sustain (S) fader all the way down and adjust the Decay (D) to taste – about 50ms gives a short, percussive hat sound. Open the Decay for a longer, open hi-hat sound.

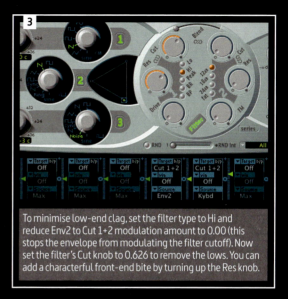

3 To minimise low-end clag, set the filter type to Hi and reduce Env2 to Cut 1+2 modulation amount to 0.00 (this stops the envelope from modulating the filter cutoff). Now set the filter's Cut knob to 0.626 to remove the lows. You can add a characterful front-end bite by turning up the Res knob.

Basic deep house tom

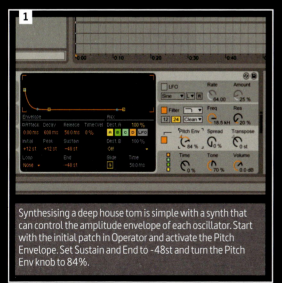

1 Synthesising a deep house tom is simple with a synth that can control the amplitude envelope of each oscillator. Start with the initial patch in Operator and activate the Pitch Envelope. Set Sustain and End to -48st and turn the Pitch Env knob to 84%.

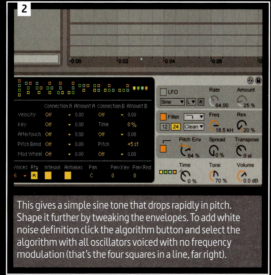

2 This gives a simple sine tone that drops rapidly in pitch. Shape it further by tweaking the envelopes. To add white noise definition click the algorithm button and select the algorithm with all oscillators voiced with no frequency modulation (that's the four squares in a line, far right).

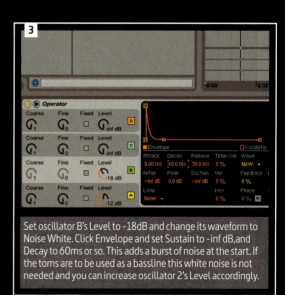

3 Set oscillator B's Level to -18dB and change its waveform to Noise White. Click Envelope and set Sustain to -inf dB, and Decay to 60ms or so. This adds a burst of noise at the start. If the toms are to be used as a bassline this white noise is not needed and you can increase oscillator 2's Level accordingly.

Layering drums

We have more sounds at our disposal than ever before. Even if your studio extends no further than a laptop and a DAW you're likely to have access to thousands of bundled drum sounds. If you have an extensive sample collection you can multiply that figure by ten.

With so many sounds, the law of averages says you should be able to find the perfect drum to fit most grooves/tracks. And even if a sound's not 100% right some tweaks to its envelope setting or tuning is usually enough to help it fit the sonic bill.

But sometimes however many sounds you audition, *none of them quite works*. The kick drum has oomph but not crunch; the snare has whack without crack. Or maybe you're a sample-eschewing sound designer who prefers every sound in their mix to be sculpted by hand.

In either case, there are two approaches to building original drum hits:

▶▶ 1: **Synthesise your own sounds**, or
▶▶ 2: **Layer existing samples** to make unique hybrids that fit the mix every time.

Drum synthesis is covered over the previous pages. Here we focus on the art and craft of drum layering.

THINKING AS ONE

Many producers end up panicking over drum layering after their first few attempts end with muddy, ill-defined results. This is often because they like a drum sound so layer it onto existing drum/s and wonder why the beat doesn't instantly sound better – two kick drums, they think, should by default be better than one.

That thinking is a shortcut to disaster. Layering must be approached with care, with an understanding of the dangers and with a clear idea of what each constituent sound is going to add to the composite final. Which is all to say, **only layer when there is a good reason for doing so**.

PHASE

The main hidden danger when layering drum sounds is **phase cancellation**, which occurs when the layered samples' waveforms are out of phase with each other.

Two identical signals are completely out of phase (aka with **negative polarity**) when their waveforms directly mirror each other. If this occurs they cancel each other out, resulting in silence.

In the real world, when layering complex drum sounds, you are not going to end up with silence. But, especially if the opening transients of a waveform set off in opposite directions, frequencies in the composite layered sound can become quieter, giving a brittle, weak sound.

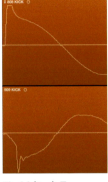

Fig 16 (*top*): Two samples with negative phase – note the way the two waveforms set off in opposite directions.
(*Bottom*): The same waveforms with the second's polarity flipped. They will now sound much fuller when triggered together.

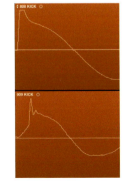

While phase cancellation can affect any layered sound, it is most noticeable when layering kicks, where even a slight drop of energy in the opening transients can badly affect the low end.

One way of checking to see if samples risk cancellation is to zoom in on their waveforms, as in *Fig 16, left*. If they set off going in the same direction you are usually safe.

A simple shortcut if they don't is to use a DAW's polarity inversion button, often (erroneously) labelled as phase inversion.

There are many plugins that also allow you to do the job, like Sonalksis' FreeG plugin.

Deciding whether the kicks work best with the polarity of one sample inverted is a simple case of trial and error: invert the polarity and if it sounds better stick with it.

It doesn't particularly matter whether you invert the polarity of the first or second kick; the effect is pretty much identical. *Bear in mind that inverting both has virtually the same effect as inverting neither.*

TIMING

When layering, the timing of the start of each sample is critical. Sometimes you'll want the combined layered hit to be a single unified sound (in the case of a kick drum, for example). At other times you may want obviously staggered layers (in the example of a lazy disco clap/snare hybrid – see *Layered EDM smash, overleaf*).

In both cases the trick to getting an effective layered sound is zooming in on the opening transients then shifting each layer in time either so they gel into a single sound or so that they hit at perceptively different times. Plugins like Sample Magic's Stacker, with its intelligent 'Scatter' functionality, make this a breeze.

NOTE Altering sample start times directly impacts on the phase relation between the samples, so, again, flip either sample's polarity to see what difference it makes.

One quick and easy way of ensuring opening transients don't hit at the same time in each layer is to employ a transient designer or compressor to change the transient make-up of each opening portion. To shift a hard-edged live snare sample slightly back from the opening portion of a layered analogue snare, for example, simply lengthen its attack. A similar approach can be taken to rebalance the energy make-up of a layer's sustain or release.

EQ: TRIMMING THE FAT

The final area to focus on is the frequency range each constituent sample occupies. When mixing two or more sounds together there's no point each one contributing the same frequencies to the composite. If too many frequencies overlap the end result will be muddy and ill-defined.

To avoid frequency doubling and masking, use **EQ bracketing** (*page 211*) to carve away the unwanted frequencies in each sound, making space for both to sit together.

If you are layering a bass-heavy 808 kick drum (for low end) with a live bass drum (for mid-tone clout), for example, you might choose to roll away the higher frequencies of the 808 while cutting the lower frequencies of the live drum for the best of both worlds – a layered kick with a subby low-end and a weighty mid punch, but without congested crossover.

TIP When applying filters, experiment with slope falloffs – too steep and you can generate unnaturally 'holey' results.

TIP If you're struggling to separate layers using EQ alone, try also using different reverb treatments for each layer. Instead of straight hall or room settings, audition early reflection programs and short reverb and chamber IRs. Placing different layers in different spaces aids separation.

PRO TIPS
KENNY 'DOPE' GONZALEZ

"'The Bomb' was done on an [Emu] SP1200 and an [Akai] S950.

"The way I used to do my beats back then, all my rhythms and my drums were in the SP, but it didn't hold long samples so all the long samples were in the S950 and I would trigger them from the drum machine. That's how that record was made – and how a lot of records were made in that time period.

"There was a certain vibe to the two as well. Today you can have unlimited amounts of sample time in a machine, but it's a different vibe to those two machines."

BUSSING

When you're happy with a layered sound, route each composite sound to a single drum bus ('kick drum group' for example). Doing this not only allows you to EQ and/or compress the layered drum as if it were one sound – giving it a single gel of glue – it also makes it easier to balance its level against other drum sounds.

TIP If you like the layered sound enough, bounce is out as a single hit and add it to your sample library.

KNOWING WHAT YOU WANT

With the theory out the way it's worth making the most important point about drum layering last: *layering is a lot easier when you have a clear intention in mind.*

If you have a live kick drum sample you like but it doesn't have the necessary low-end for the dancefloor, knowing that you need to layer it with an 808-style kick will help deliver results fast. Once you've made that call all you need to do is layer in an 808 bass drum, align the sample starts, retune, check phase, perform EQ tweaks (cutting lows from the live kick and highs from the 808) and you'll have the sound you're after.

Endless tweaking while layering wastes hours in the studio. A clear vision focuses attention on the task at hand.

// WALKTHROUGHS

Layered clap/snare combo – the old school way

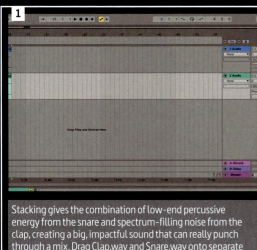

1 Stacking gives the combination of low-end percussive energy from the snare and spectrum-filling noise from the clap, creating a big, impactful sound that can really punch through a mix. Drag Clap.wav and Snare.wav onto separate audio tracks and make sure both audio clips are unwarped.

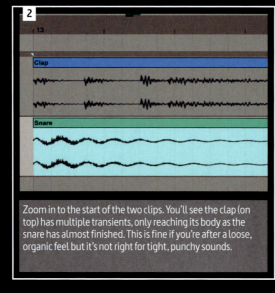

2 Zoom in to the start of the two clips. You'll see the clap (on top) has multiple transients, only reaching its body as the snare has almost finished. This is fine if you're after a loose, organic feel but it's not right for tight, punchy sounds.

3 The most elegant way to make the two sounds gel is to change the start point of the clap. Drag the clap clip's start marker to the beginning of the second transient. This gives a good balance of impact and natural feel. (An alternative for a looser feel is to drag the clap's start back in time.)

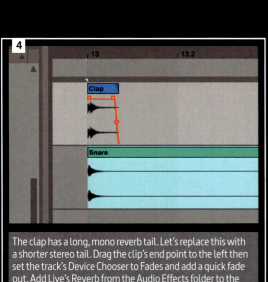

4 The clap has a long, mono reverb tail. Let's replace this with a shorter stereo tail. Drag the clip's end point to the left then set the track's Device Chooser to Fades and add a quick fade out. Add Live's Reverb from the Audio Effects folder to the clap track.

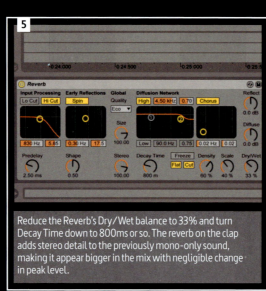

5 Reduce the Reverb's Dry/Wet balance to 33% and turn Decay Time down to 800ms or so. The reverb on the clap adds stereo detail to the previously mono-only sound, making it appear bigger in the mix with negligible change in peak level.

6 The clap is loud relative to the snare so reduce its Gain by -8dB. Another way to change the feel of the combined sound is to adjust the tuning of either element. Turn the clap clip's Transpose down to -1 for a more natural, cohesive sound.

Layered EDM clap/snare smash using Stacker

1 To produce a stadium-sized EDM smash with a swift lead-in noise build followed by a layered clap/snare impact, audition and select the following raw samples: a snare, a clap and a noise/reverb hit. We're layering them in Stacker, but any sampler will do the job.

2 Start with the noise layer. We've imported some slightly overdriven white noise and shaped it using the amp envelope. We want a speedy, ramped attack to produce the lead in – like a quick pump up. Set attack to zero, decay to 100%, decay time to around 200ms and release time to 1.

3 Next in is the snare drum. This sample has a touch of reverb for extra character. If you have a dry snare, bounce it through a hall reverb and swap it in the sampler for the dry version. Trigger the sample as a one shot.

4 The third and final element is a clap. Use one with a crisp attack transient to cut through the mix. Add reverb – a long hall or plate will do the job – and trigger the sample as a one-shot.

5 The sound comes alive when the layers are staggered. Switch to Scatter (BPM) mode and move the snare (yellow) to start an eighth of a beat after the MIDI note on. Slide the clap (green) to just before snare. The result is a combined sound where the noise (red) builds before the clap and snare hit.

6 So that the noise builds before the clap and snare hits, program MIDI so that Stacker is triggered an eighth division before you intend the snare/clap to hit. If you don't have Stacker use staggered MIDI to trigger the three different samples: noise (green note), clap (orange) and snare (red).

Chapter one
Drums and beats

Beat starters

The remainder of this chapter is dedicated to beat grids. In all, 30 grids cover a wide range of genres and styles. The grids are taken from Live but can be reproduced in any DAW. Unless specifically stated, beat grids are split into 16th note divisions (*page 26*) where a standard four-to-the-floor kick hits on divisions 1, 5, 9 and 13. Shading indicates velocity strength: dark red shows full velocity hits while lighter shading shows softer hits.

STARTING POINTS ONLY

The beats are constructed by some of the world's leading sample designers. The first step to recreating the beats is to listen to the accompanying audio and see how the grid translates to the final beat. Each beat includes information on:

▸▸ **Sound choices** – the raw source/s of samples used, whether that is drum machines, layered samples or organic drum hits from drum ROMplers and the like. Where drum machines are listed, it is easy to track down sample sets online.

▸▸ **Programming** – where the hits fall on the grid, and why.

▸▸ **Processing** – what, if any, processing has been used to shape the final beat.

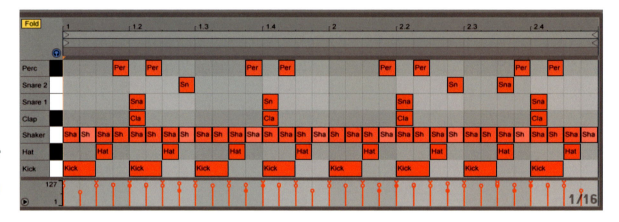

🎧
The grid for Deep Tech House (*page 60*). Note the 16th note beat divisions (each four beat bar is shaded differently). The bar numbers are indicated on the top panel; '1.3' means beat three of bar one. Full velocity hits are shaded dark red, softer hits in lighter pink.

▸▸ The percentage range for the amount of **swing** to apply.

▸▸ A suggested **bpm range** in which the genre lies and beat sounds best.

It is important to note that the grids, and all of the accompanying information, are *starting points only*. If a beat asks for a 909 snare and you think an 808 clap will suit your production better, use that. And while trying to get a beat to sound the same as the accompanying audio examples is a worthwhile exercise (and challenge), a recurring theme over the next few pages is generating **uniqueness** in a groove.

Whether that's layering samples, shifting hits off-grid, triggering multiple versions of the same hit across the stereo spread or overlaying loops, the finest beatsmiths are motivated by a desire to create original drums with unique sounds.

Finally, note that the beat grids here are for one- or two-bar grooves. While they may supply a track's main beat, to keep the arrangement fresh you will want to change things over time.

This means not only adding and dropping elements as the track progresses (you might start with a solo kick drum for the lead-in then add hats at bar 32 and a clap at 64, for example), but also programming variations every few bars.

In some cases a variation may be as simple as throwing in an extra clap or adding a drum fill to the turnaround at the end of a section. Other tracks call for more subtlety: slight changes in velocity or pitch in a beat element to keep things interesting as the track progresses, for example.

For more on the importance of change over time see The rules of mixing, Chapter eight.

// WALKTHROUGHS

Groove essentials: funky ghost snares 🎧

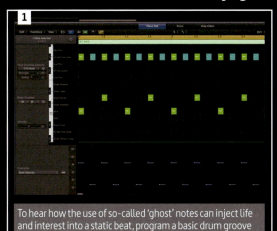

1 To hear how the use of so-called 'ghost' notes can inject life and interest into a static beat, program a basic drum groove comprised of eighth note closed hats, a kick on beats 1 and 3 of the bar, and a snare on beats 2 and 4. It's a straightforward disco-style beat that's about as vanilla they come.

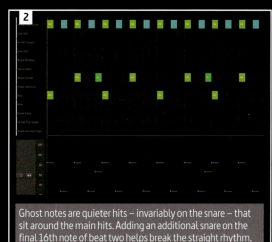

2 Ghost notes are quieter hits – invariably on the snare – that sit around the main hits. Adding an additional snare on the final 16th note of beat two helps break the straight rhythm, instantly giving the groove a more characterful 'skipping' feel.

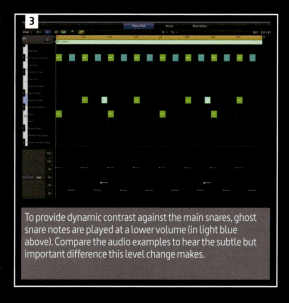

3 To provide dynamic contrast against the main snares, ghost snare notes are played at a lower volume (in light blue above). Compare the audio examples to hear the subtle but important difference this level change makes.

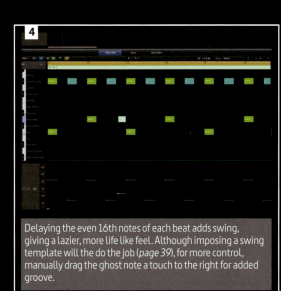

4 Delaying the even 16th notes of each beat adds swing, giving a lazier, more life like feel. Although imposing a swing template will the do the job (*page 39*), for more control, manually drag the ghost note a touch to the right for added groove.

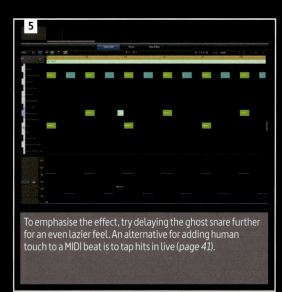

5 To emphasise the effect, try delaying the ghost snare further for an even lazier feel. An alternative for adding human touch to a MIDI beat is to tap hits in live (*page 41*).

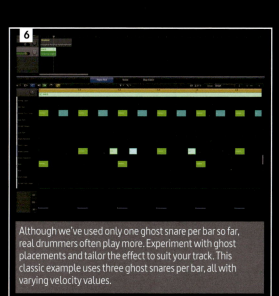

6 Although we've used only one ghost snare per bar so far, real drummers often play more. Experiment with ghost placements and tailor the effect to suit your track. This classic example uses three ghost snares per bar, all with varying velocity values.

// beat starters: House and deep house

Low tempo house Tempo: 110-115 bpm. Swing: 60-65%. Sounds: Mixed drum machine samples and live hits.

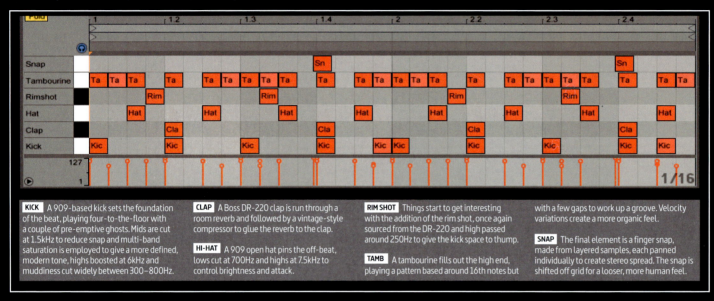

KICK A 909-based kick sets the foundation of the beat, playing four-to-the-floor with a couple of pre-emptive ghosts. Mids are cut at 1.5kHz to reduce snap and multi-band saturation is employed to give a more defined, modern tone, highs boosted at 6kHz and muddiness cut widely between 300–800Hz.

CLAP A Boss DR-220 clap is run through a room reverb and followed by a vintage-style compressor to glue the reverb to the clap.

HI-HAT A 909 open hat pins the off-beat, lows cut at 700Hz and highs at 7.5kHz to control brightness and attack.

RIM SHOT Things start to get interesting with the addition of the rim shot, once again sourced from the DR-220 and high passed around 250Hz to give the kick space to thump.

TAMB A tambourine fills out the high end, playing a pattern based around 16th notes but with a few gaps to work up a groove. Velocity variations create a more organic feel.

SNAP The final element is a finger snap, made from layered samples, each panned individually to create stereo spread. The snap is shifted off grid for a looser, more human feel.

Saturation

< When sculpting sounds, try using multi-band saturation instead of EQ. By controlling the saturation in different frequency bands it is possible not only to change the tonal make-up of a sound but also generate additional higher frequencies (*page 280*). In this example saturation is used to give a dull kick extended definition.

Soulful deep house Tempo: 110-150bpm. Swing: 55-60%. Sounds: Mainly samples of live drums from soul and jazz records.

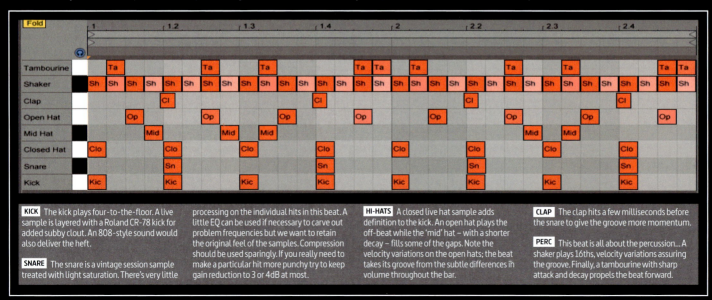

KICK The kick plays four-to-the-floor. A live sample is layered with a Roland CR-78 kick for added subby clout. An 808-style sound would also deliver the heft.

SNARE The snare is a vintage session sample treated with light saturation. There's very little processing on the individual hits in this beat. A little EQ can be used if necessary to carve out problem frequencies but we want to retain the original feel of the samples. Compression should be used sparingly. If you really need to make a particular hit more punchy try to keep gain reduction to 3 or 4dB at most.

HI-HATS A closed live hat sample adds definition to the kick. An open hat plays the off-beat while the 'mid' hat – with a shorter decay – fills some of the gaps. Note the velocity variations on the open hats; the beat takes its groove from the subtle differences in volume throughout the bar.

CLAP The clap hits a few milliseconds before the snare to give the groove more momentum.

PERC This beat is all about the percussion... A shaker plays 16ths, velocity variations assuring the groove. Finally, a tambourine with sharp attack and decay propels the beat forward.

Pinned verb

< By placing a compressor after a reverb plugin on a drum channel you can 'pin' the reverb to the sound. This works particularly well with shorter room and chamber settings.

Vintage feel

< This beat is proudly vintage in feel. Two components make it so:

Raw sounds. Sample live drums from old funk, jazz and swing records. If you're not a natural crate digger add crackle and noise to electronic hits by layering a vinyl sample.

Vintage processing. Choose vintage-style compressors and tape saturation plugins. Avoid high end boosts to retain the warmer flavours of yesteryear's productions.

21st-century Chicago house Tempo: 120–125bpm. Swing: 55-60%. Sounds: Combination of 707 and 909 samples.

Sculpting hats

> Although a standard TR-909 open hat is used in this beat, the 'closed hat' is from a sample library, sculpted using its attack and decay envelopes so that it becomes a perfect partner to the open 909. The main deciding factor when adjusting decay envelopes is the tempo of the track – sounds can be more sustained at slower bpms.

Stay unique

> Even when recreating sounds from a particular era, you still want to stamp your own individuality on a beat. In our 21st-century take on Chicago house, we've layered a 909 clap with a 707 sample to create a less familiar sound. Analogue-style saturation glues and bulks up the combined clap layer while a short delay (a few ms only) adds a phasey flanging effect.

Less is more

> Despite the fact that Big house uses seven separate elements, there are rarely more than two or three triggered on any single step. This helps to avoid making the mix too cluttered. The result is a solid, confident sound.

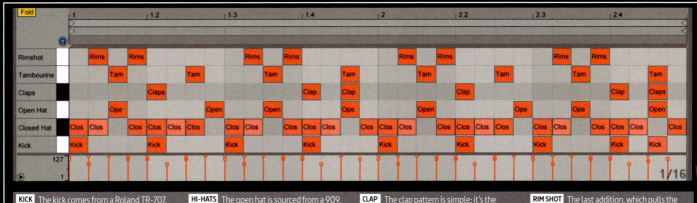

KICK The kick comes from a Roland TR-707, which gives a more plasticky sound than the house standard 909. Light compression brings out its natural weight. The four-to-the-floor pattern is supplemented with a hit into the turnaround. Note its lower velocity – it's not quite a ghost hit but is quieter than the others.

HI-HATS The open hat is sourced from a 909, a stalwart of the Chicago scene. It breaks from an expected off-beat pattern with a busier groove, closed hats playing the other 16ths. Note the velocity of the closed hat varies across the bar to add life to the pattern. Both hats are routed to the same mute group.

CLAP The clap pattern is simple; it's the processing that gives it interest – see left.

PERC A 707 tambourine, hitting the off-beat, brings out the groove. To add stereo interest two copies of the same sample are panned hard left and right, one slightly detuned.

RIM SHOT The last addition, which pulls the beat together, is a 707 rim shot. The shot plays off the tambourine and open hat to emphasise the beat's infectious syncopation. Adjusting the amount of swing dramatically affects the groove. 2-4dB worth of drum sub-mix compression glues the beat.

Big house Tempo: 123-128bpm. Swing: 55-65%. Sounds: Various drum machine samples.

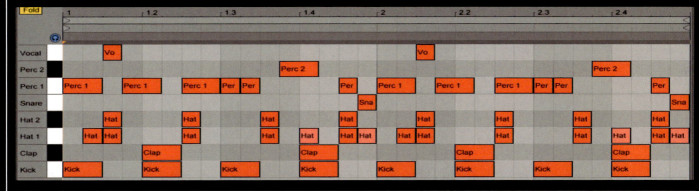

KICK A dominant kick supplies the four-to-the-floor foundation. We've chosen a sample heavy with low end and a hint of saturation to add grit. The transient section in particular is dirtier than you might expect from cleaner, more polished house production styles. This gives the kick a hard, raw edge.

HI-HATS Two hi-hat samples with distinct sounds are layered. One has a percussive character (body and weight), while the other fills in the high end with a longer release (air and crispness). The pattern is mainly based around off-beat hits with ghost notes to add a jacking feel – adjust swing to taste.

CLAP A sample of the Boss DR-110 clap plays on beats 2 and 4. The low end is rolled away from 550Hz to avoid kick frequency overlap.

SNARE The snare plays a single hit at the end of each bar, emphasising the swing and helping propel the groove into the next bar.

DETAIL A down-tuned tom sample (Perc 1) gives the beat a tribal feel, accompanied by a reversed edit of the same sound (Perc 2). EQ cuts keep the toms away from the kick. Finally, a short vocal shout ('Haw!') triggered between toms delivers both personality and old-school vibes.

// beat starters: Garage and 2-step

Rolling 2-step Tempo: 122-128bpm. Swing: 60-65%. Sounds: Mainly 808 and 909 sounds plus acoustic percussion.

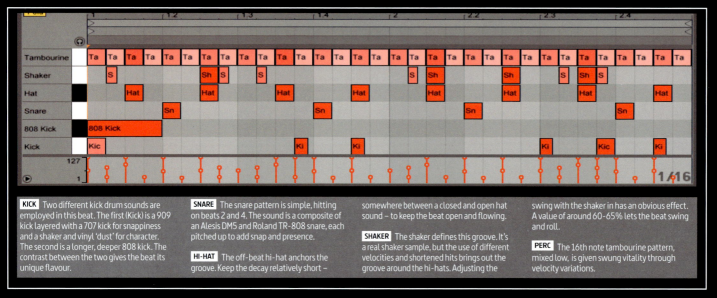

KICK Two different kick drum sounds are employed in this beat. The first (Kick) is a 909 kick layered with a 707 kick for snappiness and a shaker and vinyl 'dust' for character. The second is a longer, deeper 808 kick. The contrast between the two gives the beat its unique flavour.

SNARE The snare pattern is simple, hitting on beats 2 and 4. The sound is a composite of an Alesis DM5 and Roland TR-808 snare, each pitched up to add snap and presence.

HI-HAT The off-beat hi-hat anchors the groove. Keep the decay relatively short – somewhere between a closed and open hat sound – to keep the beat open and flowing.

SHAKER The shaker defines this groove. It's a real shaker sample, but the use of different velocities and shortened hits brings out the groove around the hi-hats. Adjusting the swing with the shaker in has an obvious effect. A value of around 60-65% lets the beat swing and roll.

PERC The 16th note tambourine pattern, mixed low, is given swung vitality through velocity variations.

Implied kick
< Note the lack of a kick on the first beat of the second bar in this two bar groove. This is standard in 2-step. The groove is implied by the other hits around it; leaving space on the 'one' gives the beat its distinctive wonky feel.

Tail lengths
< In sparse grooves, sustain and decay transients are key. Go too short and a sound loses character, too long and you can stifle a beat. Tempo is the main decider of tail length: the faster and busier a track, the shorter a sound can be.

Garage shuffle Tempo: 120-125bpm. Swing: 60-65%. Sounds: TR-909, DM5 and live percussion hits.

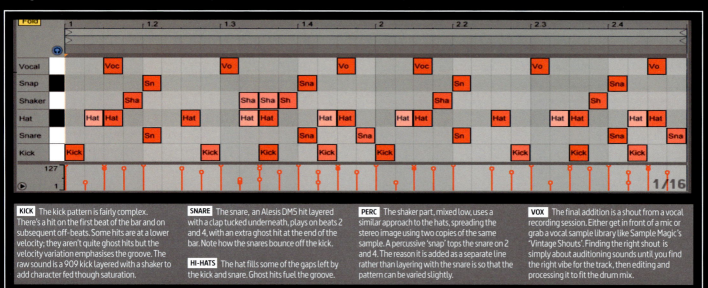

KICK The kick pattern is fairly complex. There's a hit on the first beat of the bar and on subsequent off-beats. Some hits are at a lower velocity; they aren't quite ghost hits but the velocity variation emphasises the groove. The raw sound is a 909 kick layered with a shaker to add character fed though saturation.

SNARE The snare, an Alesis DM5 hit layered with a clap tucked underneath, plays on beats 2 and 4, with an extra ghost hit at the end of the bar. Note how the snares bounce off the kick.

HI-HATS The hat fills some of the gaps left by the kick and snare. Ghost hits fuel the groove.

PERC The shaker part, mixed low, uses a similar approach to the hats, spreading the stereo image using two copies of the same sample. A percussive 'snap' tops the snare on 2 and 4. The reason it is added as a separate line rather than layering with the snare is so that the pattern can be varied slightly.

VOX The final addition is a shout from a vocal recording session. Either get in front of a mic or grab a vocal sample library like Sample Magic's 'Vintage Shouts'. Finding the right shout is simply about auditioning sounds until you find the right vibe for the track, then editing and processing it to fit the drum mix.

Stereo hats
< The hi-hat is given a stereo twist by panning two identical 909 closed hat samples hard left and right. The key to making the combined sound wide is to alter the start times of each hat in relation to the other and to add slight variations to their pitch and amp envelopes. One hat is pitched down five steps and the other four. Reverb is added to give the combined wide hat a sense of airy liveliness.

Ultra-wide clap

> To make a clap with an ultra-wide stereo spread in Bouncy retro garage we avoided a quick-win plugin like a spreader and opted instead to use five separate versions of the same 202 sample – each with slightly different tuning, ADSR envelope and sample start time – and panned them across the stereo field.

The SoundToys Decapitator was then employed to supply a whack of saturation to give the combined claps extra body. To avoid smashing the raw sound too hard, this saturation was applied in parallel with a dry/wet balance of around 20%. Last in line, a splash of room reverb gives the stacked claps a halo of depth and helps them blend into the wider beat.

Garage swing

> Garage beats typically employ heavy swing – somewhere between 60 and 65% – which can be seen (and heard) in all beats on this spread. You can either apply swing across the whole beat or manually to specific hits as in Up-front garage. Experimenting with different amounts of swing and looser timing for specific elements will change the feel of a beat and give it a unique groove.

Bouncy retro garage Tempo: 120-125bpm. Swing: 60-65%. Sounds: Various layered drums.

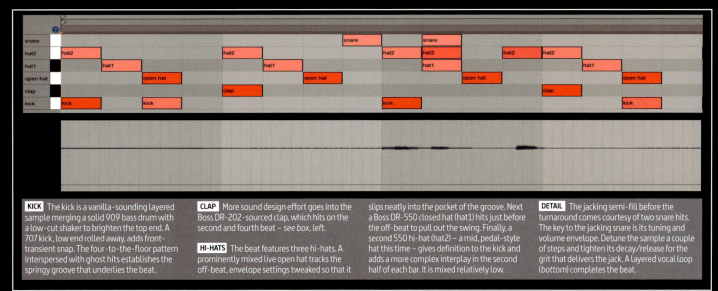

KICK The kick is a vanilla-sounding layered sample merging a solid 909 bass drum with a low-cut shaker to brighten the top end. A 707 kick, low end rolled away, adds front-transient snap. The four-to-the-floor pattern interspersed with ghost hits establishes the springy groove that underlies the beat.

CLAP More sound design effort goes into the Boss DR-202-sourced clap, which hits on the second and fourth beat – *see box, left*.

HI-HATS The beat features three hi-hats. A prominently mixed live open hat tracks the off-beat, envelope settings tweaked so that it slips neatly into the pocket of the groove. Next a Boss DR-550 closed hat (hat1) hits just before the off-beat to pull out the swing. Finally, a second 550 hi-hat (hat2) – a mid, pedal-style hat this time – gives definition to the kick and adds a more complex interplay in the second half of each bar. It is mixed relatively low.

DETAIL The jacking semi-fill before the turnaround comes courtesy of two snare hits. The key to the jacking snare is its tuning and volume envelope. Detune the sample a couple of steps and tighten its decay/release for the grit that delivers the jack. A layered vocal loop (*bottom*) completes the beat.

Up-front garage Tempo: 125-135bpm. Swing: 55-65%. Sounds: Mix of acoustic drum samples and drum machine hits.

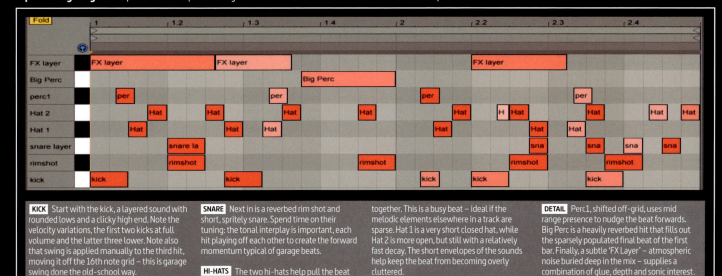

KICK Start with the kick, a layered sound with rounded lows and a clicky high end. Note the velocity variations, the first two kicks at full volume and the latter three lower. Note also that swing is applied manually to the third hit, moving it off the 16th note grid – this is garage swing done the old-school way.

SNARE Next in is a reverbed rim shot and short, spritely snare. Spend time on their tuning: the tonal interplay is important, each hit playing off each other to create the forward momentum typical of garage beats.

HI-HATS The two hi-hats help pull the beat together. This is a busy beat – ideal if the melodic elements elsewhere in a track are sparse. Hat 1 is a very short closed hat, while Hat 2 is more open, but still with a relatively fast decay. The short envelopes of the sounds help keep the beat from becoming overly cluttered.

DETAIL Perc1, shifted off-grid, uses mid range presence to nudge the beat forwards. Big Perc is a heavily reverbed hit that fills out the sparsely populated final beat of the first bar. Finally, a subtle 'FX Layer' – atmospheric noise buried deep in the mix – supplies a combination of glue, depth and sonic interest.

// beat starters: Techno and tech-house

Deep tech-house Tempo: 125-130bpm. Swing: 60-65%. Sounds: Mixture of analogue and digital drum machine samples plus acoustic hits.

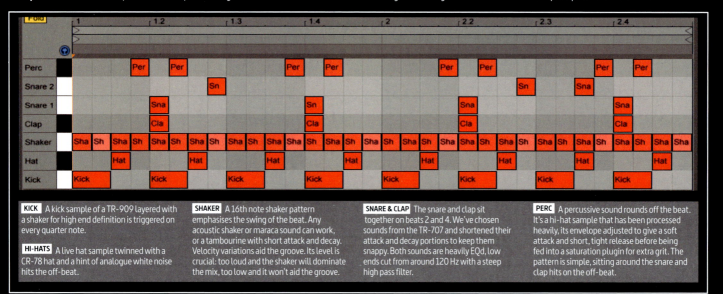

KICK A kick sample of a TR-909 layered with a shaker for high end definition is triggered on every quarter note.

HI-HATS A live hat sample twinned with a CR-78 hat and a hint of analogue white noise hits the off-beat.

SHAKER A 16th note shaker pattern emphasises the swing of the beat. Any acoustic shaker or maraca sound can work, or a tambourine with short attack and decay. Velocity variations aid the groove. Its level is crucial: too loud and the shaker will dominate the mix, too low and it won't aid the groove.

SNARE & CLAP The snare and clap sit together on beats 2 and 4. We've chosen sounds from the TR-707 and shortened their attack and decay portions to keep them snappy. Both sounds are heavily EQd, low ends cut from around 120 Hz with a steep high pass filter.

PERC A percussive sound rounds off the beat. It's a hi-hat sample that has been processed heavily, its envelope adjusted to give a soft attack and short, tight release before being fed into a saturation plugin for extra grit. The pattern is simple, sitting around the snare and clap hits on the off-beat.

Alternative ghosts

< Sometimes standard ghost snares (*page 41*) don't cut the sonic mustard. In this beat a tighter, higher-pitched sound at a low volume (Snare 2) gives the effect of ghost hits. This allows the beat maker to use a different sound while retaining the ghost effect.

Subzero minimal techno Tempo: 125-130bpm. Swing: 55-70%. Sounds: Heavily processed drum machine hits.

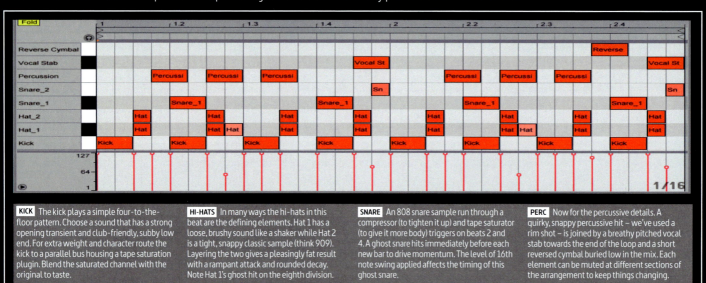

KICK The kick plays a simple four-to-the-floor pattern. Choose a sound that has a strong opening transient and club-friendly, subby low end. For extra weight and character route the kick to a parallel bus housing a tape saturation plugin. Blend the saturated channel with the original to taste.

HI-HATS In many ways the hi-hats in this beat are the defining elements. Hat 1 has a loose, brushy sound like a shaker while Hat 2 is a tight, snappy classic sample (think 909). Layering the two gives a pleasingly fat result with a rampant attack and rounded decay. Note Hat 1's ghost hit on the eighth division.

SNARE An 808 snare sample run through a compressor (to tighten it up) and tape saturator (to give it more body) triggers on beats 2 and 4. A ghost snare hits immediately before each new bar to drive momentum. The level of 16th note swing applied affects the timing of this ghost snare.

PERC Now for the percussive details. A quirky, snappy percussive hit – we've used a rim shot – is joined by a breathy pitched vocal stab towards the end of the loop and a short reversed cymbal buried low in the mix. Each element can be muted at different sections of the arrangement to keep things changing.

Up the jack

< Once you've programmed the hi-hats, you can start experimenting with swing. Higher swing values add a jacking feel to the groove.

Perc interest

< The rhythmic interplay in the percussive part plays a key role in this groove. Spice things up by automating the hit's envelope parameters over time. To add life, give it a subtle halo of reverb.

Motor city techno Tempo: 120–125bpm. Swing: 55-60%. Sounds: Roland TR-909 samples.

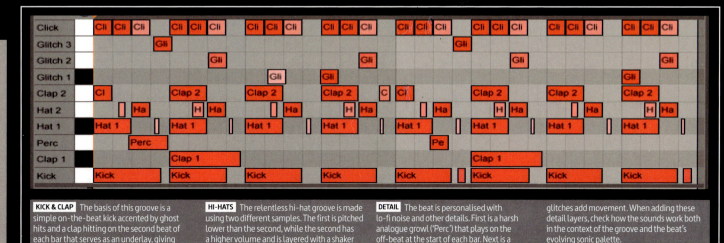

Playing it straight

> This beat is unusual in that it uses barely any velocity variations. Instead it relies on the interplay between different drum elements to provide dynamic movement. The way the rim shot and snare patterns work against each other helps fill the gaps between kicks. Note also that the rim shot doesn't ever hit at the same time as the kick – it's being used as a counterpoint rather than a reinforcing hit.

KICK The kick plays four-to-the-floor. Subtle distortion (no more than 15% wet) adds bulk, while compression reinforces the opening transient for increased punch and drive.

SNARE The snare – again treated to a dose of distortion to recreate classic Detroit mixing techniques – is a 909 sample. We've pitched it down a couple of semitones to give it a darker, grainier sound. Rolling off the high end also helps give it a less hi-fi sound.

RIM SHOT A 909 rim shot – once again, slightly distorted and tuned down a couple of semitones – helps fill out the beat. A touch of reverb, mixed low and resampled so that it becomes part of the decay of the sample, fills the beat bed with barely perceptible ambience.

HI-HATS Three 909 hi-hats are used; two different closed hats (Hat 1 has a sharp attack with lots of high end to cut through the mix, Hat 2 has a slower attack and longer decay) and a simple open hat triggered on the off-beat. To get the beat's loose, rough aesthetic we've not used mute groups – instead the tails of the open hats are allowed to sustain through the closed hats.

Grinding analogue techno Tempo: 125-132bpm. Swing: 50-65%. Sounds: Analogue drum machine samples.

Manual swing

> The Hat 2 part has manual swing applied. Although most beats use the same swing setting across all elements, techno often features different swing settings across different elements. In this case we've done it manually, but you can also do it using a DAW's swing controls (simply seperate out the part in question and apply the different swing template/timings). Try a range of values, from straight timing through to about 65%.

KICK & CLAP The basis of this groove is a simple on-the-beat kick accented by ghost hits and a clap hitting on the second beat of each bar that serves as an underlay, giving structure to the rhythmic backbone. The kick sound is a 909 sample run through saturation then mild distortion, its top end rolled away.

HI-HATS The relentless hi-hat groove is made using two different samples. The first is pitched lower than the second, while the second has a higher volume and is layered with a shaker sample. We've deliberately chosen samples without too many high frequencies in order to leave space for what's to come.

DETAIL The beat is personalised with lo-fi noise and other details. First is a harsh analogue growl ('Perc') that plays on the off-beat at the start of each bar. Next is a synthesised open ride ('Glitch 2'). Clap 2 reinforces the kick and provides a rhythmic interplay with Hat 1. Finally, the extra analogue glitches add movement. When adding these detail layers, check how the sounds work both in the context of the groove and the beat's evolving sonic palette.

CLICKS Low-level analogue clicks playing three in every four 16s glue the beat together.

// beat starters: Chillout and chillwave

Dusty hip hop Tempo: 110-120bpm. Swing: 50-60%. Sounds: Mostly organic drum samples.

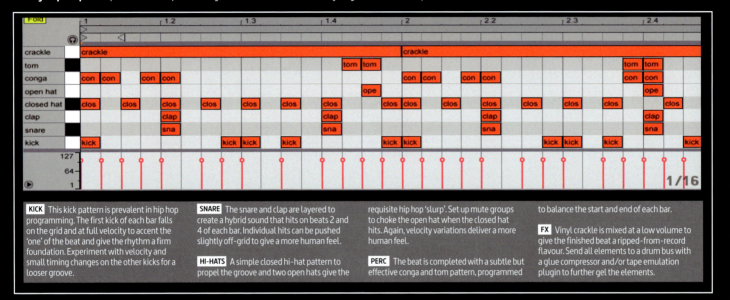

KICK This kick pattern is prevalent in hip hop programming. The first kick of each bar falls on the grid and at full velocity to accent the 'one' of the beat and give the rhythm a firm foundation. Experiment with velocity and small timing changes on the other kicks for a looser groove.

SNARE The snare and clap are layered to create a hybrid sound that hits on beats 2 and 4 of each bar. Individual hits can be pushed slightly off-grid to give a more human feel.

HI-HATS A simple closed hi-hat pattern to propel the groove and two open hats give the requisite hip hop 'slurp'. Set up mute groups to choke the open hat when the closed hat hits. Again, velocity variations deliver a more human feel.

PERC The beat is completed with a subtle but effective conga and tom pattern, programmed to balance the start and end of each bar.

FX Vinyl crackle is mixed at a low volume to give the finished beat a ripped-from-record flavour. Send all elements to a drum bus with a glue compressor and/or tape emulation plugin to further gel the elements.

Loose hats
< To give the hi-hat line an even looser feel try nudging the hits subtly off-grid and amending each hat's attack and release envelopes to sculpt the sound. See Programming 'live' hi-hats, page 21.

Chillwave Tempo: 90-100bpm. Swing: 60-70%. Sounds: Mixed digital, analogue and acoustic hits.

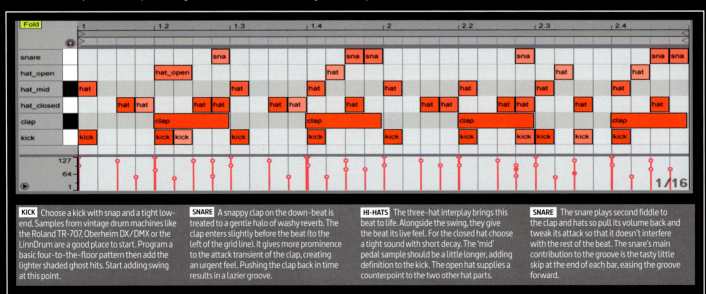

KICK Choose a kick with snap and a tight low-end. Samples from vintage drum machines like the Roland TR-707, Oberheim DX/DMX or the LinnDrum are a good place to start. Program a basic four-to-the-floor pattern then add the lighter shaded ghost hits. Start adding swing at this point.

SNARE A snappy clap on the down-beat is treated to a gentle halo of washy reverb. The clap enters slightly before the beat (to the left of the grid line). It gives more prominence to the attack transient of the clap, creating an urgent feel. Pushing the clap back in time results in a lazier groove.

HI-HATS The three-hat interplay brings this beat to life. Alongside the swing, they give the beat its live feel. For the closed hat choose a tight sound with short decay. The 'mid' pedal sample should be a little longer, adding definition to the kick. The open hat supplies a counterpoint to the two other hat parts.

SNARE The snare plays second fiddle to the clap and hats so pull its volume back and tweak its attack so that it doesn't interfere with the rest of the beat. The snare's main contribution to the groove is the tasty little skip at the end of each bar, easing the groove forward.

Live flavours
< The clap sound here was generated using a cheap mic recording a real hand clap in the studio. We experimented with the distance from the mic to balance room ambience with the direct sound to create a result that complements the kick.

Compression
> A big part of the chillwave sound is obvious, near-flatlined, compression. Send all beat elements to a characterful compressor then increase ratio and level reduction until it obviously pumps. Fine-tune the release time to the track's bpm. Note that in the audio example the compression is set to subtle for clarity's sake.

Sparse chill Tempo: 75-85bpm. Swing: 50-75%. Sounds: Mostly organic/real drum sounds – although 808-style hits can work too.

Lo-fi hats

> You can afford to get pretty lo-fi with these open hats: try sending some (or all) of the signal to an overdrive or tape saturation plugin using the tone control to shape its tonal make-up. Follow the distortion with low cut EQ to roll away any newly generated low end mud.

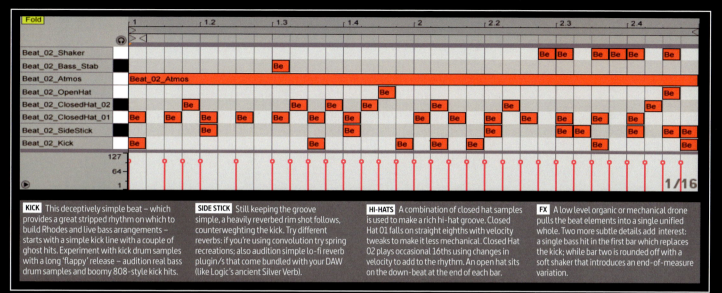

KICK This deceptively simple beat – which provides a great stripped rhythm on which to build Rhodes and live bass arrangements – starts with a simple kick line with a couple of ghost hits. Experiment with kick drum samples with a long 'flappy' release – audition real bass drum samples and boomy 808-style kick hits.

SIDE STICK Still keeping the groove simple, a heavily reverbed rim shot follows, counterweighting the kick. Try different reverbs: if you're using convolution try spring recreations; also audition simple lo-fi reverb plugin/s that come bundled with your DAW (like Logic's ancient Silver Verb).

HI-HATS A combination of closed hat samples is used to make a rich hi-hat groove. Closed Hat 01 falls on straight eighths with velocity tweaks to make it less mechanical. Closed Hat 02 plays occasional 16ths using changes in velocity to add to the rhythm. An open hat sits on the down-beat at the end of each bar.

FX A low level organic or mechanical drone pulls the beat elements into a single unified whole. Two more subtle details add interest: a single bass hit in the first bar which replaces the kick; while bar two is rounded off with a soft shaker that introduces an end-of-measure variation.

Raw 'strip hop' Tempo: 80-90bpm. Swing: 50-60%. Sounds: Mostly organic and real drum sounds.

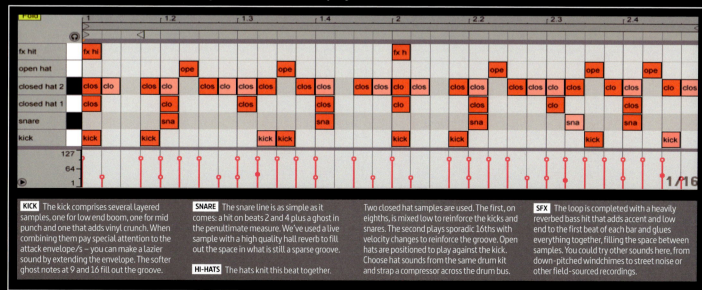

KICK The kick comprises several layered samples, one for low end boom, one for mid punch and one that adds vinyl crunch. When combining them pay special attention to the attack envelope/s – you can make a lazier sound by extending the envelope. The softer ghost notes at 9 and 16 fill out the groove.

SNARE The snare line is as simple as it comes: a hit on beats 2 and 4 plus a ghost in the penultimate measure. We've used a live sample with a high quality hall reverb to fill out the space in what is still a sparse groove.

HI-HATS The hats knit this beat together. Two closed hat samples are used. The first, on eighths, is mixed low to reinforce the kicks and snares. The second plays sporadic 16ths with velocity changes to reinforce the groove. Open hats are positioned to play against the kick. Choose hat sounds from the same drum kit and strap a compressor across the drum bus.

SFX The loop is completed with a heavily reverbed bass hit that adds accent and low end to the first beat of each bar and glues everything together, filling the space between samples. You could try other sounds here, from down-pitched windchimes to street noise or other field-sourced recordings.

// beat starters: Prog and trance

Mainroom prog Tempo: 126-130bpm. Swing: 50-65%. Sounds: Heavily processed electronic hits.

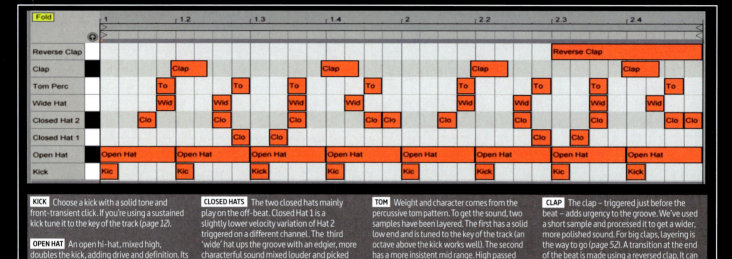

KICK Choose a kick with a solid tone and front-transient click. If you're using a sustained kick tune it to the key of the track (*page 12*).

OPEN HAT An open hi-hat, mixed high, doubles the kick, adding drive and definition. Its raw sound has a big impact on the beat's feel.

CLOSED HATS The two closed hats mainly play on the off-beat. Closed Hat 1 is a slightly lower velocity variation of Hat 2 triggered on a different channel. The third 'wide' hat ups the groove with an edgier, more characterful sound mixed louder and picked out by the swing.

TOM Weight and character comes from the percussive tom pattern. To get the sound, two samples have been layered. The first has a solid low end and is tuned to the key of the track (an octave above the kick works well). The second has a more insistent mid range. High passed kicks offer an alternative to toms.

CLAP The clap – triggered just before the beat – adds urgency to the groove. We've used a short sample and processed it to get a wider, more polished sound. For big claps, layering is the way to go (*page 52*). A transition at the end of the beat is made using a reversed clap. It can be used at the end of each turnaround.

Claps
< Try programming all elements bar the clap and then experiment with different placements for the clap hit. Some prog and mainroom house tracks place a clap on each beat to support the kick. Others don't use a clap at all.

Time keeping
< To work out exact envelope settings and tempo-matched pre-delay times, keep a bpm-to-ms calculator on hand – or flick to *Appendix 1*.

Classic trance Tempo: 125-135bpm. Swing: 55-70%. Sounds: Heavily processed drum machine samples.

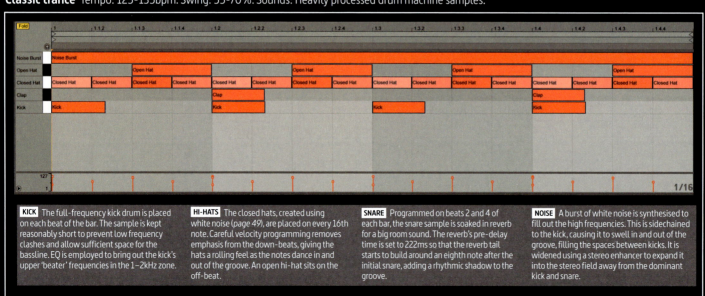

KICK The full-frequency kick drum is placed on each beat of the bar. The sample is kept reasonably short to prevent low frequency clashes and allow sufficient space for the bassline. EQ is employed to bring out the kick's upper 'beater' frequencies in the 1–2kHz zone.

HI-HATS The closed hats, created using white noise (*page 49*), are placed on every 16th note. Careful velocity programming removes emphasis from the down-beats, giving the hats a rolling feel as the notes dance in and out of the groove. An open hi-hat sits on the off-beat.

SNARE Programmed on beats 2 and 4 of each bar, the snare sample is soaked in reverb for a big room sound. The reverb's pre-delay time is set to 222ms so that the reverb tail starts to build around an eighth note after the initial snare, adding a rhythmic shadow to the groove.

NOISE A burst of white noise is synthesised to fill out the high frequencies. This is sidechained to the kick, causing it to swell in and out of the groove, filling the spaces between kicks. It is widened using a stereo enhancer to expand it into the stereo field away from the dominant kick and snare.

In a trance
< Trance beats haven't evolved much in the past few decades, and for good reason: the tried and tested combo of a 4/4 kick, open (909) hat on the off-beat and spritely hats playing 16ths is enough to provide a solid groove that fills out the frequency spectrum. Try synthesising your own hats using white noise (*page 49*). This gives full control over a groove's feel and shuffle – simply edit the MIDI velocities and change synth parameters such as velocity-to-filter and velocity-to-amp decay.

Hard styles

> Sitting somewhere between hardstyle, EDM and trance, the stomping rhythms of tunes by artists such as Showtek are particularly unique in the fact that they heavily emphasise the 4/4 pattern by placing almost all percussive elements on every beat of the bar. This marching rhythm, combined with a distorted, gabba-esque 4/4 kick, frees up room for slicing triplet synths and percussive riffs to stutter and pound through the mix.

Hardstyle-type EDM Tempo: 128–135bpm. Swing: 50-100%. Sounds: EDM-style layered samples.

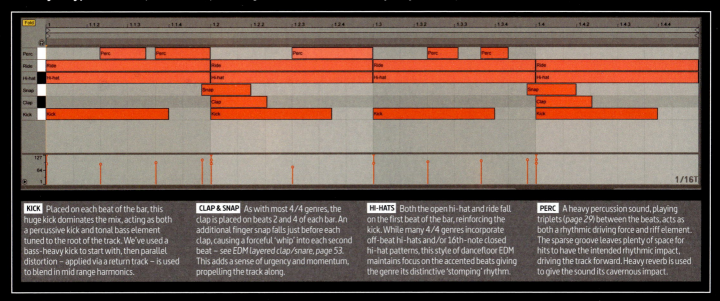

KICK Placed on each beat of the bar, this huge kick dominates the mix, acting as both a percussive kick and tonal bass element tuned to the root of the track. We've used a bass-heavy kick to start with, then parallel distortion – applied via a return track – is used to blend in mid range harmonics.

CLAP & SNAP As with most 4/4 genres, the clap is placed on beats 2 and 4 of each bar. An additional finger snap falls just before each clap, causing a forceful 'whip' into each second beat – see EDM layered clap/snare, page 53. This adds a sense of urgency and momentum, propelling the track along.

HI-HATS Both the open hi-hat and ride fall on the first beat of the bar, reinforcing the kick. While many 4/4 genres incorporate off-beat hi-hats and/or 16th-note closed hi-hat patterns, this style of dancefloor EDM maintains focus on the accented beats giving the genre its distinctive 'stomping' rhythm.

PERC A heavy percussion sound, playing triplets (page 29) between the beats, acts as both a rhythmic driving force and riff element. The sparse groove leaves plenty of space for hits to have the intended rhythmic impact, driving the track forward. Heavy reverb is used to give the sound its cavernous impact.

Jack Ü-style EDM Tempo: 128-140bpm. Swing: 50-80%. Sounds: Layered EDM-style samples and TR-808 kit.

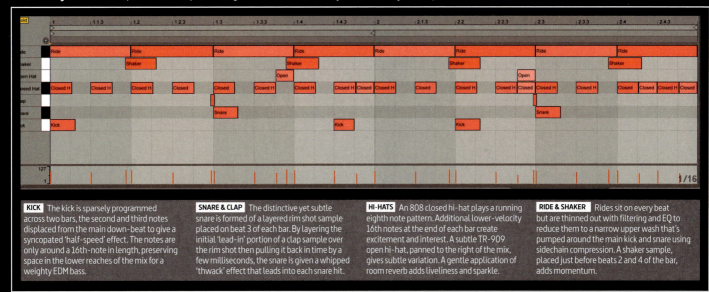

KICK The kick is sparsely programmed across two bars, the second and third notes displaced from the main down-beat to give a syncopated 'half-speed' effect. The notes are only around a 16th-note in length, preserving space in the lower reaches of the mix for a weighty EDM bass.

SNARE & CLAP The distinctive yet subtle snare is formed of a layered rim shot sample placed on beat 3 of each bar. By layering the initial 'lead-in' portion of a clap sample over the rim shot then pulling it back in time by a few milliseconds, the snare is given a whipped 'thwack' effect that leads into each snare hit.

HI-HATS An 808 closed hi-hat plays a running eighth note pattern. Additional lower-velocity 16th notes at the end of each bar create excitement and interest. A subtle TR-909 open hi-hat, panned to the right of the mix, gives subtle variation. A gentle application of room reverb adds liveliness and sparkle.

RIDE & SHAKER Rides sit on every beat but are thinned out with filtering and EQ to reduce them to a narrow upper wash that's pumped around the main kick and snare using sidechain compression. A shaker sample, placed just before beats 2 and 4 of the bar, adds momentum.

// Nu disco and indie dance

Cosmic nu disco Tempo: 120-125 bpm. Swing: 50-55%. Sounds: Based on Roland CR-78 samples.

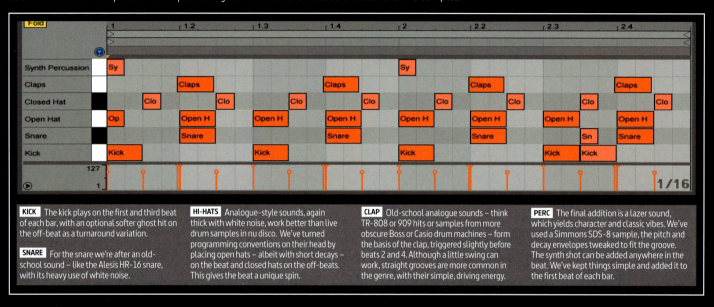

KICK The kick plays on the first and third beat of each bar, with an optional softer ghost hit on the off-beat as a turnaround variation.

SNARE For the snare we're after an old-school sound – like the Alesis HR-16 snare, with its heavy use of white noise.

HI-HATS Analogue-style sounds, again thick with white noise, work better than live drum samples in nu disco. We've turned programming conventions on their head by placing open hats – albeit with short decays – on the beat and closed hats on the off-beats. This gives the beat a unique spin.

CLAP Old-school analogue sounds – think TR-808 or 909 hits or samples from more obscure Boss or Casio drum machines – form the basis of the clap, triggered slightly before beats 2 and 4. Although a little swing can work, straight grooves are more common in the genre, with their simple, driving energy.

PERC The final addition is a lazer sound, which yields character and classic vibes. We've used a Simmons SDS-8 sample, the pitch and decay envelopes tweaked to fit the groove. The synth shot can be added anywhere in the beat. We've kept things simple and added it to the first beat of each bar.

Cosmic sounds

< Cosmic disco and related genres combine elements of classic disco with modern nu disco production techniques. This means working with contrasting sounds to craft unique hybrids. For the kick drum we've layered a subby Roland CR-78 sample with a snappier kick (TR-707, DMX or LinnDrum samples are all strong on snap). For rawer lo-fi flavours we sampled all drums into an Ensoniq Mirage (an 8-bit sampler from the mid '80s) and recorded them back into the DAW. If you don't have a suitable sampler, get the sound on *page 127*.

Nu disco: live groove Tempo: 110-120bpm. Swing: 50-60%. Sounds: Analogue hits and '80s drum machine samples.

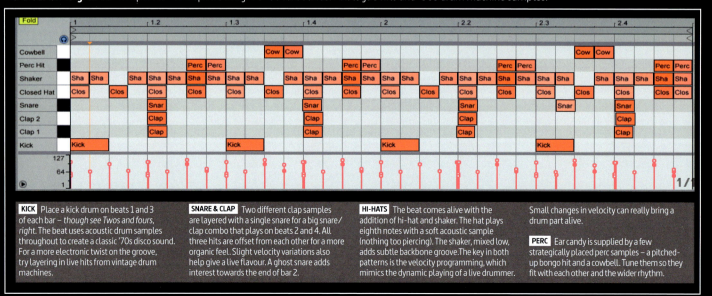

KICK Place a kick drum on beats 1 and 3 of each bar – *though see Twos and fours, right*. The beat uses acoustic drum samples throughout to create a classic '70s disco sound. For a more electronic twist on the groove, try layering in live hits from vintage drum machines.

SNARE & CLAP Two different clap samples are layered with a single snare for a big snare/clap combo that plays on beats 2 and 4. All three hits are offset from each other for a more organic feel. Slight velocity variations also help give a live flavour. A ghost snare adds interest towards the end of bar 2.

HI-HATS The beat comes alive with the addition of hi-hat and shaker. The hat plays eighth notes with a soft acoustic sample (nothing too piercing). The shaker, mixed low, adds subtle backbone groove. The key in both patterns is the velocity programming, which mimics the dynamic playing of a live drummer.

Small changes in velocity can really bring a drum part alive.

PERC Ear candy is supplied by a few strategically placed perc samples – a pitched-up bongo hit and a cowbell. Tune them so they fit with each other and the wider rhythm.

Twos and fours

< Although both beats on this page use kicks on beats 2 and 4, nu disco grooves can also use a four-on-the-floor kick pattern (either with equal volume kicks on each bar, or heavier ones on beats 1 and 3). Four-to-the-floor kicks give a solid, driving sound; two-to-the-floor a more relaxed, classic vibe.

Light touch

Tread lightly when compressing and EQing disco beats to preserve the inherent character of the original drum sounds.

Real life inspiration

> When recreating live grooves in a sequencer you need to pull off a sound choice and programming double-whammy to make the beat not only *sound* like the real deal, but also *groove* like a real life beat.

In the case of disco and indie dance this means replicating trademark disco drumming motifs such as the double snare turnaround, setting up mute groups for hi-hats and using subtle and intentional imperfections in hit placement and velocities which are typical of disco drumming.

Some programmers go further, routing velocity to attack envelopes to mimic the more transient attack a drummer gets by hitting a hat or snare harder.

Although all of these tricks deliver more realistic beats, never be afraid to layer in loops as well, as in Loose disco, *right*. Here a 'live' clap and bongo loop from a Sample Magic sample library (Vintage Breaks) is employed to infuse the beat with real-world vibes.

Ultimately even the most accomplished programmer is unable to recreate the myriad complexities of a live percussive workout. And with so many great loops available at low price points, studio time is generally best spent on other tasks.

Loose disco Tempo: 110–118bpm. Swing: 50%. Sounds: Mainly drum machine samples.

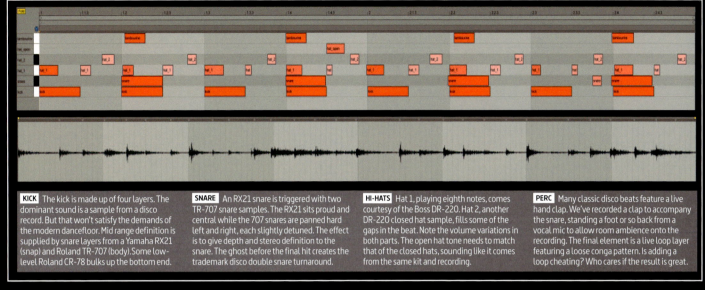

KICK The kick is made up of four layers. The dominant sound is a sample from a disco record. But that won't satisfy the demands of the modern dancefloor. Mid range definition is supplied by snare layers from a Yamaha RX21 (snap) and Roland TR-707 (body). Some low-level Roland CR-78 bulks up the bottom end.

SNARE An RX21 snare is triggered with two TR-707 snare samples. The RX21 sits proud and central while the 707 snares are panned hard left and right, each slightly detuned. The effect is to give depth and stereo definition to the snare. The ghost before the final hit creates the trademark disco double snare turnaround.

HI-HATS Hat 1, playing eighth notes, comes courtesy of the Boss DR-220. Hat 2, another DR-220 closed hat sample, fills some of the gaps in the beat. Note the volume variations in both parts. The open hat tone needs to match that of the closed hats, sounding like it comes from the same kit and recording.

PERC Many classic disco beats feature a live hand clap. We've recorded a clap to accompany the snare, standing a foot or so back from a vocal mic to allow room ambience onto the recording. The final element is a live loop layer featuring a loose conga pattern. Is adding a loop cheating? Who cares if the result is great.

Dirty indie dance Tempo: 125-127bpm. Swing: 60-65%. Sounds: Mainly vintage drum machine samples.

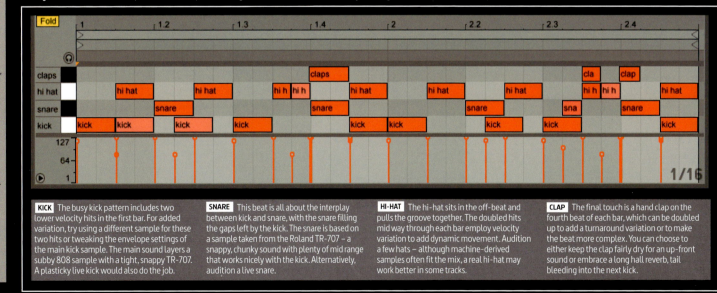

KICK The busy kick pattern includes two lower velocity hits in the first bar. For added variation, try using a different sample for these two hits or tweaking the envelope settings of the main kick sample. The main sound layers a subby 808 sample with a tight, snappy TR-707. A plasticky live kick would also do the job.

SNARE This beat is all about the interplay between kick and snare, with the snare filling the gaps left by the kick. The snare is based on a sample taken from the Roland TR-707 – a snappy, chunky sound with plenty of mid range that works nicely with the kick. Alternatively, audition a live snare.

HI-HAT The hi-hat sits in the off-beat and pulls the groove together. The doubled hits mid way through each bar employ velocity variation to add dynamic movement. Audition a few hats – although machine-derived samples often fit the mix, a real hi-hat may work better in some tracks.

CLAP The final touch is a hand clap on the fourth beat of each bar, which can be doubled up to add a turnaround variation or to make the beat more complex. You can choose to either keep the clap fairly dry for an up-front sound or embrace a long hall reverb, tail bleeding into the next kick.

// beat starters: D&B and dubstep

Raw D&B Tempo: 168-178bpm. Swing: 50-60%. Sounds: Raw live kit sounds, machine drum kick, plus dirty break/s.

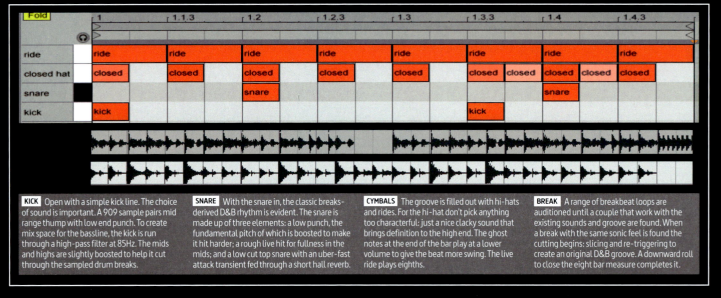

KICK Open with a simple kick line. The choice of sound is important. A 909 sample pairs mid range thump with low end punch. To create mix space for the bassline, the kick is run through a high-pass filter at 85Hz. The mids and highs are slightly boosted to help it cut through the sampled drum breaks.

SNARE With the snare in, the classic breaks-derived D&B rhythm is evident. The snare is made up of three elements: a low punch, the fundamental pitch of which is boosted to make it hit harder; a rough live hit for fullness in the mids; and a low cut top snare with an uber-fast attack transient fed through a short hall reverb.

CYMBALS The groove is filled out with hi-hats and rides. For the hi-hat don't pick anything too characterful: just a nice clacky sound that brings definition to the high end. The ghost notes at the end of the bar play at a lower volume to give the beat more swing. The live ride plays eighths.

BREAK A range of breakbeat loops are auditioned until a couple that work with the existing sounds and groove are found. When a break with the same sonic feel is found the cutting begins: slicing and re-triggering to create an original D&B groove. A downward roll to close the eight bar measure completes it.

Incessant D&B Tempo: 168-178bpm. Swing: 50-60%. Sounds: Raw live kit sounds, drum machine kick plus dirty break/s.

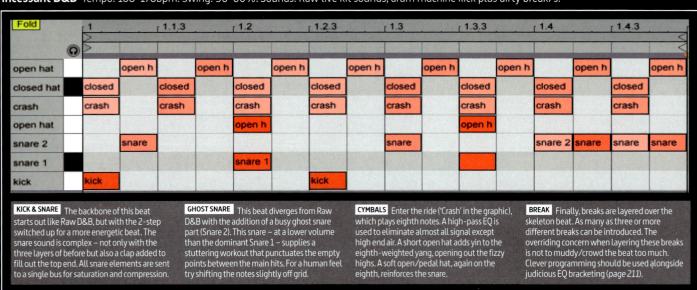

KICK & SNARE The backbone of this beat starts out like Raw D&B, but with the 2-step switched up for a more energetic beat. The snare sound is complex – not only with the three layers of before but also a clap added to fill out the top end. All snare elements are sent to a single bus for saturation and compression.

GHOST SNARE This beat diverges from Raw D&B with the addition of a busy ghost snare part (Snare 2). This snare – at a lower volume than the dominant Snare 1 – supplies a stuttering workout that punctuates the empty points between the main hits. For a human feel try shifting the notes slightly off grid.

CYMBALS Enter the ride ('Crash' in the graphic), which plays eighth notes. A high-pass EQ is used to eliminate almost all signal except high end air. A short open hat adds yin to the eighth-weighted yang, opening out the fizzy highs. A soft open/pedal hat, again on the eighth, reinforces the snare.

BREAK Finally, breaks are layered over the skeleton beat. As many as three or more different breaks can be introduced. The overriding concern when layering these breaks is not to muddy/crowd the beat too much. Clever programming should be used alongside judicious EQ bracketing (*page 211*).

Kick to fit

< Remember that when picking a kick sound you want to avoid dominating the all-important bassline. 909 sounds are good for this – 808-based sounds are generally too sub-heavy. Even with the right sound it's likely the kick will need to have its low end further tamed with EQ.

Low-hats

< In D&B beats, where kick and snare sounds are often picked to be larger that life, the hi-hat normally takes a clear (and clean) back seat. So avoid overdoing hi-hat distortion, overdrive and/or saturation.

Bus processing

< In both of these beats the programmed elements are all grouped and sent to a single drum bus where a saturator adds glue, bulk and dirt. This is followed by a compressor sidechain-triggered by the kick and snare to tuck back the between-beat rides and hats.

Don't rush!

< As in Raw D&B, auditioning is about finding a looped break whose character fits with what you've programmed. *Don't rush this stage!*

Mystik dubstep Tempo: 140bpm. Swing: 50%. Sounds: Mix of acoustic and electronic hits.

Dubby vibes

> The distinctive dubby ambience in this beat is achieved by feeding the snare drum into Ableton's Filter Delay to add a spacey echo effect. Gentle compression tames the dynamic range of the echo while a hint of overdrive after the compression delivers a gritty, retro feel. Any tape-style delay will give a similar effect.

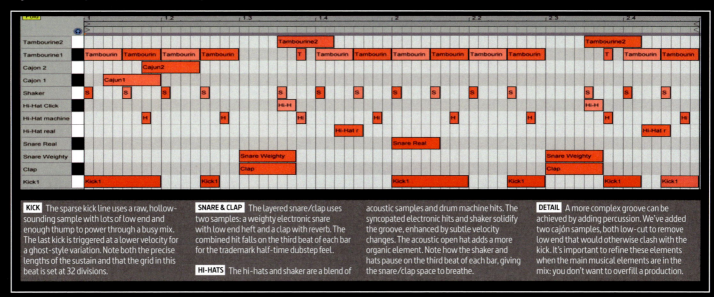

KICK The sparse kick line uses a raw, hollow-sounding sample with lots of low end and enough thump to power through a busy mix. The last kick is triggered at a lower velocity for a ghost-style variation. Note both the precise lengths of the sustain and that the grid in this beat is set at 32 divisions.

SNARE & CLAP The layered snare/clap uses two samples: a weighty electronic snare with low end heft and a clap with reverb. The combined hit falls on the third beat of each bar for the trademark half-time dubstep feel.

HI-HATS The hi-hats and shaker are a blend of acoustic samples and drum machine hits. The syncopated electronic hits and shaker solidify the groove, enhanced by subtle velocity changes. The acoustic open hat adds a more organic element. Note how the shaker and hats pause on the third beat of each bar, giving the snare/clap space to breathe.

DETAIL A more complex groove can be achieved by adding percussion. We've added two cajón samples, both low-cut to remove low end that would otherwise clash with the kick. It's important to refine these elements when the main musical elements are in the mix: you don't want to overfill a production.

Pop dubstep Tempo: 140bpm. Swing: 50-70%. Sounds: One shot samples and acoustic drum ROMpler.

Sidechain pump

> In this beat a compressor is placed on the drum bus, sidechain-triggered by the kick to make the sustained rides suck and swell around the kicks and giving a high-end rhythmic shape to the beat. It's a common technique across genres – check out the trance (page 64) and chillout beats (page 62) for more.

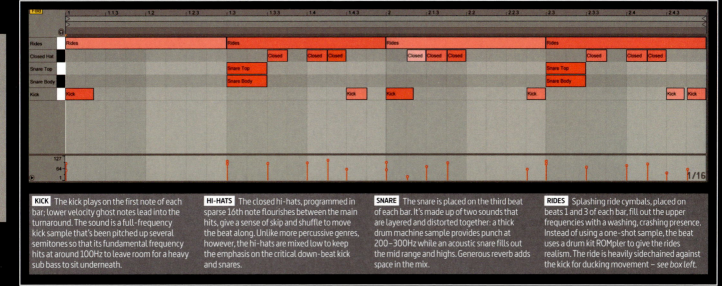

KICK The kick plays on the first note of each bar; lower velocity ghost notes lead into the turnaround. The sound is a full-frequency kick sample that's been pitched up several semitones so that its fundamental frequency hits at around 100Hz to leave room for a heavy sub bass to sit underneath.

HI-HATS The closed hi-hats, programmed in sparse 16th note flourishes between the main hits, give a sense of skip and shuffle to move the beat along. Unlike more percussive genres, however, the hi-hats are mixed low to keep the emphasis on the critical down-beat kick and snares.

SNARE The snare is placed on the third beat of each bar. It's made up of two sounds that are layered and distorted together: a thick drum machine sample provides punch at 200–300Hz while an acoustic snare fills out the mid range and highs. Generous reverb adds space in the mix.

RIDES Splashing ride cymbals, placed on beats 1 and 3 of each bar, fill out the upper frequencies with a washing, crashing presence. Instead of using a one-shot sample, the beat uses a drum kit ROMpler to give the rides realism. The ride is heavily sidechained against the kick for ducking movement – see box left.

Chapter two
Synthesis and sound design

Synthesised sounds permeate dance music.

Not only are synths able to create practically every sound the dance producer will ever need – from bass and leads to pads, drums and FX – they can also be used to process vocals and other real-world sounds.

The first devices that generated sounds using electric circuits can be dated back to the late 19th century. But it wasn't until the early 1960s that primitive synthesisers started to take off as instruments thanks to the work of pioneers like Bob Moog and Don Buchla, who created the first commercially available synthesisers and laid the groundwork for the countless other designers and manufacturers that followed.

What is synthesis? In simple terms, **it's the process of creating a sound from scratch electronically**. While acoustic instruments like guitars, pianos and violins generate sound acoustically through a physical process of plucking, striking or bowing strings, synths are entirely electrical.

Nowadays, we can take our pick from thousands of synths – either analogue or digital, hardware or software – but in the early years of synthesis the options were invariably analogue using a method known as **subtractive synthesis**. The same method dominates the synth world today.

SUBTRACTIVE SYNTHESIS

The synthesis method employed by just about every analogue synth is known as 'subtractive' because of the way it goes about creating sounds. The process starts with a harmonically rich waveform, which is then filtered and shaped, with frequencies being continually *subtracted* to give the final sound.

Those new to sound design typically start out exploring subtractive synthesis. It is the easiest method of synthesis to understand and most other methods adopt at least a few of the techniques used by subtractive synths to create their own sounds.

Virtual analogue synthesis is the most common method found in software synths. As its name suggests, it follows the same operating principles as analogue synthesis but operates in the software domain – instead of using electrical signals, sounds are created using lines of code. To the user, it works in much the same way as a real analogue synth: you'll find similar controls in a virtual analogue plugin to those you'd find on, say, a Minimoog from the early '70s.

Every DAW includes at least one virtual analogue synth. In Reason, Subtractor is the place to start. Logic offers the basic ES1 alongside the more advanced ES2. FL Studio has a selection starting with 3xOsc. Cubase has Retrologue and Ableton has Analog. If you're not happy with the sound or features of a built-in synth, popular commercial alternatives include Native Instruments' Massive, Lennar Digital's Sylenth1 and u-he's Diva.

OSCILLATORS

Oscillators lie at a synth's heart, creating the raw waveforms which are then shaped and filtered on their way to the output. Most oscillator sections allow the user to choose between a selection of wave shapes, each of which has a different sound related to its harmonic content *(see Waveforms, right)*.

The most common analogue waveforms are square (or related pulse), sawtooth and triangle. Sine waves are traditionally less common but may be found in the main oscillator options or powering the **sub-oscillator**, a section which generates an additional tone an octave or two below the main oscillator. Sub-oscillators are useful for thickening up the low end of sounds.

The (relative) new kid on the block when it comes to waveforms is the so-called **Wavetable**. Wavetables are different to the classic sine and saw waveforms in that they are made up of different evolving wave shapes. Modulating the waveform start

HARMONICS

Harmonics give different waveforms their unique sounds.

In the instrumental world a sound is made up of the fundamental frequency of the note played – for (middle) C4 this is 261.6Hz – and a series of overtones above the fundamental called harmonics that are unique to the instrument. A violin's harmonics, for example, relate to resonances in the string played, the dimensions of the instrument – even the type of wood used in its construction.

In synthesis, a synthetic waveform is made up of the fundamental frequency then multiples of that fundamental, depending on the nature of the waveform – *see box, right*. It's the unique mix of fundamental plus harmonics that make a violin sound like a violin rather than a clarinet; and a saw wave sound like a saw not a sine.

position can create evolving and complex timbres – like the now-classic dubstep bass sound (*page 110*).

In most synths oscillators can be **combined** (typically two, sometimes three or more) to produce more complex tones. Where this is possible you'll find **fine tuning** options for the additional oscillators (older analogue synths will also include tuning knobs for the main oscillator while newer models usually tune themselves automatically).

Oscillators can be **detuned** from each other by a few cents to create thicker sounds or harmonic effects. Use **coarse tuning** (usually named 'tuning' as opposed to fine-tuning) for more drastic semitone tuning steps – you might choose to transpose an oscillator down an octave to thicken its bass response or raise it by a third or fifth for a classic electro house sound.

When using pulse waves, **pulse-width modulation (PWM)** allows the symmetry of the wave to be modulated by an LFO or envelope. This alters the timbre of the pulse wave over time, giving a shifting effect which can range from subtle movement to obvious detuning. Use PWM to create shimmering pads and detailed leads.

Some synths include an **oscillator sync** setting, which allows one oscillator to act as a master, controlling the frequency of a second 'slave'. The slave is forced

Waveforms 🎧

Most synths offer oscillators with a range of waveforms. These provide the starting point of any sound and the choice of wave shape plays a key part in shaping the end result.

The **square wave** is made up of the fundamental frequency (*see left*) plus odd harmonics – which means that with a fundamental frequency of 1 kHz the harmonics fall at 3, 5, 7kHz and so on, each one at a slightly lower level than the previous.

Use for: Smooth bass and lead sounds, plus recreations of hollow reed and woodwind sounds.

Pulse waves (sometimes known as rectangular waves) look similar to square waves but are asymmetrical. A square wave is technically a pulse wave with an even 'duty cycle' – which means the high and low parts of the wave are evenly spaced. As the ratio between the high and low stages is varied, the harmonic content changes. If a pulse wave is offered, it almost always has a **pulse width control** (*see left*) to allow you to change the tone.

Use for: Pads, soundscapes and other chordal sounds, where pulse-width modulation allows the harmonic content to be modulated using an LFO, creating a shimmering movement that can add interest to sustained notes or approximate the sound of stringed instruments.

Sawtooth (saw) waves are more harmonically rich than square waves, containing even *and* odd harmonics. So with a 1 kHz fundamental, the harmonics fall at 2 kHz, 3 kHz, 4kHz, 5kHz and so on. The result is a full-bodied sound, with a harsher tone than a square wave.

Use for: Full-fat leads, aggressive basses and warm, expansive pads.

Triangle waves are the least harmonically rich of the traditional waveforms. They consist of the fundamental frequency plus odd harmonics like the square wave, but the level of the harmonics rolls away much sooner, resulting in a thinner, purer sound.
Use for: Applications where a square wave is too imposing, such as pure bass sounds, sub bass and pads.

Sine waves or sinusoidal waves are the purest waveforms,

containing only the fundamental frequency and no harmonics. They are less common on true analogue hardware synths for a couple of reasons, the main one being that they can't be filtered – attempting to filter a sine wave with a low pass filter does nothing if it's below the cutoff frequency other than reduce its volume. Sine waves are usually found in a synth's sub-oscillator section.
Use for: Adding sub bass to bass sounds and stacked synth leads, unfiltered bass sounds, piercing leads and FX.

One other option you may occasionally come across is the **supersaw wave** offered by some virtual analogue synths. This isn't technically a distinct waveform in its own right, but a digital option designed to replicate the sound of detuned sawtooth waves.
Use for: Dominant leads.

Finally, most synths offer a **noise generator** in which a stream of random numbers is set to trigger specific

bands of frequencies. White noise – which sounds like hiss – is the most common. Other shades include pink (less hissy) and brown (deep).
Use for: FX – risers, fallers, windups and so on (*page 95*) – and adding lo-fi grit to pads, keys, basses, perc sounds and leads. Use filters to shape low-level noise so it doesn't overwhelm a mix.

to reset each time the master oscillator completes a cycle of its waveform. If the oscillators are detuned even slightly, the slave generates unusual harmonics thanks to the asymmetric waveform generated when it is forced to reset part way through a cycle. The results are typically unusual, rich sounds which can get harsh or metallic at extreme detuning settings.

Cross-modulation (sometimes labelled X-mod) is another option found in some oscillator sections where the audio-rate output of one oscillator is used to modulate the frequency of another, usually resulting in clanging bell-like sounds.

Virtual analogue synths may also offer settings such as **unison** (sometimes called **spread**), which adds extra slightly detuned slave oscillators to recreate the sound of classic analogue synths. Employ unison on pads and leads to give them a thickening effect without needing to stack up multiple detuned oscillators.

FILTERS

After generating a raw waveform the oscillator on a typical synth passes signal to the filters (see Subtractive synthesis illustrated, right).

Filters are circuits that reduce the level of certain parts of the frequency spectrum. This is the most important step in subtracting harmonics from the raw oscillator waveforms to shape the harmonic content of the final sound.

The most common filter type by far is the **low-pass filter**, which you'll find on almost every subtractive synth. The filter allows lower frequencies to pass through unaffected while reducing the level of frequencies above the cutoff point. It is the starting point for 99% of bass sounds.

The **cutoff frequency** is strictly defined as the frequency at which the filter reduces the signal level by 3dB, but on hardware synths you'll rarely see any reference to specific frequencies on the filter cutoff control – it's intended to be a broad sound shaping tool rather than a precise filter like an EQ.

Resonance (occasionally known as 'peak') feeds some of the filter output back into its input, altering the shape of the filter and producing a boost around the cutoff frequency. Some filters **self-oscillate** when the resonance is turned up to a high setting – the main reason behind the screaming energy of a Roland TB-303.

Many synths offer additional filter options. These include **high-pass filters** (the opposite of low-pass, allowing just the higher frequencies through), **band-pass filters** (which allow a band of frequencies through, cutting off everything above and below the band) and **band-reject** or **band-stop filters** (which do the opposite of band-pass and are known as **notch filters** when they operate over a narrow frequency range). Some virtual analogue synths also feature a **vowel filter**, which imitates the sound of speech, Daft Punk style.

The key thing to remember is that *not all filters are built equal*. The differences between filters give each synth its personality. With vintage hardware synths this is largely due to the specific circuit designs used to create the filter/s. Each one has subtly different characteristics in terms of distortion, shape and tone.

Distinctive filters include the **Minimoog**'s thick, creamy ladder filter (named after the 'ladder' of transistors in the electrical circuit. To this day, if you see a manufacturer or developer advertise a synth with a ladder filter, chances are it's inspired by the classic Moog sound). Roland's **TB-303** bassline synth sounds totally different, squelching as the resonance is turned up. Meanwhile Korg's **MS-10** and **MS-20** feature notoriously aggressive low-pass filters which shriek and howl with self-oscillation at higher peak settings. All three are great at their specific jobs, but you'll struggle to get 303-style acid sounds out of an MS-20 or to imitate the MS-20s aggression with a Minimoog. That's why it's useful to have a range of synths to choose from.

PRO TIPS

JULIEN BRACHT

"One of my favourite synths is the lovely Korg Mono/Poly from 1982. You have four oscillators, which gives you a very large range of possibilities in terms of sound design.

"The sync and cross modulation are two of the most important features. Also the short times of the ADSR curves allow you to create very short, hard percussive sounds."

Chapter two
Synthesis and sound design

TIP You may see the roll-off or slope of a filter listed in terms of the amount by which the signal level is reduced as you move away from the cutoff frequency. This is usually expressed in *decibels per octave* (dB/Oct), but it can also be expressed by the *pole* characteristics of the filter – e.g. a '2-pole, 12dB/Oct' filter or '4-pole' filter or '24dB' filter. The rule to remember is that *the lower the number, the shallower the slope and less extreme the effect.*

Filters can be set to operate at a static frequency – you turn the filter dial to where you want it and leave it there – but things get more interesting when the cutoff frequency is controlled by a **modulation source**. In analogue synths they're modulated by a control voltage (CV) signal, which is why they're sometimes labelled VCFs – voltage-controlled filters – even in software synths. The modulation source can be an envelope generator or an LFO. Many synths also allow you to modulate other parameters of the filter such as the resonance and slope.

TIP Where a synth offers different filter arrangements – like **dual filter setups** – experiment with various routings for radically different sounds.

TIP Many synths offer a **key-tracking** control which automatically increases the filter cutoff as you play higher notes.

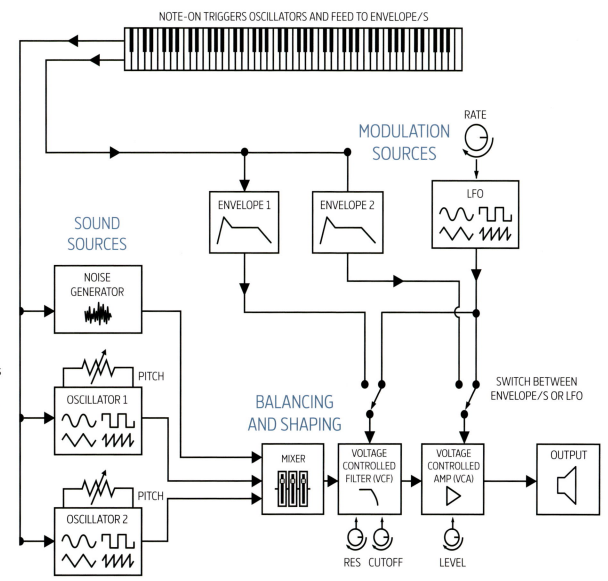

Simplified diagram of the signal flow through a subtractive synth, starting with a note-on trigger and ending at the synth's output. Diagram assumes three oscillators (one noise), and three modulators (two envelopes and an LFO).

ENVELOPES AND VCAS

When a note is pressed or MIDI note-on message is received the synth generates not only a waveform, but also one or more envelopes.

For some purposes, it's acceptable to have a sound that immediately plays at full volume when a key is pressed and instantly drops to silence when you release it (plenty of bass sounds require no further shaping), but in most cases we need a little more control.

The solution is to use an **envelope generator**, a modulator that changes a parameter over time to control the amplitude of the signal. **Voltage-controlled amplifiers (VCAs)** are the most important circuits used to control amplitude in an analogue synth. In virtual analogues, they're sometimes still called VCAs. More often they're referred to as the **amplitude envelope** or plain old **amp env**.

The most commonly found envelope generator is the four-stage **ADSR** variety (*above right*), which allows you to adjust four parameters: attack (A), decay (D), sustain (S) and release (R).

▸▸ The **Attack** stage begins the moment a key is pressed (or MIDI note-on data is received). It dictates how long the sound takes to go from silence to maximum level.

▸▸ **Decay** is the time taken for the signal to drop down to the **Sustain** level, which is the level the envelope signal stays at for as long as the key is held down.

▸▸ **Release** measures the time the envelope takes to return to zero after the finger is withdrawn from the key or MIDI note-off message is received.

A typical **string** or **pad** sound combines a long attack and release time with a high sustain, so that the sound gently swells in and is held until the keys are released, at which point it gently fades out. Punchier **bass** and **arp** sounds use short attack times with medium decay and sustain, so that the initial transient of the sound bursts through at a high volume before dropping.

Envelopes aren't just used for amplitude control. They're also one of the main tools for adding movement to a **filter** over the course of a note. While a static filter allows the harmonics of a tone to be shaped, controlling the filter using an envelope allows the filter cutoff to rise and fall as each note is played, creating movement and more harmonically interesting sounds.

Basic synths offer just one envelope generator which is shared between the amp and filter. More advanced synths offer an amp envelope plus a dedicated filter envelope. Some include additional envelopes to control other parameters.

ADSR envelope. Some older synths also include a 'Hold' stage after Sustain (ADSHR), to hold the sustain level before the release stage. There is also the rarer AHDSR which holds notes before the *decay* stage.

TIP Many soft synths offer more complex envelopes than the ADSR four-point standard. Not only are you able to dial in more envelope points, but some synths also allow you to edit curves between points, allowing for all kinds of finely sculpted transitions in the sound. *The kick drum walkthrough on page 74 shows how much flexibility is bought to sound design when curves are used in drum synthesis.*

MODULATION

Modulation is the process by which parameters like filter cutoff and oscillator fine-tuning are controlled using signals from elsewhere in the synth. Controlling amplitude or filter cutoff using an envelope generator is a simple form of modulation. But that's just the tip of the sound design

Chapter two
Synthesis and sound design

iceberg. Most soft synths allow almost any signal to modulate any parameter using a **modulation matrix** or similar signal routing section.

After the envelopes, **low frequency oscillators** or **LFOs** are the most common modulation sources. LFOs are like regular oscillators but are set to cycle below the 20Hz limit of human hearing.

The first decision when setting up an LFO is to choose its **waveform**. Options typically include the basic analogue waveforms outlined on *page 73* alongside more complex options such as reversed and inverted waveforms and random generators such as sample and hold (S&H).

The LFO **speed** controls how fast the waveform cycles, usually in Hz but sometimes in values relative to the track's tempo (eighth note, 4 bars etc). You might, for example, modulate an oscillator's pitch at a precise 16th note rate for a vibrato effect or have a filter sweep up over four bars.

NOTE Getting a hardware synth to latch to a track's tempo requires you to feed a MIDI clock signal to the synth so it knows the tempo. This happens automatically in almost all soft synths,

Note-on triggering allows the LFO waveform to be retriggered each time a note is pressed down (rather than allowing the LFO to cycle uninterrupted regardless of a new key press). Turn this on for absolute control when programming sounds and phrases that need to lock to the groove.

THE PROS AND CONS OF...
Presets

Some people look down their noses at those who use synth presets as though it's cheating to choose the pre-programmed sounds your synth manufacturer has gone to the effort of creating for users' instant gratification.

There is, admittedly, one major down side to using presets in your music, which is that the same sounds might also appear in other people's tracks. But not every sound needs to be original; entire genres have been built on the sounds of the TR-808, 909 and TB-303 without anyone complaining after all.

There are also plenty of benefits to exploring a synth's presets. The first is that most synths these days have banks of presets crafted by some of the world's leading sound designers and often one or two well-known artists.

These people have been paid to put in the hours applying their expertise to a particular synth in order to explore its potential. It seems wasteful at best – and arrogant at worst – not to take advantage of their skills and efforts.

Secondly, you don't have to use presets as they are. You can think of them as shortcuts to help you get the sound you're looking for. Let's say you want to create a thick, distorted bass patch with detuned oscillators and lots of modulation to add an imprecise, vintage feel. You could start from scratch with a blank patch, or you could scroll through presets until you find something in the right ballpark then modify it to suit your track, adding modulation and adjusting envelope settings until you've got something entirely new. In this case it's not about the journey so much as the destination. Who cares which route you took to create your patch as long as it ends up sounding good?

Thirdly, deconstructing presets is one of the best ways of learning how to get more from a synth. Load a preset you like and work backwards. What oscillator and filter settings has the sound designer employed to create the patch? How has the modulation routing been set up? Are there any tricks you can use in your own sound design efforts? Once you've figured out the techniques, initialise a new patch and try to recreate the sound. It's a great way of improving your sound design chops.

Finally, never forget that some of the biggest dance tracks of all time rely heavily on presets.

Dance music wouldn't be the same without staple sounds like the Yamaha DX100 'Solid Bass' preset or the Korg M1's 'Organ 2'. And though it might be increasingly hard to do something original with those well-worn sounds, never be afraid to turn to the classics if they work in the context of a particular track.

Presets shouldn't be a dirty word.

It's not about whether you toiled for days to create a dancefloor-filling sound. *It's that the end result fills dancefloors.* And if you've used a preset to do that, who cares? *Not us – or 99.9% of listeners.*

The **phase** control – where available – allows you to select a precise point in the LFO waveform from which to start cycling. It is typically used in conjunction with note-on triggering.

Almost all subtractive synths include at least one LFO. Some contain more, allowing multiple parameters to be controlled by separate LFOs simultaneously. In some cases you can even modulate one LFO with another before routing the result to a third destination.

NOTE When LFOs are set to operate *in audio-range frequencies* and modulate filter cutoff or oscillator pitch, the effect is sometimes known as FM or **frequency modulation**. This shouldn't be confused with the synthesis method of the same name, which is only really possible with highly accurate digital oscillators.

MONOPHONIC VS POLYPHONIC

One of the first decisions when creating a synth patch is choosing whether to use a monophonic or polyphonic synth. **Monophonic** means the synth can only produce one note at a time. **Polyphonic** means the synth has multiple 'voices', allowing it to play more than one note simultaneously (usually up to eight voices on analogue hardware synths; potentially many more on digital and soft synths). The majority of synths were monophonic until the early late '70s and early '80s because it was more complicated and expensive to create polyphonic versions: each additional voice required its own oscillator, filter, envelope generators, LFOs and VCAs. Even now, polyphonic analogue synths tend to cost significantly more than monophonic equivalents.

Some people think that monophonic synths (aka **monosynths**) are inferior to their polyphonic counterparts (**polysynths**), but it's not that simple.

The reason monophonic synths still have a place in the modern studio is that a surprising number of synth parts don't require polyphony. While chordal parts and pads obviously require polyphony, monophonic synths (or settings) are

PRO TIPS

SOUKIE AND WINDISH

"We really like the pad on 'Blockchain'. It's made with one sample. Nayan often uses an arpeggiator without note steps, so that if you hold a key longer it automatically repeats the same note. In combination with a sampler, you can find unique pads in any sample by repeating a part of the sound."

invariably a better starting point for basslines, leads and many sound FX.

Here's where monosynths have an ace or two to play. Most crucially, monophonic synths typically allow you to add '**glide**' or **portamento** to a sound, which makes the pitch slide up or down to the next note when you hit a key, rather than simply chopping off the previous note. Not only can you specify the glide **time**, you can often also specify which note you'd like to **prioritise**.

TIP Portamento is sometimes best used sparingly to highlight transitions between certain notes – often at line and phrase endings. So that not all notes glide, use automation to switch on portamento for selected notes only. Further automate the glide time for complete control.

Is analogue better than digital?

A decade or so ago one of the biggest debates in music production concerned the relative merits of analogue and digital devices. Some argued that the distinctive sounds of analogue synths were impossible to recreate digitally and that digital synths sounded cold, too precise or somehow less organic than their analogue counterparts.

Digital signal processing has progressed significantly since the turn of the millennium, to the extent that nowadays it's pretty much impossible to say that either analogue or digital is inherently better than the other. Besides, no one's forcing you to pick a side – you're free to kit out your studio with analogue, digital or a mixture of the two depending on your tastes and budget. Both approaches have their advantages, and the choice largely depends on personal preference.

A software emulation of, say, a Roland TB-303 might not sound exactly like the original analogue hardware, but it'll be cheaper, more flexible thanks to added features, more reliable and easier to use in your DAW.

Conversely, a modern virtual analogue synth like NI Massive might be cheap and flexible, but some producers find it more inspiring to work with a physical device with clear limitations that forces a specific workflow and helps shape the creative process; sometimes more options aren't necessarily better.

Chapter two
Synthesis and sound design

TIP Most virtual instruments offer polyphony – even if they're based on monophonic synths. G-Force's Minimonsta, for instance, is an emulation of the classic monophonic Minimoog, but the plugin allows you to choose anything up to 32 voice polyphony. As such, the choice between monophonic and polyphonic is up to you.

NOTE A very small number of analogue synths can also be described as **paraphonic**. This means their oscillators can produce multiple notes simultaneously, but that all of those voices are passed through just one shared filter circuit. This is mainly a cheaper way of achieving a basic form of polyphony, allowing the synth to play chords but not quite offering the flexibility of true polyphony. It can be found on vintage synths such as the Korg Poly800 and Roland RS-505, and on new models like the Moog Sub37 and Dave Smith Instruments Pro 2.

HARDWARE VS SOFTWARE? ANALOGUE VS DIGITAL?

There are two main types of synth: software and hardware. **Software** synths are computer-based synths which run either as standalone applications or, more commonly, as plugins in a DAW. They are also known as virtual instruments, soft synths and VSTs. Meanwhile **hardware** refers to physical devices such as synths, drum machines and effects which don't rely on a computer and DAW to produce or modify sounds. In the case of synths this equates to a keyboard, rack unit or desktop module.

You'll also hear people referring to synths as either analogue or digital. It's a fairly common misconception that all hardware synths are analogue, but analogue doesn't just mean that the synth is a tangible physical object. It refers specifically to the *circuitry under the hood* and the *technique used to generate sound*.

Analogue signals are continuous electrical currents which vary in frequency and amplitude. A true analogue synth processes everything in the analogue domain, starting from the oscillators, which generate an analogue signal that gets passed on to analogue filters and VCAs.

Some synths use digital or digitally controlled oscillators (which still generate an analogue wave at the output) and many now use digital envelope generators and/or LFOs. *As long as the signal path is still analogue post-oscillator, these hybrid synths can be considered to work in much the same way as their 'true' analogue forebears.*

Digital signals are nothing more than a series of pulses consisting of 1s and 0s. Digital synths generate their sounds entirely in the digital domain using complex digital signal processing (DSP) algorithms. They

TOOLS OF THE TRADE
Sequencers and arpeggiators

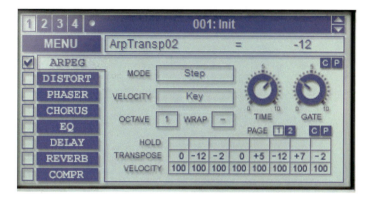

In addition to their sound shaping features, many synths feature built-in modules for creating riffs and melodies. The most common is the **arpeggiator**, like that in Lennar Digital's Sylenth1, *above*.

With the arpeggiator switched on, whenever you hold down a chord the synth plays each note back in turn. Editable options include the arpeggio **rate** (with tempo sync options usually available), **direction** (whether the notes are retriggered up the scale, down, or up and then back down) and the **octave** setting (whether the notes play in additional octaves on top of the notes held down).

Arpeggiators are simple to use and are an effective way to give standard chordal parts rhythm and movement (*page 158*).

A second, related option, is the built-in **sequencer**.

Sequencers built into software and hardware synths tend to be simple **analogue step sequencers**, which allow you to enter a series of notes that are then replayed in sync with the timing of the track.

They offer a fast, intuitive means of creating repeated monophonic patterns – melodic sketchpads that can be inspiring creative springboards as well as useful live playthings.

If a synth doesn't feature a built-in sequencer, most DAWs offer alternatives, with both Logic and Ableton boasting MIDI step sequencers and arpeggiators. Simply route the MIDI to the external synth to start jamming.

Chapter two
Synthesis and sound design

may employ any combination of sample replay, FM synthesis or circuit modelling techniques in their architecture. Only at the final stage of a digital synth are the signals converted to analogue before being routed to the audio output socket.

Virtual analogue (VA) is the term used to describe digital synths (either hardware or software) which emulate the sounds and synthesis methods of analogue subtractive synths. Although sound is generated digitally, VA synths usually offer the same controls as the analogue synths they're modelled on. VA hardware synths such as the MicroKorg and MiniNova are often cheaper than true analogue synths of a similar spec, although there are also high-end VA synths such as the Clavia Nord Lead and Roland Jupiter-80.

MIDI AND CV/GATE

When it comes to controlling hardware synths there are a couple of different options, with the approach largely determined by the synth in question. Most offer MIDI connections, allowing them to be controlled using the protocol which has been an industry standard for over 30 years.

In recent years, as more manufacturers have created new analogue synths, the old-fashioned CV (control voltage) and gate system has resurfaced. This uses two analogue electrical signals to control the pitch and timing of notes. Most manufacturers now use compatible CV/gate systems, which hasn't always been the case.

The main advantages of CV/gate are that it offers slightly more precise timing than MIDI and allows you to patch modular and semi-modular analogue synths together in interesting ways.

MIDI signals can be sent out of your DAW using a suitable MIDI interface, while CV synths require a MIDI-to-CV converter if you want to control them from a MIDI output. There are also specialist CV options such as Expert Sleepers' Silent Way protocol, which allows you to send CV signals directly out of your DAW as long as you're using a compatible audio interface.

If you want to explore the old-school approach of hardware sequencing which has grown in popularity, there are a range of options on the market. Some, such as Arturia's BeatStep Pro or smaller Beatstep offer USB, MIDI and CV options and multiple lanes of sequencing, allowing them to connect to the majority of hardware synths, or even act as an interface for sequencing soft synths within your DAW.

OTHER THINGS TO CONSIDER

▸▸ **Velocity mapping** is as it sounds – allowing note input velocities to be mapped to various parameters on the synth. Mapping velocity to filter cutoff, for example, allows you to open the filter when the keyboard is hit harder.

▸▸ **Custom wavetables** on software synths such as Waves' Codex and Xfer's Serum allow any wave shape to be drawn or an audio file to be loaded in and used as the driving oscillator. Image-Line's Harmor synth even allows image files to be used as wavetable information. *Ever wondered what a picture of your face sounded like..?*

LAST BUT NOT LEAST… THE HUMAN TOUCH

It's easy in the era of the computer studio to embrace the power and flexibility of the soft synth while overlooking the myriad workflow and performance benefits of playing you favourite synths using a keyboard.

Playing by hand, using either a synth's built-in keyboard or a dedicated MIDI controller is not only rewarding in its own right, it gives the added benefit of human timing. Tempting as it is to precisely program everything into a DAW, often the imprecision of a real performance, with the occasional happy accident, can deliver better results. Consider playing parts by hand and recording them as audio or just leaving MIDI notes unquantised. You may be surprised at the results.

CV/GATE STANDARDS

Unlike MIDI, Control Voltage and Gate isn't a fixed standard. Although there's always one connection for pitch (CV) and one for note on/off (Gate), there are a few popular implementations of both CV and Gate:

▸▸ **Volts per octave (V/Oct)** was the first CV standard with Moog, Sequencial Circuits, Arp, Oberheim and Roland adapting it.

▸▸ **Hertz per volt (Hz/V)** was used by Korg and Yamaha and a handful of other manufacturers

▸▸ **Voltage-Trigger (V-Trig or Postive Trigger)** is found on Roland and Sequential Circuits gear.

▸▸ **Short Circuit Trigger (S-Trig or Negatve Trigger)** is found mostly on Moog, Korg and Yamaha products.

Chapter two
Synthesis and sound design

TOOLS OF THE TRADE

Essential synths and emulations

Dance music might be a generally forward-thinking genre, but there have always been plenty of eyes trained on the past. Dance producers have a healthy reverence for vintage gear, and the sounds of classic synths have become staples of genres from house and techno to trance and dubstep.

The sounds of iconic machines are ingrained in dance music history. Understanding the origins of these sounds and being able to tell the difference between a Moog bass and a 303 acid line can help you get a particular sound faster.

The good news is that having an awareness of the 'top trumps' of retro gear doesn't mean you need to spend thousands on expensive kit. If you want to incorporate similar sounds into your tracks on a budget most of these synths are available as cheaper hardware clones, software emulations or multisampled virtual instruments.

Moog Minimoog Model D
The first commercially available compact synth – and still one of the best – lending itself to any style of electronic music. Released in 1970 and produced until 1981, the monophonic Minimoog revolutionised electronic music, laying the foundations for every other synth here. Renowned for its smooth, funky bass sounds and distinctive leads, Moog (pronounced 'mogue') still make a number of hardware synths which follow the pioneering footsteps of the original. Arturia make the officially licensed software emulation, Minimoog V. We like GForce's excellent Minimonsta plugin.

Korg MS-20
Released in 1978, the MS-20 (*below*) is a snarling beast of a monosynth. The polar opposite of Moog's silky offerings in terms of sound, the MS excels at raw, nasty tones thanks to its brutal low-pass filter, which can be pushed into howling self-oscillation at high resonance settings. The same filter can be found in the affordable Korg Monotron and Monotribe units, while Korg will also now sell you a faithful, if slightly smaller, reissue of the original in the form of the MS-20 Mini. In the digital domain, Korg's MS-20 plugin is a good option, but we especially like the hands-on appeal of the iMS-20 app for iPad.

Roland TB-303
The TB-303 was a commercial flop when released in 1982. The simplistic synth failed at its intended purpose: recreating the sound of a bass guitar. Its potential was only realised when Chicago producers snapped up second-hand units and abused them to create acid house. Roland's AIRA TB-3 unit is the modern successor. For a more authentic analogue clone look to the Cyclone Analogic BassBot TT-303 or any of the popular x0xb0x clones built using near-identical components to the original. Software equivalents include the D16 Phoscyon and AudioRealism BassLine 2.

Yamaha DX7
When it was released in 1983, the DX7 destroyed the competition in terms of price, polyphony and its ability to recreate real instruments. The secret? Frequency modulation (FM) synthesis (*overleaf*), the first digital synthesis approach to make a major impact on the mass market. The DX7 is the archetypal '80s synth. Special mention also goes to the DX100, a cheaper, more limited model based on the same synth architecture, which became a staple of Detroit techno. All DX synths are tricky to program. NI's FM8 soft synth makes the job slightly easier.

Roland Juno 106
The Juno 106 (*above*) is one of the most used and loved synths in the history of dance music. Released in 1984, the six voice analogue classic has a fairly limited feature set but it's almost impossible to get a bad sound from it. Maybe that's exaggerating, but the sweet spot of the Juno is broad, offering everything from superlative strings and pads to rich basses and leads. Despite reliability issues, the days of second hand bargains are long gone. Snap up a good vintage unit if you still can or give TAL's U-NO-LX plugin a go; it sounds almost identical.

Korg M1
The M1 represents one of the last great hurrahs of hardware synths before the arrival of DAWs and affordable software alternatives in the late '90s. Released in 1988, the M1 was a flagship synth at the time, cementing the popularity of the 'workstation' concept. The cutting edge sample-based digital synth architecture evolved into 1995's Trinity workstation, but the writing was already on the wall for expensive hardware synths. Even so, the M1's place in house history was assured thanks to its iconic piano sounds and much-loved 'Organ 2' preset. Korg's Legacy Collection M1 plugin offers identical sounds in your DAW.

Chapter two
Synthesis and sound design

Other forms of synthesis

This chapter deliberately focuses on subtractive synthesis (and its virtual analogue cousin) for the simple reason that *it's the most common technique used by a long way*. But it would be remiss not to acknowledge the importance of a handful of other key approaches to synthesis.

The oldest, which pre-dates the arrival of all-in-one synths by nearly a decade is **modular synthesis.** Despite playing an important role in the story of synth development, modular synths had been written off by most musicians as a relic of the '60s and '70s until the late '90s, when interest started growing again. In recent years affordable options from companies like Doepfer have helped revitalise the market.

As the name suggests, modular synths are constructed by the user from modules. The overall approach is typically analogue and subtractive, but the synth is built from individual components rather than supplied as the kind of all-in-one system typical of most subtractive synths. This means putting together a collection of synth building blocks — an oscillator here, a filter there — and linking them together using cables. The possibilities are almost infinite.

Kirk Degiorgio's Eurorack setup. Building your own modular synth is a great way to learn about complex synthesis ideas – but be warned, it's addictive…

Modular synths are comparatively expensive and can be tricky to get started with, but the potential to create something unique is unparalleled. The best place to start is the forum at muffwiggler.com and a good software alternative is u-he's ACE plugin, which offers an approximation of the flexibility of a hardware system.

A shout out also goes to **semi-modular synths**, which are typically analogue, subtractive units with patch points that allow users to customise signal and modulation routings. Unlike true modular units, semi-modular synths like the Korg MS-20, Arturia MicroBrute and Doepfer Dark Energy 2 don't require you to plug cables in to make a sound — all signal paths are also internally hard-wired — but the option's there for you to override them if you choose. The MS-20 plugin offers virtual patch cables to recreate the semi-modular experience, but the signal and modulation routing options of most software synths can match the flexibility of any semi-modular hardware synth.

FM (frequency modulation) **synthesis** was the first digital synthesis method to make an impact on the mass market following the introduction of the Yamaha DX7 (*right*) in 1983. Instead of analogue oscillators and filters, FM synthesis uses precise digital operators (essentially sine wave oscillators), which modulate each other's frequency. The audio-rate modulation creates harmonics in the output. FM synthesis excels at making bells, metallic sounds and imitations of real acoustic instruments but is notoriously difficult to program. Native Instruments' FM8 plugin is a good plugin alternative. Logic's EFM1 and Ableton's Operator are simpler versions of the same approach.

We've seen a recent resurgence in interest for **wavetable synthesis** (which uses digital oscillators, allowing complex waveforms to be constructed from huge banks of wave shapes), the brief dominance of **sample-based synthesis**, and more recently in software the arrival of **granular synthesis** (looping and replaying tiny 'granules' of sampled sounds to create unique new tones) and **physical modelling** (emulating the characteristics of physical materials from plucked strings through to struck surfaces).

Popular software synths such as Serum, Spire and Massive combine wavetables with subtractive techniques, filters and effects for broad sound design possibilities. In Massive's case, its ability to deliver ripping, vowel-shaped bass and lead sounds has followed the Roland TB-303's lead in almost single-handedly shaping the genesis of a complete dance music genre – *see walkthrough, page 110, for Massive's take on a 'talking' dubstep bass patch.*

Additive synthesis can be thought of as the opposite of subtractive synthesis. Rather than taking a harmonically rich waveform and filtering it down, additive synthesis starts with the fundamental frequency as a pure sine wave and adds harmonics and overtones on top. It's a relatively uncommon approach in hardware synths – the most common incarnation is in electric organs where 'drawbars' control the levels of harmonics in the sound. Camel Audio's Alchemy plugin (now no longer marketed) is a lot more than just an additive synth, but it's a good starting point for creating similar sounds in software.

The arrival of digital technology in the mid '80s meant that manufacturers could experiment with a range of different approaches to synthesis. It's a trend which has only accelerated with the arrival of software synths and the proliferation of plugins since the turn of the millennium. It makes today's synthesis landscape more varied than ever.

Automation and tweakability

Occasionally you may want a synth part that uses the same sound and settings for the duration of a track. Basslines are the most likely candidates for this static approach.

More often you'll want to take advantage of the numerous tweaking options available, either on real synths, where knob twiddling is a tactile pleasure, or in plugins, which provide near limitless options to change parameters on the fly using automation.

There are various ways to program tweaks using soft synths. Probably the simplest is to select a parameter then draw automation manually on a track lane in the DAW – *as shown above.*

A second option is to map parameters to MIDI controllers and then either draw those in or play them live. If you've mapped cutoff frequency to the mod wheel for example, you just need to roll up the wheel to open up a sound.

A more powerful variation on this option, where available, is to use macros to map any number of parameters to a single macro controller.

Popular synth tweaks include:

▶▶ Adjusting the cutoff frequency of an acid line.

▶▶ Changing a lead synth's envelope settings over time – gradually increase the release and/or sustain envelop towards a build.

▶▶ Tinkering with filter, resonance, pulse width and fine-tuning in a pad part to keep it engaging.

▶▶ Opening filters and raising pitch on tension-building FX (*page 96*)…

▶▶ …and the opposite on wind-downs and fall FX (*page 95*).

Chapter two
Synthesis and sound design

Synth leads and arps

LEADS

The synthesised lead is the melodic focal point in almost all dance genres.

Traditionally, a synth would take the monophonic lead above an underlying chord and bass bed to create memorable hooks. Fast-forward to today and the popularity of wavetable synthesis has facilitated the creation of timbrally complex lead sounds with ever-changing waveforms that forme the bedrock of entire genres.

KEY FEATURES

A typical lead sound features:

▶▶ **Tonal richness and/or complexity.** A lead synth is usually harmonic and interesting. Combine multiple oscillators and tune them across different octaves for bigger stacked sounds. Detune oscillators against each other or stack and detune 'supersaw' oscillators to thicken up basic waveforms and create chorus-like effects.

▶▶ **Sufficient mid range/upper presence.** Whether it's a lazy G-Funk solo or a hard-hitting EDM hook, a lead synth needs to slice through the mid range and higher mids of a mix. Blending in a noise oscillator adds bulk and bite to help give sounds definition and presence.

▶▶ **Fast attack/release.** Tight attack and release settings ensure a lead starts and ends swiftly, keeping it at the forefront of a mix. Keeping release values low also gives delay and reverb tails more impact.

▶▶ **Performance modulations.** The new-school of leads is characterised by perpetual change. Set synth parameters to be modulated by velocity, key-tracking, pitch bend and mod wheel data. This makes for expressive patches, injecting variation into the performance.

MAKE YOUR OWN LEAD

A basic PWM lead can be synthesised using any synth that features pulse width modulation. Here's how:

▶▶ **1.** Start with a single oscillator set to a pulse (or square) wave.

▶▶ **2.** Change voicing to mono or legato.

▶▶ **3.** Set the ADSR amp envelope to fast attack, maximum decay, maximum sustain and short release.

▶▶ **4.** Hook up a triangle or sine LFO to modulate the pulse width. This modulates the width of the waveform, creating a pleasing 'beating' sound.

OLD SCHOOL LEADS

Want to give a soft synth lead an analogue flavour? Try these tips:

▶▶ Detune two oscillators against each other – a few fine tune notches each way will do the job.

▶▶ Assign the mod wheel to vibrato and wiggle to taste.

▶▶ Activate legato mode then play overlapping notes for that 'sliding' effect.

▶▶ Route MIDI velocity to the attack amp so that quieter notes have a subtly softer attack.

▶▶ Assign a slow-moving sine LFO to oscillator pitch. This emulates the ear-pleasing pitch drift of early analogue synths.

▶▶ **5.** Change the LFO speed to alter the effect: slow settings sound smooth and musical; faster settings create intensity and aggression.

ARPS

Arpeggio ('arp' for short) sounds are some of the easiest to program. The difference between a typical lead and arp is simply a shorter amp envelope; arps should have an instant attack coupled with short decay/sustain and release times. Carefully shape the release portion to smooth out sharp edges.

TIP Route either **velocity** or **keynote** values to the filter cutoff. When set up, higher velocity notes or higher notes on the keyboard will open the filter more.

TIP Arps respond well to **delays**. Try tape delays that roll away the high end of repeats so they don't mask the original sound. Add reverb after the delay to push delays further back in the mix. Experiment with different delay times to the arp trigger time for interesting polyrhythms (*page 28*).

TIP To build pressure in an arp line ahead of a drop use automation to gradually open the filter and increase the amp's sustain and/or decay envelope. As the notes lengthen the mix becomes claustrophobic, ratcheting up the pressure and begging for the relief of a return to a short decay.

Basic vintage arp

1. Start a new Sylenth1 patch by clicking Menu > Init Preset. Tune Oscillator A1 down an octave and increase its Voices to 4. Change Oscillator A2's waveform to saw and increase Voices to 5. Next, turn its fine tuning to around 0.10 cents. Ensure Retrig is switched off on both oscillators.

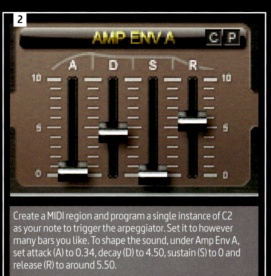

2. Create a MIDI region and program a single instance of C2 as your note to trigger the arpeggiator. Set it to however many bars you like. To shape the sound, under Amp Env A, set attack (A) to 0.34, decay (D) to 4.50, sustain (S) to 0 and release (R) to around 5.50.

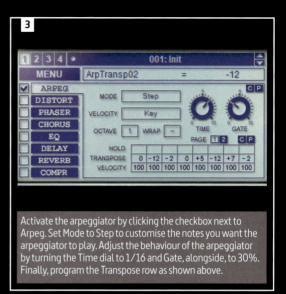

3. Activate the arpeggiator by clicking the checkbox next to Arpeg. Set Mode to Step to customise the notes you want the arpeggiator to play. Adjust the behaviour of the arpeggiator by turning the Time dial to 1/16 and Gate, alongside, to 30%. Finally, program the Transpose row as shown above.

4. Filters bring the sound to life. Set Filter A's filter type to low-pass by click/holding. Flick the switch on the right to 24 dB. Set Drive to 2.10, Resonance to 2.00 and Cutoff to 40Hz. Under Filter Control, set Cutoff to 20 Hz and Resonance to 1.00, then highlight Warm Drive.

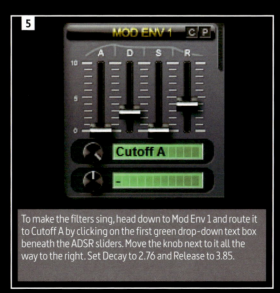

5. To make the filters sing, head down to Mod Env 1 and route it to Cutoff A by clicking on the first green drop-down text box beneath the ADSR sliders. Move the knob next to it all the way to the right. Set Decay to 2.76 and Release to 3.85.

6. To get a more vintage sound, route LFOs to modulate pitch and phase. First set the LFO 1 waveform to Lorenz and route it to Pitch A. Set Rate to 8/1T and Gain to 1.50. Then route LFO 2 to modulate Phase A using a sine wave. Move the dial alongside to 7.00, set Rate to 2/1T and Gain to 7.00.

// WALKTHROUGHS

EDM lead template 🎧

1. The secret to epic 'hands-in-the-air' EDM leads is multiple stacked and detuned oscillators – an easy job for most modern soft synths. Program a monophonic EDM-style riff on a MIDI track then load a new instance of Sylenth1 and initialise it by going to Menu > Clear.

2. In the lower right of the synth turn the Portamento dial to 0 then flip the switch to S, activating Slide mode. The glide gives the riff a lazy feel as notes bend into each other. As we're creating a stacked monophonic lead, toggle Mono Legato mode on.

3. Sylenth1 features two separate units (A and B), each offering two oscillators per unit, giving access to four separate oscillators – ideal for the rich sawtooth lead we're making. Oscillator A1 will fill the lower frequencies and underpin the patch so turn its Octave dial down to -2.

4. Each of Sylenth1's oscillators can generate up to eight unison voices to be stacked and detuned. Increase Oscillator A1's Voices to maximum 8, then set Detune to around 3.3. Back Osc A1's Volume down to about 7.8.

5. Retrig is currently switched on, meaning that each voice retriggers at the same point in the waveform with each new note. This is ideal when you want a consistent sound like a bass tone, but for a lead that relies on stacked detuned oscillators, toggle Retrig off.

6. Time for a second sawtooth oscillator. Scroll Oscillator A2's waveform to Saw and set Voices to 8, Detune to 3.5, Octave to -1, then untoggle Retrig as in step 5. The two oscillators are stacked an octave apart, filling out the frequency spectrum.

7 A third sawtooth is now added an octave above the second. Leave Oscillator B1 (accessed via the A1 drop-down) on Saw and Octave at 0. Change Voices to 8, Detune to 3.9, Volume to 8 and untoggle Retrig. With eight voices per oscillator, we now have a 24-voice lead spanning three octaves.

8 An oscillator's Stereo parameter pans its voices across the stereo field. All oscillators currently have this set to maximum. Control the effect by narrowing the spread for the lower oscillators: set Oscillator A1's Stereo to 6.3 and Osc A2's to 8.4. Leave Osc B2's Stereo at maximum.

9 Use the fourth oscillator to mix in a hint of white noise, accentuating the patch's toppy fizz to help it slice through the mix. Set Oscillator B2's waveform to Noise and Voices to 1. Adjust its Volume to add a hint of noise only – we've settled at around 1.

10 The synth's oscillators sound a little isolated and digital. Meld them together with a touch of overdrive. Activate Sylenth1's Distortion module (central panel), leave mode on OverDrive, then set Amount to 2.4 and Dry/Wet to 95%. This thickens the sound and adds character.

11 To add timbral interest, apply a small amount of the synth's phaser effect for extra movement. Activate the Phaser module and set Dry/Wet to 7%. Turn the Main Volume slider up to 6.8, compensating for the patch's slight drop in level.

12 The lead's programming is complete, but it lacks space in the mix. For a typical EDM-style pump effect, send the lead to a return track containing a lush hall reverb. A sidechaining plugin heavily ducks both the lead channel and its reverb on each beat for trademark pumping against the kick.

// WALKTHROUGHS

Funky synth brass

1 We're building a swelling synth brass patch using a plugin emulation of a classic analogue synth. Load Arturia's Oberheim SEM V on a MIDI track, import the supplied MIDI file into the track then call up Templates > Template > Init voice 1 (Sawtooth wave) patch to initialise the synth.

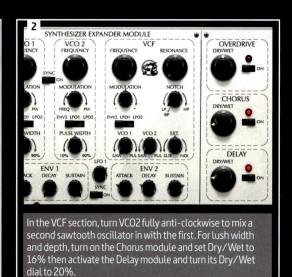

2 In the VCF section, turn VCO2 fully anti-clockwise to mix a second sawtooth oscillator in with the first. For lush width and depth, turn on the Chorus module and set Dry/Wet to 16% then activate the Delay module and turn its Dry/Wet dial to 20%.

3 On the second envelope route a subtle drifting effect to oscillator 2. Set VCO2's Freq to -7 semitones and 71.3 cents; flick VCO2's mod source switch across to ENV2; then pull the Modulation dial left to Freq: 50%. Next, set Env 2's Attack to 50ms, Decay to 192ms and Sustain to -1dB.

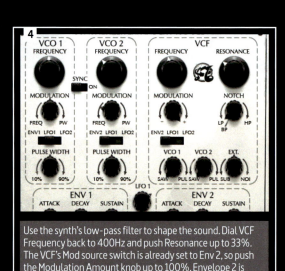

4 Use the synth's low-pass filter to shape the sound. Dial VCF Frequency back to 400Hz and push Resonance up to 33%. The VCF's Mod source switch is already set to Env 2, so push the Modulation Amount knob up to 100%. Envelope 2 is now filtering the start of each chord.

5 Now set up the mod wheel to introduce vibrato. Open the top Modulation Matrix. In the first slot set Mod Wheel as the Source and Vibrato (LFO 1) as the Destination by a small (0.024) amount. Change LFO 1's Freq to 6Hz, then automate or record in mod wheel movements.

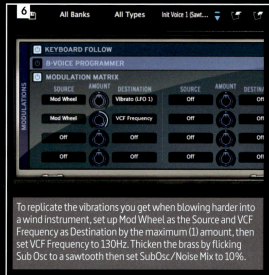

6 To replicate the vibrations you get when blowing harder into a wind instrument, set up Mod Wheel as the Source and VCF Frequency as Destination by the maximum (1) amount, then set VCF Frequency to 130Hz. Thicken the brass by flicking Sub Osc to a sawtooth then set SubOsc/Noise Mix to 10%.

Moroder-style arp

1 The arp part from Donna Summer's 1977 hit 'I Feel Love' produced by electronic music pioneer Giorgio Moroder has become an iconic disco synth sound. Open a new instance of u-He's Diva loaded into a 125bpm project then create a two-beat riff comprised of arpeggiated (*page 158*) eighth notes.

2 The seminal riff uses delay to fill the space between each eighth note to create a running 16th note effect. Load a basic delay plugin on an FX/aux track then send the arp channel's signal to this return. Set the delay's wet/dry mix to 100% wet, delay time to 1/16th and feedback to 0%.

3 Moroder originally used a Moog Modular synth to create the sound so we'll use Diva's Moog-style features to emulate the timbre. First, shape the sound's volume envelope: set ADS Env 1's Decay to 20 and Sustain to 0 to tighten and shorten the length of the notes.

4 The original riff spreads multiple oscillators over several octaves for thickness. Currently all three of Diva's oscillators are at the same pitch, so change Osc 1's Range to 16' and Osc 3's Range to 4'. Now each of the three tone generators spans a different octave.

5 To shape the tone set the filter Cutoff to 60 then modulate Cutoff using ADS Env 2 by turning the filter's Env2 (FreqModDepth) knob to 40. Set ADS Env 2's Decay to 40 and Sustain to 23 for a characterful tight pluck.

6 In the original track notes are panned to one side while delays are panned to the other. To replicate the effect pan the Diva channel to L75 and the delay return to R75. Then automate Cutoff and Env 2 FreqMod Depth to open and close the filter to recreate Moroder's live knob-twiddling.

Chapter two
Synthesis and sound design

Synth pads

The purpose of the humble pad is explained in its name. Originally pads, generated using synthesised string or organ sounds, were used to 'pad' out a sparse mix, mixed low to underpin and glue together a track's melodic elements. As synths became more powerful, pads took on more central roles until, with artists like Future Sound of London, they supplied and/or contributed to multi-layered soundscapes that became foundations of tracks in their own right.

KEY FEATURES

A typical pad sound features:

▶▶ **Rich waveform/s.** Although atmospheric 'cold' pads can be made using harmonic-free (or light) sine and triangle waveforms, warmer, fuller tones are built using square and saw waves. Add low-level white noise for old-school 'dust'.

▶▶ **Slow attack and release settings.** Pads ease in and out of the mix gradually and are designed to play for long periods. Some pads move between chords while others hold the same chord across four, eight or even 16 bar sections.

▶▶ **Movement.** To keep things interesting over long periods pads use modulation such as an LFO assigned to filter cutoff or more complex routing of velocity, aftertouch and key-tracking to parameters like oscillator pulse width, detuning and resonance.

MAKE YOUR OWN PAD

A simple pad that underpins a track's chords is easy to make using pretty much any bundled or freeware polyphonic subtractive synth:

▶▶ **1.** For a warm pad sound, start with an oscillator set to a square or saw wave. For a colder sound, try a triangle wave. Experiment with different oscillator settings to change the sound's flavour.

▶▶ **2.** Set the ADSR envelopes to taste. For a pad that gently fades in and out, increase attack and release times.

▶▶ **3.** To stop the pad from interfering with other melodic elements, use a low-pass filter and reduce its cutoff frequency until the pad recedes in the mix. Increase resonance to add a sheen of sparkle. Bracket EQ to remove unwanted low end.

▶▶ **4.** Adding a second oscillator expands the sonic palette. Not only are you able to add upper or lower octaves to a sound to extend its space in the mix, you can also start playing with the effects combined waveforms have.

OLD SCHOOL PADS

There are various techniques for giving soft synth pads an analogue bite:

▶▶ Detune the second oscillator slightly.

▶▶ Use an LFO to modulate either pitch or PWM.

▶▶ Introduce low-level white noise on a third oscillator.

▶▶ Switch on unison or layer mode to stack in detuned copies of the original sound.

▶▶ Use a saturation or overdrive plugin to introduce additional harmonics, smooth out transients and roughen up the sound.

▶▶ **5.** To add swells, use the filter envelope to change the cutoff filter's value over time. More movement can be introduced using LFOs. Start with an LFO modulating the pitch. Use a sine wave as the modulator on a slow cycle to give a gently drifting analogue feel.

EFFECTS

Many pads benefit from **chorus**, **flange**, **phase** and **ensemble** effects (*page 220*) to widen a sound, increase depth and movement and to dilute its presence, easing it back in a mix. Indeed on early pad synths such as the Juno-60 and Solina String chorus effects were bundled on board.

Although tempting to pile on **reverb**, doing so risks muddying a pad, swamping the mix and blurring detail. Gentle use of ambient settings can give a sound sparkle while automation at line ends to bring out big plate or hall tails can generate characterful 'hanging tails' with the illusion that the pad – otherwise dry – is bigger in the mix.

A **delay** with feedback is a better alternative to reverb as it allows for a cleaner sound and gives the option of setting up tempo-synced delay times.

Removing low end frequencies from both the original pad sound and its effects keeps the mix uncluttered – particularly with chords that span a wide frequency range.

Basic 'string' pad 🎧

1 Load a new patch and set the first oscillator to generate a square (or pulse) wave. This provides a rich timbral starting point rich in odd harmonics.

2 One way of adding movement to square waves is by applying pulse width modulation. This varies the width of the square wave over time, changing its harmonic content. Route (Source) LFO2 to (Destination) Osc1 Shape then set LFO2 to a gently cycling sine wave at a moderate depth.

3 Adjust the attack and release times using the amp envelope sliders. Pads typically have slow attack and release settings – let the tempo of the track dictate the settings. Next, apply low-pass filtering with a subtle bump of resonance to give a mellower tone.

Basic 'string' pad: next steps 🎧

4 To make things more interesting, introduce a second oscillator. A sawtooth wave is layered in to give a richer texture. It is tuned an octave higher than osc 1 and slightly sharpened for a thicker texture using the 'Fine' tuning control. It is mixed 45% quieter than the main oscillator.

5 A simple way to add life to pad sounds is to use subtle amounts of vibrato. Set this up using LFO1 either as a sine or triangle wave to modulate the pitch of both oscillators. At the same time use Osc 2's filter envelope to gradually open up over the course of the chord.

6 For effects, we've opted for a mix of chorus – a classic choice for string sounds, included on a lot of classic string synths – and stereo delay to bolster the stereo image. A low-level triangle sub oscillator (or third oscillator tuned two octaves down) supplies low end bulk and completes the sound.

Chapter two
Synthesis and sound design

Soundscapes

Although pads are used in all genres of electronic music, they feature most prominently in chillout, where for artists like Future Sound of London, their use became an art form in itself.

Slower tempos, fluid arrangements and sparser mixes allow for the creation of pads that are expansive, multi-faceted and detailed. Where this happens, a pad is better described as a **soundscape**.

Soundscapes may be based on traditional pads, but they are often a whole lot more. Additional layers are made up of real-world recordings, with sounds from the natural and human world injecting textures into complex combined sounds. As with many elements of sound design, the only limit to what you can do with soundscapes is your imagination.

KEY FEATURES

A typical soundscape features:

▸▸ **A pad base.** The foundation on which other sounds are laid is often a fairly simple chordal bed.

▸▸ **Additional pads.** The chordal bed is augmented with additional pad layers, either playing the same chords or, more often, different voicings (*page 151*) of those chords, including single notes. When combining multiple pads the usual layering rules apply (*page 50*): choose sounds that complement rather than clash with each another; minimise frequency overlaps; and arrange parts that weave together intelligently.

TIP When employing multiple pads, try using different synths as sound sources to widen the sonic pallette.

TIP For ease of control, send all soundscape layers to the same bus or allocate them to a single group.

▸▸ **Monophonic drones.** Sparsely programmed mono lines can be used to pick out single notes in a chord, guiding the listener's attention in the midst of big stacked chords.

▸▸ **Atonal layers.** Synth sounds based on DX-7 style FM synthesis playing long-form bell sounds (FM8 is a great source) give haunting, other-wordly tones to soundscapes.

▸▸ **Noise.** Introduce air, fuzz and lo-fi crust by adding a noise oscillator to the pad base.

▸▸ **Real instruments.** To give soundscapes organic tones, layer in real instruments. Whether they're played live or on sampled instruments, string and woodwind sounds lend themselves to layering. Tweak attack and release envelopes for smoother sounds.

TIP For a half-way house between organic and synthetic, program a 'live' string line on a sampler, then bounce out the sound, pitch it down an octave and timestretch it into something different. Placed in the mix and bathed in reverb, the sound will have a synthetic drone quality that is organic in origin.

▸▸ **Vocals.** Aaahs, ooohs and hums, mixed low, offer another means of adding human feel to a soundscape – as shown in the walkthrough, *right*.

▸▸ **FX.** With soundscapes made up of multiple layers, think carefully about which layers get ambient treatments. Adding big reverbs to sustained layers risks clogging the mix – the longer the tail, the bigger the perceived sense of space. For movement and depth, delays and chorus effects are often a better choice. Layers with higher frequencies and more detail – like bell trees – are the best candidates for verb. Consider 'hanging tails', described on page 90, to give mostly dry layers an illusion of ambience.

▸▸ **Automation.** Volume, filter and EQ automation is used to weave different layers in and out of the soundscape, highlighting not only chosen notes but also different layers throughout an arrangement.

WHAT PLAYS WHEN

The greatest pad-smiths know that when crafting soundscapes, the devil is in the detail.

Adding layers randomly results in nothing but sonic mess. Instead think forensically about what each layer is contributing and what note/s should play in each part – not only in single chords but throughout the track. Your ultimate aim is a combined sound that is greater than the sum of its parts.

In the walkthrough opposite the track's main chords (a revoiced triad with added 7th) is layered with ever simpler variants of it, including one-note parts and a fluid, but differently voiced string part.

The overall effect is of a synthetic orchestra creating a unified wash of lush movement and detail that is perpetually changing.

// WALKTHROUGHS

Building a soundscape 🎧

1 We're building a multi-textured soundscape to back a chillout track led by piano, vocals and a lo-fi beat. The foundations are laid with a simple single oscillator, sawtooth wave pad sound using Logic's basic ES1 synth to play a single backbone chord. So far, so easy.

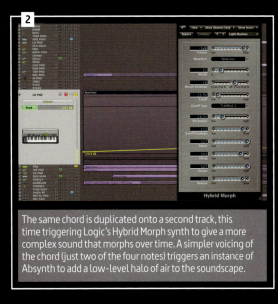

2 The same chord is duplicated onto a second track, this time triggering Logic's Hybrid Morph synth to give a more complex sound that morphs over time. A simpler voicing of the chord (just two of the four notes) triggers an instance of Absynth to add a low-level halo of air to the soundscape.

3 Organic layers are added with three single note hummed male vocal notes, low-cut, pitchshifted then pitch corrected to give them a synthesised sound that fits with the other pad elements. Heavy delays are applied, alongside volume automation so that they swell into and fade from the mix.

4 More layers are added: a chordal note 'strings' part (using Kontakt's bundled Solo Strings preset), and a single note playing an evolving patch using Logic's Sculpture. Note the different chordal arrangement on the string part, *above*, to that used in the main pad backing, to add complexity.

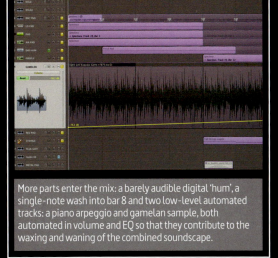

5 More parts enter the mix: a barely audible digital 'hum', a single-note wash into bar 8 and two low-level automated tracks: a piano arpeggio and gamelan sample, both automated in volume and EQ so that they contribute to the waxing and waning of the combined soundscape.

6 All elements are fed to a single bus and compressed. Different parts use different FX sends: a mix of long, lush reverb and multiple delays – pictured. Although the effects add space to the sound, restraint is key. The walkthrough mp3 plays the final soundscape in the context of the mix.

Chapter two
Synthesis and sound design

Synth FX

Sound effects (FX for short) play a pivotal role across the dance music landscape. They serve a variety of functions. They help to ease transitions between different sections of a track. They supply ear candy (*page 288*) – particularly useful during the latter stages of arrangements when FX flourishes help keep things interesting. Most of all they are key ingredients for building energy and momentum during breakdowns and into drops.

KEY FEATURES

A typical FX sound features:

▸▸ **Rich waveform/s.** For pitched sounds, saw and square waves offer the best starting points.

▸▸ **Noise.** White noise generators are responsible for all kinds of FX, from risers and falls to wind-ups. Other noise types are available (*page 73*), although they typically lack the high end of white noise which is important for getting the sound to cut through even the busiest mix.

▸▸ **Low and high end impact.** Many FX sweep between pitches: high to low or vice versa. As such they need to make an impact at both ends of the frequency spectrum; low-end energy needs to be substantial enough to make bass bins growl while the high end must hold its own as the breakdown builds. That said, for safety's sake, employ EQ bracketing (*page 211*) to roll away extreme lows to avoid expensive mishaps caused by uncontrolled bass energy.

▸▸ **Long sustain envelope.** Most synth FX are programmed to last a specific length – one, four, eight or 16 bars being the norm. This usually means setting decay and sustain to 100% and tweaking attack and release to taste. Then simply draw in a MIDI note length for the FX duration.

▸▸ **Rhythmic modulation.** The main ingredient in supersized FX is modulation. Any and every parameter is fair game for mod treatment. When building energy filters should open, pitches rise and modulation speeds increase. The golden rule is: *to increase energy open, rise and speed up; to decrease energy close, fall and slow down.* Pin movement to a track's bpm for rhythmic momentum.

TIP You can go a long way using just one modulator – for a simple pitch riser one's all you need. Things get more interesting when you increase the number of parameters being modulated, or up the number of modulators, as in the white noise fall, *right*, in which Osc1 modulates not only pitch and the noise filter but also an insert sample & hold effect.

EFFECTS ON FX

FX benefit from liberal doses of effects.

Reverb is used to add space and size. Use big hall settings or convolution IRs from spaces like cathedrals. Automate wet/dry balance towards the drop to swamp both the effect and mix in reverb before cutting the return at the moment the build ends.

Delay does a similar job but offers the ability to time-latch delay tails and throw them around the stereo spectrum.

Chorus effects add movement, width and depth. Use dimension expanders or unison-style effects combined with stereo expanders to take FX to the next level – automating their wet balance upwards towards the drop.

TIP Most synths allow you to choose either an LFO or envelope as the modulator. Both have their benefits, but envelopes tend to offer more control. You can shape, for example, how fast the pitch rises then levels off using an envelope – something you can't do without automation using a simple LFO. More envelope points offer more control.

FX TIPS

TIP Automation is an essential part of many FX, with LFO speeds and depths automated into builds to ratchet up the pressure.

TIP Add pump by using sidechain compression on sustained FX. Automate ratio and/or gain reduction to increase pump over time.

TIP Bounce down your best FX so you can use them in the future.

TIP For massive energy builds use multiple FX over different time periods. A single bar drum fill might be layered over a 16 bar pitch rise over a 32 bar reverse whoosh.

TIP Remember when building gargantuan FX that *context is everything*. There's no point in the world's biggest build transitioning into a disappointing drop. *All promise and no delivery represents an arrangement fail.*

// WALKTHROUGHS

White noise fall

1 In Massive set the wavetable in Osc1 to 'Colors' by clicking the drop-down arrow next to Squ-Swl (it's in the FX/Chords section). This is a stacked chord wavetable and isn't right for the sound we're after. So change the mode from Spectrum to Bend -/+ by clicking the drop-down next to Spectrum.

2 The noise generator is found in the bottom left corner of Massive. It's on by default but the amp is turned down. Dial it all the way up. Now in the Filter section activate a low pass filter (Lowpass 4 from the drop-down) in the Filter 1 slot. Set the cutoff frequency to around 75% and resonance to 50%.

3 We're going to use pitch and 'colour' modulation to create the fall. Drag and drop the crosshair of '1Env' onto one of the boxes underneath the pitch box on Osc1 and onto one of the boxes underneath the Color control on the noise generator (the Color control acts as a filter for the noise).

4 To set up the degree to which Osc 1 and Color are affected by 1Env, click and drag in the box to the right of the blue '1' on Osc1 until it reads -12.00. For the Color control click/drag down on '1' until the blue band goes all the way round the Color control. Next, set the 1Env ADSR attack to maximum.

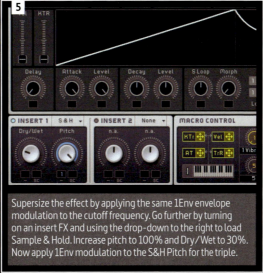

5 Supersize the effect by applying the same 1Env envelope modulation to the cutoff frequency. Go further by turning on an insert FX and using the drop-down to the right to load Sample & Hold. Increase pitch to 100% and Dry/Wet to 30%. Now apply 1Env modulation to the S&H Pitch for the triple.

6 Polish the sound with some master FX. We're using the Dimension Expander effect in slot 1 for a bigger, wider sound and Delay Sync in slot 2 with Damp notched up to 75% for slightly more high frequency presence on the delay. Dry/Wet balance is reduced to around 25%.

White noise wind-up

1 Load any synth that has a noise generator, low pass filter and LFO (we're using Sylenth), then initialise the patch (click on Menu in the centre tab and select 'Init Preset' from the drop-down). Now in Oscillator A1 click and drag up on the box next to Wave until you see the Noise waveform.

2 In the Filter A section click/drag on the box below Filter Type to activate a low pass filter then set both cutoff and resonance to around 33%. Set LFO1 to modulate Cutoff A then turn the dial alongside Cutoff A and the LFO gain, above, to 100% to hear the LFO effect in action.

3 For precise control over the wind-up effect's speed, automate the LFO rate in your DAW. Here we've upped its speed from 1/2D Hz to 1/64D Hz using a gently sloping curved increase. To give the sound more space we've also added reverb.

Pitch riser

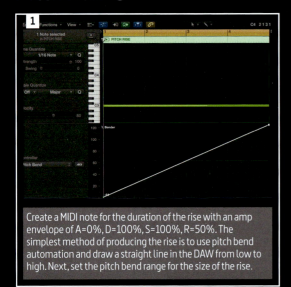

1 Create a MIDI note for the duration of the rise with an amp envelope of A=0%, D=100%, S=100%, R=50%. The simplest method of producing the rise is to use pitch bend automation and draw a straight line in the DAW from low to high. Next, set the pitch bend range for the size of the rise.

2 Almost any type of oscillator can be used, but classic risers are made using sine, saw or square waves. To add thickness to the sound try layering a couple of oscillators an octave apart. Detune one of them slightly or switch on Unison for rich, fat, chorused sounds. Add hall reverb to taste.

3 An LFO is used to make the pitch wobble as it travels up. Assign a sine or saw shaped LFO to oscillator pitch with a depth of 1 semitone. Bpm-sync the LFO rate to lock with the groove – try eighth or 16th notes. To increase the energy, automate LFO rate and depth to increase as the pitch rises.

Dub siren

1 We're using U-he's Diva to make this dub siren, but any synth that has sawtooth/square waves which can be pitch modulated via an LFO will do the job. Initialise the synth by clicking on the Patches tab then on '8 TEMPLATES' to load up the 'INIT Minimono' patch – a nice bright starting sound.

2 Click on the Main tab. To simplify the Oscillator section (we only need one oscillator) click on the drop-down where it says 'Triple VCO' and select 'DCO' from the list. The sound changes to a square wave and the oscillator section looks less like that on a Minimoog and more like a Juno 106.

3 Apply pitch modulation to the oscillator by clicking on the 'No Mod' box and selecting 'LFO 1' from the drop-down. Turn the dial all the way to the right to apply positive pitch modulation. To hear the effect turn the 'Depth Mod' control on LFO 1 all the way to the left.

4 Change the LFO waveform to 'saw down' with a sync rate of 1/1. Next click on the box alongside Rate Mod, select Velocity from the drop-down and turn Rate Mod to 100%. This gives pitch modulation a velocity sensitive LFO rate, where higher velocities produce faster LFO cycles.

5 Dub FX are naked without trademark Space Echo-style delays. Load up a tape delay, set feedback to a few notches below infinite and use low- and high-cut filters to narrow the frequency field for each repeat. Select (bpm) Sync with triplets or dotted notes to cut across the groove.

6 Because the synth and its pitch mod LFO are set up to respond to different pitches and velocities you can get a range of different sounds by tweaking the MIDI. Experiment with different pitches, note lengths and velocities. Try switching to a different LFO waveform for myriad other FX.

Deep house keys

While the use of analogue drum machines, soul tinged vocals, bouncing bass and groove-based arrangements are staples of deep house, its melodic signature is often jazz-influenced keys.

▶▶ **Chords.** Certain chords provide a mood synonymous with deep house, specifically major and minor 7ths and 9ths (*page 146*). It can be helpful to compose using a basic piano sound or initialised synth patch before moving on to synthesise the sound's tone.

▶▶ **Sound source.** There are no hard and fast rules when it comes to a sound's source tone. Rhodes and Wurlitzer VSTs give a retro feel, while simple saw-based subtractive synth oscillators provide a more current and customisable synthetic consistency to cut through a mix. Detune multiple oscillators for thickness or stack contrasting layers to combine the characteristics of each. Trigger a 'real' Rhodes alongside a synthetic sawtooth synth for the best of both worlds.

▶▶ **Subtractive filtering.** Deep house keys and judicious filtering go hand-in-hand, so get your synth or sampler's low pass filter moving with an envelope, LFO or automation. Roland's iconic Juno series of synths are known for their warm, juicy filters, so choose a synth with similar characteristics. Stick to modest resonance settings for a smoother effect.

MAKE YOUR OWN KEYS

▶▶ **1.** Start by creating a chord with four notes: the lowest the root (*page 144*), the second three semitones up, the third seven semitones up and the last 10 semitones up. This is a minor 7th chord. Turn this into a minor 9th by adding a fourth note 14 semitones above the root.

▶▶ **2.** Copy the chord over a bar or two to create a pattern over a drum groove. Transpose the entire chord at certain points to create variations, emulating the '90s technique of pitching chords up and down the keyboard in a sampler (*page 144*).

▶▶ **3.** Next, synthesise a raw sawtooth-based tone: blend two oscillators and slightly detune them against each other. Use modulation, widening and spatial effects to augment the sound.

▶▶ **4.** Pull the synth's low-pass filter cutoff right down, then modulate the filter with an envelope. To create a tight plucked sound, set the filter envelope to minimum attack, short decay, minimum sustain and minimum release. Tweak the filter envelope amount to taste.

▶▶ **5.** Automate filter cutoff throughout an arrangement, causing the sound to sweep open at key sections. Twin this with swelling reverbs and drum edits for maximum impact.

ANALOGUE GOODNESS

To inject a taste of old-school 'analogue' warmth into keys and chords:

▶▶ Run the chosen sound out of your interface and through a physical piece of equipment – budget mixing desks, hardware samplers or guitar pedals are all ideal – before recording the grunged-up audio back into your DAW.

▶▶ If you're based entirely in the box, layer low-level recordings of vinyl crackle, tape noise and electrical hum onto synthesised parts.

▶▶ Activate legato mode, then play overlapping notes for that 'sliding' pitch bend effect.

▶▶ Use saturation, warmth, overdrive and bit-crushing to dirty up chords. Apply processing in parallel to smooth the results and retain clarity.

EFFECTS AND MIXING

As the melodic centrepiece of a track, deep house chords often benefit from added width and space.

Subtle, Juno-style **chorus** can give a lush, swimming effect (use **ensemble** for more obvious thickening) while **reverb** is able to position the sound in a realistic space – audition real-life IRs like chambers and drum rooms. Apply effects in parallel via an aux send then EQ return/s to roll away bass frequencies to keep lower frequencies centred.

Rhythmic delay effects, when synced to a project's tempo, can be used to fill gaps between sparse chords. Try automating the delay's feedback amount to intensify builds or alter the delay time mid track to switch up a part's rhythm.

Stacking lower notes in a chord can lead to harmonic congestion and bloat in the low–mid region, causing frequency conflicts with other parts. **Filter out unnecessary low frequencies** with a high-pass filter, and use subtractive EQ and/or multiband compression to tame the part's 150–500Hz zone in the mix. An alternative is to revoice chords to keep a part sparse low down.

Deep house keys

1 Start with the rhythmic bare bones of a deep house track, then load a basic piano or Rhodes preset onto a new MIDI track and create a jazzy 9th chord. If you don't fancy reading *Chapter five*, load an audio file of a suitable chord and use an 'extract to MIDI' tool to separate the MIDI notes.

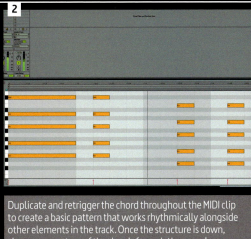

2 Duplicate and retrigger the chord throughout the MIDI clip to create a basic pattern that works rhythmically alongside other elements in the track. Once the structure is down, change one or two of the chords for variation – we've transposed the last two chords down by two semitones.

3 The basic Rhodes sound is OK but we're after a synth pluck reminiscent of '80s Chicago house. Replace the Rhodes with a VA subtractive synth like u-He's Diva and create a single oscillator sawtooth patch with square sub-oscillator for added weight. Mix in a touch of noise for extra bite.

4 A filter envelope transforms the sustained notes into filtered 'plucks'. Pull the low-pass filter's frequency down and increase the filter envelope's depth. Reduce the filter envelope's Attack, Sustain and Release to minimum and adjust the Decay until the shape of the pluck fits the groove.

5 Use chorus, reverb and/or delay to widen and thicken the patch. We've applied lush Juno-style chorus to soften the synth's timbre and spread it to the sides of the mix, then a tempo-synced stereo delay to add rhythmic taps between notes for added interest and texture.

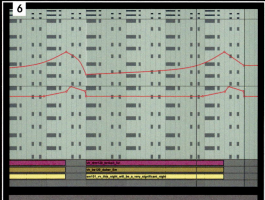

6 Finally, automate synth parameters over eight or 16 bars to give the keys evolving motion; we've altered the filter's cutoff and envelope depth here. The combination of jazz-style chords, filtered synth sound and delayed movement combine for classic vintage flavours.

Stacked EDM chords

Taking inspiration from trance, prog house and electro, the recent wave of big-room EDM features high impact synths and chords designed to fill the frequency range and command attention. The rhythmic interplay of stacked chords against a big kick define the groove.

KEY FEATURES

▸▸ **Stacked layers.** EDM leads and chords dominate the mix with unashamed power. Their weight and density is almost impossible to achieve using a single synth. Instead, producers layer contrasting synths and parts to build a single stacked mega-synth hook that's designed to dominate the mix and the dancefloor.

▸▸ **Bass layers.** Although some EDM tracks feature a bassline, others extend the frequency reach of the main synth hook into the bass zone to let the hook stack do the low end lifting. Layer in a sub to make a full-mix stack.

▸▸ **Oscillator voices and detuning.** Inspired by the mid-'90s 'supersaw' found on a few Roland synths, most soft synths allow you to stack and detune multiple saw waves against each other.

▸▸ **Rhythmic and percussive leads.** EDM styles assign the main rhythmic and percussive roles to the lead hook, which play off the kick drum to define the groove of the track. Also common is 'call and response' programming where the dominant synth gives the 'call' and a less prominent melodic part 'responds'.

MAKE YOUR OWN EDM CHORD

▸▸ **1.** First, synthesise a thick synth sound by detuning multiple sawtooth voices. Synths such as Sylenth1, Massive or Spire are ideal for these types of sounds.

▸▸ **2.** When programming MIDI notes, experiment with syncopation (*page 164*) and rhythmic unpredictability. Many EDM styles incorporate bursts of triplets (*page 29*) both as defining motifs and as spot 'FX' cuts to break the regular groove.

▸▸ **3.** Once you have your core synth timbre and motif nailed, identify missing characteristics and layer additional sounds to fill out both the frequency spectrum and stereo image across multiple octaves. Try a solid low mid layer, a fizzy higher part and even a formant-filtered vocal element until the layers gel and dominate the mix.

▸▸ **4.** Heavy sidechain compression is crucial to the EDM sound, both as a mix tool and a creative effect. Load a compressor on the synth group and use the kick drum to trigger gain reduction, causing the riff to duck, pump and swell around the kick.

LAYERING SYNTHS

Layering is the key to powerful chords. To stack like a pro:

▸▸ Think first. It's tempting to pile up synth layers, but less is usually more. Start with one core synth patch that does most of the work then add layers to enhance, thicken and fill out missing frequencies and other qualities (transient detail, stereo spread etc).

▸▸ Separate layers using filters. Layer across several octaves for a bigger sound.

▸▸ Use 'cleaner', less harmonic synth sounds to provide low end weight and solidity, then assign more harmonically complex patches to fill out detail in the mids and upper mids. Blend in white noise for fizz.

▸▸ Pull multiple layers together by bussing them to a single group before applying EQ, saturation, compression and limiting.

MIXING CONSIDERATIONS

EDM is all about the big kick drum, bassline and lead hook; so **solo these elements** and mix them to fit together. Once the key players are working as a group other sounds should slot into place fairly easily.

Whereas percussion-heavy styles such as techno employ multiple layers of mid-heavy drums, EDM uses sparse hat and ride parts that are used solely to reinforce the dominant groove interplay between kick, bass and hook. Therefore keep percussion subtle and mix it 'thin' to prevent overload in the upper mids.

TIP Big EDM synths have to combine mono punch with stereo interest. One way to keep a riff's stereo elements in check is to use a dedicated 'width' synth layer that provides the bulk of the stereo content. This maintains mono punch and fidelity for the bulk of the sound.

TIP Wash synth parts in reverb via an aux track then pump the wet signal around either the kick or synth hook using sidechain compression for another layer of controlled groove and character. Experiment with room, chamber, plate, hall and rhythmic IR settings. Filter the low end reverb return to keep the mix clean.

// WALKTHROUGHS

Stacked EDM chords 🎧

1 Lay down a beefy 4/4 EDM kick at 128bpm then load an initialised instance of Sylenth1 on a MIDI track. Program notes to ensure the chord pattern's interplay against the kick works both melodically and rhythmically. Pay attention to note lengths – tweak decay and release for tightness.

2 To synthesise a typical supersaw sound, switch all four oscillators (OSC A1 and A2 plus B1 and B2) to sawtooth waveforms and crank up each oscillator's polyphony to 16. Slightly detune each voice for girth, then deactivate each Retrig button so all four oscillators' phase is free-running.

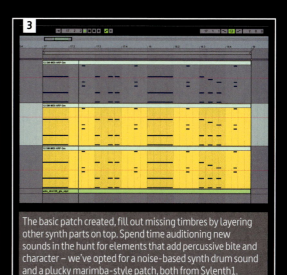

3 The basic patch created, fill out missing timbres by layering other synth parts on top. Spend time auditioning new sounds in the hunt for elements that add percussive bite and character – we've opted for a noise-based synth drum sound and a plucky marimba-style patch, both from Sylenth1.

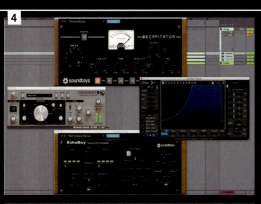

4 Send all synth layers to a single bus so you can process them as a whole. We're using parallel saturation, bit-crushing and chorus to glue the layers together, forming a united sound. Use sidechain pumping to duck the group around the kick, achieving a bouncy EDM-style effect.

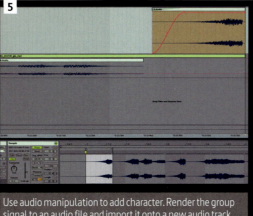

5 Use audio manipulation to add character. Render the group signal to an audio file and import it onto a new audio track. Here you can reposition notes and/or reverse them at certain points to give effects like the 'sucking' reverse that leads into the turnaround shown above.

6 Finally, add width and space by sending up to 50% of the group channel's signal to an aux containing a characterful reverb. By placing a compressor after the reverb on the aux and triggering the compressor's gain reduction via the synth group, the reverb swells between each chord.

Chapter three
Bass and basslines

The bassline is second only to the beat in most genres of dance music.

The way in which the bassline interacts with the kick drum – the other low frequency component of a mix – is so important that specific approaches to bassline programming may be the defining characteristic of an entire sub-genre – think D&B, for example, and acid house.

Basslines perform a dual **rhythmic** and **melodic** role in dance music, riffing off the kick to solidify the bottom end, underpinning overlaid musical elements and occasionally supplying melodies in their own right.

A bassline's defining characteristics are **movement** and **weight**. But bass doesn't always come easy. Mixing the low end – where the headroom-hungry kick and bass both demand room and definition – challenges even seasoned producers. Get it right, though, and the foundations are in place for a hit.

BASSLINE ARCHETYPES

Over the decades, various approaches to creating basslines have emerged, in terms of programming, sound sources and mixing. Some, like the Reese bass, are born and bred in a single genre, often before expanding into others. Others, like the classic off-beat bass, can be found in multiple genres.

The majority of basslines can be shoehorned into one of eight archetypes. These archetypes are not a definitive list of bassline types, and in reality many bass parts straddle two or more of those listed. But it's a useful starting point if you're stuck for inspiration or are looking for the perfect low end partner to twin with a floor-shaking kick.

THE OFF-BEAT BASS

The off-beat bass has been a staple part of many dance genres through the years, its roots lying in disco, synth pop and hi-NRG. It is most commonly found in trance.

With off-beat bass, notes are placed between each kick drum to deliver a driving rhythm that provides a pulsing backdrop to the production. For examples, check out the Larse Vocal mix of 'Hallelujah Anyway' by Candi Staton and deadmau5 & Kaskade's 'I Remember'.

It may be absurdly simple, but this kind of bassline *works*. And it works because the bass supplies a perfect rhythmic and tonal counterweight to even the most dominant kick drum. As such it neatly shrugs off mix and masking problems caused by frequency overlap (*page 277*). At the same time, the off-beat bass embodies movement – the kick/bass back and forth propels the groove onwards with impulsive regularity – and anchors the chord progressions unfolding above by supplying the root (*page 144*) in the most basic, but effective, way possible.

If off-beat bass feels too simple, delay can be used to create additional rhythmic interest – a classic trance trick. Set a delay time locked to the project tempo; dotted eighth note delay is a useful starting point. If that's overkill, automate delay spins (*page 187*) to pick out specific notes – the second and last in a four bar phrase, for example.

TIP If a simple off-beat bass leaves the kick drum sounding isolated, trigger the kick on 16ths – the bass pulsing at double the rate of the kick drum – and use sidechain compression to pull back the energy of the bass when the kick hits as deadmau5 does in 'Raise Your Weapon'.

ROOT RHYTHM

A more advanced take on the off-beat bass, here the bass still generally sticks to the root, but is freed from the off-beat pulse to create more interesting rhythms. The bass

STONEBRIDGE

"The 'Show Me Love' bass was a funny one. I made it first using a Korg M1, preset 16 – Pick Bass. It went well with the boogie flavour of the original. After sending the remix to Champion Records, it was rejected. I got really mad and I decided to start over with just kick, vocal and the same bassline but switched to the next preset on the M1, 17 – Organ 2, and heard the loveliest tones. I remember thinking: 'OK, this track is done!'

"In retrospect, I realise I was lucky with the kick being in the right ballpark at G and the track in D minor so the heavily tape distorted kick and organ made up the entire bottom end."

might play *on* the beat – underpinning the kick for a driving, low-end double whammy – or it may play 16ths as in Calvin Harris and Alesso's megahit 'Under Control'.

Sometimes the bass takes up a more complex pattern. In Cosmosis' 'Dance Of The Cosmic Serpent', the first two notes of the bassline – playing on the second and fourth measures of the bar – create a syncopated rhythm. The effect is to make the kick sound like it's bouncing off the kick, establishing drive in the low end.

TIP Rules are there to be broken. In Lane 8's 'Be Mine', the bass plays the root note of the chord at the same time as the kick, but with a small rhythmic flourish at the end of each bar. Meanwhile in Nathan Fake's 'The Sky Was Pink' the bass follows the root for the most part, but sometimes changes the bass a note early, creating melodic tension before resolving it into the next beat.

NOODLE BASS

The origins of the busier and more fluid 'noodle' bass lie in the funk and disco playing exemplified by the likes of Chic's Bernard Edwards (listen to the second half of Chic's 'I Want Your Love' to hear him in action) or Herbie Hancock's ARP Odyssey riffing on 'Chameleon'. Daft Punk's 'Around The World' offers a more modern example.

PRO TIPS

JORGE SAVORETTI

"'Jardin Av' [from Rosario-born Jorge Savoretti's debut album *Triskelion*] is probably one of my favourite tracks on the album, because it's a track that has a pretty straightforward groove and uplifting energy but still has its soulful edge.

"I started with this kind of raw, warm groove – as usual first the kick, then combining it with the bassline that came out of Rob Papen's SubBoomBass, which is great for those kind of basses that merge with the drums, sounding like deep toms... Once I tried it in the clubs, I knew it was gonna be one of the first tracks to make it into the final tracklist of the album."

The defining characteristic of noodle bass is movement, with the bass not only delivering an energetic rhythmic workout, but also skipping across notes and octaves. Although the bassline invariably returns to the root for resolution, it slips, slides and riffs liberally in between.

TIP Given the inherently busy nature of noodle bass, it often works best over simple, unswung, unsyncopated beats.

TIP Noodle bass takes time to program, demanding exacting attention to detail. If you have access to a bass guitar (and good player) try recording a bassline live then cutting the audio into a series of loops for further manipulation.

BASS AS LEAD

Sometimes a bassline needs to do more than underpin a track. With 'bass as lead' the bass isn't a foundational element or supporting part – *it's the star of the melodic show*, as in the all-digital Korg bass/lead organ on MK's remix of Nightcrawlers 'Push The Feeling On' or the seminal Stonebridge remix of 'Show Me Love' by Robin S (*see Pro Tip, far left*). In both cases it's the bass that supplies the hook. *Everyone knows* the 'Show Me Love' B-line.

Bass as lead is one of the key bass archetypes used in D&B. Total Science's 'Defcom 69' is a representative example of brash, heavily stacked synthesis that leaves the listener in no doubt that the bass is boss. Dubstep and EDM have taken that mantle forward.

Note that bass as lead tracks don't have to be so brazen. In Donna Summer's 'I Feel Love', Giorgio Moroder's simple eighth note bass is happy to share the melodic limelight with Summer's vocal. And in Eat Static's 'Abduction' the momentous bass steps into the limelight supported by pads and arps.

The critical sound design requirement when creating bass as lead is to ensure the bass fills out frequencies across the spectrum – which is to say, the sound not only tickles the subs, it also extends into upper octaves.

TIP Lead basses don't have to stick with the same sound throughout. In Phuture's 'Acid Tracks' the TB-303 bass undergoes filter and resonant tweaks throughout. Ditto in Aphex Twin's 'Digeridoo'. Omar-S's 'Thank U 4 Letting Me Be Myself', meanwhile, offers more subtle tweakery of the lead (and ostinato) bass.

OSTINATO BASS

An ostinato musical pattern is one that repeats (*page 160*). Ostinato bass was a staple of early jacking house, typified in 'House Nation' by The Housemaster Boyz. Wind on nearly three decades and Ninetoes' 'Finder (The Path)' makes use of an unobtrusive subby bass, which repeats while the vocals and steel drums take the lead.

Although many 'bass is lead' tracks use ostinato techniques, ostinato basslines typically take a melodic back seat, establishing a groove between kick and bass that creates movement and forward motion while eschewing the limelight. Their beauty is familiarity. By endlessly repeating, they build a low-end backbone on which the rest of the arrangement – however complex or unhinged – can be hooked.

When using ostinato bass, two things are critical: firstly, the ostinato must be tonally, rhythmically and/or melodically interesting enough to keep the listener engaged for the duration of the track; secondly, the wider arrangement demands constant change. Which means, synths, keys, arps and drums need to be constantly shifting around the repeating bass.

MODULATED BASS

Some basslines manage to pack movement, texture and dynamism into a single note. How? *Modulation*. With modulated basslines, interest is generated as LFOs, envelopes and automation tweak everything from filter cutoff frequencies to wavetable values.

Modulated basslines straddle genres, from D&B to EDM, but are most often associated with more bombastic styles, from hardcore and rave to jungle. Here, the melody of the bass part is often simple – two or three notes max – with modulation supplying the sonic changes.

Perhaps the most obvious form of modulated bass is the famous Reese sound – harsh and continuously tweaked – originally used by Kevin Saunderson under his Reese moniker on 'Just Another Chance'.

Bass modulation took a different turn with the arrival of dubstep. Skream's 'Midnight Request Line' mixes different lengths of bass note to create the precursor of what became a more overtly automated timbral 'wobble' – *the* trademark dubstep wobble – on 'Rutten'.

Modulation doesn't have to be in-your-face obvious. For a subtler variant, check out Om Unit's 'Jaguar' and Blawan's 'Why They Hide Their Bodies Under My Garage?', where gentle cutoff frequency and pitch automation throughout the track (*page 248*) give the bassline a bristling, ever-shifting momentum.

MULTI-PATCH BASS

The latest generation of basslines are the multi-patch basses of commercial dubstep and EDM and the 'cut and paste'-style micro-edited basslines of French electro.

TODD EDWARDS

"I would have to say because of how well it was received that my remix of 'As I Am' by Sounds Of One is my favourite.

"I knew once I made the bassline on my Juno-106 and made the drum patterns that I had something good. It took only 48 hours to make but it has had the most longevity of all my work."

SEE ALSO

PAGE 110 REESE-STYLE BASS

PAGE 110 TALKING BASS

PAGE 112 NU DISCO/INDIE DANCE BASS

These timbrally complex basslines owe their being to advances in digital audio. The ease with which audio can be cut and pasted coupled with the powerful routing matrices of modern synths and a greater availability of glitch plugins mean the low end can be sound-designed in ways not previously possible.

In many respects the multi-patch bass is a natural extension of the bass as lead archetype – only this time the 'lead' is made up of multiple bass sounds that are continually changing in tone, with cutoff frequency, envelopes, wavetables and FX all game for extreme tweakery. The results are the kind of basslines showcased on 'Ghosts N Stuff' by Deadmau5 and the bombastic commercial dubstep stylings of Skrillex's 'Scary Monsters and Nice Sprites'. Both tracks have informed the subsequent direction and success of EDM as an international pop genre.

For a more analogue hybrid approach, see Justice's 'Genesis', where distorted sawtooth bass parts are merged with sampled slap bass and numerous wobbles, reverses and micro-edits.

TIP The final production step to glue a complex multi-patch bassline is to add compression sidechained to the kick. Increase ratio for added pump. The release setting is critical: adjust the time so that it ducks and dives in time with the track.

Chapter three
Bass and basslines

NO BASS

Sometimes you don't need a traditional bassline at all… another mix element can do the low-frequency legwork for you.

Often this is a powerful kick drum, as in Tiga's 'Bugatti' or Lil' Louis' 'French Kiss'.

When a kick drum is used to do the combined work of kick and bass, the sustain/release of the kick is typically lengthened to fill the 'gap' of the absent bass. Because it's not competing for headroom-hungry lower frequencies the kick can be left to boom unhindered. That boom is frequently supplied either by a TR-808 kick drum – with its long trademark sustain – or a layered kick in which the sub layer is an 808.

The 808 kick, mapped to different pitches using a sampler, is also a mainstay of D&B 'basslines', where a few differently pitched 808 kicks, triggered below the higher kick drum, supply the traditional 'bassline' – a la Deep Blue & Blame's 'Re-Transitions'. Notes-wise, the usual candidates are the fourth and fifth before returning to the root.

But as long as the replacement element is rich enough in low-end energy, almost any sound can be used instead of a bass, from supplementary kicks (Maurizio 'Eleye'), to dirty glitches and FX (Mono Junk 'Channel B').

Programming bass: Which notes to play

Some basslines do no more than stick to the root note of the chord being played above. In Cosmosis' 'Dance of the Cosmic Serpent', which only uses a single chord, the bassline only ever plays one note. Where chords play a progression, as in Nathan Fake's 'The Sky Was Pink', the bassline can follow below, underpinning each triad with the root.

These simple 'rooted' basslines are not the sole reserve of the off-beat or root rhythm bass. Modulated basslines rarely feature more then three notes – and nearly always resolve (page 149) to the root.

It's easy to look down on these apparently unambitious basslines. But simplicity should never be mistaken for deficiency. In basslines, intention is all and where rhythm is the intention, a rooted off-beat bassline – even if it sticks to just one note – can be brutally effective.

If you want to add greater melodic interest to a bassline there are plenty of options. The most obvious next step is to shift a note or two to the fifth note of a scale (page 144) – an addition which works in both major and minor scales. Major or minor thirds (page 145) provide a mid-way stepping stone. Skipping briefly onto upper octaves of the root is commonplace in noodle bass workouts.

Other techniques include:

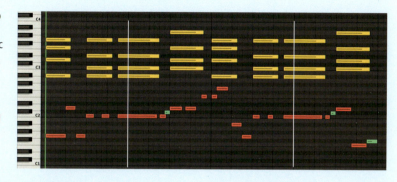

CHANGING CHORDS WITH THE BASS

Page 152 shows how a moving bassline beneath a static chord can change the chord above – a technique used to great effect in Burial's 'Archangel'.

But you can also keep a bassline moving underneath a chord progression to add the feeling of movement through the progression *without* changing the chords themselves.

Disco provides us with dozens of examples of this technique, including Sister Sledge's 'He's the Greatest Dancer' (*see image, above*).

Here the piano chords Gm7, Cm7, Dm7, are fairly static but the noodle bass jumps around underneath them, playing the 1st, 3rd and 5th degrees of the chords above. In addition, the bassline makes use of **passing notes**.

PASSING NOTES

A passing note is one that's not found in the chord – or even the scale – of the track but which 'bridges the gap' between adjacent notes in the scale. The device is common in disco.

The piano roll above highlights the passing notes in 'He's the Greatest Dancer' in green. The first passing note – the Db after the C underneath the Cm7 chord – is used to step into the following D chord. The effect is to add fluidity and movement to a part, avoiding big jumps. Because notes from outside a scale are used, they also introduce a jazzy flavour.

NOTE Passing notes aren't confined to basslines. In 'Puzzle Dust' by Dave Tipper passing notes are used in the chromatic steps that ascend and descend the G minor scale in the stacked bassline/melody to create the wonky topline.

Chapter three
Bass and basslines

Bass synthesis

The occasional live workout in a disco-influenced house or downtempo track aside, the vast majority of basslines in dance music are synthesised. Whether the archetype followed is a simple off-beat bass or a complex modulated Reese ripper, a synth is almost always the sound source.

MAKE YOUR OWN BASS

When crafting synth basslines, sound designers focus on a number of factors:

▸▸ **Switch to monophonic.** Most basslines are monophonic — with only one note playing at any one time. Traditionally bass sounds have been sourced from monosynths, making them ideal choices, whether physical or digital recreations.

▸▸ **Start simple.** The number of oscillators employed is dictated by the kind of sound you're after. A lot can be achieved with a single oscillator — see Moog bass for starters, right. For **bass is lead** sounds stack additional oscillators into upper octaves to extend the bassline's harmonic reach into territory normally occupied by the lead.

▸▸ **Add sub for bottom.** As detailed on pages 114–115, sub bass can be layered into a regular bassline by adding a sine or dedicated sub oscillator (invariably a sine wave) an octave or two below the main oscillator. For subtle bulking keep its relative volume at 20-30%.

▸▸ **Audition different waveforms.** Saw, square, triangle and pulse waves are all common choices for generating raw bass patches, with saw waves offering a fuller, rounder and warmer sound. Reserve sine waves for the sub.

▸▸ **Thicken sounds** by slightly detuning additional oscillators. You don't need to go wild here: just a few notches on the fine-tune dial is enough to add bulk and character to a sound.

▸▸ **Supersize** sounds by switching on **unison** — a one-click means of adding in multiple detuned slave oscillators to recreate the sound of classic analogue synthesis and the hard house 'hoover'.

▸▸ **Different synthesis types** have different strengths. While subtractive synthesis is the usual choice for full-bodied, Moog-style basses, for searing digital-sounding Reese and modulated bass, try additive synthesis (page 83).

▸▸ **Shape the sound.** The correct attack and sustain/release envelope settings are critical for getting a bass sound to work seamlessly with the kick drum. Extend the bass too long and you get overlaps. Too short and the mix's low-end can become gappy. At the front end, shorter attack times deliver more aggressive bass sounds — although go too short and you risk introducing clicks into the opening transients.

▸▸ The **filter** plays a key role in shaping the final bass sound: it's the famed filters of the 303 and Moog that have made them so dependable for low-end duties. Low pass filters are the order of the day here, typically with a 24dB slope. Increase **resonance** to add bite, definition and a warmer edge. Add **filter overdrive** for brasher tones.

▸▸ Wobbles can be generated by **LFOs** or **envelopes** routed to filter cutoff. Tempo-link timings to taste; modulate them for ever-changing wobble lengths.

▸▸ Particularly when using repeated ostinato patterns (page 160), **modulate anything/everything**, from envelope settings to filter cutoff frequency. For a trademark EDM-style tension builder open the attack and/or filter cutoff values of a stacked lead bass into the breakdown. Reset values at the drop.

▸▸ Use **portamento** or **glide** to transition between notes (page 78). On a monophonic part subtle amounts of glide can inject life and realism into a **noodle bass** or can be used in extremis on wonky electro belters. Don't just set the glide time and leave — automate it over time for detailed control.

// WALKTHROUGHS

Moog bass for starters

1 Create a new patch in NI Monark (any simple monosynth will do the job) by loading User Bank > INIT preset. Tune global Octave to 0 then program a simple MIDI bassline consisting of short notes. Glide is activated by default, which is causing the notes to bend into each other, so flip the switch to Off.

2 The classic Minimoog bass sound features three sawtooth oscillators, each tuned an octave apart. Change all of Monark's oscillator waveforms to Saw and switch them all on. Tune Osc 2 an octave above the first by setting its Range to 12', then set Osc 3's Range to 8'.

3 By default, Osc 3's pitch can't be played via MIDI; to rectify this, activate its Key Tracking switch (K.T.) before resetting the tune knob to 0 (centre). Now balance the three oscillator levels to taste: we've set Osc 1 to 10, Osc 2 to 9 and Osc 3 to 6.

4 Crank up mixer Load to 65% for Minimoog-style amp overloading. Now tweak the filter envelope to swiftly close the filter for the characteristic 'pluck' sound with plenty of snap and shape: set Cutoff to 1, Resonance to 5, Contour to 7, then increase the Filter Envelope Decay to 400ms.

5 In the Filter & Amp section, flick all four K.T. and Rel switches to apply filter key-tracking and increase the release time. Set the amplitude envelope settings to suit the MIDI pattern and the track's wider groove – 0 Attack, 300ms Decay and 5 Sustain gives the right amount of space between notes.

6 In Monark's B section, increase Octave Detuning to 12–2 o'clock to detune the oscillators. Now subtly adjust settings for movement – try tweaking or automating the Cutoff, Contour and Filter Envelope Decay. Finally, apply chorus or a short delay on a return to thicken and widen the sound.

// WALKTHROUGHS

Reese-style bass

The classic Reese bass sound is made by detuning two saw waves in opposite directions. In Massive, select File > New Sound. Turn Osc 2 up to maximum, Squ-Sw1, move WT-position to the right on Osc1 and Osc2 to get a saw wave, then change Osc 1's Pitch to 0.25 and Osc 2 to -0.25.

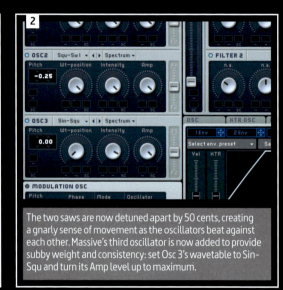

The two saws are now detuned apart by 50 cents, creating a gnarly sense of movement as the oscillators beat against each other. Massive's third oscillator is now added to provide subby weight and consistency: set Osc 3's wavetable to Sin-Squ and turn its Amp level up to maximum.

Set Voicing to Monophonic (middle panel), which adds a lazy glide. For the final touches, mix in grit via Massive's noise oscillator (bottom left) and apply width using the Stereo Expander. Processing-wise, try sending 25% of the signal to a high-passed aux containing distortion, phase and reverb.

Talking bass – The Skrillex sound

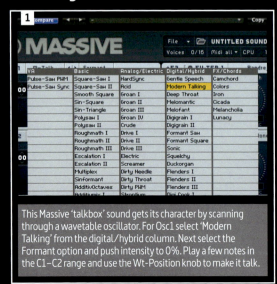

This Massive 'talkbox' sound gets its character by scanning through a wavetable oscillator. For Osc1 select 'Modern Talking' from the digital/hybrid column. Next select the Formant option and push intensity to 0%. Play a few notes in the C1–C2 range and use the Wt-Position knob to make it talk.

You can use an envelope, LFO, mod sequencer or all three to vocalize the sound. Start with a 1 over 2 note Sync sine wave LFO with Restart. Assign it to Osc1's Wt-position and increase depth to 50%. Experiment with the Wt-position and the polarity of the LFO. Also try inverting the polarity.

For more growl, load Classic Tube into the FX 1 slot. Set Dry/Wet to 25% and Drive to 100%. To brighten it, use the High Shelf EQ and boost around 5-10%. Employ a short reverb to add vibrancy. Use the Dimensional Expander in FX 2 slot with Dry/Wet and Size set to around 20% to finish it off.

Whomp robot synth

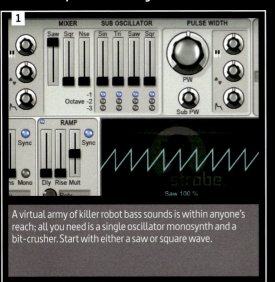

1 A virtual army of killer robot bass sounds is within anyone's reach; all you need is a single oscillator monosynth and a bit-crusher. Start with either a saw or square wave.

2 Select a 24dB low pass filter with cutoff at around 35%. To produce the vocal movement, modulate the filter with an envelope. Set the modulation depth between 60%-90% and start with a moderate attack, longer decay, minimum sustain and release at around 50%.

3 Load a bit-crusher effect. Leave the resolution at 24-bit and start lowering the sample rate. As the sound downgrades, robotic vocal overtones are introduced. Tune the overtones to match the key of the track or to accentuate specific harmonic relationships.

4 Increase resonance for a more pronounced sweep. Add overdrive either pre or post-filter to thicken up the sound. Experiment with the envelope depth and attack and decay envelopes, as well as the bit-crusher parameters: you can get big changes making tiny adjustments.

5 To lift the sound out of a busy mix, twin a low cut at around 50Hz with a hefty high-shelf EQ boost of around 4–8dB from the 4 kHz point upwards. Another tool you can use to add definition is a harmonic exciter such as the Aphex Aural Exciter or SPL Vitalizer.

6 For creative shaping, assign an LFO to modulate filter cutoff. Experiment with 1/4, 1/8 or 1/16 note bpm divisions and sine, ramp or modulation sequencers. The amount of LFO will need to be balanced with the amount of envelope; start small or the filter won't sweep through the spectrum.

// WALKTHROUGHS

Nu disco/indie dance bass

1 Modern styles of indie and nu disco often chop between sampled live bass elements and thicker synth tones to form call-and-response riff exchanges. We're starting with the weightier synth. Program a running 16th note pattern using u-He's Diva (most synths will do an equally good job).

2 Choose the 1 BASS > HS Noland SH preset. For a more authentic 'arp' feel first transpose select notes up an octave. Next, to get a tight, filtered sound that contrasts with the live bass, reduce Cutoff and increase the Env2, Emphasis and KYBD values so that the filter grabs individual notes.

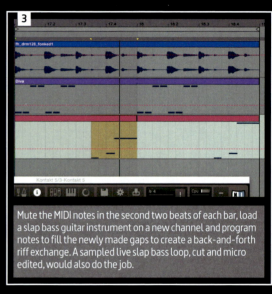

3 Mute the MIDI notes in the second two beats of each bar, load a slap bass guitar instrument on a new channel and program notes to fill the newly made gaps to create a back-and-forth riff exchange. A sampled live slap bass loop, cut and micro edited, would also do the job.

4 Now both parts are playing off each other, compare their weight and tone and take steps to bring them into line. The synth bass is thick and mono while the bass guitar is comparatively thin and wider, so we've added chorus to the synth and an EQ boost on the slap guitar.

5 Send the two bass channels to a single bus featuring a character compressor. In the style of many Nu Disco tracks, apply judicious sidechain compression – high ratio, pulling back up to 10-12dB of gain – to get the bass elements dancing around the kick. A ducker will also do the job.

6 With the basic parts working, edit the riff by altering the MIDI notes to create something more interesting. You might also want to render the bass group to audio before chopping up the file further on the timeline, creating stutters and glitches. Add a third sampled part for extra mayhem.

House organ bass 🔊

1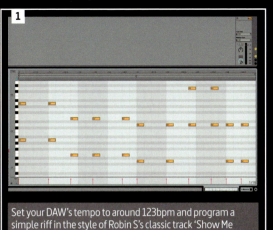
Set your DAW's tempo to around 123bpm and program a simple riff in the style of Robin S's classic track 'Show Me Love'. Initialise a new synth preset (we're using NI's Massive, but most synths will be able to tackle the job). Duplicate and stack the notes over two octaves.

2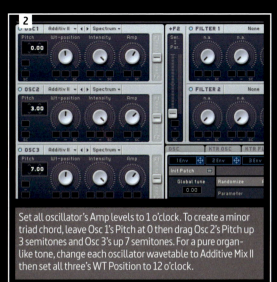
Set all oscillator's Amp levels to 1 o'clock. To create a minor triad chord, leave Osc 1's Pitch at 0 then drag Osc 2's Pitch up 3 semitones and Osc 3's up 7 semitones. For a pure organ-like tone, change each oscillator wavetable to Additive Mix II then set all three's WT Position to 12 o'clock.

3
Use a filter envelope to clamp down on each note, creating a plucky effect. Set up Filter 1 first: slide each oscillator's filter mix (to the right of each Osc) to the top, routing their signal only to Filter 1. Next, set Filter 1 to 'Lowpass 4' and its Cutoff to about 7-8 o'clock.

4
To shape the sound drag Envelope 1's (1Env) blue modulation cross into one of the empty slots below the Cutoff dial, then drag the blue ring all the way round the dial to apply full positive modulation. Set Envelope 1's Decay at around 11 o'clock and Level to roughly 9 o'clock.

5
For upper grit add a touch of noise. In Massive's noise oscillator (bottom left) change Noise type to Metallic, slide the filter mix all the way up to filter 1 (F1), then turn Color fully right and Amp to 10 o'clock. Dial Feedback to around 8 o'clock to apply grunt and weight.

6
Finally, head to Massive's FX section. Activate Classic Tube in the FX1 slot, set Dry/Wet to 10-11 o'clock and Drive to 9 o'clock. Finally, load the Delay Synced effect into the FX2 slot and set Left and Right times to 1 over 8, Dry/Wet to 10 o'clock, Damp to 1 o'clock and Feedback to 12 o'clock.

Sub bass

In most genres of music – rock, indie, metal, blues – there is a single bassline, typically supplied by a bass guitar. In dance music this main bass lead is often augmented by a lower bass part, the sub bass. While the main bassline is *heard*, the sub bass is *felt*. The low-level throb of the sub adds depth to the mix that may not be heard on iPod earbuds but which is necessary to drive the low end in a club environment – see *The low end, page 236*.

It is important to differentiate from the outset between sub bass *frequencies* (defined as frequencies below around 60Hz) and sub bass *parts, which are* specific synth tracks designed with one thing in mind: to up the ante on club rigs. The distinction shows that while any bassline may have sub bass frequencies in it, a specific sub bass part will do its thing an octave or two below the main bassline, bulking up the subsonic end of the frequency spectrum.

NOTE Extreme care is needed when creating and mixing sub bass frequencies and parts. Even high-end studio speakers typically drop away around 60Hz, and the average home studio space is unlikely to accurately reproduce frequencies as high as 100Hz (*page 260*). This means if sub frequencies are to play a major role in a mix, **use a frequency analyser** and **regularly visually A/B** your mix against one that you know translates well to a club environment. Failure to do so can lead to all kinds of problems, from creating bloated low ends to damaged speakers.

NOTE An awareness of where different notes lie on a frequency graph (*Appendix 2*), alongside an overview of how deep club rigs go (*page 236*), is essential when mixing sub bass. C1, for example, has a fundamental frequency of 32.7Hz while C0 lies at (subsonic) 16.35Hz. Given that most club rigs roll off at 30–45Hz, there's no point in programming a sub that includes C0 – it simply won't get played. **A good rule of thumb is to go no lower than E1** (43.65Hz), a frequency that will translate on all but the cheapest club speakers. This rule of thumb helps explain why so many dance tracks are made in the keys of F and G – where the root fundamentals of kick and sub hit at rig-friendly 40–50hz.

CREATING SUB BASS

There are two options for filling out the subs in a bassline.

The easiest method is to **extend the sound of the main bassline downwards** by adding an oscillator at lower octaves or a dedicated sub oscillator – see *Walkthrough, opposite*. Exactly which octave to pitch the sub in will depend on the notes played by the main bassline – but, as noted above, avoid sinking below the E1 low-water mark.

REBOOT

In Reboot's 'Just hang on' effects were use to extend the bass into the subs. "The Dreadbox Erebus delivers the bassline. On the bass I also used the Big Sky and the Eventide Timefactory to add some bottom end to make the sub area sound more spacious.

But big basslines also demand restraint: "An important step to avoid ruining the mix was the radical use of EQs to cut the frequencies below 40Hz."

When adding sub bass oscillators the best choice is invariably a sine or triangle wave. Other choices like saw and pulse waves include too many harmonics that interfere with the upper octaves.

If the main bassline is not synthesised, you can add sub bass either by layering a simple sine patch beneath the sample or live recording, or try a dedicated sub bass enhancer (*page 212*) that tracks the incoming pitch and generates a sine wave an octave or two below it.

The second, and less regular, approach is to **program a specific sub bass part** using a dedicated DAW track. In this case you end up with two bass elements: the sub and the main bass, with the sub typically playing a simpler pattern using a single vanilla sine wave. Examples of this approach include Swedish House Mafia's 'One', where a very low sub – barely audible on home speakers – is employed to shake club rigs and offer an important frequency counterpoint to the rich kick drum.

In terms of production, sine-based sub bass is simple enough that it rarely needs much in the way of additional processing. Kick-triggered sidechain **compression** can be used to keep the sub away from the kick. If using **EQ bracketing** (*page 211*) don't mistakenly roll away frequencies you want the sub to shake. Again – keep a note to frequency graph handy.

// WALKTHROUGHS

Creating an additional sub bass part

1 Our Moog bass for starters patch from *page 109* lacks power in the sub region. You can fill out these frequencies by layering a simple, weighty synth sound under the main bass. First, insert an EQ plugin and low-cut the main bass at around 100Hz with a high pass filter.

2 Duplicate the track, open an EQ and switch the high pass to a low pass filter. You now have two identical copies of the bass, the original main bass acting as the high/mid bass element, the second as a 'sub' layer. Simple filtering creates space for each in the mix.

3 An effective sub patch is typically clean and pure. Open the new 'sub' Monark instance and tailor the synth settings for maximum low frequency impact: turn Oscs 2 and 3 off, then change Osc 1's wave to Triangle. Using the same source instrument for both mid and sub keeps the sound consistent.

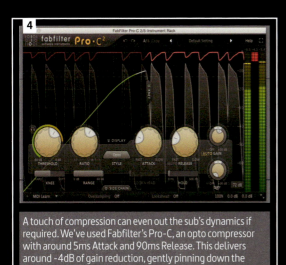

4 A touch of compression can even out the sub's dynamics if required. We've used Fabfilter's Pro-C, an opto compressor with around 5ms Attack and 90ms Release. This delivers around -4dB of gain reduction, gently pinning down the lower sub layer.

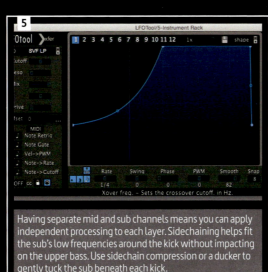

5 Having separate mid and sub channels means you can apply independent processing to each layer. Sidechaining helps fit the sub's low frequencies around the kick without impacting on the upper bass. Use sidechain compression or a ducker to gently tuck the sub beneath each kick.

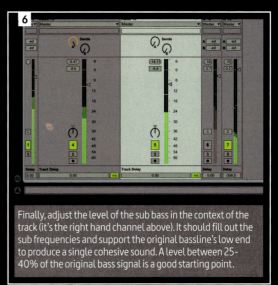

6 Finally, adjust the level of the sub bass in the context of the track (it's the right hand channel above). It should fill out the sub frequencies and support the original bassline's low end to produce a single cohesive sound. A level between 25-40% of the original bass signal is a good starting point.

Chapter three
Bass and basslines

Mixing bass

Mixing bass should be approached as part of the wider mixdown (*Chapter eight*), and detailed techniques for getting a well-balanced low end are covered in *pages 282–285*. But while general production know-how will take you a long way, there are techniques specific to mixing bass that can help both mitigate against low end difficulties and assure a bass that throbs, drives and thumps.

THE CHALLENGES

The key challenges presented by the bass when it comes to mixing are four fold:

▸▸ **It's hard to get an accurate picture of what's going on.** Inadequate speakers and/or an imperfect listening environment means mixing the low end can sometimes be an act of faith.

▸▸ **Kick and bass conflicts.** In dance music the two pivotal mix elements need to inhabit the same frequency space and work together – not fight.

▸▸ **Headroom.** Low frequencies demand more headroom. If the kick and bass are afforded too much space, the mix suffers.

▸▸ **Lost definition.** In a busy mix the bass can struggle to find identity, particularly in the radio-critical midrange.

JUAN MACLEAN

"'Happy House' [from *The Future Will Come*] is a weird sounding record. It actually has very little bass – I bet there's not much information below 80 Hz. It doesn't fit with contemporary recordings in the middle of a DJ set. It's mixed more like a rock record."

SEE ALSO

 PAGE 118 SPLITTING THE BASS

 PAGE 204 BASS IN THE STUDIO

 PAGE 256 LOUDNESS, HEADROOM AND LEVELS

 PAGE 274 MONITORING

 PAGE 274 SIDECHAIN COMPRESSION

PAGE 282 MIXING KICK AND BASS

GROUND RULES

Although experienced mix engineers often claim that production rules are there to be broken, when it comes to mixing the low end, there are certain ground rules that even they don't mess with:

▸▸ **Keep the low-end mono.** Stereo information in the low end risks phase problems that can impact on everything from vinyl cutting to the fidelity of a mix played on club rigs. For stereo basslines, split the signal – *see Walkthrough, overleaf*.

▸▸ **Keep the low-end dry.** Reverb and other ambient effects muddy the low-end and compromise mono fidelity. If a bassline requires reverb, again, split the signal first.

▸▸ **The kick and bass must work together.** Although covered in *Chapter eight*, for now suffice to say that as the foundational elements in 98 per cent of dance mixes, the kick and bass need to complement each other, sonically and rhythmically, to establish the groove and underpin the mix. Many producers begin their mixdowns by getting the kick and bass relationship right.

▸▸ **Preserve headroom where you can.** The problem with allocating too much frequency girth to the kick and bass is that there is less headroom available for the rest of the mix – which means a quieter, less punchy production.

SPLITTING THE BASS

One essential technique for giving the producer more control over the bass – and the starting point for creating 'wide' and radio-friendly bass sounds – is to 'split' the bass using **dual-band processing** (*page 118*).

When splitting, the same bass part is copied onto two adjacent tracks. The first bass part has its high end cut at 100–150Hz. The second receives the opposite EQ treatment, its low end cut at around 150–200Hz. This gives two different bands, one high, one low, that can be processed individually.

Separating the bands in this way is both a problem solver and a creative mixing gateway.

The first problem solved relates to **mono fidelity**. By retaining a low bass band you are able to mix subs in mono while adding stereo – or other – treatments to the upper band (*Walkthrough, page 118*). The second problem solved is that you are able to **precisely balance the volume of the low band** without also altering the balance of the mix-critical mid range.

From a creative point of view, once the bands are split you are free to do whatever you like with the upper band – widen it, trigger delays, automate the filter, overdrive the signal – without compromising the integrity and stability of the low-end.

TIP When employing dual-band processing, the crossover frequency – our suggested 100–200Hz – is critical, as are the filter slopes used. Rolling away each band too abruptly risks a 'hollowed middle', where a gap forms between the energy of the low and higher bands. For that reason, some overlap is usually best, coupled with sensibly gentle roll-off slopes.

TIP An alternative to splitting a single bass is to use two different bass *sounds*, one for the low end, one for higher frequencies. To set this up, cut the high end of the first bass, then copy the MIDI pattern to trigger a second mid-heavy synth (*see Walkthrough, page 119*).

DISTORTION FOR BULK

A common problem presented by basslines, particularly subbier ones, is that while they sound great down below, their reach doesn't extend much beyond the 150-200Hz zone. In a deliberately bass-heavy mix destined solely for the dancefloor this may be fine. But if a bass needs to either reach into the higher reaches of a mix (as with **noodle basslines**), dominate it (**bass is lead**) or translate for radio/earbud playback (commercial mixes) then the bass needs to have a presence in the critical mid range.

The obvious starting point when augmenting a synth bass part is to **add in higher octave oscillators**. Detune them for

PRO TIPS

SCUBA

"'Television' [from the album *Claustrophobia*] was the track that gave me the most problems technically.

"I remember playing an early version of this to George FitzGerald, who was staying at my flat at the time, and being pretty embarrassed by how it sounded – sometimes you only get an idea of what you really think of a track when you play it with someone else in the room.

"At the risk of sounding incredibly dry and technical, balancing the frequencies in that bassline was not a lot of fun."

more obvious body. Tweak upper oscillator volumes until you get a good balance with the lows. An alternative is to **layer in a second synth** playing the same progression at a higher octave.

EQ can be useful too – although most EQ models are unable to add frequencies not present in the original signal.

An alternative means of bulking up a sound is to use **distortion**. A useful tool for adding missing frequencies to any part in a mix (*page 280*), it has obvious applications for basslines where the added harmonics that distortion provides can extend the part a long way up the frequency spectrum. Experiment with anything from **mild saturation** through warm **overdrive** to raw **bit-crushing**.

TIP For more control over the distorted signal, set up the distortion on a **parallel channel** and add the signal to taste (*pages 119 and 281*). To avoid muddying low frequencies, use the **split bass technique** and apply distortion to the upper band only.

EQ

The first thing to do when mixing bass is to cut the extreme low frequencies. Although this may seem counterintuitive, by removing subsonic mud – that will never be heard or indeed reproduced (remember most club rigs bottom out at around 30Hz)

– you can free up a significant amount of headroom, which means a louder mix. A useful rule of thumb is to use a low cut filter to roll away frequencies below 40Hz.

TIP To identify the exact frequency at which to cut, note the lowest note in the bassline (sub bass included), check its frequency, then roll away all those below it.

Elsewhere, EQ is used to keep a bass sound in check against the kick and to emphasise specific tones. Note that some EQs are particularly well suited to bass sounds. Models inspired by the famed Pultec are noted for their rounded warmth on bass, as are Neve models.

WIDER BASS

For the kind of super-wide stereo floor-shaker with its roots in jungle and electro, that has become so prevalent in EDM and dubstep, start out by splitting the bass, then apply a generous dose of modulation to the upper band using a chorus, flange, ensemble or stereo widener plugin. The result? Tight, punchy and mono low end supporting a wide stereo middle.

Huge stereo floor-shakers are not just the result of split-band processing. They demand rich multi-oscillator bass sounds, often based around square and saw waves alongside multiple levels of detuning and/or unison (*see EDM lead template, page 86*).

// WALKTHROUGHS

Splitting the bass

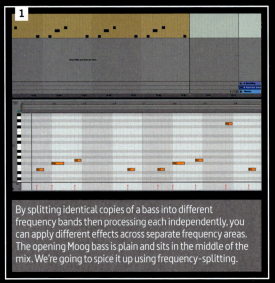

1 By splitting identical copies of a bass into different frequency bands then processing each independently, you can apply different effects across separate frequency areas. The opening Moog bass is plain and sits in the middle of the mix. We're going to spice it up using frequency-splitting.

2 Render or bounce the bass part to a new audio file, import the file into your project, then delete the source synth. Load an EQ on the audio track and apply a low pass filter to isolate the sound's low and low–mid frequencies. Tweak the cutoff frequency to suit the source material.

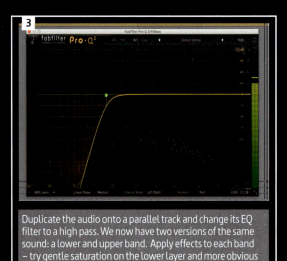

3 Duplicate the audio onto a parallel track and change its EQ filter to a high pass. We now have two versions of the same sound: a lower and upper band. Apply effects to each band – try gentle saturation on the lower layer and more obvious modulation or widening treatments on the high layer.

Stereo floor shaker

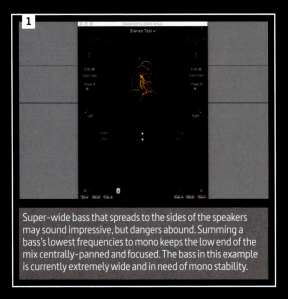

1 Super-wide bass that spreads to the sides of the speakers may sound impressive, but dangers abound. Summing a bass's lowest frequencies to mono keeps the low end of the mix centrally-panned and focused. The bass in this example is currently extremely wide and in need of mono stability.

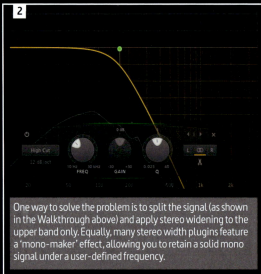

2 One way to solve the problem is to split the signal (as shown in the Walkthrough above) and apply stereo widening to the upper band only. Equally, many stereo width plugins feature a 'mono-maker' effect, allowing you to retain a solid mono signal under a user-defined frequency.

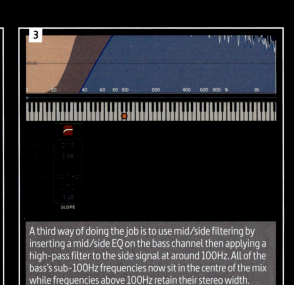

3 A third way of doing the job is to use mid/side filtering by inserting a mid/side EQ on the bass channel then applying a high-pass filter to the side signal at around 100Hz. All of the bass's sub-100Hz frequencies now sit in the centre of the mix while frequencies above 100Hz retain their stereo width.

Radio-friendly bass

1 Clean sub bass tones lack harmonics, preventing them from cutting through on smaller playback systems. By adding or accentuating a sub's upper harmonics you can increase the perception of bass on small systems. We've started with the sub bass layer from the previous walkthroughs.

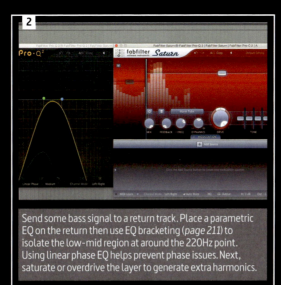

2 Send some bass signal to a return track. Place a parametric EQ on the return then use EQ bracketing (*page 211*) to isolate the low-mid region at around the 220Hz point. Using linear phase EQ helps prevent phase issues. Next, saturate or overdrive the layer to generate extra harmonics.

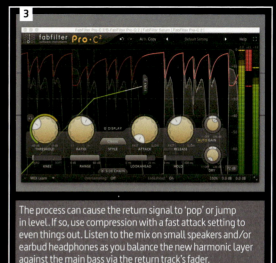

3 The process can cause the return signal to 'pop' or jump in level. If so, use compression with a fast attack setting to even things out. Listen to the mix on small speakers and/or earbud headphones as you balance the new harmonic layer against the main bass via the return track's fader.

Layered synth bass

1 Our Moog bass – currently comprised of two layers – is still missing something. To add bite, character and stereo interest we're going to overlay a new, third, bass layer using a different synth. Create a new track, copy the bass MIDI then load Xfer Serum's 'BA Feed The Mau5 factory' preset.

2 Simplify the pluck layer and tighten the sound. In Serum, turn off both Osc 2 and its reverb effect then tighten the sound's amp envelope by setting Env 1's Decay to 200ms and Sustain to minimum. Your aim with this third layer is to contribute a subtle flavour to the overall bass sound.

3 Isolate and enhance characteristics in the pluck layer that are missing in the core mid layer with the aim of creating a full-frequency '3D' bass. We've used an EQ to high-pass this new plucky layer at around 400Hz then a bit-crusher to add fizz and definition to its high end.

Chapter four
Using samples

Chapter four
Using samples

The sampler has been one of the mainstays in the development of dance music, reaching back to the 1970s.

Samplers derive their name from the process used to convert analogue audio signals into digital data. An analogue-to-digital converter 'samples' the audio at regular intervals – tens of thousands of times per second – creating a close approximation of the original signal in digital form which is stored and replayed.

Back in the day, sampling was a laborious process featuring large grey and black boxes, tiny screens, fiddly interfaces and miniscule memories. But thanks to developments in hardware and the introduction of software alternatives, using samples in a track is now painless and no longer requires detailed knowledge of the inner workings of the process. As such the sampler is just another instrument available to the 21st century producer.

Part of the appeal of the sampler lies in the diversity of tasks it can tackle. It can be used to:

▸▸ Trigger **individual sounds** – most often one-shot drum sounds. Non-looping fragments of audio – speech and FX – can also be triggered for all manner of ear candy.

▸▸ **Map a single sampled tone** – say a bass or synth sound – **across the keyboard** in a process known as **multisampling** (*page 132*).

▸▸ Play back **commercial loops** like drum or percussion loops.

▸▸ **Sample snippets from an existing record**, an approach that has formed the basis of many classic tracks.

THE EVOLUTION OF SAMPLING

The story of sample-based dance music stretches back to the late '70s and early '80s, when two influences collided to set the framework for what was to come.

The first was disco, with its culture of edits and extended remixes. Pioneering DJs like John Morales created unofficial edits of popular records, looping and repeating sections to make them more dancefloor-friendly.

The second influence was early hip-hop and its breakbeat-led DJ culture, originally based on DJs cutting funk and soul records, then progressing to the use of early sampling technology. Hip-hop production and sampling have been virtually synonymous ever since, with samplers such as the Akai MPC series, E-MU SP-12/1200 and Ensoniq ASR-10 a part of the furniture in hip-hop producers' studios.

In the mid to late '80s, house and techno producers began experimenting with similar sampling techniques, incorporating elements of existing tracks into their work. London production team MARRS scored a global hit in 1987 with the sample-based 'Pump Up The Volume', which was nominated for a Grammy. The same year Coldcut scored paydirt with their 'Seven Minutes Of Madness' remix of Eric B & Rakim's 'Paid In Full', which spliced together the original track's vocals, Israeli throat singing and a breakbeat from an obscure children's record.

Sampling comes with its share of controversy. 1988 saw the first major legal dispute over sampling in dance music when Todd Terry sampled a synth line from Reese & Santonio's 'The Sound' for his track 'Back To The Beat'. Terry came from a hip-hop background, where attitudes

PRO TIPS

JUSTICE

"In terms of sampling, our inspirations are divided into three categories. The first is when we hear something on a record and think, 'OK, that's great. Let's take a big part of it and just loop it.' That's what we did on 'Phantom', 'Stress' and 'Newjack'.

"The second category contains songs we have been listening to all year or all our lives, and which we don't actually sample. Instead, we 'mentally sample' them by adding bits that sound similar.

"The third category, representing about 90% of what we did on the first album, is 'micro-sampling'."

Chapter four
Using samples

towards sampling were more liberal. Kevin Saunderson (aka Reese), on the other hand, was furious that his work had been stolen, and retaliated by releasing 'Back To The Beat (With 'The Sound')', sampling Terry's track as payback. The two eventually settled their differences – and became friends – but the episode highlighted a key issue with sampling: when you're 'borrowing' others creative work you should be able to justify your use of samples (whether legal or not) from both a creative and an ethical perspective. If you end up in court (*page 140*) you need to be able to argue your case from a legal perspective too.

In the late '80s, commercial sample disks and CDs hit the market, offering ready-rolled – and copyright-cleared – sounds for musicians to load into their samplers. In 1990, a new company named Zero-G released 'Datafile One', the first ever dance music sample pack, sowing the seeds for what would eventually become a multi-million dollar global industry. Fast forward to the modern day and instantly downloadable sample packs are ubiquitous, with DAWs sold pre-loaded with thousands of hits, loops and FX.

A lot of sampling in the early '90s may not have been subtle, but it was effective, whether it was The Prodigy dropping huge chunks of Max Romeo's 'Chase The Devil' and The Ultramagnetic MCs' 'Critical Beatdown' into 'Out Of Space' or Joey Beltram co-opting Beastie Boy Ad Rock's proclamation: "it's the new style," for 'The Omen'.

Throughout the '90s, samplers became more powerful and affordable, spawning new trends in dance production. Commercially produced multisampled classic synths and drum machines became studio mainstays, while as the decade wore on, house wholeheartedly and shamelessly embraced large-scale sampling. Timeless classics like Stardust's 'Music Sounds Better With You', DJ Sneak's 'You Can't Hide From Your Bud' and Moodymann's 'I Can't Kick This Feeling When It Hits' are all based around samples of late '70s and early '80s disco tracks (Chaka Khan's 'Fate', Teddy Pendergrass's 'You Can't Hide From Your Love' and Chic's 'I Want Your Love', respectively).

While the househeads were weaving substantial samples into their records, D&B artists were pushing the sampling envelope in a different direction: from Goldie's timestretching antics on 'Terminator' to any number of breakbeats re-made in Propellerhead's pioneering ReCycle software, which gave producers a quick and easy way of taking a breakbeat loop and slicing it into individual drum hits to be replayed and reordered. It's an effect you can achieve nowadays in any DAW, but in 1994 it was revolutionary – a case of technology propelling a genre.

By the 21st century, new technology allowed artists to get ever more creative with samples. At one end of the spectrum was Justice's 'micro-sampling' technique, employed on tracks like 'D.A.N.C.E.', in which nearly every mix element is a tiny sample lifted from another record. 'D.A.N.C.E.' used a second technique related to sampling, in the form of the chorus melody which is lifted from the Madonna and Britney Spears single 'Me Against The Music', but sung with different lyrics. The technique is known as interpolation.

Four decades since samplers became part of the dance production landscape, sampling is as widespread as ever. Some of the biggest crossover hits of the EDM era have been heavily based on samples, from Avicii's 'Levels' with its iconic hook lifted from Etta James's 'Something's Got A Hold On Me', to Duck Sauce's Boney M-looping 'Barbra Streisand'. The underground has held it down too with tracks like Robert Hood's gospel-tinged, Aretha Franklin-sampling 'Never Grow Old' or Paul Woolford's 2013 anthem 'Untitled', which lifted a vocal line from Switch & Andrea Martin's 'I Still Love You', released less than two years previously.

To a tiny minority of people, sampling is considered cheating. We disagree. It's not the process of sampling in itself that makes or breaks a track; *it's what you do with that sound once it's loaded into the sampler.*

PRO TIPS

DANNY DAZE

Danny Daze's studio workflow is to sample single notes or short melodies from hardware synths, then edit them and replay them in Ableton: "It's really cool to sample yourself. I randomly play keys without knowing what bpm I'm playing at, then I sample that and it creates different textures and different rhythms.

"The Dave Smith Tetra was all I used on 'Silicon' aside from the kick and drums. The last one I did was a remix for Terranova which was all Moog Voyager except the drums. 'Ready To Go' was the JP-8080 – I took those bells and threw them back into Sampler, pitched them down and did a whole bunch of things to them."

The right sampler for the job

Just like synths and effects, different samplers have different characteristics and features. Choosing the right one for your needs depends on the sound and edit/replay options you want and how much you're willing to sacrifice ease of use for more advanced options.

The most rudimentary sampler of all is one that takes a single sound and pitches it up and down the keyboard to be triggered either via key presses or MIDI.

In reality, even the most basic sampler instrument on the market does a lot more than that. Ableton Live's **Simpler** is typical of a basic workhorse sampler. In addition to essential chromatic pitch-shifting, it allows you to sculpt whatever sound you load into it using envelopes.

There's a resonant filter with a range of modes and modulation options to determine how much the cutoff is affected by velocity, key-tracking and a built-in LFO. There are also three envelopes to control volume, filter cutoff and pitch. A section of the sound can be looped to extend its sustain time. There are also options such as Spread, for a unison detune effect, and Glide, for portamento.

More advanced samplers offer more complex features. The first – and arguably most important – is the ability to work with **multisampled instruments**. Here, instead of a single tone being mapped across the keyboard, different samples are triggered depending on the pitch and velocity of the notes played.

Multisampling delivers far more realistic results than single-tone mapping. Suppose you're playing a sampler instrument of an acoustic guitar. Recording a single note into the sampler and pitching it up and down to recreate the sound of the guitar's three-and-a-half octave range won't sound realistic. The solution is to use different samples for individual notes or short ranges of notes, giving a more realistic sound.

But to really bring it to life, different velocities are required as well. Playing a string harder on the guitar, the sound doesn't just get louder; its tone also changes. To some extent this effect can be replicated using a filter controlled by velocity level, but more realistic results are achieved using **velocity layers** where each note is sampled multiple times with varying intensity. Then, as the velocity of notes played increases, the louder samples are triggered. The more velocity layers there are, the more realistic an instrument.

The most fully featured software samplers, such as Native Instruments' industry-standard **Kontakt**, feature a host of other features including:

▸▸ the ability for sample-based instruments to be programmed using **scripts** which define their behaviour;

▸▸ **key switches**, which allow you to toggle from one articulation to another; hitting a keyswitch might activate vibrato for example, selecting an alternative set of samples played with vibrato.

▸▸ **randomisation/round robin playback** of multiple groups of sounds (particularly useful for drum sounds, to introduce subtle variation between repeated hits).

Although advanced features like these are rarely employed by the average producer, having them in a sampler allows for the playback of complex ready made sample-based instruments.

Samplers designed with **drums** in mind (e.g. Ableton's **Impulse**, Native Instruments' **Battery** or **Maschine**) offer slightly different feature sets, focussing less on chromatic playback and more on sculpting individual drum hits as part of a kit. Because they're designed with drum sampling in mind they offer workflow time savers like drag-and-drop to automatically assign each sample to a different MIDI note and hot-swapping features allowing you to audition samples while a track plays.

PRO TIPS

ALEX SOMERS (SIGUR RÓS)

"We did a lot of sampling on *Valtari*. While I was mixing, Jónsi, Kjarri [Kjartan] and Orri sat at the back of the studio with a [Teenage Engineering] OP-1 and recorded the sound of the speakers playing into the room.

"Then they'd slow it down or speed it up and generally mess with it, and once an hour they'd walk over to me and say, 'Hey, can we record a little overdub?' That was because they'd just written a part based on a sample of the song.

"So, that's where a lot of the unusual textures in 'Ég anda' came from – the song re-sampled."

Chapter four
Using samples

TOOLS OF THE TRADE

Samplers then and now

FAIRLIGHT CMI (1979) ⤴
The first commercially available samplers were fiendishly expensive. The pioneering Fairlight, a kind of all-in-one computer-based digital synth, sequencer and sampler, cost a staggering £18,000 in 1979. This was ruthlessly cutting-edge technology, but way out of reach to the average musician.

E-MU SP-12 (1984) AND AKAI MPC60 (1988)
By the mid to late '80s, samplers were starting to become more affordable. E-MU's SP-12 (and later SP-1200) offered an alternative to the more common keyboard-based approach, featuring pads and a built-in sequencer, primarily designed for sampling and programming drums. The concept was taken further by the Roger Linn-designed Akai MPC60, with far more sophisticated sequencing and editing options and extensive MIDI support. Both models remain popular among deep house, techno and hip-hop producers.

AKAI S1000 (1988)
The heyday of affordable hardware samplers arrived in the late '80s. Companies such as Akai and E-MU pushed the technological boundaries for their more expensive models, but also introduced increasingly affordable options. Models such as the S1000 became a mainstay in the studios of dance producers, triggering a wave of sample-based tracks. Vintage models from the time have retro appeal, with a distinctive sound that instantly evokes the era of classic house, techno and jungle. But user-friendly they are not.

NI KONTAKT (2002)
The writing was on the wall for hardware sequencers as soon as DAWs and plugins started to revolutionise music production. Software sampler plugins like Native Instruments' Kontakt changed the way we think of samplers and sampling. Whereas producers were once limited by expensive hardware, affordable software options now allow us to run countless channels of sample-based instruments in our DAWs. The change in technology also changed the way we think of samples themselves. For many producers, sample-based elements of a track are no longer something recorded from scratch, but commercially available products: complex multisampled instruments, sample packs and ready made loops.

ABLETON LIVE (2001)
For today's producers, sampling is no longer the novelty it might have seemed back in the '80s or even the '90s, when the technical challenge of using samplers sometimes overshadowed the creative process. The way we take sampling for granted is reflected in the way DAWs like Live allow samples to be dragged and dropped into an arrangement, then timestretched and pitch shifted with very little effort. Using samples is now a creative rather than a technical challenge. No matter whether you're creating your own loops, loading pre-made sounds from sample packs or working with complex sample-based instruments, today's software streamlines the technical side of the process, placing the emphasis back where it should be: on making music.

ELEKTRON OCTATRACK (2011)
You'd have been forgiven for thinking hardware samplers were obsolete in the 21st century, but there are still signs of life. Elektron's Octatrack came as something of a surprise when it was released, offering hi-res 21st century sampling options apparently inspired by the seamless looping and timestretching found in Ableton Live. It's a deep and complex machine with excellent sequencing features and a loyal following among live techno artists.

KORG VOLCA SAMPLE (2014) ⤵
At the opposite end of the scale, it's also worth checking out the affordable Volca Sample from Korg (*below*). It's a basic unit which can only sample via an iPad app, but it captures the lo-fi spirit of the bare bones vintage machines that were so important in defining the sound – and spirit – of early house, techno and hip-hop.

The old-school sample vibe

Even though samplers are digital machines, many of the now classic models had a distinct flavour to them. The limitations of early digital sampling technology had a range of effects on sound – from the perceived 'grit' of specific digital drum machines to the full-on dirt associated with low-resolution samplers. And while these may have been viewed as flaws back in the day, for today's producers they offer a characterful digital alternative to analogue warmth and fatness.

HOW A SAMPLER WORKS

What's happening inside samplers like the 8-bit Ensoniq Mirage or 12-bit Akai MPC60 to give them their distinctive sound? To turn analogue audio into a digital signal they 'sample' (aka measure) the amplitude of the waveform at regular intervals and translate this amplitude into a binary number. The speed with which this is done (the **sample rate**, measured in Hz) determines the maximum frequency that can be captured.

The second key factor is the **bit depth** – the range of numbers used to capture the amplitude at each sample point. The larger the number, the greater the dynamic range.

The dynamic range of human hearing is around 120dB (*see Levels, page 256*) while 8-bit sampling only delivers 48dB.

What does this mean for a sampled sound? As you reduce the sample rate and bit depth, you bring out more character and crunch in a signal. At 12-bit, sounds start exhibiting a rough edge. At 8-bit they fracture into digital sounding tonalities. At 4-bit the sound becomes a trashed shadow of itself. The impact on the signal of this hyper low bit depth processing is not always desirable, but in the right circumstances – like a *Whomp robot synth, page 111* – it can work sonic wonders.

CRAFTING CHARACTER

In general, the earlier (or cheaper) the machine, the lower its maximum bit depth and sample rate. 8-bit digital drum machines including the Linn LM-1 and Oberheim DMX (both introduced in 1980), used samples recorded at 28kHz or less.

But other factors shaped the sound too, not least filters. The **E-MU SP-1200** is based around a 12-bit, 26.04kHz sampling engine with a series of analogue filters. That gives it a different character to the **Akai MPC3000**, which features a 16-bit, 44.1kHz sampling engine and digital filters. There are not many plugins on the market that emulate the sound of older hardware units. 112dB's **Morgana** plugin is probably

PRO TIPS

TERRENCE PARKER

"[For the track 'Love's Got Me High'] I was watching a Jamie Foxx comedy special on HBO. Towards the end of the show he sits down at the piano and begins to play and sing… I had no idea this guy could play and sing so incredibly well. But when I heard it I immediately got the idea to sample it and make a track from it.

"I recorded the TV special on VHS tape using the highest speed to get the best quality, then sampled the parts from the VHS tape directly into my workstation.

"I created a basic drum track, arranged the samples, and played a melody around it. The rest, as they say, is history."

the best, recreating the sound of the 8-bit, analogue-filter-equipped Ensoniq Mirage. NI's **Maschine** also has 'vintage' modes. But it's easy enough to get a similar sound using a few carefully chosen effects:

▶▶ The most obvious is **downsampling** and/or **bit crushing** in your DAW.

▶▶ **Resampling** (*page 131*) allows you to reduce the sample rate and bit depth of a sample then bounce it back as lower-fidelity audio to be loaded into the sampler.

▶▶ Although you can approximate what happens when a signal is digitised, in the real world associated analogue circuitry also plays a significant role. In a typical sampler, this might include a mic pre-amp or line-level buffering amp on the input and analogue output stages. Approximate this by applying subtle analogue-style **saturation** or **overdrive** before applying the bit depth and sample rate reduction.

TIP The sound of vintage samplers wasn't just defined by the hardware, *but by the ways producers used them*. One common technique was to sample a 33rpm record at 45rpm then pitch it back down to replay it at its original speed. They did this to save memory, but it had the side effect of reducing the sample resolution. A similar effect can be achieved in software by sampling at a higher frequency then pitching it back down.

The old-school sample vibe

1 To demonstrate this tutorial we're using Massive and the 'WTZW' keys preset from its factory library. The MIDI is a chord progression in the key of A major. To process the sound old-school style we're using D16's Decimort plugin, which specialises in bit-crushing and sample rate reduction.

2 A quick online search reveals the bit depth and sample rate that classic samplers operated at. We want to recreate the characteristics of the E-MU SP-1200, which had a sample rate of 26.04–27.5kHz (we've settled at 26.10kHz) and a bit depth of 8.

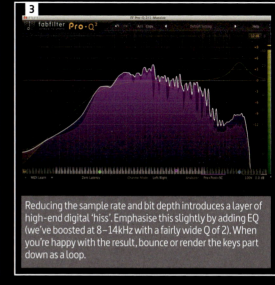

3 Reducing the sample rate and bit depth introduces a layer of high-end digital 'hiss'. Emphasise this slightly by adding EQ (we've boosted at 8–14kHz with a fairly wide Q of 2). When you're happy with the result, bounce or render the keys part down as a loop.

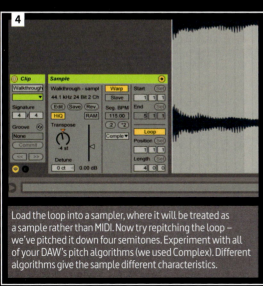

4 Load the loop into a sampler, where it will be treated as a sample rather than MIDI. Now try repitching the loop – we've pitched it down four semitones. Experiment with all of your DAW's pitch algorithms (we used Complex). Different algorithms give the sample different characteristics.

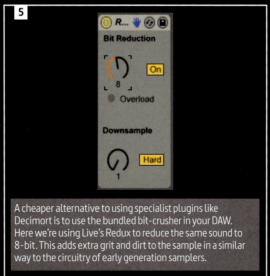

5 A cheaper alternative to using specialist plugins like Decimort is to use the bundled bit-crusher in your DAW. Here we're using Live's Redux to reduce the same sound to 8-bit. This adds extra grit and dirt to the sample in a similar way to the circuitry of early generation samplers.

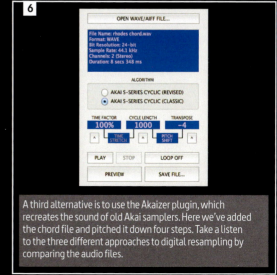

6 A third alternative is to use the Akaizer plugin, which recreates the sound of old Akai samplers. Here we've added the chord file and pitched it down four steps. Take a listen to the three different approaches to digital resampling by comparing the audio files.

Stretch and pitch

Pulling loops into time and tune is something that takes moments in today's DAWs. But in the days of hardware sampling the only way to change the tempo or pitch of a sound was to retrigger it up and down the keyboard, which affected both its pitch and length. If you wanted to speed a sample up it became higher pitched, while slowing it made it lower pitched… Which explains all those chipmunk vocals and tinny jungle breaks.

Freedom came with the arrival of Akai's S950, the sampler that introduced timestretching to the masses. Producers were finally able to change the duration of a sample without altering its pitch using an offline process. Not that the process was particularly easy; the user entered the desired duration of the sample as a percentage of the original sound's length. The sampler then generated a new sample by splitting the audio into thousands of slices and creating a new version of the sound by removing or adding copies of these slices to make the sample shorter or longer. This process – **granular processing** – is the basis for most timestretch algorithms.

TIMING IS EVERYTHING

Early timestretching wasn't nearly as transparent as it is today, and timestretching by large amounts created obvious artefacts, which artists used to their advantage. Vocals were popular candidates for extreme treatment – a la Fatboy Slim's 'Rockafeller Skank' (at around 4.30) – but drums were also stretched to good effect, as shown in Old-school melodic drum effects, opposite.

Timestretch and pitchshift algorithms are now light years ahead of where they were. They also offer a variety of modes designed to cope with different material. Most DAWs have an algorithm that preserves drum transients, while others cope better with pitched material and vocals. Try all timestretch modes on a variety of material to get an idea of what algorithm to use in a particular situation. For example, in the Old school melodic drum effects walkthrough we've used Live's Texture mode, while in Vocal effects with pitchshifting Complex Pro mode was employed to generate a different effect.

LET'S DO THE TIME WARP

It's not just dedicated samplers that have benefitted from the more complex algorithms offered by faster processing. The latest generation of DAWs feature timestretch and pitchshift on the fly, allowing producers to drop loops into a track to be automatically stretched to the project's bpm. Underlying this technology is the revolutionary concept of **warp or transient anchors** – meta markers that tell the software where beats fall. Although most DAWs handle warping automatically, with complex material – or loops with wonky grooves – you may need to move the markers manually.

PRO TIPS

REBOOT

"The idea of bringing different components and feelings together played an important role [in 'Foxfidelity', from Reboot's aLIVE album].

"There is this beach feeling, coming from live recorded seagulls, and the laid-back organs at the end of the track that kind of compete with the stronger basslines in the middle of the song: a picture that clearly reminds me of places like Ibiza during a daytime party.

"To twist up the field recordings, I timestretched the whole recording by 800% and used a texture algorithm to make it more atmospheric. The same on the radio interference, which was recorded with an Olympus LS-P2."

TIP Vibrato can sound unnatural on vocals when whole parts are sped up. To keep them sounding natural, use warping; create warp markers around vibrato start and end points (usually line or word ends) and 'pull' these vibratos back out to a more natural tremolo sound.

TIP For transparent results, solo the audio you're working on and listen to how the processing is affecting the sound. Even if you can't identify artefacts when the full mix is playing, they'll contribute to a less polished sound. To preserve transparency, don't push any algorithm too far. Whether using offline timestretching or real time warping, extreme change will increase artefacts – especially when slowing audio.

TIP Although instant timestretching and/or pitchshifting works well on most drum loops, you may get better results by slicing beats. Almost all DAWs offer automatic slicing that makes the process painless. Once sliced, the beat can be retriggered at a different tempo, and slices pitched up or down. Slicing has other benefits: you can change a sequence and alter the amplitude envelope/s of each slice (see Making your own resampled break, page 136.)

Old-school melodic drum effects

Load Ableton Live and set the project tempo to 135bpm. Drag the wr_br135_wallofbreaks.wav (from Sample Magic's Warehouse Rave pack). Take a listen to the break – it's a pretty typical-sounding breakbeat loop. Now let's get creative with some old-school repitching…

Turn up the Transpose parameter to replicate a repitched and timestretched sample. The higher the pitch, the more the beat starts to disintegrate. Set Transpose to 12, then change the Warp mode drop-down to Texture. This gives a satisfying metallic take on the sound (Pitched Break).

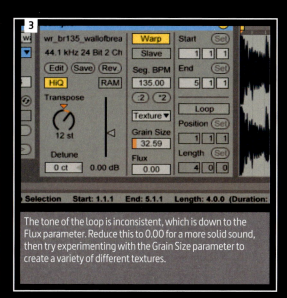

The tone of the loop is inconsistent, which is down to the Flux parameter. Reduce this to 0.00 for a more solid sound, then try experimenting with the Grain Size parameter to create a variety of different textures.

Vocal effects with pitchshifting

Drag wr_vox_oohbaby.wav onto a track, then in Clip View set Warp Mode to Complex Pro, which works well on vocals. Listen to the unprocessed vocal, then turn Transpose to +5. The vocal is pitched up, but without the chipmunk quality you get from simply speeding it up.

The transparent sound is down to the algorithm's formant processing, which you can disable by pulling the Formants fader down to 0.00. Now when you play it back the vocal gets chipmunk vibes. You can use this as an effect, as in this example, with Transpose set to -12.

Because the formant processing is disabled, the processing gives the vocal an alien quality. This works well when played alongside the original vocal. Duplicate the track and set the new version of the clip's Transpose to 0. Adjust the level of the pitchshifted track to control the strength of the effect.

Chapter four
Using samples

Creative sampling

In sampling terms, timestretching and pitchshifting offer simple creative manipulation of audio – which is not to downplay the results they can give. But when used to its full potential the humble sampler is capable of conjuring myriad sounds and effects that are impossible to create with other forms of synthesis.

Make no mistake, samplers are synths: even the most basic sampler is in essence a virtual analogue synth that uses digitally recorded audio data rather than a generated waveform. The difference between vanilla sampling and 'creative' sampling is using the instrument's filters, timestretching capabilities and amplitude, pitch and sample start point modulation to turn sounds into something more interesting than 'borrowed' loops.

Common sample manipulation techniques include:

▶▶ **Stuttered retriggers:** The trademark sound of stuttered vocal samples – effectively playing the vocal as if it were a percussion instrument – is a classic '80s trope, heard memorably on Paul Hardcastle's 'Nineteen'. The sound is easy to achieve: simply retrigger the same sample repeatedly. To build momentum, increase the pace of triggers Fatboy Slim-style.

▶▶ **Cut up vocal lines:** Sample chopping gymnastics can be taken a step further by cutting up and rearranging a loop. US garage legend Todd Edwards led the way with tracks such as his remix of St Germain's 'Alabama Blues'. With expert slicing Edwards turns vocal snippets into catchy melodies. The technique can be approached by cutting, rearranging and repitching snippets, or by assigning velocity to the sample start or end point and programming different MIDI trigger values, as demonstrated in *Cut up glitched vocals, page 196*.

▶▶ **Retriggered melody:** Vocals can be played chromatically to create melodies, as on tracks like Whistle's 'Just Buggin''. To get the sound, map a single sample across the keyboard then play a melody on it.

▶▶ **Chipmunking:** The hardcore rave scene's infamous 'chipmunk vocals' as employed on Acen's 'Trip II the Moon (Part 1)' are made by speeding vocals up to match the tempo of the track *without timestretching them*. Pitched vocals are back in vogue after a few wilderness years. Tourist's 'U', for example, uses pitchshifting and formant processing (*right*) to create lush melodic vocal textures. To explore this kind of sound, applications like Melodyne offer independent control of audio pitch, length and formants.

▶▶ **Breakbeat chops:** Undoubtedly the most influential aspect of creative sampling in dance music has been the chopping of classic breakbeats, a technique that has defined many genres, from jungle and breaks to D&B. Given its importance, it is covered in detail later in this chapter.

▶▶ **The build windup:** Assign the sample start position to a MIDI parameter such as velocity and play the sample back rapidly as the parameter is increased to create a glitchier take on extreme timestretching.

RESAMPLING

Resampling does what it says on the tin: takes a sample, processes it – often wildly – then bounces it down to be sampled and processed all over again.

It has its genesis in early D&B and garage productions, where crossfade looping and modulated resonant filtering were used to make smooth, swelling pads *a la* Photek 'Consciousness'. As filthy bass became dancefloor D&B's obsession, producers used similar techniques alongside distortion to create rich and harmonically complex bass sounds. But this time they sampled their own samples in order to process them further, as shown in *Resampling a filthy Reese bassline, right*.

Resampling allows the producer to use a practically infinite number of stacked effects; the only limit to how deep you go is your imagination… and patience.

FORMANTS

When sampling, the two most regular parameters that get changed are the pitch and length of the sample. But there's a third parameter that can be changed: the sample's formant.

Formants are the unique patterns of prominent peaks associated with harmonics in a waveform. They are integral to the character of a sound.

When pitchshifting a sound, even if the length of the sound is kept the same, the positions of the formants are shifted. This changes the character of the sound – turning a mellow male voice into a chipmunk.

Many applications, including Live, allow you to independently control formants to help correct the unnatural results of formant shifting.

Resampling a filthy Reese bassline

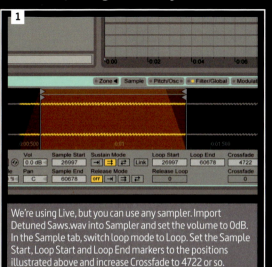

1 We're using Live, but you can use any sampler. Import Detuned Saws.wav into Sampler and set the volume to 0dB. In the Sample tab, switch loop mode to Loop. Set the Sample Start, Loop Start and Loop End markers to the positions illustrated above and increase Crossfade to 4722 or so.

2 This gives a smoothly looping sample, which we're using as the basis for our sound. Drag Saturator onto the track and set Curve Type to Waveshaper. Click the triangle button at the top left corner of Saturator's interface. This opens an extra set of controls that affect Waveshaper mode.

3 Turn the Drive knob to 18dB, set Depth to 67.2% and Period to 14.1%. This gives a crunchy, loud Reese. Now for some motion... Add Auto-Filter after Saturator, set its Filter Type to Notch and Circuit Type to OSR. Sweep the Freq as you play to bring the sound to life.

4 Sequence the sample to play C3 for four bars and automate the Freq parameter to sweep through the richest frequencies. Thanks to Live's flexible effect routing, you can easily experiment with the sound. Drag the Auto-Filter to before the Saturator to hear the difference.

5 This gives an even nastier, crustier sound – ripe for resampling. To resample, duplicate the sampler track and mute the original version. Now right-click the track name and select Freeze Track. Once that's done right-click the track name again and select Flatten Track. Mute this track too.

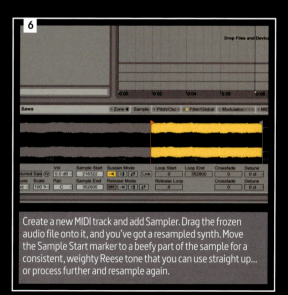

6 Create a new MIDI track and add Sampler. Drag the frozen audio file onto it, and you've got a resampled synth. Move the Sample Start marker to a beefy part of the sample for a consistent, weighty Reese tone that you can use straight up... or process further and resample again.

Chapter four
Using samples

The art of multisampling

In the most widely used sense of the word, multisampling refers to the process of loading multiple single note recordings of an instrument into a sampler in order to represent that instrument as a fully playable emulation. There are countless multisample libraries available online, putting astonishingly realistic pianos, guitars, drum kits, vintage synths and so on at your fingertips.

So ubiquitous are these libraries that there's every chance the sweeping orchestral soundtrack to the last movie you saw was entirely generated in software, using multisampled instruments in a sampler such as Native Instruments' Kontakt or Logic's EXS24.

WHY BOTHER?

Why can't you just sample a single note of the source instrument and stretch it across the keyboard rather than spend time and effort capturing multiple notes? The answer is you can... if you're not fussed about the patch sounding realistic, because even the most powerful pitchshifting algorithm can only take a pitched sample so far from its original frequency before it starts to sound obviously fake.

Then there's the crucial fact that acoustic and electric instruments are deeply nuanced in terms of dynamics and tonality, so playing a piano key gently sounds very different – not just quieter – to striking it full-force. By taking a sample of your piano every five semitones or so, at eight playing strengths, you will have enough sonic resolution to be able to lay out a convincing enough emulation in your sampler (although the most realistic VSTs will have many more than eight playing strengths).

FAR OUT SOUNDS

As an electronic music producer, you're more likely to get involved in multisampling for the creation of unique, 'unreal' sounds than the recreation of authentic real-world instruments. That might mean taking a multisampled guitar, piano or whatever, and processing it beyond recognition while retaining its fundamentally melodic nature, or working found sounds (*page 228*) into playable instruments that sound like they come from another world.

Your main allies in such endeavours are a sampler's layering tools and effects. Multitimbral samplers like Kontakt, which mix multiple sampling engines in a single multi-channel instrument, enable disparate snippets of audio to be layered on top of each other then mangled using pitchshifting, timestretching, filters, looping and more, to be brought together as a single, cohesive sound that amounts to more than the sum of its parts.

Effects can be applied either within the sampler or via separate plugins (or both). At the top of the list for transforming real world tones into hyper-real noises are filters, distortion, delays and modulation processors (chorus, phasing and flanging). In the walkthrough opposite, we combine a multisampled synth with a heavily processed vocal sample in Kontakt to make a unique new instrument.

TIP Before you spend money on a professional orchestral strings library, check that your DAW doesn't already have one included. It might not be as detailed as a third-party offering, but for a background riff, is it really going to matter?

TIP If you regularly multisample, investigate applications that automate the process, such as Skylife's powerful SampleRobot.

TIP When layering samples (*page 50*), ensure that every element in the stack makes a worthwhile contribution to the overall sound. Use filters to reduce overlap.

TIP Many samplers offer a range of timestretching and pitchshifting modes. Read the manual and make sure you understand the strengths and weaknesses of each for different types of sound.

PRO TIPS

MAELSTROM

"I like to resample a lot, which means I'll run a drum hit through a reverb, then sample the reverb tail, reverse it and use it as an instrument, or run a synth line through a delay and sample the feedback to start writing something off grid with it.

"For me, sampling is an instrument – it's a way of turning things upside down or getting out of situations where I know I have something interesting going on but I'm kind of stuck with it, so I'll end up using it as a sample, or making a multi-sample instrument with the original source to approach it with a different angle."

Making a custom multisampled instrument

1. Start by creating a MIDI clip containing a linear progression of full velocity triggers placed every few semitones from C3 to C5. The sound we want to multisample is from Xfer Records' Serum. Serum's output is recorded as a single audio clip, which is then sliced into individual notes in an audio editor.

2. Each note is saved as a separate sample then dragged into Kontakt and set up as contiguous keyzones, with each zone centring on its sample's root pitch and extending one to three semitones. We've only recorded a single velocity layer so we don't need to worry about 'vertical' zoning.

3. Now you can use Kontakt's editing and processing features on the raw Serum samples. First hit the Reverse button in Kontakt's Source panel. The tails take too long to come in, so access Kontakt's Wave Editor and pull the sample End points back to shorten them.

4. Next, loop each sample to prevent the longer notes stopping abruptly as playback reaches the end point. Increase the X-Fade parameter and switch to forward/backward loop mode (so that the playhead reverses direction at either end) to smooth the loop point transitions.

5. Add a second layer using a vocal sample. Dragging it into Kontakt's interface loads it on a new sample module set to the same MIDI channel so they trigger together. Kontakt's DFD mode sounds wrong, so choose Tone Machine mode, which pitches samples up and down without timestretching.

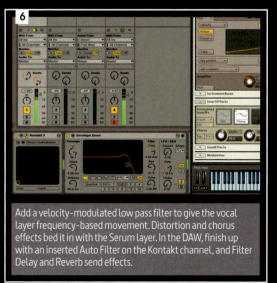

6. Add a velocity-modulated low pass filter to give the vocal layer frequency-based movement. Distortion and chorus effects bed it in with the Serum layer. In the DAW, finish up with an inserted Auto Filter on the Kontakt channel, and Filter Delay and Reverb send effects.

Chapter four
Using samples

Amen to that: the last word on breaks

At the end of 2015, thousands of musicians across the world pooled their cash to ensure one of dance music's little-known superstars was finally recompensed for six seconds of drumming. His name? Richard Spencer. His claim to fame? He was front man of The Winstones and copyright owner of the iconic 1969 track 'Amen Brother' – source of the most famous breakbeat in history. The act was a recognition of the iconic importance of what *The Economist* called "a short burst of drumming [that] changed the face of music".

A 'breakbeat' is the drum part of a song played alone during an instrumental 'break'. In 'Amen Brother' the guitars, organ, bass and brass take a six second break at 1.26 to allow drummer Gregory Coleman to do his thing. His four-bar drum solo forms the famous 'Amen' break, which has appeared in sampled form on 2,000 plus records.

'Breaking' the rhythm away from a more regular beat can be as simple as replacing the second of each four-to-the-floor kick with a snare drum – think 'Billie Jean' – and as complex as rich 2-step grooves featuring double kick drums and a programming grid filled with snare rolls and ghost hits.

The break has been embraced by producers in numerous genres. With the advent of the sampler, early hip-hop producers began sampling breaks from '70s funk, soul and disco records, re-pitching, slicing and looping them using early Akai and E-MU samplers to create rhythmic beds over which melodies and words were laid.

It was the start of a long journey in the breakbeat's percolation of dance music that led to its uptake first in electro-funk, then rave, jungle and D&B, and finally the myriad genres under the broad church of 'breaks' – with acts including The Prodigy, Leftfield and The Chemical Brothers taking it to a new level of accessibility. Elsewhere, the breakbeat's legacy lives on in the raw, funky shapes of drum grooves in genres from 2-step through broken beat to chillout.

DEFINING CHARACTERISTICS

Although dozens of breaks are considered part of the 'classic' repertoire – Amen, Funky Drummer, Ashley's Roachclip – they share a number of common characteristics. Specifically they were all:

▸▸ **played by a real, talented, drummer**,

▸▸ **recorded with mics onto tape**, and

▸▸ **mixed using analogue desks and outboard**.

ZERO CROSSINGS

When setting sample start, end and loop points – whether you're dealing with one-shots, loops or multisamples – use zero-crossing points (i.e. where the sample waveform crosses the line of zero amplitude) to avoid unwanted clicks at the start and end of samples.

Many samplers offer a 'zero-crossing snap mode' to make the process quick and painless.

An alternative is to increase a sampler's amplitude envelope attack and release parameters or the audio clip's fade handles to manually smooth the start and end of samples.

These three facts have a number of implications that give the breaks an authenticity that blows away anything that even the best beatsmith can coax from their sampler:

▸▸ **Human groove:** There is no grid or metronome in operation, just the drummer's natural timing. Consequently some hits fall directly on the grid, but most are subject to carefully swung micro variations that alter the timing from hit to hit.

▸▸ **Real drums:** Not only does a top drummer know how to set up and tune their kit to get world class sounds, but when striking a real kit repeatedly, each hit is unique. Differences in the strength of the hit, the drummer and a stick's position on the drum all change from moment to moment, meaning you never get the same sound twice.

▸▸ **Studio recordings:** The drum kits were mic'd in unique configurations designed to enhance certain characteristics of the drums. Each mic introduced a unique character to the sound, as did the pre-amps, the sound of the room, the recording medium and the way in which the engineer mixed the mic channels and processed them in an analogue desk. Add in the fact that the drums were tracked to tape – often run hot – using all-analogue signal chains before being pressed to vinyl supplied layer

Chapter four
Using samples

upon layer of additional compression and pleasing saturation.

The combination of raw drumming talent and studio technique means that simply lining up kick, snare and hat samples onto a grid will only get you so far; the magic is in the mix, the groove, the processing, and the expression and variation of the hits – which is why many producers choose to slice up original breakbeats rather than recreate their own.

BREAKDOWN

If you do want to take on the challenge of creating your own break – or using breaks-style patterns in your own beats – start by analysing a raw breakbeat in an audio editor.

Fig 1, top right, shows the waveform for James Brown's 'Funky President' break – a single showcase bar of unadulterated funk. Look at it carefully against the 64 division grid. Note that certain hits fall wildly off-grid in places. Particularly noticeable are the snare drums, which are both delayed (aka swung, *page 38*) by different amounts.

Also note how the down-beat kick is bang on the grid whereas all the other elements are a bit late. This is likely because the kick in the original groove was slightly before the beat, but as it's been sampled and cut right on the beat, everything else feels late.

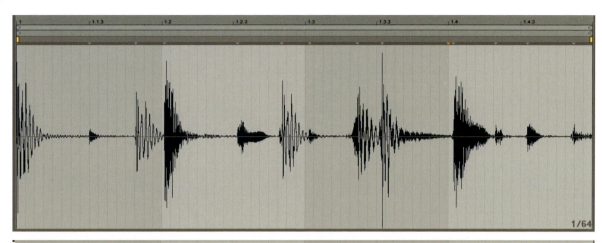

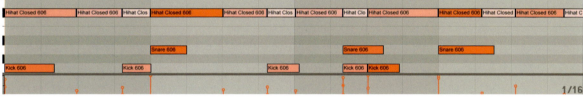

These timing differences – which play a key role in a beat's funkiness – need to be tamed to some extent for the dancefloor – DJs are unlikely to thank you for releasing a track that has kick drums that hit off- beat. So when working with classic breaks rule number 1 is to use warp or transient markers to ensure every kicks hit on the beat. It is in the space *between* the beats where you can let loose with swing and groove.

You can get further information about a groove by extracting the groove to MIDI. Fig 2 shows the same beat translated to MIDI. The resulting MIDI part gives a more

🎧⏺
Fig 1, top: Waveform for James Brown's 'Funky President' against a 64 division grid.

Fig 2, bottom: The same beat, extracted using Ableton's 'Convert to New MIDI Track' function – note the velocity differences.

transparent picture of the timing variations in the groove against a 16th note grid.

The MIDI file clearly shows that the high velocity hits – in dark red – are tight and form the main backbone of the groove, the off-beat hi-hats are fairly close to the grid, while the 16th note hats and ghost snares/kicks are more heavily swung by varying amounts (it's likely the last hat in the loop is swung too far and would require correction).

Using an extracted MIDI pattern and velocities gives a useful basis for creating your own breakbeats, explored in *'Making your own resampled break', overleaf.*

// WALKTHROUGHS

Make your own resampled break

1. To emulate the sound of a classic break sampled from vinyl find a breakbeat sample you like the feel of and extract it as a MIDI clip (page 45). This loop is from Sample Magic's Vintage Breaks Vol II sample pack. Check out the audio (db_kurtisbreak) and MIDI in the audio folder.

2. With the MIDI file placed on an instrument track in Logic Pro X, open an instance of Drum Designer with the 'SoCal' kit loaded. Now we have the groove and dynamics of the original sampled loop playing a completely different set of drum sounds. Tweak the drum sounds to taste.

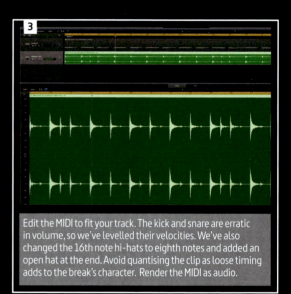

3. Edit the MIDI to fit your track. The kick and snare are erratic in volume, so we've levelled their velocities. We've also changed the 16th note hi-hats to eighth notes and added an open hat at the end. Avoid quantising the clip as loose timing adds to the break's character. Render the MIDI as audio.

4. For vintage-style compression, we've added an emulation of the classic UA 1176 (page 214) with a ratio of 8:1 coupled with a medium attack and fast release to up the impact of the transients. The 1176 is famed for adding not-so-subtle colour, increasing vibey authenticity.

5. We want our drums to sound like they were recorded to tape, with all the noise and temporal fluctuation that implies, so we've loaded u-he's Satin. For an oxidised vibe switch to Vintage Tape Mode and increase the Hiss and Wow & Flutter values in the Service panel.

6. IZotope's free Vinyl plugin emulates the crackle and warp of the vinyl to which our fictitious breakbeat would have been pressed. Set the Year and RPM knobs to 1970 and 45 respectively. The impact is profound – particularly at the lower end of the frequency spectrum.

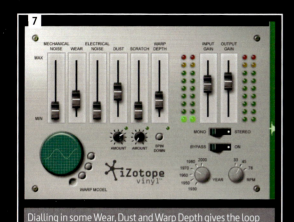

7 Dialling in some Wear, Dust and Warp Depth gives the loop more vintage flavours. The level has dropped by 3dB as a result of Vinyl's processing, so up the Output Gain. If the vinyl processing diffuses the low end, apply it in parallel to upper-split frequencies only (see *page 118* to set this up).

8 With the break processed, render it with its effects. Our intention is to use it in a D&B track. We could have edited the MIDI to create a unique D&B groove, but for old school authenticity we're doing it by slicing the processed audio up and rearranging it.

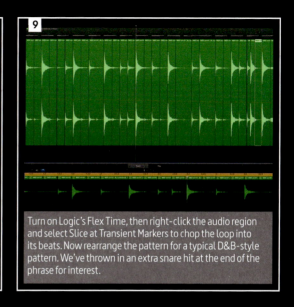

9 Turn on Logic's Flex Time, then right-click the audio region and select Slice at Transient Markers to chop the loop into its beats. Now rearrange the pattern for a typical D&B-style pattern. We've thrown in an extra snare hit at the end of the phrase for interest.

10 The basic groove now complete, use Logic's Join option to merge the slices into a new audio region. The result is a re-sequenced drum loop with an organic feel in terms of rhythm and timing, steeped in crusty old school production goodness.

11 There are two options for speeding the break up to 170bpm. For true retro timestretching, reach for Logic's Speed (FX) Flex Mode, which pitch shifts the audio up as the project tempo is raised, in the same way as a turntable or early sampler (*page 126*).

12 For a more breaksy sound, choose Rhythmic Flex Time mode, which keeps the loop at the same pitch regardless of the tempo.

Mixing samples

When it comes to the mix, the treatment of samples mainly depends on whether the sound has already been processed.

If you're using a **commercial sample library** – a string or drum library, say – or you've **sampled a sound yourself** – from a synth or using found sounds – you can usually treat it the same way you'd treat the original sound source. Compression, EQ and other effects are all fair game.

Things are different if the sample is **lifted from an existing recording**. Whether you're taking a hit or a longer loop, the sound you're sampling is likely to have already been compressed, EQd, mixed and mastered as part of the original mix. As such it is usually unnecessary to repeat the process. Indeed it can be counterproductive; compressing an already heavily compressed kick drum, for example, is likely to kill the dynamics in the sound.

The same applies to commercial sample packs that typically offer polished, ready-to-use sounds which have already been heavily processed. That's not to say you can't tune a sample, shape its envelopes or remove frequencies that don't fit your mix – indeed, you should be doing all of these – but avoid applying compression and/or EQ out of habit.

ISOLATING SAMPLES

Sampling from a commercial recording poses an additional problem: **it is very difficult to isolate individual parts from a mix**. One of the most asked questions online is: 'How do I extract a vocal from a recording?' Most of the time the results aren't great unless you have an instrumental mix too, when **phase inverting** one of the tracks can be employed – see Walkthrough, right.

Non-vocal parts are even tougher. No matter how hard you try, you're unlikely to get the part as clean as you want. That floor-rocking bassline you want to incorporate into a track, for example – even if it appears to occupy a distinct frequency range – will likely overlap with the kick in the low end and multiple synth and drum elements higher up the frequency range. The only neat solution is to find a section of the track where the element you want to sample plays solo. But it's not often you get that luxury.

In these cases, the usual techniques for semi-isolating a signal are to use **EQ bracketing** (page 211) or **bandwidth splitting** (page 118) to filter out frequencies above and below the target range – see Walkthrough, right. So if you just want the bass you might roll away signal around 200Hz. But it's a compromise, and you'll almost always end up with material outside of the target area. Sometimes the best option is to embrace the bits you don't want. Make them an integral part of the sonics of your track. A good example is the breakbeat from 'Think (About It)' by Lyn Collins, sometimes known as the 'Yeah! Woo!' break due to the vocal overlapping the drum break. The intrusion of the vocal hasn't stopped the break being sampled and used on hundreds of tracks by everyone from Venetian Snares and Squarepusher to Katy Perry and Miley Cyrus.

Prepping samples

You've scoured YouTube, dosed up on cult movies and listened to the funk output of the 1960s. Finally you've found the killer sample... There are now four steps to prepare the sample for use:

▶▶ **1: Trim**: Once you have the unedited source audio – as a recording into your DAW, an mp3, or any other kind of audio file – trim out the section you want. For basic editing purposes your DAW or the free Audacity (Mac, PC and Linux) is sufficient. For a one-shot sample, trimming the sound out of the recording is simple. Just set the trim points around the sample. If it's a loop, ensure the end point is in time so that the sample loops cleanly.

Tip / When trimming one-shots, particularly drum sounds, don't trim too tight. There's a lot of information in the first waveform cycles before the bulk of the sound hits. Equally, removing too much tail can leave you with an unpleasantly dry and snappy sound – sometimes the dusty, crackly tail is what a production calls for.

▶▶ **2: Normalize**: Normalise the sample to peak at 0dBFS.

▶▶ **3: Fades:** To avoid unwanted clicks, check the sample starts and ends on a 'zero crossing' (the point where the waveform crosses the zero axis). If you can't find suitable zero crossing points, apply short fades to the start and end.

▶▶ **4: Save (as Wav)**: Save your new sample in a suitable file format for your sampler. 24-bit Wav is often best – it's the uncompressed audio file format compatible with just about all audio software.

SEE ALSO
PAGE 34 — EXTRACTING THE SNARE FROM A DRUM LOOP

// WALKTHROUGHS

Isolating a bassline

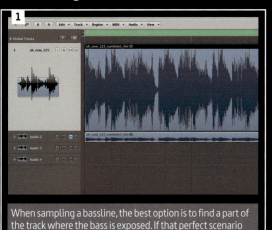

When sampling a bassline, the best option is to find a part of the track where the bass is exposed. If that perfect scenario doesn't exist it needn't be a problem. Here's the loop we're starting out with: a fully mixed and trimmed loop, with bass, music and beat elements all present.

We're approaching the isolation job using a split frequency approach. Start by duplicating the mixed music loop onto a second DAW track. Next, use high cut EQ to remove all signal above the bass frequencies (we've chosen a cutoff point of 186Hz with a 36dB/Oct slope).

On the second track cut out everything below a similar point – we've opted for 200Hz with a relatively gentle 18dB/Oct slope to avoid a 'hollow middle'. A steeper cut is then also applied to frequencies slightly above the previous 186Hz. Both tracks are then balanced to taste.

A-cappella extract – aka isolating a vocal

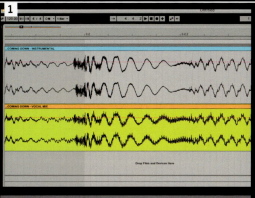

Isolating a clean vocal from a mix to produce an *a cappella is* possible – but you need an instrumental mix too. Start by creating two audio tracks, one for the vocal mix, one for the instrumental. Line up the files using the waveforms. The more exact the alignment, the better the result will be.

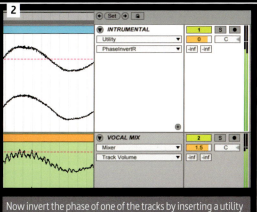

Now invert the phase of one of the tracks by inserting a utility plugin and turning on 'phase invert' for both right and left channels. If the tracks are perfectly aligned they will cancel each other out to produce silence, with the single different element – the vocal – left pretty much untouched.

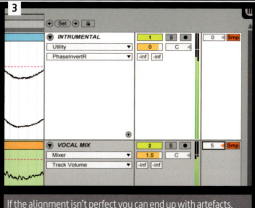

If the alignment isn't perfect you can end up with artefacts. To fine-tune the alignment use the 'track delay' parameter set to 'sample'. As the tracks get closer to perfect alignment the spectrum is filtered from low to high frequencies until the vocals are left untouched.

Chapter four
Using samples

The rights and wrongs of sampling

KEY QUESTIONS ANSWERED

I've found a sample in a commercial song that I want to use in my own track. Do I need to clear it?
It doesn't matter if you want to use a beat, *a cappella* or musical loop, *using another person's original sound recording without prior permission constitutes copyright infringement.*

Sampling without permission infringes copyright in three ways. Firstly, it is a breach of copyright in the **original sound recording**. Secondly, it is a breach of copyright in the **underlying music** (and, where applicable, lyrics) and thirdly, it constitutes an unauthorised use of one or more of the **performances** in the original work, such as a riff, hook or drum part.

Does this apply to *all* samples? Are short samples like drum hits OK?
In UK law, under the Copyright Designs and Patents Act 1988, in order for infringement to take place a 'substantial part' of a copyright work must have been used. Substantiality in UK law differs somewhat from its US counterpart, the doctrine of 'substantial similarity'. Moreover, US copyright law permits the defence of 'fair use', which has been invoked in a number of cases – although not always successfully.

So what is a 'substantial part'? The UK case of Produce Records Ltd vs BMG Entertainment Ltd (1999) established that **a 7.5 second** sample of 'Higher And Higher', a track originally recorded by The Farm, constituted infringement when appropriated by veteran Latino duo Los Del Rio for their summer hit 'Macarena'. In Ludlow Music Inc vs Williams (2000), a **two-line lyrical 'sample'** of the song 'I'm The Way' written by Loudon Wainwright III formed the basis of a dispute, with the judge ruling that the extent of the copying was substantial, "although not by much".

So is sampling a single drum hit OK? The answer can be no more certain than 'probably'. Copyright owners would have a tough job proving the use of a single drum hit was 'substantial' and there is the additional practical fact that if a drum sample is layered and tweaked it is nigh-on impossible to identify its source. *But* that won't shield you from court action if a copyright holder takes exception to your usage. Nor does it mean a judge will side with you if a case ever proceeds that far.

What about classic breaks?
Breakbeats – like Amen – have been sampled so many times in old and nu-school breaks and D&B that they sometimes feel as if they are part of a legitimate sample cannon. But they enjoy no dispensation from copyright and very few judges would take the line that the use of a full break was not 'substantial'.

What happens if I cut up/re-order or otherwise disguise a sample?
If no-one notices your sample use then you are likely to get away with it. Certainly you have a far better chance of dropping beneath the legal radar than those who use samples as they are. But if your disguised sample *is* identified then the ramifications for infringing copyright remain the same.

What happens if I I'm caught out?
If you are deemed to have breached copyright then a judge can make a number of demands. You might be required to pay a significant – perhaps unreasonable – percentage of royalties to the copyright holder. A stubborn publisher may demand 50-100 per cent of the publishing income for the privilege of using their words or music, something the Verve learned the hard way when, following the release of *Urban Hymns* in 1997, they were obliged to hand over 100 per cent of the royalties for 'Bittersweet Symphony' to Abkco Records.

In more extreme cases, an artist can be forced to withdraw a record from sale completely. In 2003, Indian composer Bappi Lahiri and Saregama India Limited sued Dr Dre and Universal Music for $500 million

SAMPLE NOW, PAY LATER?

Millions of artists around the world get away with copyright infringement every day – some of it blatant. The truth is that if your sample use isn't spotted by the copyright owner/s (or if they notice it and decide not to challenge you) then even though you may technically be breaking the law, you're unlikely to face consequences.

Be warned, though, that the moment the track in question blows up and you find yourself with a hit on your hands, you can pretty much guarantee the arrival of a legal letter. And publishers will be considerably more punitive in what they demand if you haven't gone about seeking permissions in what they and the law consider the 'right way'.

Chapter four
Using samples

over the use of an unlicensed sample on 'Addictive', the debut single from Truth Hurts' album *Truthfully Speaking*. Dre was also given an injunction preventing continued sale of the record which by then had shifted more than 200,000 copies.

I'm going legit. How do I legally clear a sample?
The good news is that most labels, publishers and artists are happy to give their permission to artists looking to re-work their music – for a fee. All you need do is track down the copyright holders.

Before doing so it's worth recapping the different royalties we're talking about. First, you'll need to find out who the original **writer(s)** of the work are, and which **publisher(s)**, if any, represent their interest or share of copyright in the song. Once you know the publisher and authors, you provide them with a copy of your new record, a copy of the original sampled record, and an isolated copy of the sample in question. The publisher is then in a position to consider price, contact the original composer(s) for permission(s) and start negotiations over copyright ownership and royalty splits on the new record.

Next, the **record company** must be asked for permission to use the **original sound recording**. Master rights have their own price tag, and sometimes artists or labels will refuse to give their permission to use a sample. If no permission is given, or the price tag is too high, you needn't abandon a project: as long as you can license the publishing rights, **sample recreation companies** like Replay Heaven should be able to construct an authentic-sounding reproduction of the recording.

It sounds like a lot of work.
It can be. The good news is there are agencies that will happily do this legwork for you, albeit at a price. Clearance companies like Sample Clearance Services can usually negotiate better rates than individual producers. These companies often also help with legal advice and expertise in dealing with overseas labels and publishers

How much will all this cost?
How long is a piece of string? Sample clearance companies usually charge a flat fee – somewhere between £275-£400 for a straightforward job. But that's just for *their* services. The fees to clear the samples themselves will be considerably higher and will depend on everything from the notoriety of the original record to the prominence of the sample in the new record, as well as your profile as an artist and likely sales of the new record.

For a track using a brief clip of a recording you may be able to settle at around £2,000-3,000. For more significant uses, the sky's the limit; Puff Daddy's 'I'll Be Missing You', which sampled the Police smash 'Every Breath You Take', costed a reported £500,000 in publishing royalties.

Are samples from sample libraries safe?
It depends. Reputable libraries ensure that all samples are 100 per cent copyright cleared. Less reputable ones don't. And even among reputable names, *check every license* before using a sample from a pack; some libraries carve out exemptions in their licence agreements that you wouldn't expect.

What about if I don't want to release the track? Do I still need permission to put it on SoundCloud or YouTube?
In theory, yes. Any track containing an uncleared sample should not be uploaded to the internet. Although largely untested legally, under UK copyright law putting a track online – even if not traditionally 'released' – would constitute a violation of the 'making available' or 'communication to the public' right which covers distribution via electronic means. In the US the Digital Millennium Copyright Act 1998 provides explicit protection against illegally downloading and distributing music. This means you need written permission from all copyright owners to use any samples contained in the track – including movie dialogue and speeches etc – even if you have no intention of making money by releasing a track.

(C) IN YOUR OWN TRACKS

If a track that *you've made* or remixed has been released by a record label, then you might still need permission – from that label – to upload it to sites like SoundCloud and YouTube.

Likewise if you had a publishing deal when you recorded the track, or are a member of a rights organisation like the PRS, or have already licensed your track to another user. All of these reasons may lead to unintentional infringement of copyright by uploading.

Uploading short excerpts instead of full tracks will put you on safer legal ground, but you're best off getting written permission from the label/publisher before doing even that.

Chapter five
Theory crash course

Chapter five
Theory crash course

Dance producers run a seamless gamut from grade eight theory masters...

...to those without any formal musical training at all, and tracks can employ compositional techniques from the kind of musical flourishes employed by Wagner and Bach to atonal noises and glitches above a pounding beat.

Although dance circles are still largely free of snobbery over the use, non-use or *abuse* of musical theory, understanding the basics of chord structure, scales and a few classic, if not *classical*, techniques for introducing tried and tested rhythmic and musical motifs to tracks can only be a good thing, expanding the musician's compositional palette and allowing greater control over a track's mood, energy and emotional shape.

This chapter doesn't claim to be an all-you-need guide to music theory, and if you're interested in deepening your knowledge, there are resources out there aplenty. But it does outline key principles, shows how to make use of them practically and relates theory to a range of example recordings.

KEYS AND CHORDS

Let's start at the beginning, with the blank keyboard or piano roll. The first terms you need to understand are 'scale' and 'key'. A **scale** is a series of notes ascending or descending the keyboard in pitch order, the first note of which (called the **tonic** or **root** note) defines the **key** of the scale.

The easiest scale (and key) to get to grips with is C major. C major (referred to as 'C' in notation) uses all the white keys on a keyboard and none of the black 'flats' or 'sharps'. The standard C major scale starts at C and ends at the C above, passing through, in order, D, E, F, G, A and B – see Fig. 1.

RELATIVE MINORS

The C major scale is easy to play and has a cheerful feel. For the kind of darker, more moody sound you find in most dance tracks, a better bet is often a minor scale.

Each major scale has a **relative minor** that uses the same notes but which starts and ends at a different place on the keyboard. In the case of C major, the relative minor is A minor (notated as Am), which starts and ends not on C, but on A.

Fig 2 shows the same notes of the C major scale, but with the different A minor start and end points highlighted in red.

Fig 1 (*top*): The scale of C major, starting and ending on C (shown in red).

Fig 2 (*bottom*): Natural A minor scale (starting and ending on the red As). It comprises the same notes as C major.

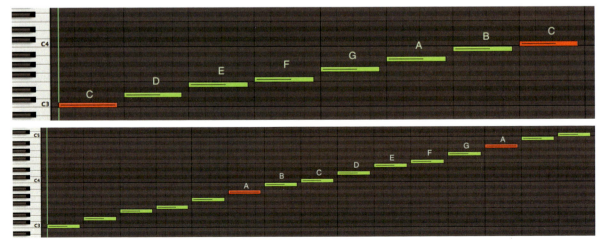

/ the secrets of dance music production

Chapter five
Theory crash course

MODES

By starting and ending a scale at a different point on the keyboard you can generate a range of different moods from the same series of notes. The standard major and natural minor scales are just two of seven **modes**.

If you play the notes of the C major scale but start and end on the following notes of the scale, you get these different modes:

- C – **Ionian** (standard major)
- D – Dorian ● Dorian Mode.mp3
- E – Phrygian ● Phrygian Mode.mp3
- F – Lydian
- G – Mixolydian ● Mixolydian Mode.mp3
- A – **Aeolian** (natural minor)
- B – Locrian ● Locrian Mode.mp3

Each mode has its own mood, with Aeolion the most widely used in dance music. For more mystical eastern vibes, take a listen to Kryptic Minds' 'Organic', with its introductory flute solo that makes effective use of the Phrygian mode.

TERMS OF THE TRADE
INTERVALS & SEMITONES

The term 'interval' describes the distance between pitches, typically notes in a scale.

A semitone is the distance from one note on the keyboard – including the black notes – to the next.

A tone comprises two semitones.

↻
Fig 3: C chord with E as the major third (left). Cm chord with Eb as the minor third (right). ●

↻
Fig. 4: The seven triads of C major. ●

MAJOR AND MINOR CHORDS

A **chord** is a 'stack' of notes played at the same time. Some of these stacks sound great, others less so, which has given rise to a long list of commonly used chords.

The most basic chord types are **major** and **minor** chords, the former sounding more upbeat than the darker minor. Whether a chord is major or minor is generally determined by the most 'descriptive' **interval** of the scale, the **3rd**.

In the case of C major the 3rd is E, in C minor Eb. The interval from C to E (four semitones) is known as a 'major third', from C to Eb (three semitones), a 'minor third' (Fig 3, below).

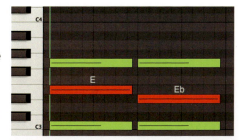

TRIADS

A chord can contain as many notes as you wish (on a piano the upper limit is the number of fingers that can be laid on the keyboard at any one time), though the most common is the **triad**, which contains three notes: the root, 3rd (major or minor) and 5th note of the scale.

Ascending the major scale in triads, you get seven chords. These form the basis for the chords conventionally available in that key.

In the case of C major (Fig 4, below), these are C major, D minor, E minor, F major, G major, A minor and B diminished, notated as C, Dm, Em, F, G, Am, Bdim respectively.

A **diminished triad** is one in which the fifth, rather than the third, is flattened. Because the fifth of a B minor or major triad is F# – a note not available in the key of C – the B triad that occurs in the key of C major has to be referred to as a diminished triad. Note that these are the same chords available in the relative minor (A minor).

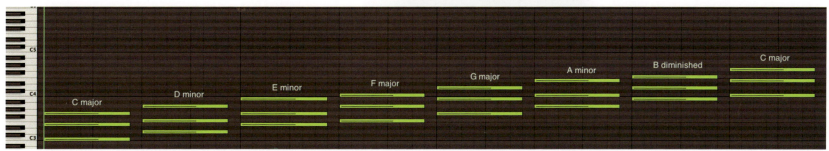

the secrets of dance music production /

BEYOND THE TRIAD: 7THS AND 9THS

You can get a long way in composition with no more than a handful of triads; just ask any number of trance or mainroom producers (and indeed, folk, country, pop, R&B and rock composers).

But things become more interesting when you add notes above a simple triad. These richer chords owe much to our musical heritage, with blues, jazz, soul and disco each gifting their own sonic flavours to the dance songwriter's arsenal.

The easiest amendment to the simple major triad is to add a 7th above the 5th (B in the case of C major, see Fig 5). This produces the popular **major 7th** 🎧 (maj7) chord – the jazz-influenced mainstay of a-million-and-one deep and disco-house tracks.

Minor 7ths 🎧 (m7) are just as simple, only this time the minor 3rd determines which note forms the corresponding 7th, lowering it by a semitone. In the key of C the minor 7th chord consists of C, Eb, G and Bb (Fig 5).

If you're of a deep or classic house writing persuasion, spend a little time experimenting with 7th chords – both major and minor. For a starting progression try Fmaj7 – Em7 – Fmaj7; it's easy to play but with the right soft-synth or Rhodes sample it can sound great. The Masters at Work classic 'To be in Love' is a showcase in how to make the most of lush sevenths.
🎧 *Check out the MIDI track in the Walkthrough folder and turn to page 155 for the full MIDI note notation.*

Inserting 7th chords into an arrangement is a fail safe way of giving tracks an authentic classic house feel, but you can widen your writing palette further by adding a 9th or two.

In many ways 9ths are easier to work with than 7ths as the note added is the same regardless of whether the original triad is major or minor. In the case of C major or minor the 9th is D, generally played an octave and a tone above root C.

The classic **minor 9th** 🎧 (m9) chord is heard regularly in dance music with the kind of dark, heavily reverbed chord stabs found in techno and dub techno.

🎧
Fig 5 (*left*): To create major 7th and 9th chords start with a standard triad (C, E and G in C major) then place a major 7th on top (B) to create a Cmaj7 chord. Add the 9th above this (D) for the soulful Cmaj9.

(*Right*): The Cm7 and Cm9 chords differ in two ways: the initial third is a minor third (Eb rather than E) and the 7th is a minor 7th (Bb rather than B).

SAMPLED CHORDS

The technique of sampling a chord and mapping it across the keyboard to be triggered by a sampler has played a central role in countless house and UK garage hits – think Soul 2 Soul's 'I Feel Love' and Todd Edwards' 'Steal Your Heart'. As the same chord is triggered at different pitches, the harmonics are shifted up and down to create that unique 'sampled' sound.

But there is an alternative to triggering a single chord in this way, which is to actually *replay* the chord at different points on the keyboard. Example 🎧 Sampled C minor 7.mp3 reveals what a Cm7 chord sounds like as it moves up and down in pitch. In the first pass the same minor seventh chord is played on a keyboard at various pitches (Fig 6, left). Second time around the same progression uses a single sampled Cm7 chord (Fig 6, right). The difference is striking, the second giving a classic old-school flavour brimming with tasty harmonics.

Chapter five
Theory crash course

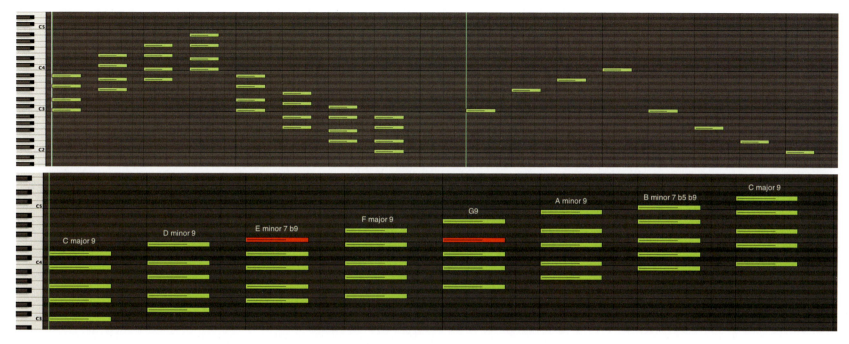

What's happening here in theory terms? If you look again at the triads available in the key of C major (*page 144*), you can see that a major triad can only be played on C, F or G (I, IV or V) and stay in key. Hence, a sampled major triad whose root note is played on any other note than the first, fourth or fifth degree of the major scale will be out of key; if the root is D, for example, you end up playing a D major triad, the major third of which is F# – a note not present in C major.

Things get more awkward when sampling more harmonically complex chords like 9ths as the intervals that make up the chord are increasingly less likely to stay in key. *Fig 7* shows all of the 9th chords ascending in the key of C major. To keep the third chord on the E in the key of C major, an F has to be used as the top note rather than F#. This means you can't play a standard minor or major 9 chord but instead have to play a b9 chord, with F (highlighted in red) as the 'flattened' 9th of E. Problems arise again with the fifth chord, where the minor 7 above the major G triad makes it a dominant 9th. While three different chords in the key of C can stay in key when playing major triads, when playing major 9ths only two chords – I and IV – can stay in key.

This example reveals how limiting it can be sticking to rigid theoretical rules. In this case, they can be solved in a moment by

Fig 6 (top): The difference between replayed and sampled chords: First time around the same minor 7 chord is triggered at various pitches, specifically Cm7, F#m7, Am7, Cm7; Cm7, Gm7, D#m7, Cm7. On the second pass the same sampled chord is triggered at C, F#, A, C; C, G, D#, C.

Fig 7 (bottom): Why only two 9th chords can stay in key.

retriggering sampled chords old-school style and ignoring whether the constituent notes remain in key when played at different pitches. Theo Parrish's 'Ebonics' is a case in point. Here a sampled minor 9 chord is triggered at six different pitches – the chord itself acting as melody. The consequence is that a number of intervals in many instances of the chord are technically out of key, but the result isn't discordant nastiness – it's a unique, dark, feel that gives the track its character.

Which is all to say that while some knowledge of music theory can be useful, a willingness to break the conventions often delivers more interesting results.

Chapter five
Theory crash course

Chord progressions

INTRODUCTION

There are a large number of dance tracks that riff around a single chord. But you can significantly up the emotional ante by employing chord **progressions** or sequences. Because each chord supplies its own unique feel, you can begin building arrangements that toy with tension, anticipation and resolution. Progressions across all genres use similar principles.

Before looking at common progressions, it's important to understand how different chords are described.

Spend more than a few minutes studying music theory and you'll be confronted by rows of roman numerals. This **numerical system** is a simple way of notating chord progressions in terms of each chord's distance from the scale's root (*page 144*).

In the case of C major, the numbers and chords are shown in *Fig 8, below*, with F sitting at position IV and G at V.

The chords in a C minor scale are shown in *Fig 9, below bottom*. While the first chord is still recognised as being chord number I in the scale, the 'i' is written in lower case this time to show it is a minor chord. By using lower case numerals for minor chords and upper for major, it's easy to differentiate between the two, a common example progression being I, IV, V, vi, I.

Fig 8 (*top*): The triads of C major, notated as numbered chords.

Fig 9 (*bottom*): The triads of C minor.

The beauty of the number system is that it allows musicians to easily move a progression into a different key if they want, for example, to ensure a song falls within a singer's natural vocal range.

CIRCLE OF FIFTHS

We now know how to notate chords, but how do we know – of the hundreds available for use – which chords will work when arranged into progressions?

The answer, like much in music, is largely down to trial and error, but a useful tool for identifying chords that might work in a sequence is the 'circle of fifths', *Fig 10*. Moving clockwise around the cycle, the key goes up in fifths for both major (on the outside) and minor (inside).

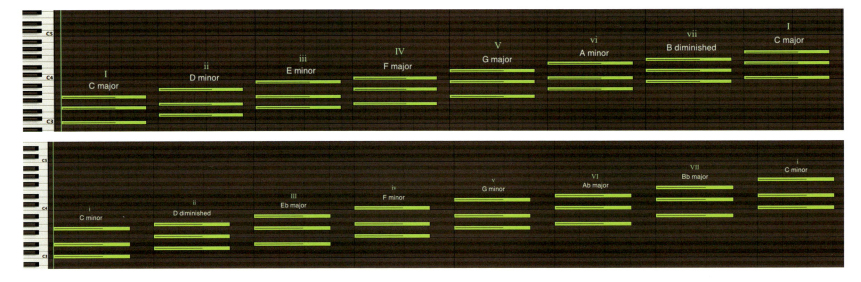

Chapter five
Theory crash course

The circle (sometimes known as cycle) of fifths is, among other things, a great tool for working out the chords in a given key. Using the key of C major as an example, the notes either side of C denote the other two major chords in that key, F and G (numerically IV and V). The note on the inside of the circle is its relative minor, Am (vi). The two chords on either side of that (Dm and Em) are the other minor chords that occur in the key (ii and iii).

The same works inversely for minor keys: in E minor for instance, the Bm and Am chords are both minors, G is the relative major with C and D the other two available major chords.

What use is the circle in practical terms? When crafting a chord progression, if you choose a root key and extend out in short steps along both the inside and outside of the circle, you'll end up using chords that are almost guaranteed to work well together. The further you stray from the root key, the less comfortably chords will sit.

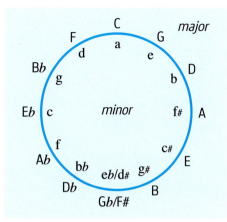

Fig 10: The circle of fifths, showing major chords on the outside of the circle and minor on the inside. Note that the 7th triad in a major scale (and the 2nd in a minor) is diminished. It sits two to the left (anticlockwise) of the key.

Fig 11: Demonstration of anticipation and resolution in the key of A minor.

ANTICIPATION AND RESOLUTION

The best experiences in life – eating, travel, partying, sex – are about anticipation followed by payoff. The same is true in music and, directly or indirectly, the majority of successful chord progressions rely on the twin musical concepts of anticipation followed by resolution. Those that resolve unexpectedly, delay their resolution or do not resolve at all are often even more powerful.
The fact that the mind of the listener naturally anticipates a chord progression resolving can be used to great effect.

'Tristan Und Isolde' by Wagner is a great example of this, notable when it was first played for its long, unresolved, tension-building progressions, and while harmonically a good deal more complex than anything an electronic music producer is likely to attempt, it's a superlative example of the power that anticipation and resolution in music can have.

A chord progression is said to 'resolve' when it progresses from a chord suggesting anticipation to a chord suggesting stability and 'closure' – which is almost always the tonic/root chord of the scale.

If you play a simple progression in A minor, for example (Fig 11), you can hear how the third chord, F major, leaves the listener anticipating a resolve to the root chord of the scale. The listener's expectations are satisfied when the chord progression resolves to A minor at the end.
Nicky Romero's 'Like Home' offers a

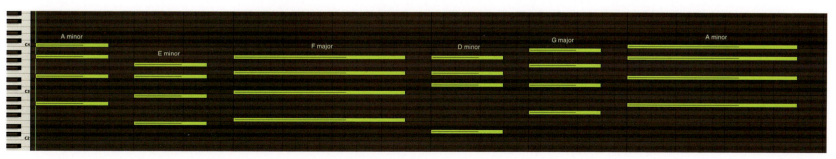

Chapter five
Theory crash course

real-life example of the same kind of movement. The Bb major chord builds anticipation towards the Dm resolution (by way of C major) (*Fig 13, below*). Incidentally, the first C major chord provides a good example of a chord **inversion**, explained in detail below.

But resolution doesn't always have to feel this comfortable. For a less predictable example, listen to the sampled vocals that form the introduction to the Black Box classic 'Ride On Time'. During the words '...*love away*' the progression resolves from Dm7 b5 to a straight Am (*Fig 12, right*). The unusual resolution surprises the listener, as the b5 in the Dm7 b5 chord would conventionally place the progression in the key of C minor rather than A minor.

A third example of a progression that riffs on the natural anticipation of resolution can be found in the verses of the Zedd track 'Spectrum' (*Fig 13, bottom*). After the second instance of the Bb chord, instead of resolving to the expected Cm (the track is in the key of C minor), it resolves to C *major*. The major 3rd, responsible for this unexpected uplift, is highlighted in red. While classic vi–I and IV–V–I progressions

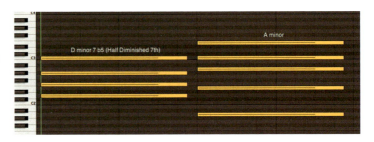

Fig 12: Dm7b5–Am from 'Ride on Time'.

**Fig 13 (*top*): Nicky Romero 'Like Home'.
Fig 13 (*bottom*): Zedd 'Spectrum'.**

are surefire chordal winners for floor-filling anthems, these examples show that the transition from anticipation to payoff can be turned around to bring moments that surprise too, toying with expectations and often extending the euphoria.

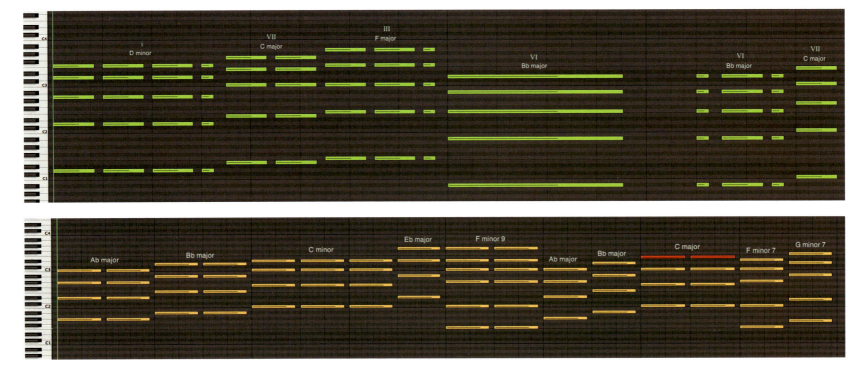

Chapter five
Theory crash course

Taking chords further: voicing and inversions

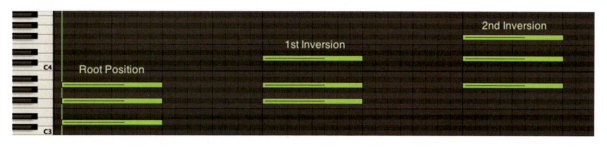

INTRODUCTION

Chord progressions can be further developed using alternative **voicings** and **inversions** of chords.

Ordinarily a triad's lowest note is the root. In the case of a D major triad in 'root position', for example, D is the lowest note.

Voicing simply means changing the order of notes or 'voices' that make up the chord and a chord is said to be **inverted** when the lowest note isn't the root. The same D major chord can be voiced differently by moving root D to the top of the chord and making the chord's lowest note its major 3rd, F#. This creates a **D major 1st inversion** (Fig 14). If the next interval in the chord (the 5th, A) is used as the lowest note, the chord becomes a **D major 2nd inversion**.

Rearranging chords using inversions gives the composer far more freedom when crafting progressions, generating subtly different moods from the same set of notes and, significantly, allowing progressions to flow more easily, avoiding big jumps in pitch that can give a disjointed feel.

An illustration of the effectiveness of inversions can be seen by returning to Nicky Romero's 'Like Home' and re-voicing it so that the original chords as outlined in Fig 13, opposite left, are played as triads in root position (Fig 15, below) rather than as the inverted originals. Comparing the two versions of the track demonstrates how much more musical a progression can be when triads are revoiced using inversions; the feel of the original phrase is more natural and fluid, with none of the second version's awkward jumpiness.

🎧
Fig 14 (above): The triad of D major in root position and with its two inversions. 🔴

🎧
Fig 15 (below): A simplified rewrite of Nicky Romero's 'Like Home' that eschews inversions in favour of straight triads, the root placed at the bottom of each chord. Compare this with the same chord progression using inversions in Fig 13, opposite. Note that the octave bassline has been removed in this example, leaving just the basic triad chords on top. 🔴

There are also good mix reasons for choosing inversions over triads, namely that you have far greater control over which notes are played and therefore which areas of the frequency spectrum an instrumental part is allowed to inhabit. So if you find that a keyboard, for example, is straying too far into bass territory, a simple re-voicing of the chords to shift the notes up may be all that's needed to solve frequency overlaps.

A common compositional technique is to shift the bass off the root and onto another note of the chord to create an inversion. Look again at the original notation of 'Like Home' and note how the E in the bassline inverts the C major chord above (even though the chord itself doesn't shift). Using voicing also allows for the epic-sounding upward projectory from D minor to F major by way of E rather than root C.

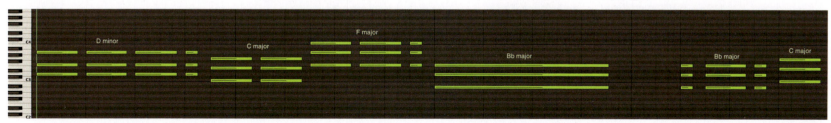

Chapter five
Theory crash course

CHANGING A CHORD WITH THE BASS

Adding basslines that toy with inversions is one way of breaking away from simple rooted chords. But you can open up a whole range of new flavours by writing basslines that use notes not found in the chords above at all.

A good example of this is found in Burial's 'Archangel'. The opening chord of the main sample, shown in *Fig 16*, is Cm. However, the use of Ab – a note not found in a C minor triad – in the bassline in the next four bar section (shown in red) changes the combined chord to an Ab major 7 (Abmaj7). In this instance, the bass note introduces a different and unexpected flavour to the chord.

'Verbena Tea' by Teebs is a second, beautifully simple example of how a bassline can change the feel of the chords (or in this case, *chord*) above. The chords for the verses are displayed in Fig 17. The progression uses a simple sustained D# minor triad throughout, forming the top three notes of each chord. However, the context of this repeated triad is changed by the notes of the bassline. In the first two chords, the D# minor triad forms the upper notes of a Bmaj7 chord. In the third, the D# in the bassline puts the chord in root position. In the final chord, the bass slips down to G# to form a G#m9 chord.

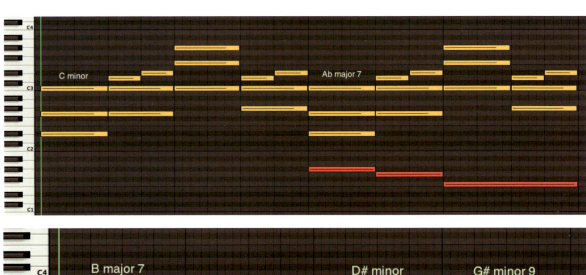

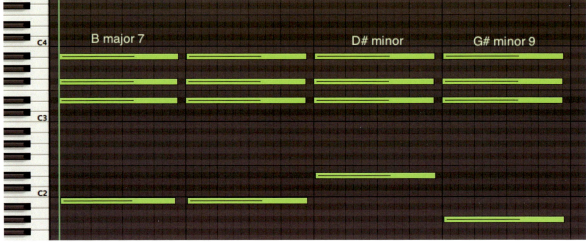

Note: The lack of minor 3rd in the G#m9 means the chord could also be notated as G#m9 (omit 3) – signifying the omission of the 3rd in the chord.

It's worth studying the scores of disco classics in the Chic/Sister Sledge vein for masterclasses in how an energetic, ever-moving bassline can dramatically change

Fig 16 (top): Chords for 'Archangel' by Burial. Note the red-shaded bassline.

Fig 17 (bottom): The simple but beautiful 'Verbena Tea' by Teebs, the bass used to change the chords.

the feel of the often simple chordal guitar and keyboard progressions above.

Although using a bassline to alter chord progressions is fairly common, other instruments can be used to the same end. Burial, for example, could just as effectively have replaced the bass sound with a low string sample or pad drone.

Chapter five
Theory crash course

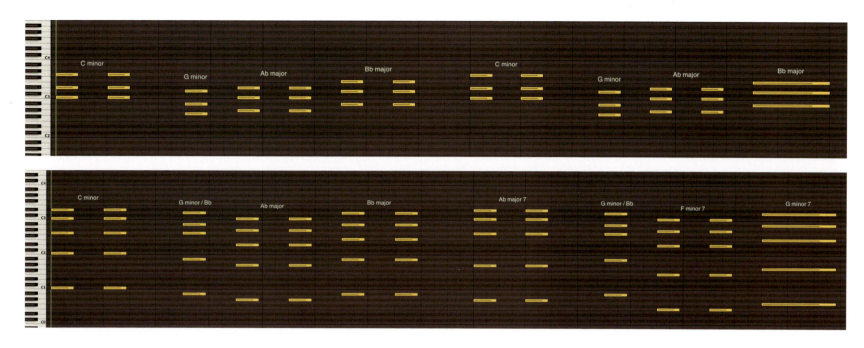

THEORY INTO PRACTICE

Let's use a couple of the techniques outlined so far to create variations on a simple chord progression.

Fig 18 shows a simple progression using the triads i-v-VI-VII in the scale of C minor. The chords are all shown in root position. Take a listen to the MIDI file; it's a nice enough progression but it lacks movement and variety.

There are a number of ways to develop the sequence so that it sounds more fluid and engaging. As the progression pretty much repeats itself, you can also use the bassline to create a variation in the second half of the phrase while still maintaining a sense of continuity.

Fig 19 shows a refined version of the same progression. First time around, the chords are kept the same only with different voicings, allowing a smoother transition between each chord.

But that's not all that's changed. The bassline adds further interest, with the descending C, Bb, Ab in the bass creating a 1st inversion of the Gm chord and allowing a flowing progression between the chords. So-called 'walking' basslines like this are common across the musical landscape –

Fig 18 (*top*): Before – a simple i-v-VI-VII progression in C minor. This is the file 'Example progression' in the Walkthrough folder.

Fig 19 (*bottom*): After – a mix of inversions and the addition of a moving bassline has transformed the vanilla original into something more fluid and interesting. 'Example progression 2' in the Walkthrough folder.

Paul Johnson's classic 'Get, Get Down' is *the* definitive example.

To add further interest the second time around, a number of chords are changed by virtue of non-root notes in the bass part. So the Cm chord from the first turnaround becomes Ab7 when the bass reaches down to Ab rather than sticking to root C. Meanwhile, the ascending F and G bass notes in the final two chords turn the Ab and Bb triads to Fm7 and Gm7.

The example shows how by using a mix of revoicing and bassline movement a simple chord progression can be transformed into something far more interesting.

More chords and progressions

11THS AND 13THS

While 7ths and 9ths open up thousands of compositional avenues, there's no reason to stop there – you can keep stacking up notes to create ever more complex chords, the jazzy, soulful flavours of which are used across the house and downtempo landscape. Generally speaking, where the 2nd, 4th or 6th notes of the scale are added to a 7 chord above the octave of the root note, they are referred to as the 9th, 11th and 13th respectively, *see Fig 20, right*.

ADDED TONE CHORDS

But there are other means of introducing new flavours to chords that don't rely on moving upwards in the scale. An **added tone chord** refers most commonly to the addition of the 2nd, 4th or 6th degree of the scale to a regular triad chord – typically *in the same* octave. Added tone chords differ from 9, 11 and 13 chords in that they don't contain the 7th of the scale. So an 'Eb minor add2' chord (*Fig 21, right*) comprises the root (Eb), the 3rd (F#), the 5th (Bb) and the added 2nd, F. The result is a complex, dark – oppressive even – chord, the kind used by techno and adventurous D&B producers.

You can hear a sampled Eb minor add2 chord in Theo Parrish's 'Command Your Soul' in the piano lead.

SUSPENDED CHORDS

A suspended or 'sus' chord, is a chord which ignores the minor or major 3rd and contains the root, fifth and the 2nd or 4th note of the scale in between. The lack of a minor or major third creates anticipation, making the chord feel as if it is moving somewhere.

In the Theo Parrish example noted above, if the same chord had the minor 3rd (Gb) omitted, it would be an Eb sus 2, or Eb suspended 2nd chord (*Fig 22*). (And if the 4th note had been used instead, the chord would be an Eb sus 4). The common feel of these sustained notes is the lack of completion – they cry out for resolution.

IN PRACTICE

The Kerri Chandler track 'You Are In My System' (*Fig 23, opposite*) makes generous use of sustained chords alongside inversions and 7ths, bringing together much of what has been discussed in this chapter. The sampled 3rd inversion m7 chord is still in key when played on the Eb as the 5th chord of a natural minor scale is also a minor 7. The inversion itself places the 7th right beneath the tonic note of the chord, creating a sound typical of disco and house

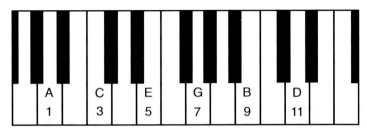

Fig 20: An Am11 chord in root position – the additions of the second and fourth note of the scale (B and D) above the 7th forming the 9th and 11th respectively.

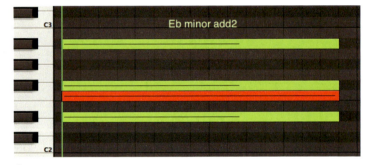

Fig 21: An Ebm add2 chord features the root, 3rd and 5th (in this case Eb, F# and Bb) with the added 2nd, shown in red, F. Note that if the F was an octave higher, the chord would be an Eb minor add 9 chord. If the F was an octave higher *and* the minor 7th, Db, was also present, the chord would be a standard Eb minor 9.

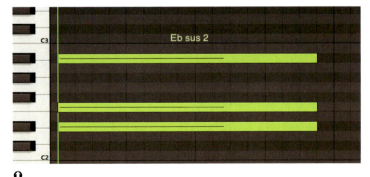

Fig 22: Eb sus 2 featuring the root, Eb, the 2nd (F) and the 5th (Bb).

Chapter five
Theory crash course

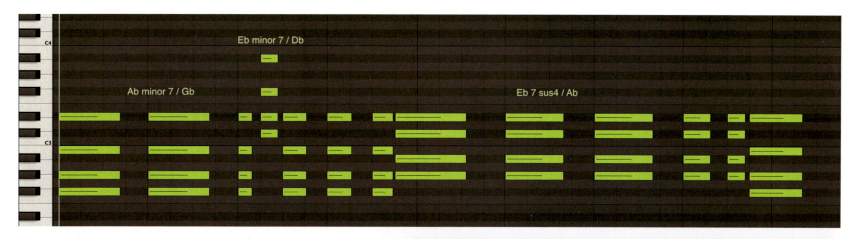

chords. Another example of a 7 inversion creating this same kind of sound is found in the opening inverted D7 in 'Rain', also by Kerri Chandler, which is voiced A, C#, D, F#.

Naming the Eb dominant 7 sus4 chord in the second half of the phrase is tricky. The position of the Eb in the Ab minor scale suggests it is a minor chord – Eb is the 5th note in the Ab minor scale, so the chord on that note of the scale would generally be referred to as Eb minor. In addition, the 7th of the chord is a minor 7th. However, the inclusion of the 4th, Ab, in place of the minor 3rd, Gb, makes the chord a suspended 4th – specifically a first inversion Eb dominant 7 suspended 4th, or Eb7 sus 4 / Ab.

Chic's 'Good Times' (*Fig 24*) and the MAW classic 'To Be In Love' (*Fig 25*) both showcase a range of more harmonically complex progressions.

Fig 23: The chords of 'You Are in My System'.

Fig 24: 'Good Times' by Chic. Disco loveliness exemplified.

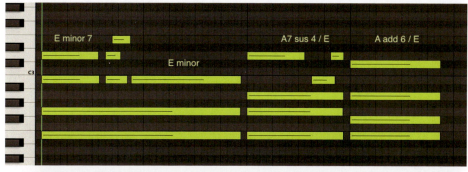

Fig 25: A prime example of more harmonically complex 9, 11 and 13 chords in action – the 'MAW Dub' version of Masters At Work's 'To Be In Love'. The chords shown are those that make up the opening string progression. The Cm13 chord – voiced C, Eb, G, Bb, D, F, Ab – contains every note of the C minor scale.

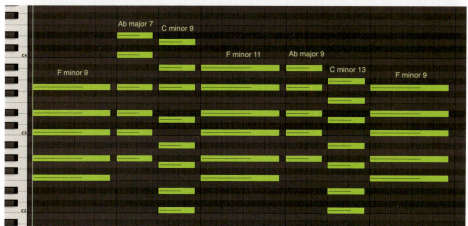

the secrets of dance music production /

Chapter five
Theory crash course

Melodies and toplines

You're not going to write a club-rockingly fantastic topline by following a set of theoretical guidelines. That said, there are a range of techniques that crop up time and again in both underground and crossover hits. An understanding of how they work can help when crafting melodies and give insights into how they might be developed further.

CONTRARY MOTION

The term **contrary motion** describes the movement of two melodic parts in opposite directions.

In dance music, which typically deals with fewer melodic parts than orchestral arrangements, instances of contrary motion tend to occur between the bassline and lead. The Prodigy's 2009 hit, 'Invaders Must Die', is a good example.

Here the driving bassline initially descends in pitch while the lead that enters at 0.42 moves upwards (*Fig 27, below*). The contrast in melodic trajectories creates an extra lift in the progression. Although both melody and bassline are strong in their own right, when played together the contrary motion adds a new dimension to the track.

For another striking example return to Burial's 'Archangel' from the 2007 album *Untrue*, where the string sample (taken from Harry Gregson-Williams' score for a cut scene in the game 'Metal Gear Solid 2') runs in contrary motion to the bass.

The ascending pattern of the top melody is C, D, Eb, and Ab – notes 1, 2, 3 and 6 of an ascending C minor scale (*Fig 26, above right*). The simplest potential bassline would follow an ascending pattern starting on the C – effectively mirroring the lead. But Burial takes the contrary route instead, bass moving down the C minor scale from Ab through G to F. The increased sense of tension as the melodies work against each other results in a complex, moody combined sound.

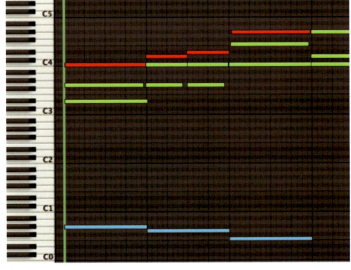

Fig 26: Burial's 'Archangel', melody in red and contrary bass in blue.

Fig 27: The Prodigy's 'Invaders Must Die', bass in yellow, lead in red.

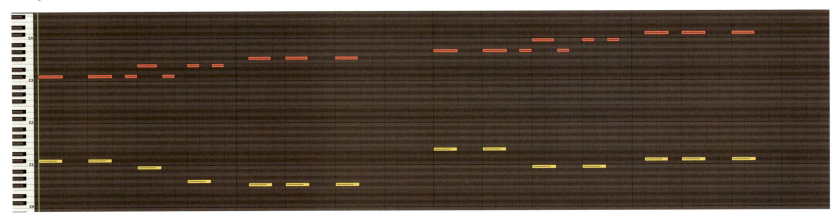

Chapter five
Theory crash course

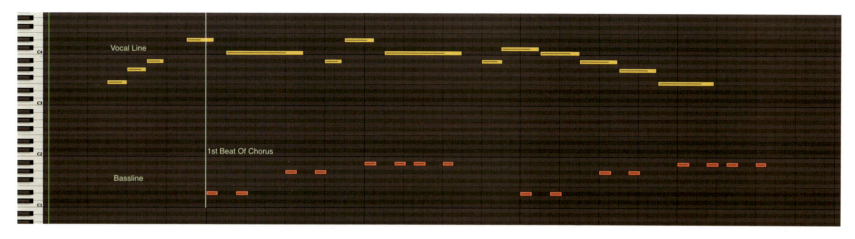

ANACRUSIS

An **anacrusis** is a note or series of notes in a melody that occurs before the first beat of a bar. The musical device can be used to lead a listener into a chorus or melody line, to generate a brief sense of anticipation, to provide continuity between musical phrases – or it can just give a tune an extra 'catchy' element, the ultimate precursor to an ear-worm-style chorus hook.

Commonly cited examples are found in the songs 'Happy Birthday' and 'We Wish You a Merry Christmas', in which the start of each chorus – the words "Happy" and "We" respectively – occur before the first downbeat of the line. In the Beatles' 'Yellow Submarine', the words "In the" form the anacrusis before "town" hits on the beat.

In dance music, a more relevant example can be found in the vocal part of the chorus

◯ Fig 28: Disclosure, 'You and Me'. Vocalist Eliza Doolittle's "So please don't let" enters before the first beat of the chorus.

◯ Fig 29: Anucrusis in Pendulum's 'Slam'.

to Disclosure's track 'You And Me' featuring Eliza Doolittle (Fig 28). The first four words of the vocal line – "So please don't let go, 'cos you know, exactly what we've found" – occur before the first beat of the chorus, leading into the 'drop' of the first beat.

You can see above how this technique works in conjunction with the bass (which drops out temporarily to up the tension), and hear how it makes the transition from the long build to chorus even more impactful. Incidentally, the second half of the phrase features an example of contrary motion between bassline and vocal.

But anacrusis doesn't have to be confined to vocal parts. Fig 29 notates the catchy lead melody line from Pendulum's 2005 anthem 'Slam', where the first three notes of the melody (it hits at the 1.36 mark) anticipate the first beat of the track's 'chorus', which enters on the fourth note of the melody line.

the secrets of dance music production / 157

Chapter five
Theory crash course

ARPEGGIOS AND ARPEGGIATORS

The term **arpeggio** is derived from the Italian *arpeggiare* meaning 'to play the harp'. It refers to the technique of playing through the notes of a chord one after another rather than all together.

The audio example 🎧 Chord/arpeggio Cmaj 7.mp3 (*Fig 30*) features a C7 chord played as a one-shot covering two octaves voiced C, E, G, B, C, E, G, B. Second time around the same chord is played but this time arpeggiated – first going up the scale, then back down.

A commonly used technique in classical music, arpeggios allow the composer to give chords movement. Where an arrangement lacks momentum, arpeggios can be used to rhythmically shape melodies. Famous examples include Chopin's 'Op. 25 # 12 'Ocean' Etude' and Scharwenka's 'Piano Concerto #1 in Bb Minor'. In the pop world, REM's 'Everybody Hurts' and Louis Armstrong's 'What a Wonderful World' both feature prominent arpeggios.

In dance music, where rhythm often trumps melody, custom-built arpeggiators on synths and soft synths give producers the means to create often complex arpeggios at the touch of a button. Indeed many arpeggiators allow you to break up and mess with chords in ways that would not technically be referred to as arpeggiated –

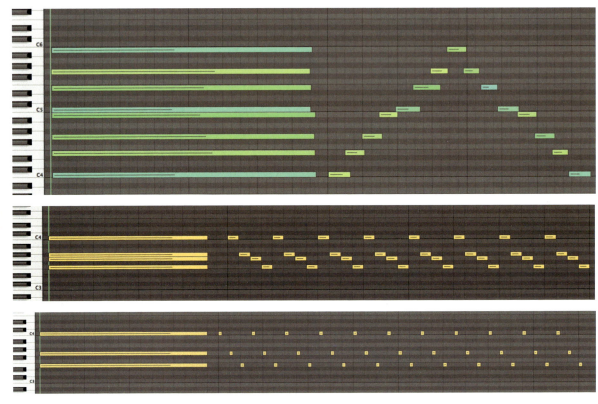

such as triggering the whole chord on each step of the arpeggio.

Accent, envelope and swing functions on many arpeggiators give them additional rhythmic flexibility, allowing producers to beef up the rhythmic credentials of synth lines in parallel with – and sometimes in lieu of – more traditional beat elements.

A simple but effective example of an arpeggio is found in Burial's track 'Loner', from the *Kindred* EP. At around 1.23 a

🎧
Fig 30 (*top*): A C7 chord, played as it is and then arpeggiated up and down. 🎧

Fig 31: The downward Fm add 2 arpeggio from 'Loner'. 🎧

Fig 32 (*bottom*): Frankie Knuckles' 'Your Love'. 🎧

downwards-arpeggiated F minor add 2 chord plays. The piano roll in *Fig 31* shows the chord and then the arpeggiated version as it sounds in the track. Like many arpeggios used in dance music, the repetition of the downward phrase means it is also an example of **ostinato** (*page 160*), its 16th note rhythm adding momentum and a driving energy to the track.

'Your Love' by the late Frankie Knuckles, also uses a downward arpeggiated chord, this time a 1st inversion C major. What's

Chapter five
Theory crash course

interesting here is the rhythmic interplay between arpeggio and beat. You can see from Fig 32 (left) how the first note of the arpeggiated chord – the C – lands on the beat every three bars, rather than the expected four. This rhythmic juxtaposition (a form of **polyrhythm – page 28**) adds interest and unpredictability to the progression, toying with listener expectations and rejecting convention.

ARPEGGIOS – NEXT STEPS

Daft Punk make frequent use of classical composition techniques, like the arpeggiated lead line from *Discovery*'s 'Aerodynamic' (Fig 33, below) that in his book *We Are The Robots* author Alan Di Perna brands as "impossible, ridiculous Yngwie guitar arpeggios".

Part of the reason Di Perna calls them impossible is because both the order of notes and the notes themselves would not (and could not) feature in any sequence triggered by an arpeggiator. The B minor, G# diminished and A major chords in the progression, for example, each play with an alternating pattern, whereas the third chord, E minor, plays a straight up/down arpeggio pattern. Rather than sustaining the same arpeggiated chord over a changing progression, 'Aerodynamic' takes classic arpeggiation as a starting point then re-sequences the chord progression to turn the expected patterns – both metaphorically and practically – on their head.

It's likely Daft Punk achieved the end result by playing the 'arpeggios' on a guitar – thus bypassing the limitations of a mechanical arpeggiator. But you could get a similar result by starting with 'vanilla' arpeggiation then sampling, cutting and re-arranging the sequence. The moral of the tale? Many compositional techniques can be used as starting points on which to stamp your style.

(Incidentally, Daft Punk's love affair with the humble arpeggio doesn't end with 'Aerodynamic'. You'll find simpler – and truer – arpeggios in the laid-back 'Voyager' too at the 2.14 mark.)

PRO TIPS
REBOOT

"To get the lead sound [on "Piece of Cake" – from the *Alive* album], I mainly used the Access Virus TI with its great arpeggiator. To modify the hook and keep it vibrant, I added some random MIDI note fills in Ableton."

Fig 33: The 'impossible, ridiculous' arpeggios in Daft Punk's 'Aerodynamic'.

WHAT ARE THOSE..?
Chord progressions

Avicii – 'Levels': **i-III-VII-VI**

Nicky Romero – 'Like Home': **i-VII-III-VI**

Swedish House Mafia – 'Don't You Worry Child': **VII-i-VI-VI**

Disclosure – 'You and Me': **iv-VII-i-i**

Burial – 'Archangel': **VI-V-iv-iv**

Black Box – 'Ride On Time': **i-III-VI-VII**

N-joi – 'Anthem': **i-VII-IV-VII** (note how the IV chord being a major rather than a minor puts the piece in a Dorian mode)

Nicky Romero & David Guetta – 'Metropolis': **VI-VII-i-vVI-v-iv-iv**

Daft Punk – 'Around The World': **v-VI-i-i**

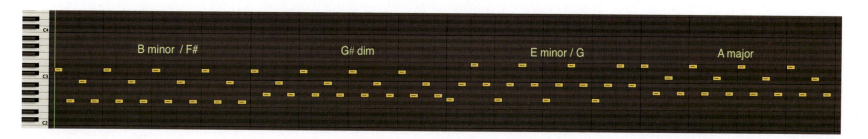

Chapter five
Theory crash course

OSTINATO

An **ostinato** is a melodic or rhythmic motif that repeats. Alternatively referred to as a 'riff' or 'hook', an ostinato is the part of a composition that listeners latch on to, that they remember, and in some cases, that they sing along to. An ostinato is often the defining motif of a song, used to establish familiarity and create continuity between different sections of a track.

It's no exaggeration to say that without ostinato, there's no dance music; repetition is in the DNA of the entire body of electronic music, the occasional exception of wayward ambient excursions aside.

By definition, tracks that contain repeated melodic loops use ostinato. Technology delivers ostinatos too – 16 step sequencers like those in the Roland TB boxes were created to produce repeating patterns, and in genres like psy and goa trance, as well as acid house, ostinatos are ubiquitous.

'Dance Of The Cosmic Serpent' by Cosmosis features a number of ostinatos playing

Fig 34 (*top*): 'Dance of the Cosmic Serpent' – at the 0.58 mark – features three separate ostinatos. Here the bass is highlighted in red and the two different synth parts in yellow and blue.

Fig 35 (*bottom*): The overlaid mallet ostinato that plays in the intro to Prodigy's 'Out of Space'. As the chords shift ever-upwards, the melody repeats, giving a sense of cohesion and tension to the track.

simultaneously in different instrumental parts (Fig 34). The combination of repeating synth riffs and largely syncopated off-beat bass above the pounding four-to-the-floor kick and rhythmic stereo delays give a relentless, hypnotic feel to the track that is characteristic of psy trance.

While this obvious use of ostinato can be brutally effective, there are more subtle uses for ostinato too, most powerfully to link different parts of a track together and supply melodic continuity. Fig 35 shows the chords during the introduction of The Prodigy's 'Out of Space' (13 seconds in), with the synth mallet ostinato over the top. Despite the changing string chords beneath, the ostinato builds cohesion by repeating the same melodic topline.

A more ambitious use of ostinato occurs at 1.35 (*Fig 38, opposite right*). Here the underlying chord sequence doubles in pace and changes from the ascending pattern that plays beneath the intro, yet the same plucked ostinato is used – pushed back in the mix – to ensure melodic continuity, relating the 'chorus' back to the opening of the track. When the original chords return at 1.48 this second potentially drastic backing change is softened by the overlaid ostinato. There's something clever about using ostinatos like this. The producer is indulging in a little compositional showing-off – which is never a bad thing.

Ostinato for continuity is a perennially popular device. In 'Levels' by Avicii (*Fig 36*), the arpeggiated Db minor / Db minor 7

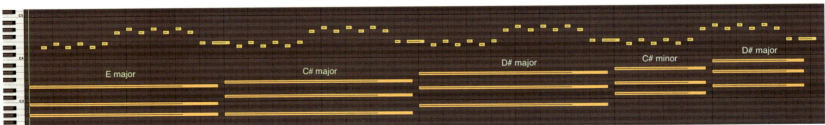

Chapter five
Theory crash course

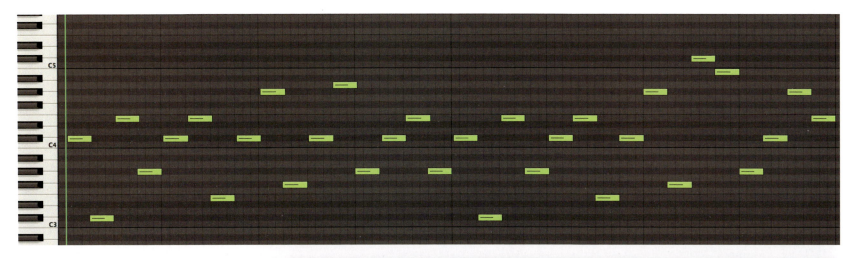

16th-note secondary motif supplies support to the lead riff. It has the effect of providing continuity between verse and chorus. Note, for example, the anticipation of the drop evoked when it enters at 2.25 and the continuity it delivers at 2.40 as it plays on as part of the full-bodied chorus. It's a simple little part – as many ostinatos are – but its contribution is pivotal to the flow and emotional punch of the track.

Although ostinatos are most commonly used for toplines, they can be found in other parts too. In Mr. Fingers' 'Mystery Of Love' (*Fig 37*) a Roland TB-303 plays an ascending ostinato bassline that repeats throughout the track, anchoring everything that occurs above. Playing non-stop for close to 7 minutes, the bassline's driving simplicity – and hypnotic groove – allows Mr. Fingers to mess with all kinds of rhythmic and melodic interplay above.

Fig 36 (*top*): Piano roll of the arpeggiod ostinato in Avicii's 'Levels' – for a secondary part, its contribution is pivotal.
Fig 37 (*middle*): The driving bassline from Mr. Fingers' acid classic 'Mystery of Love'.

Fig 38 (*bottom*): The ostinato topline from the middle section of 'Out of Space' – with the changing chords below.

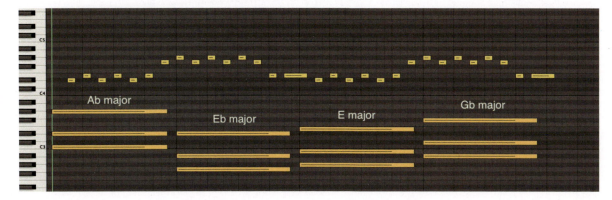

the secrets of dance music production /

Chapter five
Theory crash course

Putting ideas into practice

With a broad introductory understanding of a range of popular compositional techniques under our belt, let's put them into practice.

For the sake of demonstration, a number of ideas discussed over the past few pages have been incorporated into the relatively short 🔴 Example track.mp3. As a consequence it's a necessarily obtuse example – in any normal track you'd only pick one or two devices to use, and they'd be spread over a much longer time frame.

SAMPLED CHORDS

The basis of our track is a sampled minor 7 chord (🔴 Sampled Bm7 Chord.mp3) played using a jazzy organ patch. It is retriggered using the chord progression outlined in *Fig 39*. Because the track is in a minor key, we know from *page 146* that to keep the sampled chord in key it needs to be played on either the 1st, 4th or 5th degrees of the scale. The track is in B minor, making the 1st, 4th and 5th degrees of the scale B, E and F# respectively.

The track is built around a simple i-v-iv progression (which translates as Bm7, F#m7, Em7), but by occasionally triggering the sampled chord on passing notes (*page 107*) as we move between the 'main' notes of the progression, the chord is occasionally and briefly shifted out of key for classic garage house vibes.

OSTINATO

The track also uses an ostinato 🔴, shown in *Fig 40* below, which repeats during the intro above the Bm7 and the Em7 chords, increasing the anticipation through the build and continuing during the 'verse' section of the track.

ANACRUSIS

Note also the use of anacrusis in the ostinato – highlighted in red in *Fig 40* – the

Fig 39 (*top*): Trigger points for our sampled minor 7 chord. 🔴

Fig 40 (*bottom*): The simple ostinato that plays over the Bm7 and Em7 backing chords. Note the anacrusis highlighted in red. 🔴

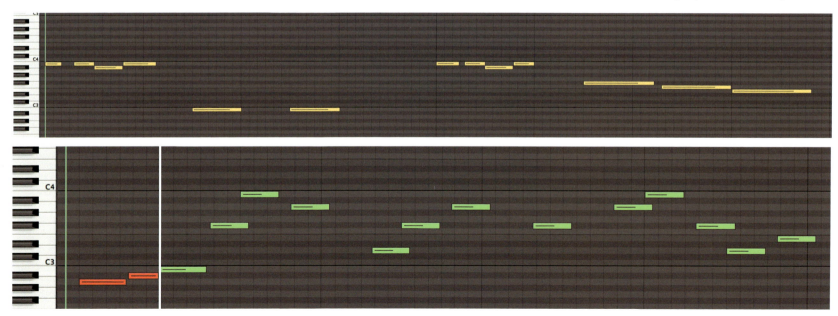

Chapter five
Theory crash course

leading A and A# occurring before the first beat of the bar. When using hardware or software sequencers, invariably constructed around the 16-division paradigm, it is all too easy to get straitjacketed into writing to four bar measures when pushing a note or two outside of the construct can deliver anything from increased anticipation and a deeper sense of movement to memorable signature motifs. At the very least, this kind of compositional ear candy will help keep listeners engaged.

CONTRARY MOTION

Once the full track is in and pumping, a second topline is introduced to keep things fresh. This additional melody – highlighted in *Fig 41* in orange – doesn't play throughout; it only enters the arrangement on every fourth bar. You can see from the piano roll how the melody moves up in pitch while the sampled chords shift down. The contrary motion between the two parts adds movement, lift and drive, aiding the all-important sense of anticipation and subtly building momentum as it eases into the next bar.

Using melodic flourishes sparingly in this way offers an alternative to a standard drum or FX fill; you still get transition momentum without an arrangementally disruptive fill.

Fig 41 (*top*): On every fourth bar, a melody (in yellow) rises in contrary motion to the falling sampled (red) chord progression (the ostinato is shown in green). Note that for illustrative purposes, the sampled chord progression is shown an octave higher than it actually plays.

Fig 42 (*bottom*): The two chords that feed the arpeggiator.

ARPEGGIATION

About halfway through our example track, it's time to bring another part in. The listener's engagement is in danger of waning so now's the time for something new – an extra melodic lift. Enter an arpeggio, mixed deliberately low so that it takes a secondary role to the lead ostinato.

The arpeggiator, set in 'down' mode, repeatedly cycles through the notes of the two simple input chords (*Fig 42*). A moderate amount of swing (set by ear) is applied to reinforce the groove of the beat and help glue the arpeggio to the rhythm.

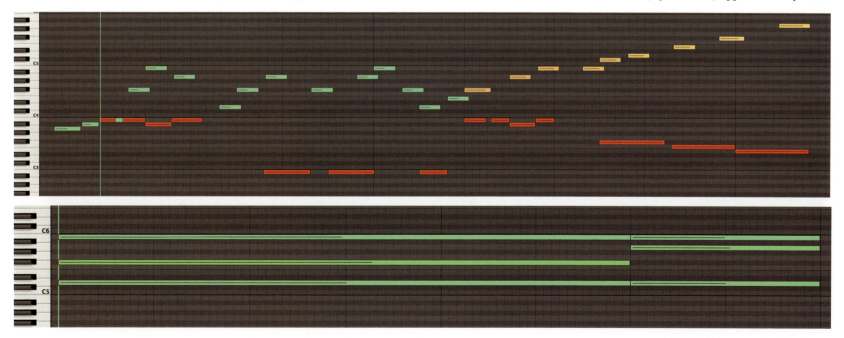

Chapter five
Theory crash course

Syncopation

Syncopation is a term that describes the accentuation or 'stress' of a normally weak off-beat that has the effect of disrupting the prevailing rhythmic flow. Its purpose is to break regularity and toy with the listener's rhythmic expectations. Its effect is often one of forward-momentum and in dance music it is one of the fundamental techniques used to add movement and **groove** (*page 38*) to a track.

Before moving any further, it's worth recapping some **Chapter 1** terminology. In a standard 4/4 rhythm, the **down-beat** occurs on the first beat of the bar, with the 'weaker' second and fourth beats considered the **off-beats**. Where the pulse of a normal beat sits on either the emboldened **1** – 2 – **3** – 4 or **1** – 2 – **3** – 4, in a syncopated off-beat rhythm the pulses occur on the second and fourth beats: 1 – **2** – 3 – **4**.

Syncopation is often confused with **swing**, but while swing describes the *shifting of* off-beats by varying degrees (*page 38*), syncopation *accentuates* them without necessarily shifting their timing.

Like swing, syncopation is best understood by using it. One way to do so is by grabbing a TR-909 (clone, plugin or original), program a simple beat, then add the in-built accent to hits on off-beats. Doing so increases the volume of the accented hit/s, changing the flow of the rhythm and adding an element of momentum and funkiness not there before.

A simple syncopated beat is shown in *Fig 44*. We've started with a straight kick–snare–kick–snare pattern overlaid with closed hi-hats playing 16ths. Then a number of the closed hats have been replaced with an accented open hat (shown in red) to create a more syncopated feel. Finally, a number of the 16th closed hats have been removed – mainly after the open hats. This heightens the effect of the syncopation.

Although the use of syncopation is commonplace in beats, it can be used in melodic parts to build rhythmic interest too. A good demonstration of this is the introduction to Survivor's 'Eye Of The Tiger' (*Fig 43*). Here the guitar plays muted 16ths, clearly accentuating the first 16th of each bar (highlighted in orange on the piano roll, where the yellow notes represent quieter notes). When the main guitar comes in for

Fig 43 (*top*): Piano roll for 'Eye of the Tiger'.

Fig 44 (*bottom*): Simple beat with open hi-hats highlighted in red. Note their positions – invariably on off- or down-beats. The Walkthrough folder includes a swung version of the same beat.

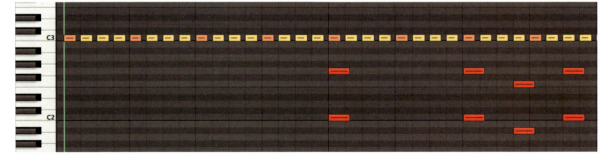

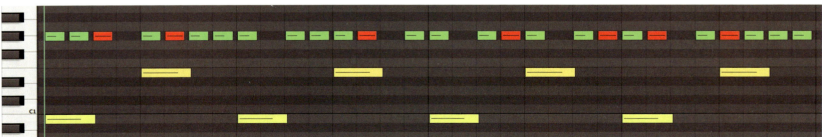

Chapter five
Theory crash course

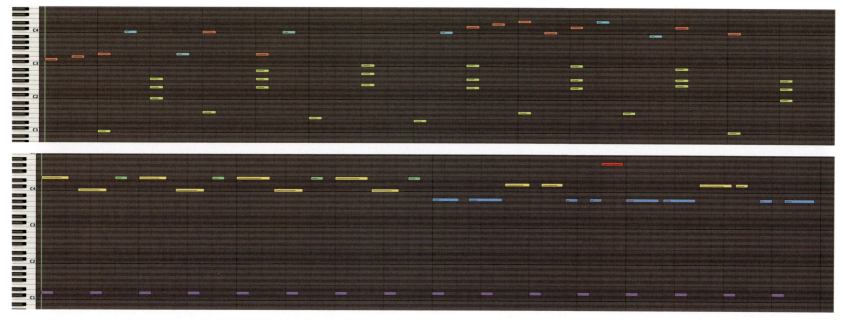

its raucous stabs, the first two chords hit on the down-beat. The third accentuates the off-beat, breaking the rhythm pattern established by the muted guitar and giving the intro its memorably syncopated feel.

A second example comes courtesy of Scott Joplin's 'The Entertainer', a simplified version of which is shown in *Fig 45*. Ragtime, like jazz and ska, makes heavy use of syncopation, with the left hand 'bass' piano part commonly playing to the beat while the right riffs with the off-beats.

The melody, shown in red, includes a number of syncopated notes that accentuate the off-beats, highlighted in blue, while the left-hand part plays bass and chords on the beat in typical ragtime style. Even though the piano roll is quantised to rigid 16ths, the syncopated interaction between the left and right hand parts is enough to create a sense of free movement and dynamism.

As in the beat example, it's worth repeating that the *omission* of notes playing *on* the beat is as important as the notes that play *off* the beat in creating the syncopated feel. This is explained by expectation; when the listener expects a note and it doesn't come – but is then supplied a measure later – the result is a momentary anticipation/resolution payoff. Returning to the piano roll, you'll see examples of other syncopated notes in the melody playing

🎧
Fig 45 (*top*): 'The Entertainer', left hand in yellow, right hand melody in red. The blue highlights indicate syncopated melodic elements.

Fig 46 (*bottom*): Bonobo's 'Cirrus', kick in purple and the different chimes in yellow, green, blue and red. Note how many of the yellow and blue chimes land on the 16th just before the subsequent on-the-beat kicks.

off-beats, but as they have notes on the 16ths either side of them they don't accent the off-beat as strongly as those which stand alone – and consequently don't deliver the same level of syncopation (bar nine is an example).

Bonobo's track 'Cirrus' from the *North Borders* album, features examples of multiple syncopation (*Fig 46*). The different bells and chimes sampled in the introduction play on different 16ths of the bar, interacting with the four-to-the-floor kick to make a patchwork of carefully controlled rhythmic interplay. Once again, the gaps between the notes are as important for creating the syncopated feel as the notes themselves.

Chapter six
Vocals

Chapter six
Vocals

This chapter opens with a caveat: *you don't need vocals in dance music.*

The majority of dance output steers clear of vocals, and the advantages for doing so are numerous: no sourcing of vocalist/s, no mics, no lyric writing, no retuning or re-timing, no studio egos to placate… the list goes on. Which means if you're making music that has no demand for vocals you can skip this chapter.

It should be noted that by vocals, we don't just mean full 'song' workouts featuring a traditional verse and chorus paradigm. Dance producers have been rejecting that convention for years using creative effects to mangle vocal lines, from talk boxes and vocoders to sample manipulation and distortion.

Nor do you need to go down the full-on studio recording route: you can sample phrases from online videos, use *a cappellas*, talk down a phone or program vocal synths to generate the magic ingredient.

If even that feels a stretch too far, the use of cut-up vocal lines as rhythmic elements is commonplace not just in techno and tech-house but mainroom styles too. Introducing a single syllable of vocal to a groove introduces a human element that you can't coax from a machine.

There are numerous benefits to using a vocals in a dance track.

Firstly, and most importantly, it's the easiest way of **saying something** as an artist – quite literally through the lyrical content. For some, the message of the song is throwaway (we'd never look to Paul Johnson's 'Get Get Down' for learning life lessons). Others, like James Teej and Roy Davis Jr (*Pro Tips, right*), find inspiration for their words in "love, loss and life's light and dark moments," and "love, umoja and peace" respectively. For producers wanting to explore story and emotion, vocals offer the perfect vehicle.

Secondly, it's an easy way to **make your tracks stand out** from the crowd. It takes time, effort and expense to track a memorable vocal. Producers who go this extra mile are invariably rewarded. Thirdly, **it's satisfying**. Adding a vocal to a song adds another dimension to it, and crafting a memorable lyric before recording a fantastic vocal performance can be a deeply rewarding. It's also fun – especially when collaborating with vocal talent.

Finally – and there's no point ignoring the fact – **you're unlikely to score a major hit unless your track features vocals**. List the biggest crossover acts of the last two decades. Then ask if their hits have used vocals. David Guetta? Check. Air? Check. Disclosure? Check. It's no surprise that the highest earners of Deadmau5's career have been tracks with vocal toplines (Haley Gibby on 'I Remember' and Rob Swire on 'Ghosts N Stuff'.)

In many cases, the addition of a vocal is enough to transform an underground hit into a chart juggernaut. Spiller's 'Groovejet' had been doing the club rounds for months before Positiva roped in Sophie Ellis-Bextor (with a little help from lyric supremo Rob Davis) to weave the breathy topline that transformed the Italian DJ's sample-heavy disco cut into a worldwide hit. Equally, adding a pop vocal to their EDM banger was enough to transform Avicii and Nicky Romero's 'Nicktim' into the UK chart topper 'I could be the one'.

The listening public thirsts for *songs*, even from dance artists, and if you're sitting on an underground hit there's one shortcut to the golden payoff/sellout: a winning vocal topline. If you're making music to get rich ignore vocals at your peril.

PRO TIPS

JAMES TEEJ & ROY DAVIS JR

Where do lyric writers find inspiration? For James Teej, "my travels and life's experience.

"Stories and memories of love, loss, and all of life's light and dark moments are what I gravitate to when getting inspired lyrically."

Roy Davis Jr, meanwhile, finds himself "going back in time to listen to Stevie Wonder's 'As' or Bob Marley's 'Could You Be Loved' to bring me back to a great feeling, but I also look to what I fight and stand for – love, umoja and peace, with a dash of wisdom for all mankind."

Chapter six
Vocals

Vocals are the element that won't go away. They've been a consistent part of the dance music landscape since its inception. Their presence spans all genres and styles and, though there have been periods of heavy use (like the mid '90s disco-house resurgence) followed by periods in the wilderness, the wilderness years never last long and it's only ever a matter of time before vocals find their way into the latest emerging trend.

TYPES OF VOCALS

Vocals in dance music can be split into three broad types: song vocals, riff vocals and glitched vocals.

Song vocals are the most traditional, taking their inspiration from other musical styles and embracing a verse/chorus and occasional middle eight structure. Production is typically kept clean with a lead vocal supported by any number of harmonies, ad-libs and double-tracks. Lyrics are important, as is a high calibre vocal performance.

Riff vocals are simpler, abandoning structural norms and featuring instead short clips of sung or spoken word content. These brief vocal elements become hooks pivotal to the structure of the track. To ease the potential monotony of repeating the same line, any number of production tricks can be used to keep things changing, from

TEN OF THE BEST
Vocal performances

1. Nightcrawlers - 'Push The Feeling On' (MK Dub Revisited)

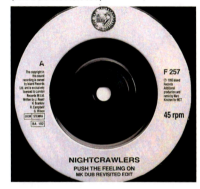

Featuring one of the earliest, and still devastatingly effective, examples of the chopped-up vocal loop, 'Push The Feeling On' has reportedly been reworked more times than any other lyrical line in dance music history.

2. Daft Punk - 'Around The World'
NME's entry No. 21 in the '150 Best Tracks of the Past 15 Years', Bangalter and de Homem-Christo's house classic is a supreme example of nonsense vocals with no variation playing a defining role in a track. The track kick-started a generation of vocoder- and talkbox-led vocal soundalikes.

3. Massive Attack - 'Teardrop'
The Bristolian trip-hop genre-definers' finest hour came with *Mezzanine* and its downtempo lead single 'Teardrop' featuring lyrics straight out of the Bob Dylan school of ambiguity. Penned and sung by Cocteau Twin Elizabeth Fraser, the words were inspired by the untimely death of her ex-lover Jeff Buckley.

4. Jon Cutler feat. E-Man - 'It's Yours'
Cutler hit paydirt in 2001 with 'It's Yours', the spoken word Chez backroom classic that went on to break the UK Top 40. But if Cutler crafted the sparse background, it was 'E-Man' (aka Eric Clark) who provided the sonic foreground, with a fine set of spoken-word lyrics, "Chasing beats through ghetto streets..." Sublime.

5. Justice - 'D.A.N.C.E.'
Gaspard Augé and Xavier de Rosnay managed to pull off two coups with their 2007 Michael Jackson-inspired hit. Firstly, by borrowing song titles from MJ's catalogue, they ensured the track's lyrics retained credibility. Secondly, by recruiting school children to sing them, they avoided having to feature a guest vocalist. The result? The most broadcast track of 2009 on French radio.

6. Underworld - 'Born Slippy .NUXX'
The euphoric turned mayhemic paean to insobriety, 'Born Slippy's semi-sung/shouted lyrics were delivered in a single take. The Joycian stream-of-consciousness lyrics capture the fragmented experience of a night's heavy drinking. "I was walking around Soho with a notebook and camera, just observing things," recalled singer/songwriter Karl Hyde, who even today regrets the fact his anti-booze rant is seen by many as a hedonistic celebration of 'Lager, lager, lager".

7. MJ Cole - 'Sincere'
The vocals from Cole's seminal UK garage hit were sourced from a sample CD and then re-sung by Nova Casper. The result? Lyrics of stark simplicity that have stood the test of time: "Don't do it / Be sincere..." Proof, if any were needed, that simple is often best.

8. Kaskade - 'It's You, It's Me'
Sometimes you only need one verse to say what you want to say, as in Kaskade's enduring beach-house epic, with Joslyn (Petty) providing the breathily gorgeous vocals to the perfect West Coast mix of substance and style.

9. Mr Fingers - 'Can You Feel It?'
The 1998 vocal remix is an all-time classic treatise and codification of all that house music represents, including one of the more memorable lines in the genre: "Let there be house!"

10. First Choice - 'Let No Man Put Asunder' (Frankie Knuckles Remix)
This 1983 disco-house colossus – featuring what is thought to be the most sampled *a capella* of all time – became a soundtrack to the early days of the disco revival, with lyrical invocations of love, spirituality and sex defining an awaking genre.

Chapter six
Vocals

automation (Mylo's 'Drop the Pressure' is a good example here, with the vocoder tuning automated to both keep things changing and to ratchet up that pressure) to glitching. But change is by no means essential, as Daft Punk displayed so effortlessly in 'Around The World'.

Glitched vocals (*page 196*) have enjoyed widespread use in recent years, with large swathes of the sample industry lining up to supply producers with single-loop bars of mangled vocals that can be layered with beats to supply organic elements to the groove or even, if they're unique or memorable enough, a track's topline.

Within these three types of vocals there are a range of approaches a producer might take to originate vocal content:

Do it (all) yourself: If you've got the talent, there's no reason why you can't write your own lyrics and melody before recording it in your own studio.

Use a session singer: A variant on the above for those who have the song-writing skills but not the vocal talent; you write the lyrics and melody then bring in a vocalist to sing it. They may contribute their own ideas during the session too.

Get a third party to write the topline: Probably the most common approach is to build the backing track then give it to a vocalist/topline writer for them to come up with the melodic content/lyrics/both. You will usually have to concede some of the publishing rights, but giving your creation to a singer experienced at writing memorable melodies could turn your near-miss into a hit.

***A cappellas*:** A quick online search will reveal thousands of vocal *a cappellas* in Wav and mp3 format that can be imported into a production. The legal ramifications of weaving a Beatles' vocal part into your dubstep banger could lead to anything from court action to donating all of your royalties to Michael Jackson's estate (*page 140*), but only if the track hits the big time, and if you're not planning a release, experimenting with an *a cappella* allows you to hone your vocal arrangement and production skills. It can also be a useful creative springboard: some producers like to build a song around a third party vocal then remove these placeholder vocals and record new ones against the backing track.

Samples: The number of good vocal sample libraries can be counted on the fingers of one hand, but there *are* some out there and even the worst examples occasionally provide melodic inspiration when you're struggling with ideas. Using copyright-cleared samples has the benefit of being legally legit, with phrases that have usually been well recorded by high calibre singers. Re-tuning and re-phrasing

SEE ALSO
PAGE 139 ISOLATING VOCALS

It is possible to isolate a vocal *a cappella* from a commercial release if you have an instrumental mix of the track as well as the full vocal mix. In this instance it's simple enough to get a clean extraction of the vocal – you just use phase invertion techniques to cancel out the backing track.

A similar result may be possible if you don't have an instrumental-only mix by finding a vocal-free section of the backing within the vocal mix. As long as it has the same instruments playing then a clean extrraction should be possible.

Audible artefacts are often due to differences in the mastering between the vocal and instrumental mixes.

samples (*pages 128–129*) opens new creative avenues. You can't go far wrong with the Sample Magic series of vocal packs (samplemagic.com/genres/20/vocals/), many of which are recorded by top session artists.

Movies, TV and radio shows: The web has given producers access to billions of hours of raw media, from the obscure to the cultish. Who would have thought, for example, that the 'speed stacking girl' would be the voice behind the punk hookline 'OMG' used by Skrillex? As with *a cappellas,* there are obvious legal implications with 'borrowing' such clips (someone will own the copyright and if you want to exploit it, you will need permission to do so), but you can steer clear of the law by restricting yourself to royalty-free archives of media in which the lifetime of the copyright has expired.

Speech synthesis: Most computers offer in-built speech synthesis capabilities, Stephen Hawking-style. Creating vocal lines in this way is easy. The results are, however, variable, somewhat clichéd and legibility is not always assured.

Other ideas: If none of the above suggestions appeal, there are a range of other methods for generating unique vocals to suit all budgets:

▸▸ Onionz and Joeski had success by using

JUSTICE

Struggling to write great lyrics? You're in good company. Speaking about the genesis of Justice's 2007 hit D.A.N.C.E., Xavier de Rosnay admitted: "For us, writing the words is really tricky because we don't want to make them too serious, too complicated or too pretentious. But we also don't want to come up with stupid dance music lyrics like 'Share your ass, you look beautiful'.

"At least the music of Michael Jackson is something we believe in, so we built the lyrics of D.A.N.C.E. around the titles of his songs."

---

the humble **mobile phone** to capture the 'Hold On To Your Love' vocals, with a local Queens singer performing down the line which was captured by switching the phone to speakerphone and mic'ing it up. The result? A thin, distant-sounding vocal that is unashamedly lo-fi.

▸▸ At the other end of the scale was Justice's recruitment of a **school choir** to perform on 'D.A.N.C.E.' at London's Air studios. Featuring complex orchestration and a big budget, the production was both time-consuming and expensive – though the results speak for themselves.

▸▸ A cheaper and less headache-inducing approach than recruiting under-eights to your production cause is to raid their toy cupboards instead (with permission, of course!). **Devices** like Texas Instrument's Speak & Spell may have an army of admirers in the circuit-bending community, but they serve vocal producers well too.

▸▸ If you own a **field recorder,** try leaving the studio and record real-world vocals. Transport hubs, cafés, galleries and beaches all provide hotbeds of conversation, though you often have to wait a while before you get a golden quote. For melodic lines, grab surreptitious recordings of buskers (though, once again, be aware of copyright and publishing implications).

▸▸ Finally, why not audition a son/daughter, mum/dad, significant other to say or speak the phrase you want vocalising? Once in a while getting **someone unfamiliar with recording** to supply vocal content can yield surprising results.

SETTING UP A RECORDING

Whether you're recording at home or in a pro studio, unless you're deliberately after a lo-fi sound, your aim will be the same: the best quality performance you can capture. The main variables when doing so are the quality of the vocalist, sound of room and quality/suitability of microphone (almost always in that order). Working in a studio's professionally treated vocal booth makes the job easier, but with a little investment and the right acoustic considerations there's no reason why you can't get release-quality results at home.

PREPARATION

The first 20 minutes or so of a vocal recording session is usually spent setting up (engineer) and warming up (vocalist). Typical preparations include:

▸▸ **Selecting the right microphone for the job.** Different voices respond better to different microphones. Audition all likely candidates before deciding on the one most suited for the session. The usual way of doing this is to set up two or three models in front of the singer and record the same vocal line on all of them. A/B between the different audio files to select the best mic and don't assume the most expensive will sound best. A noteworthy *Sound On Sound* magazine 'mic shoot out' – search for it online – found that for certain vocalists £150 mics outperformed those that costed thousands. It's also worth noting that microphone choice is to some extent dictated by style: the Shure SM-7, for example, is a regular first choice for spoken word vocals due to its specific mid and higher mid-heavy EQ curve.

▸▸ **Preparing the signal path.** Some engineers have a favoured chain of outboard featuring an EQ and compressor alongside a mic pre-amp. The compressor reduces the risk of clipping on the way into the audio interface – though the additional headroom supplied by 24-bit recording has negated the need for this to a large extent.

Although by all means experiment with outboard if you're booked into a pro studio, you can get excellent results by running a reasonable mic directly into a good interface. Doing so gives you the added freedom to experiment with different EQ and compression treatments (using software or hardware) when the vocal recording is complete without requiring you to commit at this early stage.

▸▸ **Getting the headphone mix right.**

Chapter six
Vocals

A good vocal recording begins with a good headphone mix. Indeed many A-list producers argue that *the* secret to a fantastic vocal performance is the quality of the performer's headphone mix. Take your guidance from the singer about what they want to hear. Usually they will ask for volume adjustments – both to the backing track and their own voice – but it's not unusual for them to want reverb applied to their voice or to hear more or less of specific mix elements.

To add reverb to the vocal part in the headphones, use a post-fade aux send on the track being recorded or insert a temporary reverb plugin on the vocal channel. To stop latency becoming a problem bypass all processor-heavy effects (many DAWs have a specific low-latency mode). This reverb will not be recorded, of course; it's simply there to help the singer feel comfortable. Monitoring the vocals directly from the sound card instead of via the DAW outputs can also negate the issue of latency. This works well with DSP-driven interfaces such as the UAD Apollo and when using outboard EQ and compression.

▶▶ **Setting the recording level.**
High-quality recordings are achieved by running each piece of equipment in the chain at its optimum signal level – that is to say at as high a level as possible while leaving enough safety margin (headroom) to handle unexpected peaks (*page 257*).

When recording digitally (at 24-bit) this translates to leaving around 12–15dB of headroom on signal peaks. *Bear in mind that when a performer gets into their zone and begins to sing out, the volume of their voice will increase – especially in builds towards the chorus or during ad-libs.* Ensure you leave enough headroom for these unplanned peaks and keep an eye on recording levels throughout the session. Having to discard a fantastic take due to digital clipping is a rookie's error.

TIP If you want the singer to give a louder performance, turn down the vocal level in their cans fractionally. (Though don't go too far or you'll force them to scream.)

▶▶ **Having a final run-through**, to make sure the recording level is where it should be, that the singer is happy with the headphone mix and that the fidelity of the audio you're capturing is pristine. Listen to the recording in isolation to check there are no unwanted artefacts or spurious noises. Be particularly mindful of jangles from jewellery, the noise of toes tapping – even the ticking of a watch can make its way onto a recording. Another potential source of unwanted noise is rustling lyric sheets. To stop this, tape the words to a wall or music stand rather than letting the singer hold them. Last but not least, switch phones to silent!

When you and the singer are both happy to proceed, it's time to press record...

THE RECORDING

The order in which you record vocal parts in a project will be dictated by the song and the vocalist. Take your cues from both.

You invariably get the most natural results by recording **single takes** – i.e. full performances – that start at verse 1 and continue to the final words of the last chorus. Weak words and phrases can be overdubbed if necessary. Where you have a track governed by a traditional structure and the vocalist is confident with the material then by all means give this a go.

But dance producers often work with vocalists who are less confident with the material (some session singers only hear the material on the day of the session, as was the case with Martina Topley-Bird's vocals on her recordings for Tricky) meaning it can be more effective to record a **verse or even line at a time**. This kind of approach is unlikely to generate the most organic result and if you're not careful it can end up sounding like obviously different takes stitched together. To avoid this, ensure the singer maintains the same position before the mic between takes and give them the sound of their own voice in the section before you want to drop in so they can continue with the same style and energy.

TIP To ensure you get all the material you need, make a list before the session of the

PRO TIPS

BREACH

On Breach's 'Jack', Ben Westbeech recorded his own voice using a Neumann U47 FET running into a Neve 1073 followed by a Steven Slate Audio Dragon and then a custom-built dual channel LA-2A.

Once recorded the vocal was re-pitched then fed back out of the DAW to be treated with the 1073 for a second time before being fed through a Fatso and then back into the LA-2A.

"It's all about resampling and processing again and again. That's the way you're going to get a sound that's hard to find," he notes.

Chapter six
Vocals

minimum vocal part/s required for each track. There's nothing worse than realising you've forgotten a pivotal hook or ad-lib when the session is over.

TIP A good way of ensuring you've got a good take of every phrase is to print a copy of the lyrics then cross off sections when you're happy with the results. Give spare copies to the vocalist and engineer to keep everyone on track.

TIP Ensure you've got at least two solid takes of the chorus. Although it's tempting to copy and paste the same chorus throughout a song, having variations helps to maintain listener engagement.

It is normal to complete the lead vocal before moving onto double-tracks, harmonies, ad-libs and so on. When overdubbing these elements, set up a vocal '**anchor**' on top of which additional vocal elements are recorded. The usual way of doing this is to spend a few minutes while the singer is having a breather to make an early but accurate comp (*page 174*) of the best sections of the lead line which are then used as the anchor. This anchor is fed into the headphone mix for the singer to record over. Failing to provide a good quality anchor can mean the singer performs to potentially out-of-time and out-of-tune takes, making your life immeasurably harder when it comes to editing the vocals.

Double-tracks are identically sung copies of the same melody that give a lush, ensemble-type feel to vocal lines. Typically used during choruses, they can occasionally sound good in verses too. To record a double-track, simply feed the lead vocal anchor into the singer's headphones and get them to sing along to what they hear as precisely as possible.

Harmonies are usually (but not always) rhythmically identical but melodically different lines. It can be tough identifying good harmonies; working out parts before you begin the session saves valuable studio time. The most obvious harmonies are

The Neumann (valve) U47: the grand-daddy of vocal mics.

TOOLS OF THE TRADE
Vocal mics

Although not right for every singer, the **Neumann U87** can be relied upon to deliver a flatteringly bright, punchy and modern sound on most vocals across a range of musical styles.

The **Neumann U47** – probably the most famous of all vocal mics – delivers a warm, rounded tone. An original will cost a fortune and require regular servicing. Some modern clones are arguably just as good.

A more affordable option is the hugely popular range of **Rode** mics, including the **NTK**, which offers high quality recording to those on a budget.

Audio Technica's **AT2020** also proves that quality doesn't need to cost. Its ability to place a vocal at the front of a mix can be useful in busier productions and its slightly breathy tone often works on lush trance/prog vocals.

Shure's **SM-7/SM-7B** is popular among hip hop artists. If you're dealing with spoken word vocals, give it a spin. Its upper mid lift can help vocals cut through the mix, while the low end remains solid.

When price is no object, the **Sony C800G** can deliver beautifully crisp results and vocals that truly cut – it's the modern pop and hip hop sound *par excellence,* with spoken artists from Kanye West to Eminem regularly claiming it's the best in show. At around $10,000 a pop, it's a definite luxury.

Of course, if you're after a superstar mic on a budget you can always **hire one in** just for the duration of a session.

How a well-recorded vocal should look – a healthy signal level with plenty of headroom to take unexpected peaks into account.

octaves above and below the main vocal line, both of which can be fed into the mix at a low volume to bulk up a vocal section. Lines based around thirds and fifths are also good starting points. If a singer is struggling to sing a harmony line try dramatically reducing the volume of, or muting, the lead line. Alternatively, lay down a keyboard part playing the desired harmony and get the singer to sing along to that.

To build big harmony-rich **chorus** blocks, try doubling and potentially tripling every line, including the lead anchor. You can go further by adding overdubs while varying the position of the vocalist in front of the mic (some takes nearer and some further away) and also their tone and register (nasal, breathy, deep etc) to create the illusion of many different people singing. This is how Michael Jackson recorded many of his vocal ensembles. When doing so, ensure each overdub is super-tight against the anchor or you can end up with loose and scrappy results (or a mammoth re-timing job ahead).

Ad-libs – the noodles and wails that can be dropped into builds, choruses and intros – are best left to last. Create a rough mix featuring all vocal elements for the singer to record over. It's also worth capturing at least one pass sung to the backing track alone. If you have a chorus playout don't scrimp while recording: ensure you have more than enough ad-libs to choose from.

TIP It's hard to know when to stop pushing a vocalist for an even better take and move on to something new. Some producers go to arduous lengths during vocal sessions, generating upwards of 20 or more takes for each line. Although some singers undoubtedly need more time than others to nail a performance, if your track count is running into double figures regularly you should probably spend more time rehearsing or rethink either your choice of singer or the arrangement itself.

TIP Beware the law of diminishing returns when recording vocals. Singers only have so much energy and you'll notice their voice starting to tire during demanding sessions. The best takes often occur early in a session. Don't waste that energy and don't think that by over-rehearsing you'll necessarily get better results.

VOCAL PRE-PRODUCTION

If you're lucky enough to work with the world's finest vocalists then you may be able to skip this section. But even then, probably not. Vocal pre-production has played a pivotal role in the mixing process for decades. In the past, the time was mainly devoted to **compiling** a single master from various takes (Don McLean famously recorded 24 takes during the 'American Pie' sessions). Nowadays it begins with the same comping process but may also include **retuning** and **re-timing**.

NOIR

"I love when HRRSN sings, with his heart almost popping out of his body, but he must have hated me at some point in the process of making 'My Fault' 'cause I kept pushing him to sing better and write more..."

It's worth noting that none of this is mandatory. If your track requires a vocal that is deliberately loose, lazy and live, you may choose not need to do any editing. But this would be an exception. In today's production environment rare indeed is the vocal performance that hasn't been given some Auto-Tune or Melodyne fine-tuning. And if the track is aimed at a crossover chart audience then the demands are even higher: the public is now so used to artificially tuned vocals that severe re-tuning is often called for.

The typical pre-production process runs as follows:

▸▸ **Initial compilation (comp) of the different vocal takes.** Line up all vocal

WHAT IS..?

The perfect take

The 'perfect take' is a mix of 'soul', intelligibility and technical accuracy. Of these, soul – the inherent *humanity* of a performance – is usually the most important.

Utilities like Melodyne offer today's producer the tools to pull a technically imperfect performance into tune and time. But nothing except a fantastic vocalist can deliver a spine-tinglingly memorable performance that engages with the audience. That is what you want to capture with the 'perfect' take.

This means if your singer is 80 per cent of the way there technically and 100 per cent there in terms of soul, keep on recording. You may need to do some editing afterwards, but you're capturing the stuff that will make the record stand the test of time.

Chapter six
Vocals

Typical vocal recording setup. Whether you're recording at a pro studio or at home, the principles for getting a good recording are the same.

the secrets of dance music production /

takes starting at the same place and listen to each solo'd and against the backing track to identify the best phrases. Using the sequencer's edit tools, cut out weaker lines until you're left with a single comped vocal.

▶▶ **Set fades** between different audio regions to remove clicks and pops.

▶▶ When you've finished compiling the master take, it's time to begin **detailed 'forensic' editing work** on both tuning and timing. Seasoned vocal producers invariably turn to Melodyne at this point, but other tools are available, not least VariPhrase in Cubase and a combination of Flextime and Flexpitch in Logic. Ableton Live's warping and transposition editing tools are also up to the job: they are powerful enough for technical work as well as ripe for experimentation. Several warping algorithms are offered, all producing sonically different results while clip-based editing makes it easy to produce variations and the freedom to arrange them in the sequence.

TIP Pitch correctors are used in one of two ways. Utilities like Melodyne and Auto-Tune in Graphic mode are programmed just like note sequencing. When you're done editing, the part is then bounced and re-imported into the mix. Meanwhile Auto-Tune in Auto mode and utilities like Pitch Corrector in Logic work as insert plugins in real-time. Although real-time pitch correction has its place – particularly on vocal parts that are reclined in the mix – on exposed lead lines the more natural and forensic capabilities of an offline editor is the better option.

By this stage the vocal should be sounding pretty good. If there's no other vocal material in the song then your job is done. If, however, there are double-tracks, harmonies or ad-libs then these will need to be comped, re-timed and re-tuned in the same way, this time using the comped lead vocal as an anchor.

TIP In large-scale projects featuring dozens of multi-tracked vocals, a utility like VocAlign can help shift multiple parts into time against a single anchor. To nudge the tuning into pitch you can use instances of Auto-Tune on select tracks with different retune speeds to thicken the sound. Taking

SOUKIE & WINDISH

"For the vocal recording on 'Head up my Dear' we used the combination of a Neumann M149, Amek 9098 and CL-1B, which clearly points out every detail of the voice... This is the first time we put the vocals really forward and loud."

Getting more from singers

Your job as producer is to get the best possible performance from a singer. A large part of this will be down to their talent, of course, and how familiar they are with the track. But it's also down to the producer and their 'bedside manner'. Golden rules include:

BE CONSTRUCTIVE WITH CRITICISM
Performers – like anyone else – respond best to positive feedback rather than negative. If you do have criticisms, ensure you are clear about what you feel is wrong and offer achievable solutions ("I think if you sing softer we'll get better results,") rather than plain criticism ("Your voice sounds grating.")

MAKE SURE THEY ARE REFRESHED
Have water on hand. The temperature of drinks is important: too cold and it can affect the vocal cords, while too hot can also cause problems. Tepid water, however nasty it sounds, is best. A bag of cookies on hand is never a bad idea either.

TAKE REGULAR BREAKS – especially if the singer's voice shows signs of fatigue or when a specific take is causing major headaches.

DRINK AND DRUGS ARE BEST LEFT OUT OF THE STUDIO
Although you may occasionally get inspiring results when a singer is part-way through a binge, it is the exception to the rule.

KEEP THINGS RELAXED
Recording sessions – particularly when you're on a tight time or financial budget – can be hard work and stressful for both producer and performer. That doesn't mean they can't also be fun. Piling the pressure on a vocalist to get the perfect take is unlikely to help matters. It's better to create an atmosphere that is creative and relaxed.

IF SOMETHING'S NOT WORKING – the tuning of a particular word, a lyric that won't fit – then consider a workaround. Stumbling blocks only become hurdles if you let them. Where the material allows it, try rewriting a line or editing lyrics to make them easier for the singer to deliver rather than force something that doesn't come naturally.

ALL THAT SAID, never settle for second best. Use any and every effort to help the singer deliver their best. And when you think you have the perfect take, try for one more; once confident with a part a singer is often able to perform something even better.

Chapter six
Vocals

PRO TIPS

TRICKY

Never underestimate the unplanned magic that can happen when a talented singer stands before the mic.

Tricky's 'Black Steel' session was notoriously freeform, with Martina Topley-Bird's vocal contributions pretty much improvised on the spot.

Recalls engineer Mark Saunders: "She sang to this loop with no music to guide her, yet she came up with this melody that had such a great vibe.

"She came up with all the songs' melodies and not one of them did she work out beforehand."

---

this kind of approach rather than re-pitching and timing every take using Melodyne can save hours and the end result is not usually noticeably different – particularly if the vocals are mixed low in a busy mix.

TIP Although it is common to spend time correcting the pitch of vocal parts, timing is often overlooked. It is easy to forget, when concentrating on the bass and drums, that **vocals are prominent contributors to a song's groove**. Ensure line entries occur where they should and pull lagging syllables into time.

TIP In projects featuring complex vocal arrangements the comping process can get messy, spawning dozens of audio tracks. To keep things manageable, undertake vocal pre-production in a different project using a bounce of the music as a backing track and only export the vocals you need back into the main project.

TIP Keep all rejected takes on hand until you're finished with a track, and even then keep them backed up. You never know when you may need to revert to previously discarded takes.

VOCAL PRODUCTION

The vocal production process involves taking the final comped and tuned vocals and treating them in any number of ways to help them sit/shine in the mix. Most vocals are treated with EQ, compression and some form of reverb, although even these are not essential and, in dance music, where anything goes, more extreme effects may be employed to create memorable vocal hooks and riffs.

There are no uniform rules on how to treat vocals; the track and the vocal performance dictate the treatment. Some vocal lines demand no more than light compression and a splash of reverb. Others call for overdrive, limiter/s, delay/s, multiple EQs and more in the effects chain. In general, the more plugins you use, the less natural the result will be.

TIP Before adding any effects, program in a rough pass of level automation so that the vocal sits at a consistent level relative to the mix for the duration of the track. This initial automation will reduce the amount of time you spend adjusting the vocal level as you work through mixdown. It can be fine-tuned later.

EQ

EQ is used in three ways to treat vocals:

1. Corrective – to remove unpleasant and unnecessary frequencies from the signal,

2. Enhance / Sweeten – to shape the overall tone of a signal (e.g. more air),

---

TOOLS OF THE TRADE
Vocal editors

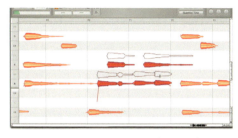

MELODYNE
Market-leading tuning and timing correction software that allows for detailed editing of both single lines and multiple parts. Although it takes time to master, it's pretty much essential if you spend a lot of time on vocal productions.

AUTO-TUNE
The original retuner, which started life in hardware form. Its beauty is its simplicity: just insert the plugin on a vocal track, select the key and adjust correction speed to taste. Go fast and hard to get 'that' artificial effect. For more comprehensive Melodyne-style control (without the timing editing), switch to graphic mode.

VOCALIGN
Offline utility that allows the rhythmic content of a single anchor track to pull other tracks into time. A useful time saver when dealing with large numbers of double-tracks and harmonies.

Chapter six
Vocals

SPOKEN WORD VOX

If a sung melody isn't right for a track but you still want the human factor, then a spoken word vocal might be the answer. These can range from the simple (Paul Johnson 'Feel My MF Bass') through the ambigious (Nina Kraviz 'Ghetto Kraviz') to the dramatically iconic (Chuck Roberts' "In the beginning there was Jack" monologue on Mr Fingers 'Can You Feel It') and downright offensive (Johnny Dangerous 'Beat that Bitch [With a Bat]'.

Although rap artists sometimes favour different mics (the Sony 800 in particular), the techniques used for mixing spoken word vox are pretty much the same as for sung vocals.

Many of the tracks mentioned above use recurring motifs. The trick here is picking a phrase that is ear-wormingly catchy and which fits the wider groove like a glove (words are rhythmic mix elements too).

3. Effect – to radically change the frequency characteristics of a signal (as in the case of 'telephone EQ' – page 194).

While performing any kind of frequency tweaks remember the golden EQ maxims: **cut narrow, boost wide** and **cut is more natural than boost** (page 210).

When **cutting frequencies** start by removing unnecessary lows. Vocal recordings often include low-end content like breath blasts and mic stand noises that are unnecessary and consume headroom. To lose them, set up an 18dB high-pass filter then increase the cutoff frequency into the 60-100Hz zone until you hear a marked change in the tonality of the sound. When you reach this point back down a little. In the context of a final mix, you may find yourself rolling away as high as 300Hz – especially in a busy arrangement.

To **remove unpleasant rogue frequencies**, often caused by the room in which the recording was made, set up a parametric EQ with the ability to fine-tune the cutoff point, dial in the narrowest possible Q value and then use the 'search and destroy' method (page 211) to identify unwanted peaks. These peaks are normally fairly obvious, identified by a ringing, wailing sound that sticks out when you dial through the frequencies. Use a graphic display to help identify where surpluses of signal are concentrated. When you find a rogue frequency, widen the Q a little then dial in a dip of between 3–10dB to control it. A/B between the original signal and treated one to check any changes you make help rather than hinder the sound.

'Usual suspect' areas that cause problems include:

▸▸ **150–400Hz:** Boxiness – reduce here to open the sound.
▸▸ **1–1.5kHz:** Nasal frequencies and 'honkiness' – often the result of a poor recording environment.
▸▸ **2.5–6kHz:** Ringing and unpleasant higher-mid peaks.

TIP Where unwanted peaks are only found in specific phrases (when the vocalist moves into a more nasal register to sing a high note, for example), **dynamic EQ** can be useful as it only notches out (or boosts) select frequencies when they exceed a given threshold in the same way as a de-esser.

To **shape the tone** of a vocal part, use the best 'sweetening' EQ you have; a clone or plugin version of the Pultec EQP-1A or Neve 1073 is a good place to start. Classic EQs for tone shaping tend to employ wide, carefully sculpted bell curves that sweeten (or soften) the most flattering musical frequencies. In the case of vocals the main areas of interest are typically:

▸▸ **200–600Hz:** Warmth/body/chest
▸▸ **2.5–6kHz:** Presence/articulation
▸▸ **8–10kHz:** Brightness/air.

TIP When adding air, a boost of between 1–2dB is usually enough. Beware of going too far: excessive high-end boost exacerbates sibilance and can result in a grating mix.

TIP To add low-end body to a vocal without piling on the EQ, try an enhancement tool like the Little Labs Voice of God or a sub bass/harmonic synthesiser like the Aphex Aural Exciter. **Used sparingly** these can sometimes be all you need to give a touch more girth and confidence to a lackluster vocal.

TIP At the other end of the spectrum, for added high-end air and sparkle, specialist EQs like UBK's Clariphonic and effects like the Aural Exciter can help open out a sound and give it an airy sheen. Again, **use in moderation.**

TIP Where either the backing orchestration or tone of the lead vocal changes between the verse and chorus (there might be a whispered style in the verse and a more energetic sound in the chorus, for example) use different vocal EQ treatments for different sections. You can either do this using automation or by splitting the verse and chorus vocals onto separate audio tracks and treating each independently.

Chapter six
Vocals

When **radically changing** a vocal part using EQ, go wild with the settings. The point here is not to polish a natural sounding performance but to transform it into something different – the more extreme the better. The most common example is the much-used 'telephone EQ' effect (*page 194*), which combines a sharp low-pass filter at around 350–900kHz with a high-pass in the 2.2–2.5kHz region. Follow this with a compressor and bit-crusher to accentuate the effect.

TIP Effects like telephone EQ are often most effective when used sparingly on select phrases or automated vocal spins. For a masterclass in using these techniques in ambitious vocal arrangements, listen to any number of R&B and pop chart hits.

DYNAMIC PROCESSING

Vocals are inherently dynamic, with changing levels of energy reflecting the emotional highs and lows of a song. These variations in volume present a challenge to the producer, with louder peaks sticking from the mix and softer parts masked by the backing track. There are two main approaches to solving this common problem:

▶▶ **Level automation** – Programming volume changes so that the vocals sit at a controlled level in relation to the backing track.

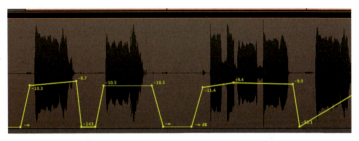

🎧 Level automation of a vocal line. Note the volume dips during pauses to reduce the level of breaths. Automation can be a laborious job, with some vocal producers inserting hundreds of nodes to get the best from a performance.

Note that you don't have to remove or quieten breaths. Some songs leave them in and heavily compress them as an effect.

▶▶ **Compression** – A similar result, but level control is performed automatically by the compressor.

▶▶ Many producers use **a mix of both**, treating an already automated signal with one, and occasionally more, instances of compression.

Regarding **automation**, there's not much to say. Simply program the required volume changes onto the vocal line. Typical tweaks include dipping the volume for breaths while raising it for lost/low level/softer words and line-endings to maintain energy.

An alternative option is to use a **vocal rider**, like Waves' Vocal Rider plugin, which uses a sidechain feed from the backing track to automate the vocal level to a consistent volume. Automation can be exported from the plugin to be tweaked manually.

Vocals are run through a **compressor** in almost all dance mixes. Not only does the compressor keep levels in check, reducing the dynamic range of a vocal to help it sit in the mix, it also subtly – or not so subtly

TOOLS OF THE TRADE
Vocal compressors

UA / TELETRONIX LA-2A
Simple and highly effective, the 50-plus-year-old LA-2A's warm and flattering compression curves have been treating vocal performances for generations. Gain reduction is performed by a light-dependent photocell which provides the musical two-stage release drop-off. Can also be used in Limit mode (flick that switch) as the last plugin in a vocal effects chain.

UBK FATSO
For vocals with balls, a more tape-effected performance or to inject a breath of analogue-style warmth to a cool digital recording, this brown wonder box and its plugin equivalent, the UBK-1, can do spankingly good things. Smooth and Glue settings are both good starting points.

TUBE-TECH CL 1B ↻
High-end sheen and gloss are the order of the day with this popular Danish studio staple. If you've marvelled at the vocal sound on a pop or R&B mix in the last five years, chances are there's been a CL 1B somewhere in the signal chain. Also available in plugin form.

the secrets of dance music production /

Chapter six
Vocals

QUICK GUIDE

The pro studio

If you choose to record in a pro recording facility there are a few tips to help you get the most for your money:

CHECK the studio has a suitable recording space and at least a couple of quality vocal mics. Some producers demand eye contact with the singer when recording. If that's you, check the studio is set up suitably. A short pre-visit to check the facility is never a bad idea.

YOU CAN OFTEN SAVE money on studio space by booking late cancellation slots or recording at unsociable hours. If you're on a tight budget enquire about deals.

SHOP AROUND; there are fewer musicians booking studio time these days which means you can often get a good deal. That said, you usually get what you pay for...

BE CLEAR when booking the session what you want from it ("I'm recording a solo vocalist and want to take away 24-bit Wav files.") It can save both time during setup and will help ensure you take away exactly what you need.

DON'T SCRIMP ON TIME. Although you don't want to spend more money than you need to, false economies abound if you rush a session. Ask the vocalist how much time they normally take to record a song, adding in time for warm up, a break or two, and the tracking of ad-libs, double-tracks and so on. Between two and four hours per track is usually about right.

IF THE STUDIO HAS A RANGE OF MICS, TRY THEM ALL. Spend ten minutes at the start of the session identifying which mic suits the vocalist best. A good studio should also be able to rent in any mic you particularly want to use.

EVEN IF YOU USE A PRO STUDIO for the recording, it is worth meeting the vocalist at your own studio first for a run-through to check they are comfortable with the material, that harmonies are worked out (record them to your phone and take them with you) and that the songs are within the singer's range.

TREAT EVERYONE WELL including the intern/ assistant/tea-boy/girl.

USE THE ASSISTANT/ENGINEER. They will know more than you about the recording space and they're there to help.

– changes the shape and tone of the vocal signal, adding colour and anything from attack and body to bulk.

There are no fixed rules when it comes to compression. Everything from the choice of unit, through the method of compression (*page 214*) to the attack, release and ratio settings will be governed by the performance, backing track and kind of vocal sound you're after.

When choosing a **style** of compressor, VCA compressors like the Neve 33609 tend to produce more transparent, less coloured results than compressors based around tubes (Manley Vari-Mu), FETs (1176) and optical circuits (LA-2A), although a small amount of compression colour on vocals is often considered a good thing.

A useful starting point when compressing the lead vocal is a reasonably fast **attack** time (around 10-25ms) to allow transients at the start of words through, and, if the unit allows it, an auto **release** time that alters depending on the material passing through it. Where this isn't available, try a fixed time of 100-250ms. Attack and release times should be adjusted by ear to ensure they work with the vocal and that any pumping effects introduced 'breathe' in time with the track's tempo.

The amount of compression required will vary hugely. Start with a **ratio** of between 2:1 and 4:1 (lower for gentler results) and gain reduction of between 3–5dB. When a more assertive sound is required, a high-end compressor may be able to handle gain reduction levels of up to 8–10dB without much trouble. After that pumping artefacts will become obvious.

TIP If you can't hear the effect your changes to the attack and release times are having, increase the threshold and ratio until the results of tweaks become obvious. Set the values as you want them then return the ratio and gain to their original values.

Where a single compressor is not able to handle a dynamic vocal without compromising it to an unacceptable degree, try adding a **second compressor in series** to pull back volume spikes that the first misses. This second compressor can be set more aggressively with a higher ratio as it will only treat a small number of 'spiky' phrases. Compressor number two can be bypassed using automation when not required.

A more appropriate result can sometimes be achieved by following the first compressor with a **limiter** instead.

To add bottom-up girth to an underwhelming vocal part, try using **parallel compression** (*page 275*). The idea here is to increase the level of low volume phrases

REDLIGHT

Often the journey from conception of a lyric to the final recorded vocal is a long one, as Redlight noted when speaking about the making of his album *X Colour*. "For the track 'Me & You' I was in New York and met up with ASTR. It was real early one winter morning and I had to walk through really deep snow to get to a little studio in the bottom of someone's yard in Brooklyn.

"I wrote the top line with them, recorded some of the vocals in a cupboard, came back to London, rewrote the track underneath the vocal, caught a vibe, then went back out to New York and re-recorded the vocals in a proper studio. Then I came back to London and mixed it."

---

while simultaneously reducing dynamics in high volume ones.

Set it up by feeding some of the signal via an aux send to a bus which houses the 'parallel' compressor. The parallel compressor (pick one with an assertive character) should be set with a high ratio reducing around 15-25dB worth of gain. Mix this hyper-squashed signal with the original vocal at a low volume then balance the two vocal channels to generate a combined sound that delivers a magic mix of detail, dynamics and assertiveness.

SIBILANCE

Sibilance (the excessive prominence of 'S' and 'T' sounds in the 3–8kHz frequency range that translate as sizzling Ss and shredding Ts) is a perpetual pain in the asssssss for vocal producers. It can be caused by anything from bad mic technique to a poor choice of mic – even the shape of a singer's mouth plays a part. It is an inescapable by-product of modern recording and mixing methods, with our taste for ever brighter and more forward-sounding vocal parts.

Sibilance is best tackled at source – i.e. during the recording itself. Although there are technical solutions for reducing sibilance, including placing a pencil vertically in front of the mic diaphragm, more often than not using a mic that accentuates less of the high end or altering the position of the mic in relation to the singer's mouth will do the job.

If you have to deal with sibilance in the mix, there are a number of approaches that can help:

▸ Use **level automation** to reduce the relative volume of S sounds,
▸ Avoid too much **high-end EQ** gain,
▸ Roll away highs in **reverbs** and **delays**, or automate them so Ss don't ring out,
▸ Reduce the amount of **compression** on vocal parts,
▸ Use a **de-esser** (*page 217*).

A **de-esser** is a tool primarily designed to deal with the specific problem of sibilance in vocal parts.

The objective of de-essing is to reduce only the problematic frequencies that lie in the sibilant range while leaving the rest of the signal unchanged. To set up a de-esser, identify the target sibilant frequency, widen or narrow the band then reduce to taste. With careful setup, only the undesired sibilance is caught and the rest of the signal is left untouched. An 'audition' button makes the selection process easier by allowing you to hear the target frequency being reduced in isolation.

Not all manufacturers use the same technical process to de-ess. The majority opt for frequency-conscious dynamic compression to duck the unwanted material. Others, like SPL's De-esser, introduce the selected sibilant frequencies back to the original signal with an inverted polarity so that they cancel out a percentage of the offending S sound. If all this sounds a bit technical, the end result is the same – less sibilance.

TIP The general target ranges for sibilant frequencies are 3–6kHz (male) and 4–10kHz (female).

TIP There is a world of difference between cheap and more expensive de-essers. Use the one that sounds smoothest and most natural on the sibilant material.

TIP Use automation to reduce the de-esser's effect (or bypass it altogether) when sibilance is not present to stop it from impacting on the rest of the vocal signal.

TIP It is not uncommon for a vocal to have more than one sibilant frequency. In such cases, try two – or more – de-essers in series.

TIP It is easy to go too far with de-essers, generating unnaturally lispy results. Use them carefully and sparingly, only removing narrow notches of signal. Regularly bypass the effect and A/B against well produced vocal tracks to check you're not making things worse.

TIP Compression and high-end EQ boosts both make sibilant problems worse. Sometimes to resolve sibilance all you need to do is ease back on both.

TIP De-essers usually work best last in the vocal processing chain, after EQ and compression.

AMBIENT AND SPATIAL EFFECTS

Reverb and/or delay help vocals settle into a mix and give them a sense of liveliness without which they sound uncomfortably dry.

When choosing **reverb**, you can go down either the convolution or algorithmic/synthetic route (*page 222*). Although the former sometimes fits the bill – particularly when using shorter room and chamber settings featuring real-world settings from the world's finest recording rooms – the sound and flexibility of a good quality algorithmic reverb is usually the preferred option when treating vocals.

Room and **hall** settings both deliver good results, with room settings generating a shorter, more intimate sound. But probably the most widely used reverb type on vocals is the **plate** setting popularised by classic units like the EMT 140. Other choices include digital recreations from units like the EMT 250, Lexicon 224, 300 or PCM 96 and Bricasti M7.

When you've found a reverb character that suits the vocal you are mixing, it's a case of simply tweaking the parameters to help it fit the mix (it's one of the few occasions where preset surfing is both legitimate and useful). Key tweaks include:

▶▶ **Pre-delay.** Increasing the pre-delay time helps ease the ambience away from the dry vocal to keep it at the front of the mix. Listen carefully to the timing: you don't usually want the reverb to enter the mix after a delay that's out of kilter with the song's tempo.

▶▶ **Early reflections (ERs).** Bright-sounding ERs (*page 223*) breathe life into a signal in a subtle way. Shaping the ER tonality using reverb filters changes the character of a vocal part in a similar way to EQ.

PRO TIPS

NOIR

"The hardest part [when writing 'Explode'] was getting the arrangement right and make room for both melodies and Chris's lovely vocal hooks.

"I played around with the arrangement and used my ears for what I felt sounded good: where in the story would there be room for melody and words?"

▶▶ **Length/tail.** Tweak to taste bearing in mind the tempo of the song. Longer values make a sound 'bigger', while making it less immediate and prominent in the mix.

▶▶ **Low/high-cut filters.** Left uncontrolled, reverb can contribute to a messy mix, especially if multiple instances are used across different parts. Filter out unnecessary frequencies on the reverb return to keep the mix uncluttered. Start by rolling away lows (below around 100Hz) and cutting highs from 5hKz or so to reduce tinny/spitty sounds that follow bright consonants (Ps, Ts), as well as sibilant resonances.

Although you may get the result you want with a single instance of reverb, some producers use more than one, combining them with subtle delay/s. Vocal ambience that is both up-front but with a defined tail, for example, is achieved by combining

Make way for the vocals

If a vocal sounds great in isolation but you find yourself making endless EQ tweaks while trying to fit it in the mix, it may be the wider arrangement that is at fault rather than the vocal itself. Remember that a typical vocal occupies a large amount of frequency real estate making clashes with other melodic parts, including synths, keys and percussion, inevitable. A busy mix will present even the most competent mix engineer with a challenge. Solutions include:

▶▶ **SENDING ALL MELODIC ELEMENTS** that clash with the vocals to a single 'music bus' then using EQ to carve out a gently sloping notch at the frequency that contains the bulk of the vocal energy. If that doesn't work, you can increase that separation by applying a similarly gentle EQ boost to the vocal at the same frequency.

▶▶ **RETHINKING ARRANGEMENT** decisions to mitigate clashes. You may decide to shift a synth down an octave, for example, so the two parts occupy different areas.

▶▶ **CHANGING CLASHING SOUNDS.** If the snare hits at the same frequency the vocal shines in, either tweak the snare EQ or change the sound altogether.

▶▶ *REMOVING* **CLASHING PARTS.** It's the nuclear option, but in a vocal-heavy mix nothing is more sacred than the vocal.

Chapter six
Vocals

OSKAR OFFERMANN

You can get memorable vocals with no more than a phone, a girlfriend and one's own voice. On the track 'August '14' on *Le Grand To Do*, Offerman uses two different vocals. The first "is my ex-girlfriend singing another song, pitched differently. It was a song which Edward and I played in our DJ sets and she wanted to know what it was, so I had her voice message on my phone for a while and found it much later and played around with it.

"The other vocal is me. I like the idea of this sort of dialogue between the two of us."

a short room setting heavy on ERs with a longer hall/plate tail. In general, the simpler and sparser a track, the simpler and sparser the vocal ambient treatment can be.

NOTE With bright reverb treatments, use a de-esser before the reverb to eliminate sibilant build-up in the ambience. *This de-esser won't alter the original vocal.*

NOTE Too much reverb pushes a vocal back in the mix, robbing it of its usual space at the front. To avoid this, try reverb settings that are heavy on ERs (rather than tail) and substituting reverb for subtle delays.

If reverb is causing more problems than it's solving then you don't have to use it. **Delay** does a similar – sometimes better – job. Try slapback delay in a busy arrangement with an energetic vocal. Mixed low, stereo ping-pong delays can help settle an epic vocal into a busy mix.

The critical setting when using delay is the delay time, which is usually synced to the tempo of the song. When the delay time feels right, increase the number of repeats to taste. Two or three semi-audible repeats is usually all you need, but you may choose more in complex arrangements or for epic trance and prog vocals.

As with reverb, EQing the delay return helps control the tone of repeats. Reducing lower frequencies frees low end headroom

while shaving highs stops the delay from interfering with the unaffected vocal. A more natural approach is to use a **tape-style delay**, which includes degradation of the repeated signal as standard, with each repeat losing a little more high end.

TIP To get the right balance between too much and too little reverb and delay, increase the relevant return until there is obviously too much effect in the mix, then pull it back down until there is obviously too little. Settle on a value in the middle. Leave the fader for a bit, then return to it later, easing it down by a dB or so to see if it has an obvious impact. If it doesn't, set the fader at this new lower value.

MODULATION AND CHARACTER EFFECTS

Although most vocal parts require little additional processing, more esoteric effects that are sometimes bought to play include:

Overdrive/tape saturation: where a vocal needs more bulk, running some of the signal to a parallel overdrive or tape saturation plugin can have the required effect.

Bit-crushers: If subtle overdrive doesn't do the job, try a bit-crusher. Used subtly it can generate a more solid vocal. Push it to the extreme for ever more deranged, lo-fi and robotic results.

Chorus: Although chorus effects on the lead vocal usually undermine its mono fidelity, 'smearing' its pivotal place in the mix, gentle chorus can be useful on harmonies and chorus parts to keep them from interfering with the lead vocal.

Other stereo effects: Wideners and stereo enhancers may be used on harmony and chorus blocks to tease a little more artificial width from a stereo group. On lead lines, as with chorus, you risk destabilising the part. Generally, stereo effects are either best used sparingly or as an obvious effect.

'Character' plugins: like Noveltech's Character and Aphex Aural Exciter can bring a tired part to life. Although results are hit and miss, a small boost of 'character' (supplied on a parallel bus or treating at most 10-20 per cent of the signal) may help a vocal stand out in a mix. Such effects are best used sparingly or as a last resort.

'WTF' vocal effects: A **formant shifter** can transform a man into a woman and vice versa without altering the pitch – good for adding extra character to backing vocals, especially when the lead vocalist is performing all the vocal parts. At extreme settings formant shifters generate robot voices. Try a **ring modulator** for more classic robot sounds. The rotary **Leslie cabinet**, derived from classic organs, creates a warm, warbly psychedelic effect. Used sparingly it adds trippy character.

Treating vocals

STARTING POINTS FOR DIFFERENT SOUNDS

The following starting points and associated walkthroughs come with this caveat: *95 plus per cent of mix decisions depend on the choice of vocalist and their performance in front of the mic. You will not get a tender chillout vocal from a big-voice disco diva, and vice versa.* Assuming you start out with a well-recorded raw vocal with a style that suits the intentions of the mix, production treatments include:

PROG LEAD VOCAL

To get the big, ethereal, trancey kind of sound exemplified in Kaskade and Deadmau5's 'I remember' start as follows:

- **Employ assertive compression**. These kinds of vocals can't be allowed to get lost in the mix. Instead they need a constant dynamic that is almost unnaturally flat. Begin with a ratio of 3 or 4:1 reducing the signal by 4-6dB and then increase both to taste. If doing too much with a single compressor has negative effects, try two in series. Follow this with a limiter.

- For added bulk, consider adding a **saturation or overdrive plugin** on a parallel bus fed by 10-50 per cent of the original signal.

- Use **two reverb settings**, one a room setting, heavyish on ERs, the second a longer plate with a lush tail. Send both reverbs to a single bus that is compressed to make the tails even more defined.

- To stop a big reverb/delay tail from interfering with the lead vocal, use a **ducker** triggered by the vocal to push the reverb volume down when the lead is in.

- Stereo or ping-pong **delays** add more scale to the vocal line and help it blend deeper into the mix; roll away highs to keep the dry vocals prominent.

- Use **automation** to send specific words and line endings to an obvious delay/reverb bus.

- **EQ** for presence and air.

GUTSY DISCO

The feel-good diva disco tones of an Angie Brown-style performance can benefit from:

- **Volume automation** and **light compression**. Remember that compression reins in dynamics – which is precisely what you don't want to do with an explosive disco performance. If you need additional bulk consider parallel compression.

- Parallel saturation or overdrive may help fill out the important lower mids.

- When **EQing**, don't lose too much low end – that's where a lot of a vocal's natural energy lies.

- Keep **reverb** settings short and sparse, using a mix of ERs and room sounds with judiciously applied pre-delay to keep the vocal where you want it: at the forefront of the mix. Where a bigger sound is required, a small amount of plate can help, but **delays** (including slapback) are often more appropriate.

PUMPING CHILLWAVE

Throw all the traditional rules out to get the huge, pumping style popularised by Washed Out; standard good practice has no place here.

- **Cut** as high as 200-450Hz when rolling away lows to create a brittle sound.

- Follow this with a big **reverb**; halls and plates will both do the job, as can lo-fi choices like spring reverbs. Avoid pre-delays; the reverb is part and parcel of the vocal sound itself, not an additional effect. The tail should be long and defined without being over-messy. Play with the low and high cut filters to shape the reverb tone.

- After the reverb add **heavy-duty compression in line,** triggered by an on-the-beat kick. Start with a ratio of around 3:1, reducing as much as 12dB of signal for

ALEX SOMERS (SIGUR RÓS)

"For the vocals that Jónsi recorded at my studio I used a tube U47, which is so flattering on his voice. It has a beautiful mid-range and, whereas a lot of modern condenser mics are overly bright, old Neumanns sound so good.

"Jónsi sang the songs all the way through, doing just one take, or a second one that we could comp from if there was a phrase we didn't like. He also did a lot of backing vocals, and those were recorded really fast – once he came up with a backing vocal line, he'd do four performances straight away, and I'd then pan them left-right-left-right to get a wide, choir-like effect."

Chapter six
Vocals

a pumping sound. The attack and release values are critical: the vocal should pump in time with the song's tempo.

▶▶ Tape **saturation**, at quite extreme levels, gives an organic warmth to the sound (and at higher levels, a desirably lo-fi result).

BACKING VOCALS

The trick with backing vocals (BVs) and harmonies is to give them a defined presence in the mix without allowing them to dominate the lead vocal. This can be achieved by:

▶▶ Rolling away some of the higher and lower frequencies using **shelving EQ**. You don't need to be extreme here; just make sure BVs have less presence than the lead.

▶▶ Using **more extreme compression** (higher ratio, more signal reduction) than on the lead vocal; don't worry about losing some of the natural dynamics of the performance as the lead will carry the bulk of the energy.

▶▶ Using less reverb on BVs than on the lead. In vocal arrangements that have a large number of BVs/harmonies the mix can get clogged by too much reverb triggered from the different vocal lines.

▶▶ Using a touch of chorus or ensemble to subtly diffuse the stereo focus of the BVs.

DOUBLE-TRACKS

The treatment for double-tracks is usually the same as for a single tracks – only repeated. Indeed, if the treatment is too different you risk jeopardising the doubling effect.

Process the main vocal line first and when you've got the sound you want copy the channel strip to the doubled track. Assign both doubles to the same fader group or bus so that both are controlled with a single mouse movement.

You may need to reduce the amount of reverb and/or delay on each channel as you're effectively doubling the amount in the mix by multiplying the track count. Avoid chorus effects on doubles; the doubling effect provides a pseudo-chorus feel anyway making additional processing redundant.

The main consideration with double-tracks is panning. Common conventions **include:**

➲ panning at **2 and 10 o'clock** or somewhere thereabouts,

➲ panning **wide** (though you'll need near-flawless doubles),

➲ each track **panned to centre** (in these instances reduce the level of the qualitatively weaker double).

Of these, the first option is the easiest to get sounding right. Panning both to centre risks introducing phase effects if the takes are too identical, while with hard panning it's too easy to disassociate the two parts, leaving a gap in the middle of the mix.

↻ There's no reason why you need to stop at double-tracks. Some producers use **triple-tracks** with the lead anchor in the centre supported by low-level doubles panned either side. This solves the 'missing middle' problem and allows you to use slightly different (and less processor hungry) effects on the supporting tracks.

NOTE It's a rookie's mistake to think that doubling makes for bigger sounds. In fact, the opposite is almost always true. And though doubled vocals can sound *sublime*, they will never sound as *big* as a single well-performed vocal mixed loud and proud at the front of a mix. If a single take works best but you still want to include doubles, you can use them in the chorus or to highlight specific phrases. Or take the triple-track approach with the lead vocal considerably louder than the supporting tracks which are then used to add almost imperceptible spatial support to the lead.

TIP You can create fake double-tracks by copying a vocal line onto a new track, delaying it by a few ms (start at 30) and using a pitch-shift or pitch-correction

// WALKTHROUGHS

Vocal sound: Gutsy disco 🎧

1 Gutsy vocals start with a solid vocal performance. Here's the dry audio played alongside the mix sounding nice enough but sticking out sorely.

2 To sweeten the sound the Pultec gives a gentle boost at 100Hz while a more significant, and wider, boost opens up the voice at 5kHz. The CL 1B with a slow attack, slow release and a ratio of 2:1 shaves off no more than 5dB of signal. Last in chain is an LA-2A in limit mode reducing a final 1dB.

3 Settling this vocal into a busy mix requires a mix of reverb (two types, one roomy EMT-250 plus a long tail from Logic's Space Reverb) and delays, with a stereo delay set to 1/8 Note Dotted. To bulk up the vocal even more a small amount of signal is routed to a parallel bus featuring a 1176 clone.

Vocal sound: Pumping chillwave 🎧

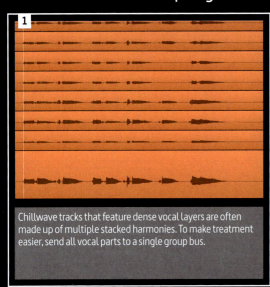

1 Chillwave tracks that feature dense vocal layers are often made up of multiple stacked harmonies. To make treatment easier, send all vocal parts to a single group bus.

2 Radical processing is the name of the game. A big chapel-style reverb, reversed, goes first in chain, followed by EQ to roll away the lows, a de-esser to control the Ss and then a compressor acting almost as a limiter – with an 8:1 ratio and swift attack and release trimming 5-6dB of signal.

3 Next up, a tape delay adds movement (before the compressor), while a Spreader adds width. Finally a tape emulation plugin, driven hard, infuses the vocal block with fuzzy-round-the-edge warmth. A number of aux sends feed additional delays and reverbs to fit the sound into the mix.

Vocal sound: Prog-style lead

1 The double-tracked vocals in this track have already been comped and edited for pitch and timing using Melodyne. They are panned pretty hard left and right. The slight variations between the two give them a wide chorus effect.

2 We are after an up-front sound with an obviously compressed effect. This is achieved using a compressor (optical model) with a reasonably high ratio – around 3:1 – trimming around 5-8dB from peaks. A slowish attack (13ms) allows opening transients through to retain intelligibility.

3 Ambient effects are supplied from three sends. The first feeds a stereo delay, the second a long, bright plate. The third feeds the pictured Space Echo. The dry sound is now backed by a lush halo of ambience and cascading delays.

4 Another aux feed is set up on each double track. The left feed is slightly delayed and phased then pitched up 7 cents. The right is delayed by a different amount then pitched down -6 cents. These subtly pitch- and time-shifted tracks are mixed back in low to provide 3D bulk and interest.

5 A stereo bounce of the vocal double-tracks is treated to reverse reverb (*page 194*), which is placed on a new track then heavily compressed and widened. Mixed at around 20% of the volume of the lead vocal, it lays down an ethereal pad-style base on which the leads sit.

6 Finally, details are added in the form of delayed vocal spins (check the words 'blew' and 'love' that fill gaps in the vocal line). You can set these up using automation but we added a new track with edits of the audio. The main vocals are then EQd and de-essed to round off the sound.

Chapter six
Vocals

plugin at a low retune rate to slightly change its tuning over time in the way a singer would when doubling. (*See Fake double-tracks, below*).

CHORUS VOCAL BLOCKS

Multi-tracked vocal blocks are typically sent to a stereo vocal bus for combined processing. Usual bus treatments include:

▸▸ **Bus compression**, with a suitably gluey SSL-style bus compressor (medium attack and release), ratio of 3:1 or above and signal reduction to taste. The specific treatment will vary depending on how dynamic you want the part to be – there's no point in flattening or robbing the opening attack transients of an energetic diva chorus for example. Start by reducing 2–3dB of signal and increase to taste.

▸▸ **EQ** to sweeten and trouble-shoot the layered signal. Where a lead vocal needs to shine above the chorus block, reduce highs. Shelve away lower frequencies (anywhere up to around 250–350Hz) to alleviate low-end congestion.

▸▸ **De-essing**, to significantly reduce multiple instances of sibilance. The usual approach here is to allow one or two chorus parts to carry the Ss and then reduce them heavily in the others either using a de-esser or volume automation; any undesirable audio artefacts introduced by the de-esser are masked by the louder lead vocal (and the Ss in that). Out of time sibilant and plosive consonants (Ps, Bs etc) should be aligned before mixdown. Having multiple consonants hitting at different times across different vocal tracks seriously hinders intelligibility.

// WALKTHROUGHS

Fake double-tracks

1. Select the track you wish to artificially double and copy its contents and channel strip onto a second track.

2. On the duplicate track, first insert a delay plugin (or manually delay the audio file) set to around 25-45ms. Then add pitch correction to slowly retune the duplicate. We've used Logic's Pitch Correction with a response time of 378ms set with a chromatic scale.

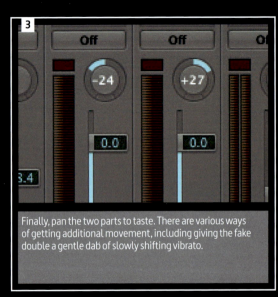

3. Finally, pan the two parts to taste. There are various ways of getting additional movement, including giving the fake double a gentle dab of slowly shifting vibrato.

▸ A single common **reverb** treatment – often a hall or plate. As a general rule, the higher the track count in a vocal block, the less reverb you'll need on the block.

AD-LIBS

Ad-libs are normally treated in a similar way to the lead vocal, with different EQ settings if the ad-lib is sung in a different register. If ad-libs are battling for space against the lead – a common problem in a busy mix – then it can be a symptom of arrangement overcrowding: ad-libs shine best when the lead vocal is absent.

Where you need both in at the same time, try:

▸ ducking the volume of one against the other;
▸ shifting the stereo placement of both to increase separation;
▸ treating the ad-lib to a lift from a 'character' plugin to differentiate it in the mix.

Automating levels rather than bashing the life out of them using an overbearing compressor will help retain energy if the ad-lib is dynamically rich.

EAR CANDY

To retain sonic interest in a vocal part – particularly if it repeats during the arrangement – you might introduce automated delays, reverb builds, spoken word shadows and EQ effects. For further inspiration, check out hip hop and R&B tracks that feature melodic vocals alongside spoken word elements: R&B producers have been dealing with multiple vocal parts in complex vocal arrangements for decades. Common techniques include:

▸ **Echoed words:** Where a noteworthy word or phrase comes before a pause in the vocal part, you can fill the gap by repeating the last words using an echo or delay plugin. To do this, automate the delay so that it only switches in to repeat the word/phrase you wish to highlight.

▸ **Spun delays:** A variant of the above where you effect the delay return to add interest. Try anything from telephone EQ to hard-tuned Auto-Tune.

▸ **Reverb highlights:** Decide on a word or phrase that you want to receive the 'big verb' treatment then automate a reverb plugin to switch on for the word/phrase in question with a 50 per cent or thereabouts wet/dry balance. Unusual convolution impulse responses can deliver leftfield flavours to a vanilla vocal line. For variation, automate the wet/dry balance over time.

▸ **EQ highlights:** As above, but use (radically) different EQ like telephone EQ to highlight select phrases.

▸ **Reverb builds:** An effective trick to ratchet up the tension, automate an increase in the level of the reverb return over a period of time (1, 2, 4, 8 or even 16 bars) so that the previously up-front vocal becomes more cloudy in the mix as a reverb halo builds around it. When the vocal is all but lost in reverb clouds (helped by EQ automation to reduce the mids and highs), kill the automated reverb send so that the vocal returns to where it was: bright and in-your-face.

▸ **Spoken word ghosting:** You'll need to be in at the recording stage to make this work. Get the vocalist to perform a spoken word double-track against the sung lead vocal and then introduce it into the mix at specific points to add bulk or create 'ghosting' ambient effects.

▸ **Effected cast-offs:** Unique timbres can be generated using rejected takes to feed a reverb instead of the retained vocal line. Here place a rejected take on a track, reduce its volume to zero then use a pre-fade send to feed a reverb. The result? The lead vocal is given a reverb treatment from a different vocal take. It's a subtle effect but in the right track can give unique results.

The golden rule when using any of this vocal ear candy is – for the most part – to *use it sparingly*. Overdoing a single technique, or using too many different ones, risks arrangement and listener fatigue.

MARC KINCHEN

The godfather of the cut-up vocal sample, Marc Kinchen's catalogue includes the iconic remix of the Nightcrawlers' 'Push The Feeling On'.

How did his trademark vocal technique originate? "I was getting asked to remix songs that I didn't really like or songs where the melodic line wasn't strong enough, so I basically tried to create my own hook by chopping the vocals.

"Probably the first or second time I did it, I was like, 'Oh... This works.' Then I realised, 'This works every single time.' Even now if I'm doing a song that's really great I still do it anyway because it makes a second hook."

Chapter six
Vocals

Vocal effects

Much of what has been written so far in this chapter has been about capturing and treating a 'traditional' vocal performance.

But the vocal story doesn't need to go like that, and dance musicians have been steering vocals down more creative avenues for decades. Devices like talk boxes and vocoders have been embraced to make melodies of words, Auto-Tune has been abused to the point of cliché and samplers have been used and abused to give new life to weary vocal samples. If you like the idea of an obvious human element in a track but don't want to go down the usual sung or spoken-word route then the only limit is your imagination.

Vocoders are electronic devices, originally designed to encode speech, that imprint the sonic character of one signal (the 'modulator') onto that of another (the 'carrier'). They do this by dividing the signal of each using a series of band-pass filters and then recombining them to produce the final effect.

Although almost any kind of signal can be used, most commonly the modulator is a vocal and the carrier is a synth or rich pad so that when different notes are played the vocal part is given a melodic or chordal sound such as on Mylo's seminal 'Drop the Pressure'.

🎧 **The Vocoder 2000 from EMS, the 16-band British classic from the late 1970s, widely considered to be one of the finest ever made. A second-hand model costs a small fortune.**

There are any number of reasonable vocoder plugins, including native ones in Logic, Live and Cubase SX. Typically these are placed on instrument tracks with the modulator signal fed via sidechain from a vocal audio track. Chords or melody lines are then programmed on the vocoder instrumental track using MIDI. Depending on the settings used, you can get anything from clear 'electrified' vocal sounds to chordal pads that bear no resemblance to the original vocal line (*Vocoded vocals walkthrough, page 197*).

Although simple enough to set up, getting good results from a vocoder is not quite as easy, involving a certain amount of trial and error. For the best results:

▶▶ **Speak clearly into the mic** when recording. The more articulate the initial recording, the more recognisable the mixed signal will be. This means enunciating clearly, keeping the vocal volume as constant as possible and ensuring consonants are in exactly the right place.

▶▶ **Use a compressor to even out vocal levels**. Be extra careful when tweaking the attack and release settings that you don't inadvertently weaken line beginnings (which means a longer attack time to let word starts through). A transient designer can sometimes help bring out detail.

▶▶ **Remove all breaths** and other parts of the performance that aren't essential. Remember you aren't looking for a natural sound with a vocoder; edit the audio with brutal singularity.

Talk boxes, frequently confused with vocoders, are different devices. An effect that allows a musician to modify the sound of an instrument being played by altering the shape of their mouth around a plastic tube mouthpiece, it is almost certainly a talk box that is responsible for Daft Punk's 'Around the World' vocal (which was subsequently *treated* with a vocoder).

Originally popularised by guitarists such as Peter Frampton, the talk box has a more guttural 'vowely' effect than the vocoder and can give a more intelligible vocal sound. The sticking point is that talk boxes are difficult to use and there are not many plugin incarnations that come close to offering the same sound – although NI's The Voice does a reasonable job.

▶ **TIP** Daft Punk, it is rumoured, used the 'Hard Brass' preset of a Yamaha DX100 – the same synth and preset used by Roger Troutman – to melodise their talk box tones.

// WALKTHROUGHS

The chorus block 🔊

1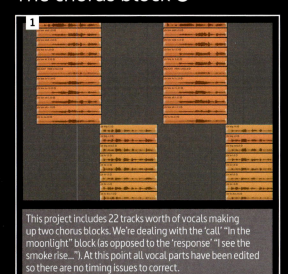
This project includes 22 tracks worth of vocals making up two chorus blocks. We're dealing with the 'call' "In the moonlight" block (as opposed to the 'response' "I see the smoke rise..."). At this point all vocal parts have been edited so there are no timing issues to correct.

2
The double-tracked lead anchors are the first to be processed, with a similar chain to the Gutsy disco lead vocal (*page 186*); that is, some gentle Pultec sweetening (with less bottom end than the verse lead) and the same CL 1B and LA-2A compression/limiting combination as before.

3
The harmonies are all sent to a single bus. On the bus a Pultec removes a significant amount of low end before an SSL bus compressor followed by an LA-2A on Limit mode reduces dynamics. Last in chain is a stereo spreader to give slightly more width to the combined signal.

4
Now for the ambient effects, which are the same bussed effects as on the lead vocal: a roomy EMT 250 and a longer plate. Just as important is the space-filling stereo delay with timings tweaked so that the delays hit just off the beat, and filters set so that the delays don't interfere with the toplines.

5
To give even more prominence, depth and movement to the chorus, a feed is sent from the harmony block to a delay line with a long delay, generous feedback and a telephone-style (reverbed) EQ. Although it may sound overkill out of context, in step 6 things start to make sense.

6
With the full mix playing you can hear how the large reverbs and delays do their job. The only last tweak – to help the 'answer' lines stand out above the 'moonlight' calls – is to run them through the Fatso and give them a wide 8kHz boost. Volume automation completes the picture.

Chapter six
Vocals

Auto-Tune and similar retuning devices have been performing extreme vocal processing duties since Cher opened the world's then-innocent ears to the hard-tuned sound of 'Believe'. Thus spawned a new vocal production epoch, the effect used most famously on Romanthony's voice in Daft Punk's 'One More Time'.

The hard-tuned effect is easy to achieve: simply push retune to the max and remove all vibrato. A more precise result is achieved by programming the desired melody using Graphical mode. (*Hard Auto-Tune, right*).

But Auto-Tune can do considerably more than the tired hard-tuned sound. How about copying the same vocal part across multiple tracks to create virtual electronic choirs by programming different melodies on each instance of Auto-Tune? Or programming melodies outside of the singer's natural range to create other-worldly textures? Or feeding non-vocal material to Auto-Tune for artificial melodics?

Melodyne can be abused too. Extreme retuning effects in the same vein as Auto-Tune are achieved by removing all internal pitch drift. Shifting the formants outside their natural range can also deliver unusual and often interesting results.

◊ The Rocktron Banshee – a modern incarnation of the often unstable talk boxes of old.

Trashy lo-fi vocals are made using **distortion** and associated effects.

For a gentle fuzzy-edged sound, employ **light overdrive, amp simulators or overloaded tape saturators**. For more messed-up results try **distortion** units and **bit-crushers**.

EQ can be used to further shape the sound (phone-style EQ filter treatments combined with distortion sounds suitably brash).

To make trash tones more interesting, **automate** distortion/bit-crushing parameters. Change the bit rate on a bit-crusher during a phrase or across an eight bar section for engaging results. Remember that distorting a signal compresses it and can result in grating sounds: keep a subtractive EQ handy at the end of the FX chain and beware of over-filling spaces in a mix.

TIP Unique 'trash vocals' can be created with no more than a mic, an instance of Auto-Tune (or similar pitch corrector) and a distortion plugin. Simply record a sung phrase. Use pitch correction to pull it into tune. Then copy the audio onto three or four tracks and on each instance reprogram the pitch to create an artificial 'choir'. Finally send all choir parts to the same bus and run through distortion for a punk-style 'trash choir'.

For vocal mayhem or to generate new ideas from a vocal phrase load up a **glitch plugin** like blue/Illformed's Glitch 2 or iZotope's Stutter Edit. Send a vocal performance or pre-cut vocal loop through it, bounce it down then sift through the results: there's invariably some inspiring audio wheat among the chaff.

A more refined version of the above, used across a range of genres to bring human elements to a groove, is to use a **sampler** to trigger short bursts of a sung or spoken word audio file in time with a beat.

Routing velocity to the sample start point then changing the MIDI velocity of each note is a great way of sprinkling a beat with snatches of chopped up vocal, which can be as minimal or hooky as you like (*Cut up glitched vocals, page 196*). For source material use anything from short samples to longer *a cappella* phrases. Or just hook up a mic and record an original phrase yourself. Also try spoken word phrases and bounced-down chorus blocks.

The fact that these percussive vocals are controlled by MIDI means you can have additional fun by messing with the MIDI sequence itself. Cut, paste and re-arrange notes to generate whole new sequences. Adding pitch-bends (with pitch bend wheel routed to pitch) can introduce

Chapter six
Vocals

anything from subtle movement to wobbly fills. Experiment also with extreme retuning, moving the same note through different octaves or creating whole new melody lines based around interesting vocalisations.

Although these kinds of sampler techniques are surfing something of a production wave, you can embrace a more retro vibe by taking inspiration from older vocal **resampling** tricks. It may been done to death, but sample retriggering (re-re-retriggering – Fatboy Slim-style), if done creatively, can still generate solid hooks (simply drop a vocal phrase into a sampler and then retrigger it at ever quicker intervals to increase energy towards a drop).

Another technique made possible by early generations of samplers was **digital time-stretching**. Effective for generating both lo-fi vocals and fractured alien-style speech, it has been largely ignored as a technique for the past few years (and is therefore ripe for rediscovery).

The technique is simplicity itself. Every DAW includes some form of timestretch facility. Simply load in a vocal file and start stretching (or shortening). Experiment with low bit-rates and poor quality stretch algorithms for lo-fi results.

Finally, although an oldie, **reverse reverb** can sound great on vocals (*Reverse reverb vocal walkthrough, overleaf*). The effect, which bestows a sweepy, sucking reverse tail to the front of a vocal line, is achieved by reversing a dry vocal, adding reverb, bouncing the result, then reversing the bounced file again before lining it up alongside the dry original. For best results experiment with the reverb settings and align the reversed file carefully.

// WALKTHROUGHS

Hard 'Auto-Tune'

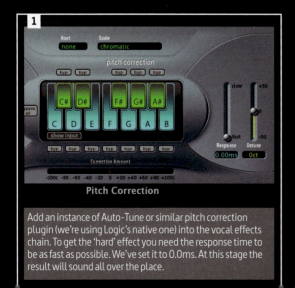

1. Pitch Correction
Add an instance of Auto-Tune or similar pitch correction plugin (we're using Logic's native one) into the vocal effects chain. To get the 'hard' effect you need the response time to be as fast as possible. We've set it to 0.0ms. At this stage the result will sound all over the place.

2. If you know the track's key, set its root note and scale type in the correction plugin. If you don't, experiment with different settings until you get a result that shifts notes into the places you want them. In this instance the scale that works best is an F melodic minor scale.

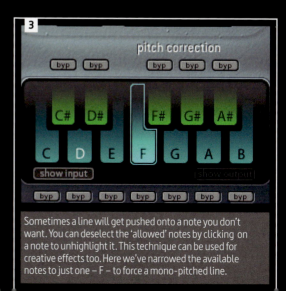

3. Sometimes a line will get pushed onto a note you don't want. You can deselect the 'allowed' notes by clicking on a note to unhighlight it. This technique can be used for creative effects too. Here we've narrowed the available notes to just one – F – to force a mono-pitched line.

Reverse reverb vocal

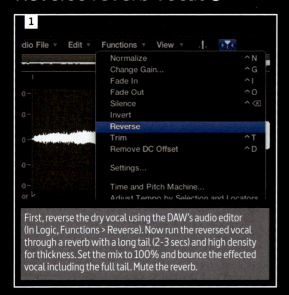

First, reverse the dry vocal using the DAW's audio editor (In Logic, Functions > Reverse). Now run the reversed vocal through a reverb with a long tail (2-3 secs) and high density for thickness. Set the mix to 100% and bounce the effected vocal including the full tail. Mute the reverb.

Reverse the dry vocal file so that it plays the correct way round again then import the reverbed audio file onto a new audio track and reverse that as well.

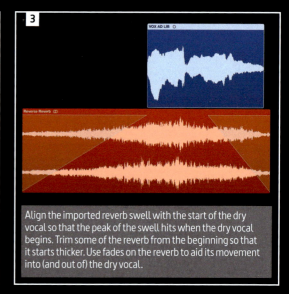

Align the imported reverb swell with the start of the dry vocal so that the peak of the swell hits when the dry vocal begins. Trim some of the reverb from the beginning so that it starts thicker. Use fades on the reverb to aid its movement into (and out of) the dry vocal.

Telephone EQ

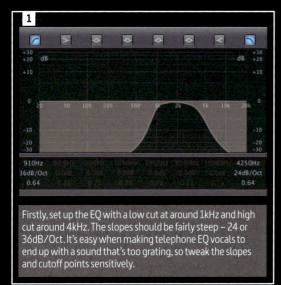

Firstly, set up the EQ with a low cut at around 1kHz and high cut around 4kHz. The slopes should be fairly steep – 24 or 36dB/Oct. It's easy when making telephone EQ vocals to end up with a sound that's too grating, so tweak the slopes and cutoff points sensitively.

To add more presence and grit – modelling a proper old-school telephone – low-level distortion is added. The sound is further shaped using the Tone control. The result is a little spiky so we've made a precision cut at 3kHz to control a band of wayward upper mid frequencies.

A more subtle effect is the 'telephone EQ spin', where select words are sent for a delayed EQ treatment. In this instance the words 'sand' and 'built me' are sent to a 'spin' effects bus on which sits the telephone EQ, a tape delay, flanger, panner and compressor that pulls the signal together.

Vocal transition riser

1 Load a vocal sample onto an audio track or load in a sample into a sampler and trigger it with MIDI. We're using a vocal loop from Sample Magic's 'Nu Disco' sample pack, and have edited the region down to the first vocal stab.

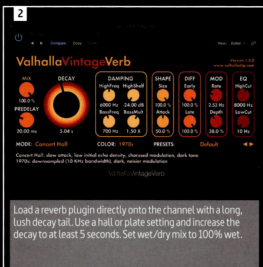

2 Load a reverb plugin directly onto the channel with a long, lush decay tail. Use a hall or plate setting and increase the decay to at least 5 seconds. Set wet/dry mix to 100% wet.

3 Bounce out the reverbed audio, allowing plenty of time to capture the reverb tail. Import the bounced audio on a second track then reverse it. At this stage we already have a perfectly useable vocal riser, but a few extra tweaks will take it to the next level.

4 In Ableton you can directly pitch audio regions. In Logic, right-click on the newly imported audio region and select 'Convert to new sampler track'. Check 'Create zones from regions', uncheck 'Create '1 Shot' zones' and hit OK. An EXS24 sampler is loaded with a MIDI note triggering the rise.

5 Apply pitch bend to the MIDI region by double-clicking on the region to bring up the piano roll (shortcut: press P), then draw in an upwards pitch bend.

6 A filter cutoff rise is used to emphasise the rise. Turn EXS24's filter on, set cutoff and resonance to around 15%. Add an automation lane in Logic and draw in filter cutoff automation to open the filter as the sound pitches upwards. Finally, add reverb to smooth off the end of the rise.

// WALKTHROUGHS

Cut up glitched vocals

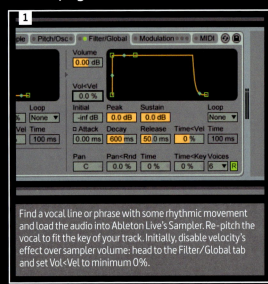

1 Find a vocal line or phrase with some rhythmic movement and load the audio into Ableton Live's Sampler. Re-pitch the vocal to fit the key of your track. Initially, disable velocity's effect over sampler volume: head to the Filter/Global tab and set Vol<Vel to minimum 0%.

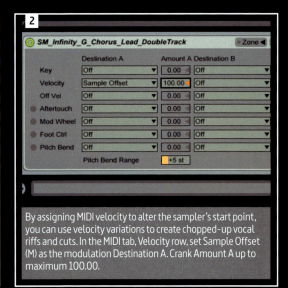

2 By assigning MIDI velocity to alter the sampler's start point, you can use velocity variations to create chopped-up vocal riffs and cuts. In the MIDI tab, Velocity row, set Sample Offset (M) as the modulation Destination A. Crank Amount A up to maximum 100.00.

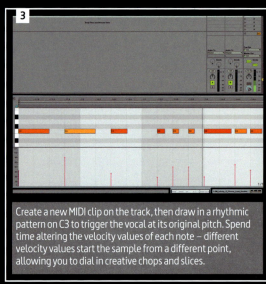

3 Create a new MIDI clip on the track, then draw in a rhythmic pattern on C3 to trigger the vocal at its original pitch. Spend time altering the velocity values of each note – different velocity values start the sample from a different point, allowing you to dial in creative chops and slices.

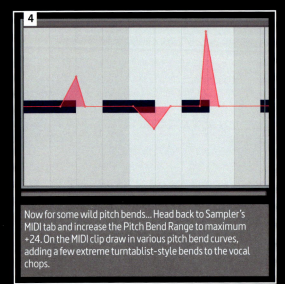

4 Now for some wild pitch bends… Head back to Sampler's MIDI tab and increase the Pitch Bend Range to maximum +24. On the MIDI clip draw in various pitch bend curves, adding a few extreme turntablist-style bends to the vocal chops.

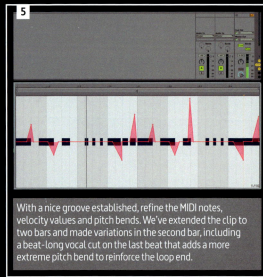

5 With a nice groove established, refine the MIDI notes, velocity values and pitch bends. We've extended the clip to two bars and made variations in the second bar, including a beat-long vocal cut on the last beat that adds a more extreme pitch bend to reinforce the loop end.

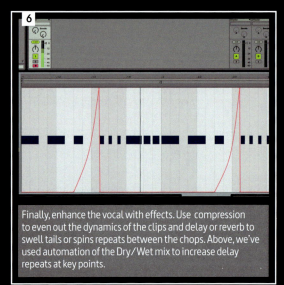

6 Finally, enhance the vocal with effects. Use compression to even out the dynamics of the clips and delay or reverb to swell tails or spins repeats between the chops. Above, we've used automation of the Dry/Wet mix to increase delay repeats at key points.

Vocoded vocals

1 A vocoder needs two signals to work its magic, a carrier – typically a voice – and a modulator – usually a synth. Most vocoders have inputs for both signals, while some, such as Logic's EVOC 20, have the synth built in. Because of this, routing the signals is different in each DAW.

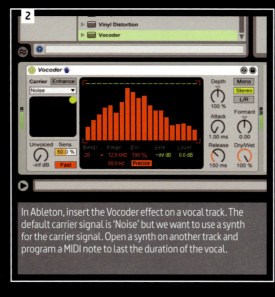

2 In Ableton, insert the Vocoder effect on a vocal track. The default carrier signal is 'Noise' but we want to use a synth for the carrier signal. Open a synth on another track and program a MIDI note to last the duration of the vocal.

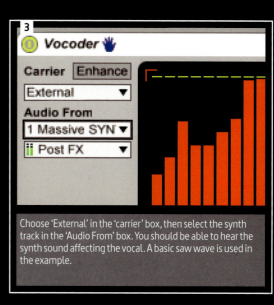

3 Choose 'External' in the 'carrier' box, then select the synth track in the 'Audio From' box. You should be able to hear the synth sound affecting the vocal. A basic saw wave is used in the example.

4 We are going to mix in some of the noise carrier to help make the vocals more understandable. This is built into most vocoders. In Live it's called 'Unvoiced'. Increase this to bring out the clarity and definition of the tone. In this example it is increased to -20dB.

5 To make the vocoder 'sing' the line needs to be programmed into the synth track. Chords can be input in the same way. Synth tricks such as portamento, vibrato and slides can all be used to produce vocals with movement.

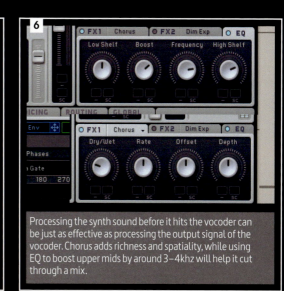

6 Processing the synth sound before it hits the vocoder can be just as effective as processing the output signal of the vocoder. Chorus adds richness and spatiality, while using EQ to boost upper mids by around 3–4khz will help it cut through a mix.

Chapter seven
The studio and its tools

Chapter seven
The studio and its tools

The studio is the most important space in the producer's world...

...and whether that studio is a dedicated room with racks of synths and several pairs of monitors or no more than a laptop and a second-hand pair of speakers, it's the place where the creative magic happens.

It's also a place where vast amounts of time and effort can be wasted.

BEFORE WE BEGIN…

We open with a caveat: *there's no such thing as the perfect studio*. Even the control rooms of Abbey Road – which represent millions of pounds worth of investment – have their idiosyncrasies.

Lower down the food chain, most of us make do with a spare bedroom or shared space in a lounge or garage. Even if we're lucky enough to have a dedicated room to mix in, it's unlikely to have been built with music production in mind – the average household space is rarely of the dimensions or construction that lends itself to trustworthy sonics.

This matters, because **a mix can only be as good as the sound you hear**, and if you're not hearing an accurate representation of what's going on in your DAW then the cuts and boosts, the edits and tweaks – the thousands of decisions performed during mixdown – will be performed half 'blind'.

The most important thing your production/mix space must do is facilitate the creation of music that sounds good to the listener. This becomes immeasurably more difficult if you can't properly *hear* that music.

A poor listening environment can be blamed for two recurring – and sometimes debilitating – complaints expressed by both rookie and experienced producers.

The first is that **no matter how many tweaks you make to a sound, it never seems right**. You might add high end to the snare and increase its attack only to find the result gritty and abrasive which leads you to pull back the highs again. This kind of circular decision-making is commonplace when you can't trust the mix you're hearing and end up dwelling on different pieces of misinformation each time it's played.

The second is **the curse of the untranslatable mix**. In this scenario the mix sounds OK in your own studio, but take it elsewhere – most importantly, when playing it on a club sound system – and it falls apart, with holes and spikes appearing in pivotal frequency spaces: uneven bass, a jarring middle, and so on. The feeling of taking your hard-won creation outside of the studio to be faced with its imperfections in all their dubious glory is one every producer experiences at some point.

The good news is that with a little time, knowledge and expenditure everyone can improve their studio sonics. The results are mixes that are clearer, fuller, easier to pull together and – crucially – translatable. **It is no exaggeration to say that improving your listening environment will do more to benefit your mixes than any number of new plugins or outboard investments.** This fact alone makes the next few pages some of the most important in the book.

GOLDEN EARS

Having access to a great studio is of limited benefit if you don't trust your ears.

The best chefs have palates refined over years of tasting. They are able to take a spoonful of pasta sauce, identify the ingredients and tell intuitively what it needs in terms of seasoning – a pinch more salt, one more basil leaf.

So it is with record producers. The best in the business have 'golden ears' refined through listening intensely to – and working on – thousands of records.

Fortunately all of us can train our ears by doing more of the thing we love… listening to music.

On the most neutral speakers you can, listen to mixes you admire. Listen intently to what's going on in key frequencies; to ambient treatments; to the effects used… Over time you'll develop better critical listening skills.

Chapter seven
The studio and its tools

WHAT YOU HEAR IN THE STUDIO

When you listen to a pair of speakers in the studio what do you actually hear? You hear the direct sound of the mix, but you also hear reflections of the mix as it bounces off hard surfaces in the room, including the walls, ceiling, desk and cupboards. All of these reflections colour the sound reaching your ears – some more strongly than others – building misinformation which in turn leads to poor mix decisions.

Almost every project studio has an uneven frequency response, with some frequencies sounding louder than others from the position of the mix engineer. These noticeable volume spikes generally occur in low and lower mid range frequencies and are therefore particularly problematic for dance producers. They are mainly caused by two acoustic baddies, **standing waves** and **flutter echoes**.

When sound leaves the speaker, hits a wall and then bounces back it causes a pattern of constructive and destructive interference as some of the reflected sound wave peaks combine with the direct peaks to augment certain frequencies while some peaks meet reflected troughs and cancel each other out. The specific patterns are governed by, among other things, the setup of the speakers and the dimensions of the room. At lower frequencies these peaks and troughs are said to '**stand**', creating **resonant room modes**. The result? Some frequencies are emphasised while others seem to disappear altogether, making dips and troughs in what would be an ideally flat frequency response. If left untackled they can make informed mix decisions very difficult.

At the upper end of the frequency spectrum **flutter echoes** occur when waves bounce between parallel walls or wall and ceiling, combining to form a high pitched 'ringing' sound – the kind you can hear when you clap your hands in a confined hard-surfaced space.

All of these reflections need to be bought under control so that you're hearing the most accurate portrayal of the sound coming from the speakers possible.

TIP Unsure whether your studio has standing waves? Although specialist test equipment like KRK's Ergo System can help identify problems, you can do a simpler (and free) diagnostic test by programming a MIDI sequence triggering a sine wave to play equal velocity chromatic notes in ascending order from C0 to C4. Then sit back and listen for noticeably loud notes. If you find one, it's a sign of a resonant frequency that will require tackling. (If you can't tackle it, then at least you know where a weak point in your room is and can mix to compensate accordingly.)

MONITORING

Legowelt (aka Danny Wolfers)
"I have a lot of monitors set up. They each have their own character and after working with them for some time I know what I should listen for and how to make the mixdown better. What we've got is a bunch of Dynaudio BM5s, Alesis Monitor One MK2s, Yamaha HS50s, Bang & Olufsen hi-fi speakers from the '70s and a grotbox and monitor controller from Behringer."

Zombie Nation
"We have three sets of monitors but that's just because we both had the same system when we moved in. We don't have all of them plugged in. The Quested 3110s are excellent – the perfect speakers. I always liked the [Quested] 2108s but they weren't sufficient for me on the volume side. I was always killing the tweeters. Before those I had Dynaudio BM5As. I found them to be like a smaller version of the Questeds."

Chapter seven
The studio and its tools

IMPROVING ACOUSTICS

A good listening environment is one in which reflections are controlled so that **all frequencies decay at the same time** (a reverb decay time of between 0.3–0.5 seconds). This means taming both higher frequencies and the more difficult lower ones, as well as dispersing reflections which would otherwise form room modes.

In the quest for the perfect room there are two key weapons in the acoustician's armoury, diffusers and absorbers, each of which deal with a specific problem:

▶▶ **Diffusers** scatter sound energy over a wide angle rather than bouncing it back like a mirror. They randomise hard reflections that might otherwise confuse stereo imaging and cause flutter echo. The simplest kind of diffuser is an irregular solid surface, often made from different height wooden blocks fixed to a flat panel. Usually these are sited on the back wall of a studio – scattering the sound waves that come directly from the speakers – or on the ceiling just behind the mixing position.

▶▶ **Absorbers** are panels of porous material such as mineral wool or open-cell foam that absorb sound energy, reducing reflections and ambience in the room.

With absorbers, size matters. For it to be effective an absorber needs a thickness

The diffuser on the back wall of Florian Miendl's Berlin studio. "This is my self-constructed quadratic residue diffuser made of 284 wood parts," he says, "it diffuses the frequencies bouncing back behind me."

...And Florian's absorbers. "My side wall absorbers which absorb frequencies from 20kHz down to about 250Hz. I've got more on the ceiling. They've made a big improvement to the sound in my studio; I can't live without them any more."

comparable to a quarter wavelength of the sound being absorbed. At 1kHz, for example, where the wavelength is 340mm, the absorber must be at least 85mm thick. What does this mean for the non-technically-minded? First, to get an even spread of absorption across the frequency spectrum, you are likely to need at least two different thicknesses of absorber. Second, the lower the frequency, the larger the absorber required.

(In fact, it's not quite that simple as sound waves rarely hit absorbers head-on. Instead they arrive from various angles. The more oblique the angle of approach, the greater the thickness of material the sound wave has to pass through, meaning absorbers are effective down to a lower frequency than their thickness suggests.)

The granddaddy of absorbers – specifically engineered to deal with frequencies below 100 or so Hz – is the **bass trap**, an absorber-on-steroids with dimensions to match. Frequently sited in the corners of studios (to take advantage of the oblique approaches of waves), commercially-made traps feature heavy membranes above the usual porous absorbers.

TIP Some companies offer 'absorbers on legs' – absorbers that can be moved around. These are ideal if your studio is located in, for example, a spare bedroom and you need to be able to free up space.

Chapter seven
The studio and its tools

WHERE TO PLACE ABSORBERS

You don't need to cover every available space with absorbers. In fact doing so is not recommended – you end up with a dark, oppressive sound that is unlikely to translate. Aim instead for a coverage of around 20 per cent of wall space – you should notice a big difference.

But which 20 per cent? When deciding where to locate absorbers your aim is **to reduce the effect of room reflections from the perspective of the mixing position**.

There is a tried-and-tested method of deciding where to place absorbers. Get a volunteer to move around the front of the room holding a mirror held flat against the wall while you sit in your mixing position. Wherever you see a reflection of one of your monitors in the mirror you need to place an absorber to reduce the reflections bouncing directly back at you.

In most rectangular rooms, these mirror points are found on the **side walls between the mixing position and the speakers** and **behind and between the speakers**. Look up and you'll find one on the **ceiling** too.

Don't worry about the floor – aside from the obvious impracticality, we're so used to hearing floor reflections that our ears naturally tune them out.

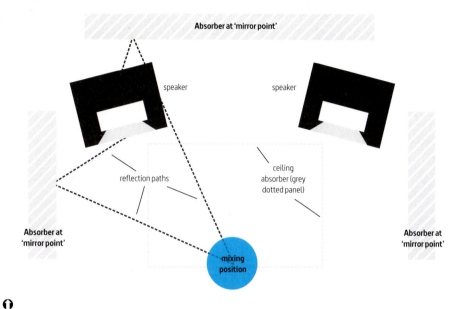

Absorbers placed wherever a mirror would show a reflection of the speaker, including on the ceiling. Note also the monitor placement, with the listener forming an equilateral triangle with the speakers.

Where the **back of the room** is also reflective, placing absorbers there may help, although the more usual choice is a **diffuser**. If the back wall has shelves or cupboards packed with stuff, that's normally enough to guarantee a good amount of scatter.

SPEAKERS AND HEADPHONES

High quality headphones (*page 260*) are good for working late at night when you don't want to disturb others and for forensic mix work – they're strong on detail – but mixing entirely on headphones is not recommended. Stereo imaging sounds very different on 'phones than it does on speakers and you may also find that bass frequencies vary according to how the headphones fit your ears. Which means by all means use headphones when you're on the road or for late-night writing sessions, but when it comes to mixdown proper, treat your mix to the benefit of a reasonable pair of speakers too.

Hi-fi speakers are generally designed to flatter the music fed to them for the consumer market. The same is true of

DIY TREATMENT

Although investing in acoustic treatment is almost always money well spent, if you're handy with a hammer and saw you can save yourself a good few hundred pounds by doing things yourself.

DIY diffusers are easy to make. Simply buy a solid (ply) backing board and affix different height blocks cut from 100mm square timber – *see Florian Meindl's home-made version opposite for inspiration.*

To make a DIY absorber, put 30 or 50mm mineral wool cavity wall insulation blocks into 100mm deep wooden frames where the wool is flush with the front of the frame so as to leave an air space behind. Cover the construction with a porous fabric such as cotton or polyester.

Wear gloves and a dust mask when handling mineral wool or glass fibre as the fibres cause skin and lung irritation.

computer speakers, which are sold mainly into the gaming market. Studio speakers, or monitors, on the other hand, are generally designed to be as accurate (and unforgiving) as possible to give a true picture of your mix.

Almost all studio monitors are **active** designs, meaning they have an in-built amplifier for each driver. They often also feature back panel controls to shape their tonal response.

When choosing speakers for a studio, the main considerations are usually how **hyped** you want them to be, how much **bass extension** you require, and how **enjoyable you find them to work** with (there's no point investing in a pair of expensive speakers if you don't like their sound – you'll be spending *months, probably years* with these guys!)

As a rule, the bigger the monitor, the lower the bass response – which on face value might seem an indisputably good thing for a dance producer.

But tread carefully: you can end up investing in a speaker that is too big for a room and consequently creating all manner of soupy acoustic problems. Instead measure the space and settle for a speaker that fits it better. A typical domestic room rarely requires a speaker driver of more than 5–8 inches in diameter.

Given the importance of bass in dance music production some people choose to invest in a **subwoofer**. Again, tread carefully. Remember the ideal studio environment is one in which all frequencies are present in equal measure – a truly balanced sound. By introducing a sub to the mix you can upset this balance and – ironically – end up producing mixes that sound balanced in your own studio but which are bass light elsewhere. (You may also end up requiring a lot more bass trapping to absorb the additional low-end frequencies being blasted into the room). Your best bet – unless you know exactly what you're doing – is normally a pair of the best monitors you can afford with as full a frequency response as possible.

TIP Many pro studios have a second (or third) set of **'grotbox' speakers** that are run alongside the main full-frequency speakers. Having a pair of speakers with limited bass response can help perfect the middle and upper parts of a mix. In commercial studios the weapons of choice are invariably Auratones – notoriously unforgiving speakers that hype the mids and highs. Unless you do a lot of work for third party clients or regularly mix for radio there's not much need for a dance producer – who's more interested in the low end than the mids – to have a set of grotboxes. But if

Yamaha NS10s: Old-fashioned by modern standards but still popular with some engineers.

you visit a pro studio and wonder why they have a pair of rough sounding or old fashioned speakers like NS10s in pride of place, now you know...

ROOM & SPEAKER SETUP

Having a decent pair of monitors is a good start, but it's only part of the story. You also need to ensure they're set up correctly in relation both to your listening position and the room itself.

▸▸ The golden rule when positioning speakers it to **form a roughly equilateral triangle with the speakers to the left and right corners and you in front**. The tweeters should be pointed directly at your head in both the horizontal and vertical planes. Most monitors include setup information to help with placement.

▸▸ Ideally, **speakers should be placed on solid isolated stands** filled with sand so that they can't move.

▸▸ If you have to place speakers on a **desk**, the desk should be as solid as you can make it – wall bracing may help – and with **isolating speaker platforms** like the Auralex MoPADs beneath the speakers. Any vibrations generated by the loudspeaker drivers which cause the cabinets to move will compromise the sound and result in a less defined bass end, so ensure those cabinets stay still.

▶▶ **If possible, avoid placing speakers low down at the back of a deep desk** as you'll hear strong reflections from the desk's surface which will compromise the clarity of the mix. If you have no choice, the sound can often be improved by using the monitors' half-or quarter-space setting.

▶▶ **Avoid siting speakers too close to a wall** or to wall corners. In both cases you'll be introducing more reflections (from the back of the speakers) to your listening position; where a speaker is sited very close to a wall the reflected sound can reinforce the bass end by up to 6dB. Even pulling speakers away from the wall by a few inches is enough to focus the sound in a meaningful way. Where you have no choice but to have them near-flat against a wall, many monitors offer back-panel switches that adjust the bass response to compensate for such placement.

▶▶ **Point speakers down the longest dimension of the room** (rather than across it). In smaller spaces the bass end is better behaved when the speakers face the length of the room.

▶▶ **Avoid a layout that has you sitting mid-way between the front and rear walls**, especially in very small rooms. It's asking for mode-related problems.

▶▶ **Ensure that speakers aren't positioned exactly mid-way between floor and ceiling**.

TIP The modal peaks and troughs are least severe around a third of length from the end of a room (specifically, 38 per cent of the way down). This is the best place to sit and listen.

FINALLY... ERGONOMICS

The dedicated producer spends long hours in the studio. Now, more than ever, the computer represents the hub of the studio, which means lots of slouching, sitting and staring, with the odd mouse click. It's the perfect recipe for **back pain**, **repetitive strain injury**, **carpal tunnel syndrome** and the kind of workplace injuries you'd normally associate with an office job.

Although investing in a chair over a yearned-for piece of outboard is an unwelcome proposition to even respectable gearsluts, failing to take care of yourself is plain daft – there are more enjoyable ways of suffering for your art than developing a sore neck and arthritic fingers.

A **height-adjustable office chair** and **desk** with built-in keyboard/mouse shelf are pretty much essential, encouraging good posture and raising you to a comfortable level relative to the desk. Next, focus on optimising the **configuration of your most-used computer equipment**: keyboard, mouse, MIDI controller/s and screen. Place the screen on a stand or improvise by raising it on a pile of books if necessary.

Those who produce on **laptops** typically run into the most problems. When using a laptop at a desk the head is typically angled down, often with elbows forced back and wrists bent – it's the stuff physios have nightmares about. Where possible, use an **external keyboard and mouse**, and buy a laptop stand to raise the screen to eye level.

Once you've sorted the basics, set about optimising the rest of your studio. Being comfortable with the position of all regularly-used gear has major benefits. Putting synths, controllers, effects and other hardware in easily accessible places around your central monitoring area speeds up workflow and allows you to focus on what really matters. For example, if you're right-handed, put knob-laden hardware on your left – allowing you to play and tweak while you click at the same time. If it only saves you five minutes a day, in a year you'll claw back 30 hours.

Finally, never underestimate the myriad benefits of **regular breaks**. Ten minutes away from the studio every hour or so will get you out of the same physical pose, will rest your eyes, and – crucially – will allow your ears to 'reset'… which means better mixing decisions.

KNOW YOUR ROOM

All advice on these pages is in many ways less important than the single overriding maxim to **know your room and speakers**.

In the project studio you're always going to be fighting a losing acoustic battle. Instead of despairing, simply make yourself aware of the limitations of the speaker/s and room and mix accordingly. So if you know the bass is boomy at 80Hz, pull back that frequency slightly when mixing to compensate.

Confidence in your speakers and room is something that builds over time when you take your music to other spaces that expose the flaws in your listening environment. Take comfort from the fact that some of the best music is mixed in substandard environments. But – crucially – it's mixed by producers who know their speakers and room inside out.

Chapter seven
The studio and its tools

The dance producer's studio

ESSENTIALS AND BEYOND

The good news is that you can make great dance music with nothing more than a laptop, bundled software/a trial version of a DAW and a reasonable set of headphones. Every day plenty of people do just that. Talent is about nurturing ideas and an ear for what's going to rock the clubs; there are plenty of wannabees who spend tens of thousands on dream studio setups who have yet to produce a memorable track.

Which is not to say investment won't improve the quality and fidelity of your mixes. A mid-range pair of studio monitors should be considered one of the first upgrades, along with an audio interface. Both will reap immediate sonic rewards.

After that, the route you take while expanding your studio will depend on your personal passions as a producer and musician. If you love old analogue synths then you'll prioritise spend there. If you regularly record vocals, a reasonable mic will be on your early wish-list. As this spread shows, there are plenty of ways to part with cash on the never-ending road towards the 'perfect' studio.

EARLY DAYS

When you're starting out, you can make perfectly good dance music using a laptop, reasonable headphones and an entry-level DAW with a few loops and freeware soft synths.

NEXT STEPS

Adding an audio interface and a pair of monitors will deliver tangible rewards to mix quality. A few higher quality soft synths and FX will expand your sonic palette.

SOLID SETUP

With the basics covered, the next steps are usually to invest in higher quality monitors and a better audio interface while expanding software offerings and adding a few key pieces of hardware – a synth, control surface or potentially a mic. A higher spec computer will allow you to work on more demanding projects.

Chapter seven
The studio and its tools

DREAM STUDIO

When the royalties start rolling in you can start making the incremental moves towards the kind of studio any self-respecting gearslut dreams of...

$ – 100s
$$ – 1,000s
$$$ – 10s of 1,000s

$ **DIY acoustic treatment:** If your room sounds bad then no amount of quality gear will enable you to make good recordings or mixes.

$$$ **Fully treated room:** It'll cost a lot, but getting your studio acoustically treated can be the wisest money ever spent in the studio.

$$ **Better speakers:** The sky's the limit here with some of the best in class costing the same as a second hand car. Coupled with acoustic treatment, quality monitors will significantly increase the fidelity of your mixes. A high-end pair of headphones to check details is also important.

$$ **Second set of studio monitors.**

$$ **Dedicated studio computer.**

$ As much **monitor display area** as you can accommodate. Two large screens are often more useful than one huge monitor.

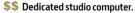

$$ **High quality audio interface:** As with mic pre-amps, the differences between audio interfaces may seem subtle but the better the digital/analogue converter circuits, the smoother and more refined the sound of your mixes will be.

$ **Hardware monitor control device:** Once you start upping the number of listening devices in the studio, you'll need a quick and powerful means of controlling them. Although some audio interfaces offer monitoring controls, many don't, and those that do may not do all the things you need.

$$ If you regularly record vocals or other acoustic instruments then a range of **high-end mic/s** will improve recordings and widen your sonic palette.

$$ **Quality mic pre-amp:** Although an entirely unsexy investment, when you have a few serious mics you are likely to want to twin them with better pre-amps.

$ **Range of quality plugins:** These days there's little to choose between the performance of better plugins and dedicated hardware. Essential early upgrades will be at least one high-end reverb, EQ and compressor alongside a few soft synths and drum machines.

$$ **A drum machine.** Or two.

$$ Single pieces of **quality outboard** like compressors, limiters and exciters.

$ **Comfy chair:** Never underestimate its importance!

$$$ **Collectable vintage outboard.**

$$ **Hardware synths:** both old and new.

the secrets of dance music production /

Processors and effects

INTRODUCTION

A good mix can be transformed into a great one with a handful of quality effects.

Processors (like compressors, EQ and limiters) and **effects** (reverb, distortion, chorus and so on) are the spices in the sonic soup that do two things. On the one hand they **enhance** sounds – refining and shaping them so they fit the mix. Their second role is more creative: **altering** sounds to make new and original textures, warping tepid grooves into mighty pumps; glitching, morphing and re-pitching.

Effects bestow width and depth, sparkle and life, giving 2D mixes a third dimension. Picture the same cityscape on an overcast day and then bathed in the hues of a summer sunrise – that's the difference effects can make to a mix.

ROUTING: INSERT VS SEND

There are two ways that effects can be added to an audio channel in a hardware or DAW mixer.

The simplest is to **insert** the effect onto the audio channel itself. The insert point on a hardware mixer adds effects 'in-line', processing the whole of the signal flowing through it. EQs, compressors, panners and pitch correctors are the most regular insert effects, used to process 100 per cent of a signal rather than part of it. In DAW mixers there's often more flexibility, with plugins of traditional insert processors like compressors offering a wet/dry balance so that only part of the signal is treated.

The second way is to place an effect on an **aux** (or **auxiliary**) **bus**, then route a portion of the signal to it using a **send**. This allows you to send as much or little signal as you wish to be effected and to balance the amount of effected signal (known as the 'return' level) in the mix.

The key point here is that the dry signal still flows to the master bus as normal; the desired proportion of wet effect is then *added to it*. This is different to a channel insert, where the *entire channel signal* is processed.

There are two advantages of using send effects on an aux bus. The first is practical. Even in today's era of super fast processing, using the same processor-heavy reverb to treat several signals, rather than using the same reverb multiple times on different track inserts, saves CPU resources. The second is that the use of a handful of common effects across a mix (usually a couple of reverbs and a delay) can improve mix coherence, imprinting the same sonic character on a range of dispirate signals and placing sounds that may have different sources (a synth, a music loop and a vocal for example) into a single acoustic space.

It's worth noting that a signal can be sent to a bus 'pre-' or 'post-fade' (that is, before or after the channel's volume fader). In pre-fade mode, the signal is sent to the effect at a set level regardless of the fader position. Although most useful when setting up headphone mixes, a pre-fade send can be ideal when all you want is the effected sound without any dry signal.

ROUTING: SERIES AND PARALLEL

There are two other terms you'll find in this book and the world of mixing when discussing effects routing: use of effects in series and in parallel.

Using effects **in series** is easy enough to understand. Instead of placing just one compressor, for example, on a channel's insert point, two are inserted, one after the other.

Parallel processing takes a different approach, placing the effect or processor on an aux channel instead of the insert point. Effectively this splits the audio signal onto two parallel paths, with the parallel-processed sound blended back into the mix

---

WHAT IS..?
Aux vs bus

The terminology of effects can be confusing – a sitation not helped by the different and often interchangeable terms used by both hardware and software manufacturers through the years.

A **bus** takes signals from multiple sources, combines them and sends them to a single destination.

An **aux send** is a control on the mixer that allows you to route a variable amount of a channel's signal elsewhere on the mixer – usually a bus.

An **aux channel** is another channel on the mixer into which you can insert processors or effects – or indeed send signals to further aux channels.

Still confused? The important thing is that ultimately buses and auxes do the same thing – that is *route signals elsewhere*.

Chapter seven
The studio and its tools

alongside the unadulterated 'dry' sound. Typically, the signal on this parallel bus is radically treated – smashed and beefed to the max (see *parallel compression, page 275*) – so that when it is mixed back in with the dry signal you get the best of both worlds; the dynamic original signal plus the flattened and up-front parallel signal.

While compression is the most common candidate when parallel processing, limiters, distortion (to generate additional harmonics) and EQ have applications as well. Parallel processing is used to treat drums, vocals (*page 187*), bass (*page 115*) and many other signals.

GROUPS

Another common use for aux buses is to treat multiple signals, or **groups**.

A typical dance mix may have as many as 20 or so faders controlling different drum tracks. Once you have a good relative balance between these tracks, you can make life easier for yourself by routing the different constituent parts to a new 'Drum Group Bus'. When grouped, you can change the level of the whole drum group by using a single group fader rather than shifting each one of the 20 around. You can also process the bus too – adding glue compression or using EQ to re-tone the full drum section. *For more on grouping, see Chapter eight, page 263.*

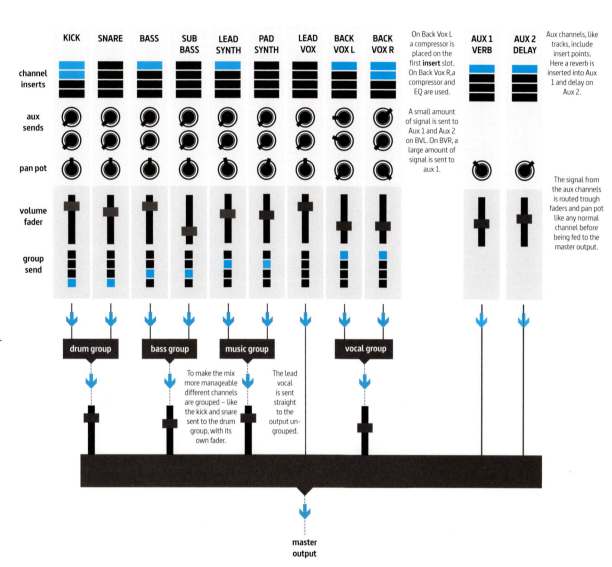

Diagram of a simplified DAW signal flow showing insert and send FX, groups and internal routing. For clarity's sake some elements – like the aux sends on groups – have been omitted.

Chapter seven
The studio and its tools

EQ

WHAT IS IT?

EQ, short for equalisation, is a process that uses filters to shape the tonal characteristics of a sound by cutting or boosting the volume of select frequencies within it to balance the whole. So if a snare needs more low end weight or a synth is too fizzy in the high end, EQ can be used to change the frequency balance of the sound.

TYPES OF FILTER

Because EQ is used for so many different tasks, there are a range of different filter types that specialise in performing distinct jobs. The main types are:

Shelving filters: The simplest filter of all, commonly used in hi-fi equipment tone controls. With a high shelf filter, the frequencies above the designated position are boosted or cut while the rest of the spectrum is left untouched. With low shelf fiters only the portion of the spectrum below the frequency point is affected.

High and low cut filters: These allow you to set the frequency at which a signal is cut. A high cut filter (called a low pass on many synths) passes frequencies below its cutoff point and reduces those above. A low cut filter (or high pass) does the opposite.

Bell filters: Named due to their characteristic bell shapes, bell filters allow you to boost or cut frequencies around a centre frequency. They often allow the user to adjust the centre frequency, bandwidth and the amount of boost or cut.

Parametric EQ: The most flexible of all EQs, the parametric EQ uses bell filters where all primary parameters – amplitude, centre frequency and bandwidth – can be changed. As such, it can be used in a general way for tone shaping or with pinpoint accuracy for surgical edits. Most DAWs' native EQ plugins offer several bands of parametric EQ alongside low and high cut filters and/or shelving filters.

CONTROLS

Centre frequency: Sets the frequency, in Hz, at which to cut or boost.

Bandwidth (or 'Q'): The width of the frequency range being treated, centred around the centre frequency. The higher the Q value, the tighter the focus of the filter. Some EQs offer such precise Q settings that only a single note is affected.

Gain/boost/cut: Increases or decreases the volume of the selected frequency range. If significant changes are made you may need to adjust a track's volume to compensate.

Slope (dB/Octave): On filters and shelving EQs the slope value dictates how steeply the shelf falls or rises, and therefore how abruptly frequencies are effected. A 24dB slope is steep, the signal falling away at the reate of 24dB per octave while a 6dB slope drops gently, giving more natural results.

WHAT IS IT USED FOR?

EQ is typically used in one of three ways:

1. Tone shaping – to sculpt the overall balance of a signal,
2. Corrective – to remove unwanted frequencies from a signal,

THE GOLDEN RULES OF EQ

There are two maxims that have governed EQ use since the year dot:

Cuts sound more natural than boosts.
This is particularly true of digital EQ – analogue EQ is more forgiving of big boosts.

Cut narrow, boost wide.
Narrow boosts create resonant peaks that are unnatural sounding and can cause ringing. For a smooth-sounding lift, use a wide (low) Q.

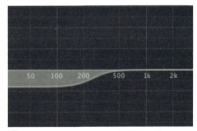
🎧 Shelving filter cut at 250Hz: Note the gentle roll down to the level shelf.

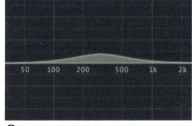
🎧 Parametric bell filter showing a wide 5dB boost (low Q) at 300Hz.

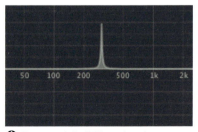
🎧 Parametric bell filter showing a very narrow boost (high Q) at 300Hz.

3. As a **special effect** – as in the case of 'telephone EQ' (*page 194*).

When performing **corrective EQ**, the two main tasks are **bracketing** and **forensic cuts**.

Bracketing (aka 'top and tailing') uses low and high cut filters to remove unwanted or unnecessary parts of the frequency spectrum from a signal (*walkthrough, page 265*). A recorded vocal part, for example, will often include spurious sonic content as low down as 20–30Hz (rumble and vibrations that travel up the mic stand) which, if kept, can interfere with other low frequency parts like the kick and bass. Given the low frequencies in the vocal do nothing but take up headroom and confuse the lower reaches of a mix, a low cut filter can be employed as high up as 80–120Hz to remove them – even higher on backing vocals (*page 191*).

It is not just the low end we need to be vigilant of though. There is often just as much unwanted activity in the high end, which can be removed using high cut filters so that instruments that *should* inhabit the space – shakers, hi-hats and so on – can do their job without battling other parts.

Bracketing EQ can be effectively used on a range of parts – from synths and drums to FX and basslines. Some producers use it on almost every channel.

When deciding how far up to cut, a good starting point is to keep edging up the cutoff frequency until you can hear an audible change in tone, then back down a little.

Forensic cuts are used to tame unpleasantly rampant rogue frequencies that may be present in a signal. Although more common in recorded material (where frequency spikes relate to the acoustics of the room in which the recording was made), spikes can still be a problem in samples and VST-generated instrumental lines.

Rogue frequencies are typically identified either by looking at a spectrum analyser to see obvious buildups or by using the so-called '**search and destroy**' (aka 'boost and sweep') technique (*page 231*). Here you use a parametric EQ with a very high Q, turn the boost way up, then cycle through the frequency spectrum to identify areas that contain too much activity. When you find one it's usually obvious: it will ring out in an unpleasant way. You can then make a precision cut at that frequency, widening the Q to taste.

TIP Different EQ models do very different things. For detailed 'micro'-level frequency tweaks, an EQ like the Cambridge (*see right*) is ideal, while for wider 'sweetening' (adding a sheen of air for example), a Pultec or Neve treatment is more appropriate.

TOOLS OF THE TRADE

Equalisers

Pultec EQP-1A
The studio world's favourite tone-shaping tool with a pedigree that stretches back to 1951, the Pultec EQP-1A has sweetened the highs and beefed up the lows on more records than any other EQ unit. Although unsuitable for forensic tweaks, for general tone shaping this is the best in class. Has been emulated in plugin form a thousand times over.

Cambridge EQ
For precision frequency control, the oft-modelled Cambridge EQ is as good as it gets. Featuring five bands of switchable parametric or shelving EQ plus high and low cut filters (17 types!), there are few jobs the Cambridge can't tackle.

Neve 1073 and 1081
Originally designed for Neve mixing consoles, the EQ is now available in plugin form. Great for tone-shaping and the 1081's filters are solid bracketing tools too.

Fabfilter Pro-Q
A leader of the new school of EQ featuring a beautiful GUI, massive flexibility (up to 24 bands) and a pro sound. Pre and post analysers plus mid/side processing give it extra clout.

Your DAW's EQ
Never underestimate the power and flexibility of a DAW's bundled EQ. Plugins like Ableton's EQ Eight deliver results far beyond their price.

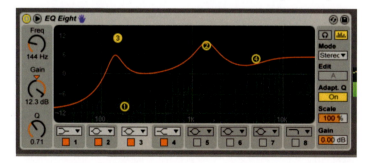

Chapter seven
The studio and its tools

Tonal enhancers

WHAT ARE THEY?

Tonal enhancers generate additional frequencies not found in the original signal in targeted areas of the mix. Although EQ can be used to increase the level of frequencies *already present* in a sound, where frequencies are *missing altogether* a tonal enhancer generates them artificially. A tonal enhancer might be used to help a lightweight kick deliver a lower punch or a subdued hi-hat slice through a busy top end.

SUB BASS ENHANCERS

Sub bass enhancers, or subharmonic synthesisers, generate additional frequencies at the low end of the audio spectrum. Most DAWs include one, with third party offerings including the bin-blitzing dbx 120A.

These enhancers work by analysing the pitch of the signal passing through them then generating a synthesised waveform (usually a sine wave) an octave or two lower that is fed back into the mix.

Although most commonly used to thicken kick drums and basslines, sub bass enhancers can benefit other parts too, including toms, synths – even thin vocals.

CONTROLS

Octave/ratio: Selects the number of octaves below the original signal the synthesised signal will be.

Centre: On complex material this helps steer the tracking frequency to the optimum range for clearer results.

Bandwidth: Allows fine-tuning of the width of the generated waveform.

TIP Sub bass enhancers work best on material that has a clear pitch. On complex tones, the results tend to be more rumble than tone.

WARNING Enhancement in the sub bass area should be approached with caution. It is easy to accidentally push levels too far and end up generating inaudible low-end that consumes precious headroom (*page 257*) – especially if your monitoring setup is less than ideal. The secretive nature of how specific enhancers treat material means you're never certain what is being done so keep a spectrum anaylser open when tweaking controls to give you a clear visual picture of the impact tweaks are having on the low end of a mix.

TIP Given these inherent difficulties, it's often best to consider a workaround. Kick drum lacking oomph? Use another sample or layer what you have with a booming 808 kick. Bassline not shaking the subs? Layer it with a sub bass to underpin the main bass (*page 115*). Even mixed low, this should be enough to deliver the missing bottom end.

EXCITERS

Where sub-bass enhancers work on the lower end of the spectrum, exciters are used to bring sparkle and air to the upper regions of a mix.

Exciters generally use parallel distortion and filtering to generate even order harmonics (*page 72*) above the source material. They can be used to add sheen to lacklustre keys, synth and guitar parts as well as air on vocals. They can help pick lifeless percussion out of a mix and give bite to dead hi-hats and shakers.

As with sub bass enhancers, **exciters should be used with care**. Overuse risks listener fatigue and can lead to a 'race to the top' – with ever more high frequencies being added to a mix.

Ultimately exciters – like sub bass enhancers – are most usefully viewed as problem solvers of last resort, standby solutions for when all others have been tried. As such, use enhancers to help the few parts they treat stand out from the wider mix.

ACCIDENTAL LEGACY: THE APHEX AURAL EXCITER

Although there are a number of exciters on the market today, they all owe a debt to the very first – the Aphex Aural Exciter (AAE) – which was reportedly invented by accident.

The AAE takes a signal, feeds it through a high-pass filter, heavily distorts and compresses it, then feeds the newly generated harmonics back into the mix, extending the harmonic reach of a sound by over an octave.

/ the secrets of dance music production

Compression

WHAT IS IT?

Compression reduces the dynamic range of an audio signal, changing the relationship between its loudest and quietest parts and shaping its transients in the process. Alongside EQ and reverb, the compressor is one of the three most used tools in a producer's armoury. It can significantly improve a mix by bringing details into focus, giving bulk and body to sounds and controlling the dynamic range of a signal so it avoids clipping and sits better in its sonic surroundings.

WHAT IS IT USED FOR?

Compression is used in three ways, which are intrinsically linked:

▸▸ **Dynamic range control** – controlling peaks, reducing volume fluctuations and, after gain, producing higher average levels,
▸▸ **Sound shaping** – altering a sound's envelopes,
▸▸ **Sound colouring** – changing the tone of a sound.

When treating a single short sound like a kick or snare compressors can **change the shape** of the sound in dramatic ways, accentuating the click at the front of a kick drum, for example, or increasing sustain on a snare. For denser material like vocals, a compressor is used to **even out volume over time**, helping to keep a part at a steady level to fit a mix. In both cases, the compressor itself may also **colour** the signal passing through it.

CONTROLS

Threshold: Level (measured in dB) at which the compressor begins reducing signal volume. Signal below the threshold passes through untouched; that which exceeds it is compressed.

Ratio: Amount of gain reduction applied to the signal above the threshold. At a ratio of 1:1 there is no reduction. At 3:1 an input level of 3dB over the threshold is required to generate 1dB worth of level above the threshold. As the ratio increases above 10:1 the compressor begins to **limit** the signal (*page 216*) until the signal becomes so squashed it is said to be **brick wall limited**.

Attack: Length of time it takes for the signal to be compressed to a specific amount of gain reduction after the input signal exceeds (and keeps exceeding) the threshold, measured in milliseconds (ms). Longer attack values preserve early transients (like drum attacks) by delaying the onset of compression. Digital compressors can '**look ahead**' for instantaneous attack times, something analogue units can't do.

Release: Time (in ms) that it takes for the compressor to return to 0dB worth of gain reduction after the signal has returned below the threshold. The release setting has a major impact on rhythm and motion in a track, with a fast release time pulling the 'background' forward, sometimes resulting in a pumping sound. Be careful about setting release too long; it leads to a situation where the compressor isn't able to catch up and react to the input signal, resulting in an immediate squash followed by an unnaturally slow ramp back up.

Knee: Sets the behaviour of the compressor as the input signal approaches the threshold. On a hard knee setting, the compressor only works once the signal breaches the threshold. With a soft knee, the compressor starts acting as the signal level *nears* the threshold – increasing the ratio upwards until the threshold is passed and the full ratio is applied. Soft knee curves are more suited to subtle signals that don't need to instantly cut through a mix like vocals and synths. Hard knee settings preserve transients. If in doubt, the compression knee rule of thumb says: *for banging mixes, go hard*.

Make-up gain: Since the compressor reduces peak levels, the net result is a lower output level. Use make-up gain to push the volume back up. Some compressors offer **auto make-up** gain by default so that the new peak level matches the old one.

DYNAMIC RANGE

The term dynamic range refers to the difference between the softest and loudest parts of a signal. If a vocal line peaks at -5dB and the quietest at -20dB, the dynamic range of the signal is 15dB (*for more on loudness and levels, see page 256*).

To see what a compressor is doing to the volume use a level meter with both **Peak** and **RMS** readings. The **average level** between the lowest and highest volume is called the RMS and is closely related to how our ears experience sound.

A compressor reduces a sound's dynamic range by pulling back the volume of the loudest parts, thus lowering the Peak level. The RMS can be increased using ratio and make-up gain.

The difference between the Peak and average (RMS) is known as the **Crest Factor**. The larger the Crest, the greater the dynamic range.

Gain reduction: This meter shows how much the signal level is being reduced in dB.

TIP Although you can raise a track's fader to increase the volume of a signal after compression, it is good practice to use make-up gain to get the same subjective volume with the compressor bypassed and switched in. Doing so allows you to make informed decisions about what the compressor is doing rather than falling into the common trap of thinking what sounds loudest sounds best.

Auto release: You won't find this control on every compressor but where you have the option Auto sets the compressor so that it constantly monitors the incoming signal and modifies the release time on the fly depending on the material. It is most useful on complex material like vocals and bussed groups where attack and decay characteristics are constantly changing.

Sidechain input: The sidechain input – which in normal use is constantly assessing the level of the material passing through it before passing it onto the variable-gain amplifier – can be switched to route an external audio signal for the compressor to 'listen' and react to.

Although any signal can be routed to the sidechain – including EQ, to force the compressor only to respond to sounds over a certain frequency, for example – in dance music the most common sidechain feeder is a four-to-the-floor kick drum. The regular punch of the kick fires the compressor into action delivering either a mild 'breathing' sound or the now classic pumping effect made famous by a generation of French house producers.

TYPES OF COMPRESSOR

Not all compressors are created equal. Indeed over the decades a number of different technical means have been employed to offer the same end goal of reliable gain control.

Some compressors, like the LA-2A, use a light element and **optical cell** to deliver its highly musical program-dependent release, while **VCA** compressors like the SSL Bus Compressor use integrated voltage (solid state) controlled amplifiers (VCAs) for their faster response time and transparent gain reduction. The legendarily expensive (and heavy) Fairchild 670 does the job using an array of **valves** (or **vacuum tubes**) while **FET** (Field Effect Transistor) compressors like the UA 1176 eschew valves in favour of (cheaper) transistor circuits.

* Note: Compressor recommendations here do not require the real thing. The vast majority of plugins are modelled – however loosely – on a few original units. So where there is a recommendation for the LA-2A any kind of 'opto' compressor – including native DAW models – will provide a good starting point, as will any number of plugin models, from the UAD 'original' through the Waves CLA-2A and NI's VC2A to Cakewalk's CA-2A.

FOUR OF THE MOST USED...

Compressors*

The piece of outboard that has surely graced more hit records than any other: the understated, flexible and silver-fronted **LA-2A**. Can generate transparent and musical results on a wide range of material, from vocals to bass.

Universal Audio's **1176 Peak Limiter**, first introduced in 1966, is probably best known for the energy and high-class grit it bestows, a musically-pleasing push of tone in the lower mids. Think big, but also think intimate. That's the 1176's dichotomous charm.

The **G-Series Bus Compressor** from Solid State Logic is famed for its stylish-as-hell bus compression, either on sub-mixes or the master bus. For 'glue' purposes, it reigns pretty much supreme: a holy grail compressor that makes a mix louder and punchier while imparting an expensive, modern-sounding cohesiveness.

Loved and hated in equal measure, the **Alexis 3630** defined the pumping sidechain compression sound which became a trademark of French house in the late '90s. But there were complaints too: distortion, noise and a habit of making everything sound lifeless. The updated 3632 fixed many of these issues.

These different models affect sounds in different ways. VCA compressors are generally more transparent, tube compressors have a warmer sound, FET models are fast and clean while optical models are known for their denser character.

This means that a compressor suited to one application – adding more definition to a bass drum, for example – may struggle to add glue on a mix bus. Choosing the wrong compressor for a task can end up doing more harm than good so invest time learning how all the compressors at your disposal affect material so that when a job needs doing you'll already have a shortlist in mind.

STARTING POINTS

Many producers have 'go-to' compressor choices for different applications. If you don't yet, here are some starting suggestions: (Almost all of these compressors have plugin equivalents.)

▶▶ **Kicks and snares:** FET (1176) compression offers anything from snap and punch to transient-destroying smash. Use a dbx-160 for accentuating 'pop' at the start of sounds.

▶▶ **Drum bus:** For gentle glue, opt for an SSL-style bus compressor. For something more raucous audition an Empirical Labs Distressor or Fatso.

▶▶ **Parallel drum bus:** For assertive smash, a 1176 driven hard can do the job, as can other character ball-boxes.

▶▶ **Basslines:** The LA-2A and CL 1B are both admired for lower-end treatment, bestowing bulk while nesting dynamics. For a more assertive sound, try a Distressor, Fatso or 1176.

▶▶ **Vocals:** The usual suspects here are the LA-2A (smooth) and 1176 (for a more aggressive sound). For the sheen of modern pop production, try a CL 1B.

▶▶ **Master bus:** Your choice here will be dictated by the sound you're after. Master 'smash' can be delivered by a pair of Distressors. Gluey warmth is the domain of the Neve 33609. If you're after a more transparent glue SSL-style bus compressors (including Ableton's 'Glue') are the way to go.

TIP If a single compressor is not able to control a signal's dynamics without introducing undesirable side effects, try adding a second compressor after the first. The ratio on each can be reduced, alongside the amount of signal reduction. Using two in series reduces the amount of work each has to do, generating a more natural result. It can also shape signals in a more refined way, the first compressor bringing out a sound's transient punch while the second shapes its decay and release.

QUICK GUIDE

Compressor settings* (and why they might work)

KICK DRUM
Gain reduction 2-8dB **Ratio** 2:1-4:1
Attack 2-20ms **Release** 0.6ms
Attack is key here, affecting both the punch and weight of the sound. Too fast an attack time will hammer the pivotal opening transients.

SNARE
Gain red. 2-8dB **Ratio** 3:1–5:1.
Attack 0.5-120ms **Release** 5-180ms
Changing the attack time alters the relative level of the transient at the start of a snare; to accentuate the transient, use a slow attack. To emphasise the sustained 'ring' of a snare, use a faster release.

UP-FRONT VOCALS
Gain red. 2-6dB **Ratio** 2:1-5:1
Attack 10-25ms **Release** 0.5ms
To position the vocal at the front of a dynamically flat mix start with a medium ratio and enough gain reduction to sit the vocal comfortably without sapping its energy. If you set the attack time too fast, the compressor will pull back on line openings before they've had a chance to be enunciated properly.

BASS
Gain red. 3-6dB **Ratio** 3:1-8:1
Attack 0-30ms **Release** 0.5-2s
For busier, more dynamic basslines, lower the ratio and ease back on gain reduction.

MIX BUS GLUE
Gain red. 2-5dB **Ratio** 1.1:1-2:1
Attack 0.1ms **Release** Auto
A relatively gentle treatment for subtle gluing. Note the Auto release setting which is well suited to complex (bussed) material.

MIX BUS MAJOR PUMP
Gain red. 4-10dB **Ratio** 5:1-10:1
Attack 0.1-0.3ms **Release** Auto
The ratio is increased and threshold lowered to deliver audible gain pumping. As the ratio increases, transients have less impact. With highly audible pumping, the release time is crucial: play with it until it 'breathes' in time with the tempo of the song.

PARALLEL SMASH
Gain red. 15-20dB **Ratio** 10:1-inf:1
Attack 0.5-20ms **Release** Auto

* Note 1: These are starting points only. **You will always need to alter the settings** depending on the material, choice of compressor and what's happening in the wider mix.

* Note 2: When using samples, particularly drum samples, bear in mind that they are likely to have been compressed already – often multiple times. Samples from leading retailers can typically be used without additional processing.

LIMITING

Sometimes a compressor – even on its highest ratio setting – cannot be relied upon to deliver the level of dynamic control required. When you need to guarantee that *no* peak sneaks past the threshold, reach for a limiter.

A limiter is a specialist compressor with a super-fast attack time and a high ratio (at least 10:1, more usually upwards of 20:1), which effectively flattens the signal at the threshold point, eliminating the risk of clipping. Because attack and ratio times are invariably fixed, the main controls are:

Threshold: Level in dB at which the limiter kicks in. Any signal above is flattened.

Release: How quickly the limiter reacts to incoming changes in volume. As with a compressor there is a midway point between too fast (the sound becomes thick and overbearing) and too slow (shorter transients are blurred).

A limiter is commonly used after a compressor in mastering, the compressor bringing peaks under control and the limiter catching speedy transients that the compressor misses. It can also be useful on buses (including the master bus) to help gel grouped elements together. Some producers use it *in extremis* to create very loud, very flat masters.

WARNING Because signal above the threshold is flattened against the 'brick wall' of the limiter, transients are smashed into submission. Although some producers make this effect part of their trademark sound, it can be harsh and fatiguing, the ironic result being a sound that has less impact and less energy than one that has not been so heavily limited – of which much more in **Chapter eight**.

MULTI-BAND COMPRESSION

A multi-band compressor splits a signal into two or more adjustable frequency bands and applies compression to each independently. This allows you to compress different parts of the audio spectrum using tailored compression settings.

Although multi-band compressors can look overwhelming, they really aren't; once you've mastered a single-band compressor you know all you need to know about setting up its bigger sibling.

The most common use for multi-band compression is to balance headroom between frequency bands. Inbalances can occur on the drum or master bus where a dominant kick or bass part causes a single-band compressor to pull back the whole signal, resulting in the masking of higher frequencies. A multi-band gets around this single band limitation by allowing the engineer to dial in heavy, high ratio compression on the low end to tuck it in, while allowing the rest of the material to breathe in a less controlled way.

Setting up a multi-band compressor to contain a dominant frequency band starts with marking the edges of the offending territory by adjusting the **crossover frequencies**. It can be helpful to solo the specific band while tweaking the compressor to produce the desired amount of control. Next, move on to the next band/s and repeat. Finally adjust the make-up gain of each band to restore balance across the spectrum. Most often called upon for mastering duties, other uses for the multi-band include:

▸▸ **increasing detail** in a part's specific frequency range and focussing it in the mix. Loops from sample libraries are good candidates for this kind of detailed tone-sculpting since you can't adjust the levels of individual elements within them.

▸▸ **controlling problem bands** of 'rogue' frequencies, as in the case of a percussive part with an abrasively harsh upper mid-range for example, where you can set one of the bands to rein in the level of the offending part while leaving the rest of the signal untouched (this technique is used in many **de-essers)**. In such cases, using a multi-band to duck the offending frequencies is often more effective than trying to EQ them out.

QUICK GUIDE

Parallel compression

While compression is typically used in-line as an insert effect, it can also be applied 'in parallel' on a send.

Originally pioneered by New York engineers, parallel compression allows the dry, more dynamic signal to be blended with a highly compressed, transient-smashed parallel copy to deliver a magic mix of the best of both worlds.

The process has become such a staple of modern mixing that some compressors have a wet/dry control to make the job simpler.

Used commonly on basslines, drum busses, synths and a range of other signals, the technique is covered in detail on *pages 275-276*.

DE-ESSER

A de-esser is a specialist tool primarily used to tame sibilant 'S' and spitty 'T' frequencies in vocal parts.

Excessive sibilance can build up in vocal recordings for all kinds of reasons, including an unsuitable choice of microphone, poor singing technique and over-zealous EQing and compression. In all cases, sibilance is best tackled at source – during the recording itself (*pages 175, 181*). Where this isn't an option a de-esser can be used to forensically pinpoint over-sibilant frequencies and reduce them without impacting on the rest of the signal.

Most de-essers are single band compressors that act on a narrow frequency range, leaving the rest of the signal unchanged. The band is used to hone in on and reduce the offending S frequencies (somewhere in the 4–10kHz zone depending on the vocalist). Others use polarity inversion techniques to switch the selected frequency band out of phase. Whichever method is employed, the usual controls are:

Detection frequency: Central frequency that triggers the ducking process.

Target frequency: Central frequency to be ducked (in most cases you'll want the detection and target frequency to be the same).

QUICK GUIDE
Expanders

An expander can be thought of as the opposite of a compressor, increasing the dynamic range of a signal rather than reducing it. As a consequence, the expander's controls mirror those of a compressor.

Although expanders are rarely used in day-to-day dance music production, they can be useful for opening up signals, giving more dynamic life to an overcompressed loop or a flattened vocal part you've receive for a remix.

Sensitvity/release time: How quickly the de-esser reacts – think of it as the equivalent to a compressor's release setting. Use longer values for slower tracks.

Strength: Controls how much ducking occurs.

Setting up a de-esser can be tricky. For the most transparent results, use the smoothest de-esser you can afford and tread lightly to avoid generating unnaturally lispy results. *(For more tips on tackling sibilance see page 181.)*

TIP De-essers can also be used for controlling spitty high-end frequencies in percussion and hi-hats.

NOISE GATE

A noise gate monitors the level of signal passing through it. When the level exceeds the threshold, the gate opens, allowing the sound to flow through. When it drops below the threshold the gate closes again, shutting off the signal flow.

Back in the day, noise gates were used with microphones and guitars to mute low volume signals, reducing the amount of low-level hiss, noise and rumble hitting tape during gaps in performances. They are still used in this way, silencing audio between vocal phrases, for example, or gaps between percussive hits.

But they have more creative uses too. By running a percussive pattern into the sidechain input of a noise gate, a sustained pad or vocal line can be turned into a pulsing, rhythmic part, a technique common in trance and mainroom house. Controls include:

Threshold (dB): Minimum signal level required for the gate to open.

Reduction/attenuation level: Volume of signal when gate is closed. The default position is 0dB (silent), although it can be varied to reduce volume to any other level.

TIP Where a gate allows negative attenuation values, it will *increase* the volume of a sound when the signal fed to the sidechain is absent. Doing so turns the gate into a ducker.

AHR envelopes: Attack, hold and release values can be altered in the same way as a synth's envelope to shape how the gate impacts on the material each time it opens. Attack sets the time it takes for the gate to transition from closed to fully open once the signal exceeds the threshold; release (or decay) applies a smooth fade out.

TIP Listen out for clicks and pops when setting up noise gates – particularly with super-fast attack times. To mitigate against clicks ensure that **Lookahead**, if offered, is switched on.

// WALKTHROUGHS

Group compression: drum bus

1 Start with a drum mix comprised of several individual elements, then route each drum element to a single drum bus group or channel. This process varies among DAWs. In Live select the chosen channels then hit Ctrl/Cmd-G to add them to a single group.

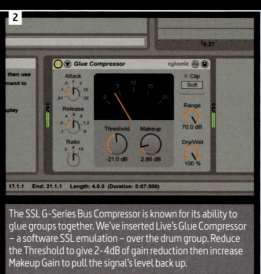

2 The SSL G-Series Bus Compressor is known for its ability to glue groups together. We've inserted Live's Glue Compressor – a software SSL emulation – over the drum group. Reduce the Threshold to give 2-4dB of gain reduction then increase Makeup Gain to pull the signal's level back up.

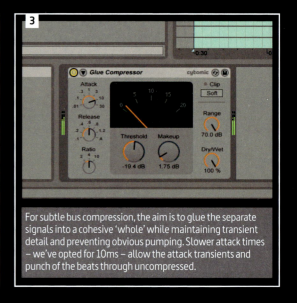

3 For subtle bus compression, the aim is to glue the separate signals into a cohesive 'whole' while maintaining transient detail and preventing obvious pumping. Slower attack times – we've opted for 10ms – allow the attack transients and punch of the beats through uncompressed.

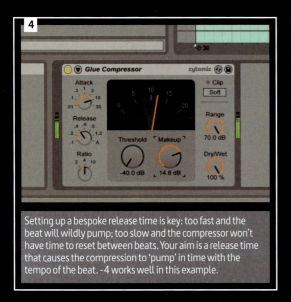

4 Setting up a bespoke release time is key: too fast and the beat will wildly pump; too slow and the compressor won't have time to reset between beats. Your aim is a release time that causes the compression to 'pump' in time with the tempo of the beat. -4 works well in this example.

5 When compressing a bus, bass-heavy elements like kick drums can create unwanted pumping across the whole group. Some compressors feature a sidechain filter allowing you to remove bass from the signal triggering the gain reduction. Alternatively, remove the kick from the group.

6 Although bus compression is generally used to give subtle cohesion, you may wish to apply more forceful compression for obvious character and pump. Here we've crunched the drums with 10dB of gain reduction and reduced the Dry/Wet balance a little.

Parallel compression: drum bus 🎧

1
Parallel compression involves mixing a heavily compressed copy of a signal alongside a second, usually uncompressed, version. Start with a drum mix made up of multiple tracks and route all drum signals to a single group or bus as in Step 1 of the Group compression walkthrough opposite.

2
Insert a compressor plugin on an aux/return track then send the drum group signal in parallel to this return. Apply heavy-handed compression (high ratio) to squash the parallel signal. Use a fast attack time to emphasise body/sustain, or a slower attack for more punch and attack.

3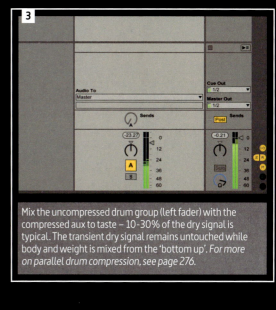
Mix the uncompressed drum group (left fader) with the compressed aux to taste – 10-30% of the dry signal is typical. The transient dry signal remains untouched while body and weight is mixed from the 'bottom up'. *For more on parallel drum compression, see page 276.*

Extreme pump compression: master bus 🎧

1
Although not a technique that can be applied to every track, in some cases an extreme dose of compression applied to the master bus can add rhythmic pump and character to a lifeless mix (or sub group). To do so, insert a ballsy 'character' compressor plugin (*page 214–215*) on the master channel.

2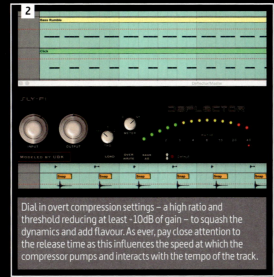
Dial in overt compression settings – a high ratio and threshold reducing at least -10dB of gain – to squash the dynamics and add flavour. As ever, pay close attention to the release time as this influences the speed at which the compressor pumps and interacts with the tempo of the track.

3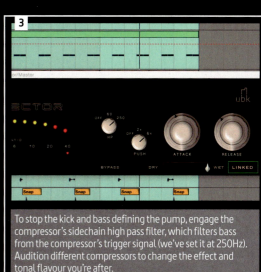
To stop the kick and bass defining the pump, engage the compressor's sidechain high pass filter, which filters bass from the compressor's trigger signal (we've set it at 250Hz). Audition different compressors to change the effect and tonal flavour you're after.

Modulation and pitch effects

When a choir performs, the different vocalists deliver their lines with slight variations in pitch and timing, creating a combined sound that is richer than a solo singer. A similar effect is achieved mechanically by mixing identical copies of the same signal together then delaying one of them, with chorus, flangers and phasers all using slightly different methods to achieve a range of unique modulation effects that add movement, colour and depth to a mix.

CHORUS

When chorus is created artificially, a signal is split and mixed with a slightly delayed version of itself. The delay time is modulated by an LFO to give the effect of subtle pitch-shifting. When the two signals recombine they produce a sound with a desirable wavering quality.

Many analogue synths have built-in chorus effects, including the Roland Juno-60 and Juno-106.

Roland were also responsible for the Dimension D Chorus (*above right*), widely recognised among chorus aficionados as the best chorus unit ever made.

Chorus is used on pads and keys to add depth and, on stereo signals, to add width. Because it has the psycho-acoustic effect of diffusing a signal's focus, chorus can also be used to push elements back in a mix. It plays a near-mandatory part in the creation of big stacked synth sounds in D&B, prog and trance. Used subtly (wet level of no more than 5-10 per cent), it can also bring a touch of interest to background vocal parts. Settings include:

Depth/intensity: Controls the amount of perceived detuning.

Rate: Speed of the LFO. A fast rate at low intensity produces a shimmering effect; a slow rate with high intensity results in thick detuning – ideal for brazen lead synths and brass.

Delay/predelay: Delay time between the original and effected signals. The longer the delay time, the less focussed the result.

Mix: Sets the wet/dry balance.

Ensemble effects combine not just a single delayed copy of the original signal, but many, with additional LFOs used to modulate the extra voices. The resulting sound is richer than that of a single chorus. Ensemble plugins usually offer the same controls as straight chorus effects but with an option to change the number of voices.

🎧 Roland's Dimension D, released in 1979. A studio stalwart that does just one thing – sublime chorus – with four 'Dimension' settings offering a range of lush, uber-wide results.

TIP Chorus and ensemble effects that allow different offset times to be applied to the left and right channel delays can be used to increase the stereo width of a signal; simply apply slightly different values to each side.

VIBRATO

Take away the contribution of the dry sound from regular chorus and you're left with a very short delayed signal to which pitch modulation has been added. This is vibrato. It can sound beautiful on Rhodes and organ parts, and synths that require organic movement.

FLANGE

The crazier cousin of chorus was originally produced by running two identical tape recordings of the same sound together then leaning on one of the tapes to slow it down by a fraction of a second. Today it is created by reducing the delay on a chorus device (typically 20-30ms) to less than 15ms then adding a feedback control. The distinctive 'plane taking off' sweeping sound is caused by comb filtering between the original and delayed signal intensified by the

PRO TIPS

SOUKIE AND WINDISH

"We use the Roland Dimension D chorus effect and Lexicon's PCM 42 for delay effects. The combination of these two tools makes a sound so much better."

feedback applied from the output back into the input.

Flange is a mainstay effect of techno production, where it is used most prominently on hi-hats. It can also add interest to transition effects including crash cymbals, white noise whooshes, reverse builds and other high frequency audio to create a rushing, sucking quality without affecting the pitch. Controls include:

Depth/intensity: Sets the range of the sweep. Reduce to zero for metallic resonances.

Speed/rate: How quickly the LFO sweeps through the spectrum. Increase the value for a more chorussy sound.

Feedback/regeneration: Increases the intensity of the effect by emphasising the resonant frequency. At high values comb filtering becomes obvious.

Phase invert: Some flangers enhance the stereo image by inverting the phase of the dry and effected signals. This produces a noticeable change in the quality of the harmonics.

NOTE When using modulation effects, remember to check the mono fidelity of the mix – many of these effects introduce/rely on phase cancellation. For this reason if using modulation effects on sounds that demand a solid low end (kick drums, basslines), *split the signal first (page 118)*.

TIP Insert a chorus or flange plugin before bussed reverb and delay effects to diffuse and add interest to the ambience.

PHASE

Often mistaken for a flanger because of its similar sweeping sound, phasers take a feed from the original signal and run it through an all-pass filter to alter its phase before mixing it back again. When the signals recombine, the frequencies that are out of phase cancel each other out. The LFO controls the speed at which the frequency sweeps up and down.

The phaser's character and the intensity of the effect you get depends on the number of all-pass filter stages used. The more stages, the more pronounced the result, with two- and four-stage phase giving a gently shifting effect that is ideal for pads.

12-stage phase is sharper and more defined with the resonant frequency clearly highlighted. This more extreme effect can be used on percussive parts or to introduce harmonic content to a dead sound. Aside from the number of filter stages, the phaser shares most of the same controls as a flanger.

PITCH SHIFTING

Doing exactly what its name suggests, a pitch shifter changes the pitch of a signal. It can be used for simple re-pitching – to transpose a vocal part into a different key for example – or to thicken up sounds. Very small amounts of pitch shift can be used in place of chorus effects, usually combined with a few ms of delay. Controls include:

Shift: The amount of transposition, measured in semitones for large steps and cents (100 cents=1 semitone) for micro-pitching. It is possible to write new melodic lines by automating this value.

Scale: Intelligent pitch shifters can be programmed to harmonise to a set scale.

Type/algorithm: Most pitch shifters run different algorithms optimised to process different kinds of material. Common types include 'complex polyphonic', 'vocal' and 'drum'. Audition all available options before making a final decision.

Formant: Affects the tone of the shift and can alter the perceived gender of a vocal to make it sound more male or female.

NOTE Automation of a pitch shifter is a simple way to make a melody from a sustained single synth note. Use lo-fi algorithms for unique effects.

Reverb

Reverberation – reverb for short – is a natural phenomenon caused when sounds reflect from surfaces, often in complex ways. You hear it when you clap your hands in an empty room, tunnel or hall.

Reverb has been a studio staple since the earliest days of recording, with production maverick Phil Spector using Gold Star's echo chambers to bind his legendary 'wall of sound' together as far back as 1962. Later in the '60s it was homemade echo rooms in the attics of 2648 and 2652 West Grand that supplied the trademark reverb to recordings on Berry Gordy's Motown label, heard loud and proud on hits from The Four Tops, The Supremes and Marvin Gaye.

Since then, reverb fashions may have changed (gone is our love affair for big '80s-style washes and hair), but our appetite for it hasn't waned, with ambient effects used for a range of applications across dance music production, including to:

- 1. add **life** and **sparkle** to a sound,
- 2. bring **cohesion** to a mix, and
- 3. generate **space** and **depth** in a mix.

Exactly *why* a mix sounds better with reverb is a question even academics struggle to answer. Some of it is likely cultural; Western nations associate music listening with live performances that happen in clubs and halls awash with natural reverberation; for cultures that listen to music outside our reverbed mixes probably sound strange.

If reverb's a cultural hang-up it's one that's near impossible to shake. Try bypassing all ambient effects in a mix and see how it sounds. Chances are it sounds sterile and lifeless, which is enough to illustrate the point. In the end, who cares what the psycho-acoustic reasons are for explaining why reverb makes records sound better? *It just does*, and for the purposes of mixing, that's enough for us.

Sounds become richer and harmonically brighter when fed through short reverbs. With longer ones, signals becomes diffused, their contours blurred so that they seem to come from further away. This allows the producer to push parts back in a mix and is one of several tools used to create a three dimensional mix (*page 240*).

Although in the past no more than one or two reverbs were used in a mix, placed on buses so that groups of signals could be given the same treatment, DSP advances allow today's producer to use different reverbs on every channel. Not that this is recommended: usually one short room and one longer plate/hall on buses bolstered by a couple of insert verbs on specific parts is more than enough to do the job. Throwing too many ambient flavours into the mix is likely to muddy and confuse it.

TYPES OF REVERB

Plate: Plate reverb was originally created by vibrating a thin suspended steel plate and then amplifying those vibrations, as in the legendary EMT 140 (*below right*). Most plugins offer a plate setting, with a sound that is rich and smooth without suggesting any specific acoustic space.

Spring: Most commonly found in guitar amps, the spring was once the poor man's plate, a single coil vibrating to supply the ambience.

Algorithmic: Probably the most ubiquitous of all reverb types, algorithmic (or synthetic) reverb uses complex algorithms and multiple delay circuits to recreate what happens in nature. Simulations of different spaces – including halls, rooms and plates – are supplemented by a range of controls to help shape the final sound. The Lexicon 224 is probably the most famous incarnation of (digital) algorithmic reverb.

Convolution: The latest chapter in the reverb story is convolution reverb, which uses samples of real-world spaces that are imposed onto signals to treat a sound with, for example, the ambient characteristic of the Taj Mahal, the London Tube or a famous live room. Because convolution uses samples of real spaces (known as impulse responses or IRs), it is the most realistic of all reverbs but also the least flexible.

Interior of the *very* heavy (270kg) EMT 140, introduced in 1957 and probably the most loved plate reverb of all time. Its lush tones are modelled in hundreds of plugin tributes, including the official one from Universal Audio.

Convolution reverb entered the market to fanfare – suddenly producers had thousands of stunningly realistic reverbs at their fingertips – but they have their limitations. Firstly, convolution reverb does not do non-linear movement like the organic 'Spin and Wander' modulations introduced by Lexicon. Nor are IRs particularly flexible. The samples on which they are based can be timestretched, filtered and pre-delay added, but that's pretty much it. Digital reverb is generally more flexible, offering a degree of control that by definition convolution plugins can't deliver.

The trade-off between the two choices is realism versus control, natural verses synthetic, and in the end it's a case of getting to know the tools at your disposal and picking the right one for each job.

CONTROLS

Early reflections (ERs): Contribution made by the initial reflections that bounce off surfaces closest to our ears.

Time/length/decay: How long it takes the reverb to fade away after its initial build. Generally speaking, the bigger the space, the longer the tail. The longer the tail, the further away the treated part will sound.

Pre-delay: Gap between the dry sound and first reflection. A little pre-delay helps to seperate the dry sound from the reverb and

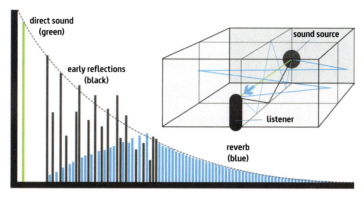

Diagram showing how reverb occurs in nature, with the direct sound (green) hitting a few moments before the early reflections (grey) begin. Shortly after the ERs hit, the complex reflections and re-reflections that we call reverb (blue) start to build, rising to a peak before tailing off slowly as the reflected sound energy is soaked up in the room. Most digital reverbs allow you to blend different amounts of ERs and reverb. A greater balance of ERs make a signal sound closer.

can be used to keep even fairly wet signals towards the front of a mix. Pre-delay can be timed to the tempo of a track.

Density: Controls the quantity and thickness of reflections. High values sound smoother as they are composed of more reflections. Reduce the amount for a rawer, more lo-fi sound.

Diffusion: Rate at which the complexity and distribution of the reflections build after the initial sound.

Filter settings: Most reverb units offer low and high cut filters. These help shape the tone of the reverb – keeping the tail from interfering with the original sound – and also reduce the amount of headroom-reducing mud in a mix.

STARTING POINTS

Vocals: Anything goes here. Plates give lush, often bright, reflections. Hall settings work well too, offering a mellower flavour. The problem with both is that they can push the vocal too far back. For a more up-front sound, use a balance of heavy ERs and a short, room-based tail.

Snare: For a live 'drum-room' sound, use a room or cabinet setting or an IR sampled from a real recording room. Use longer hall/plate settings, decay timed to tempo, for long, smooth tails that bleed into the next kick hit. Classic '80s-inspired 'smash' is achieved by adding a gate after the reverb.

Kick: In the majority of dance mixes, avoid reverb on the kick. It muffles low frequencies and muddies the mix.

Percussion: Convolution reverbs can do good things to congas, bongos, shakers and synthetic percussion. Pick a drum room IR with a short ambience that adds life without clouding the sound.

Hi-Hats: respond well to short, bright ambient treatments – although reverb is by no means essential.

Pads: It's easy to go too far with pads, adding long hall and plate reverbs thinking you'll get a bigger sound. The truth is usually the opposite: sounds that take up a large amount of space already need little in the way of additional reverb. Delay settings are often more effective – especially ping-pong and modulated settings.

Echo and delay

Echo and delay are variations of the same naturally occuring effect. An echoed sound repeats after a set time and continues to repeat until it fades away.

Echo and delay serve many purposes. Subtle echoes can be used to smooth out vocals and lead lines, helping them sit in a busy mix. Delays can add interest and movement to transient percussive parts and enhance the groove of drum beats and hi-hat lines. They play an essential part in supersized FX and are frequently used alongside or instead of reverb to create depth and space in a mix.

Very short delay times are also the basis of a range of effects like chorus and flange (*page 220*). Variations of both can be made using delay plugins.

Although straight 'vanilla' echo is useful in its own right, delay effects come in a range of other flavours

Ping-pong or **stereo** delays pan repeats across the stereo spectrum automatically. Seperate delay times on each side are required for true stereo operation.

Even more sophisticated echo patterns can be generated using **multi-tap delays** like Logic's Delay Designer and Waves' Supertap. With these, each tap can be given a different delay time (and often unique stereo placement and filter values). The ability of multi-tap delay plugins to sync to tempo make them ideal for creating rhythmic sequences that can be automated to turn what was a simple sequence into a living, breathing and ever-evolving groove.

NOTE *Don't overdo stereo delay effects.* Some club rigs are wired in mono and those that do operate in stereo are unlikely to give listeners the full effect unless they happen to be standing (and not moving) directly between the two speakers. At the very least, check the mix's mono fidelity to ensure you're not losing important stereo detail.

Tape echo plugins model a range of classic tape echo units. These devices, like the Echoplex Tape Echo, worked by recording a signal to tape then replaying it a short time later using one or more playback heads. Because the tape could be saturated, each repeat become more distorted and lo-fi, with less high end, giving the echoed material a fuzzy organic flavour. There are a range of tape delay plugins on the market that model everything from the degree of saturation to effects like wow and flutter.

Grain delay is an effect based on real-time granular resynthesis that is mainly geared towards creating experimental textures and glitch effects.

CONTROLS

Time/groove: Either measured in ms or as a factor of the groove such as eighth or 16th notes. Many units also offer triplet, dotted note and swung options.

Feedback/regeneration: The number of repeats, from one to infinite (or 100 per cent). Digital delays remain crystal clear while tape echoes start to distort on higher settings. For full-on dub, pick infinite. EQ the return to taste.

EQ/filter: As with reverb, most delay effects include built-in high and low cut filters to shape the tone of the echo. It is good practice to thin out echoes by rolling away unnecessary low and high end signal. This does three things: it stops the delayed sound from interfering with the original signal; it helps bed the delay into a mix; and it preserves headroom.

TIP Delays cry out for automation. To get the classic 'crash fading to infinity' effect, set delay time to eighths (or dotted eighths) and feedback to infinity then automate the delay volume so the echoes slowly fade to silence.

TIP Although tempting to sync all delays to a track's bpm, you can pull them out of the mix and give them more character by shifting them slightly off-tempo. Try automating the delay time too.

REVERB VS DELAY

Although different effects, both reverb and delay do similar things to signals – settling them into a mix and giving them a sense of liveliness, movement and foundational glue. So which to use? The answer often lies in the drawbacks one or the other brings to the table.

On vocals, for example, delay may be favoured over reverb to bestow a sense of movement without receding the part in a mix, while sometimes just a dash of light reverb can be enough to lift a tired percussion line out of the mix.

Stereo effects

Stereo effects are used to add width and diffuse the focus of parts you want to ease away from more important mix elements.

WIDTH ENHANCERS

Width enhancers use mid/side processing to reduce the volume of the mono part of the sound in the centre (middle) of the mix. As this decreases, the signal in the extreme left and right (sides) of the stereo spectrum becomes more prominent, creating the impression of a wider sound. Push it hard enough and the sound stage appears wider than the speakers themselves.

Enhancers work best on pads and other sounds that contain a significant amount of stereo information. Backing vocals and harmonies can also benefit from a subtle stereo push.

Since they reduce volume at the centre of the stereo field, stereo enhancers are rarely used across full mixes, buses or on sounds that rely on a solid central presence like drums and bass.

Controls include:

Mono width: Makes the image wider by reducing the volume in the centre.

PRO TIPS
PETAR DUNDOV

"To add dimension [to the lead sound on 'Before it all ends'], I recorded a couple of takes [on the Prophet-600] in different octaves, mixing them down in hard left and right pan positions.

"I prefer this technique over chorus since the P600 is always slightly detuned, so you can never get two identical takes and the result is a huge stereo width of sound."

Bass: Helps preserve the bass component by leaving lower frequencies untouched.

WARNING *Remember to regularly check mono compatability when using width enhancers.* Because mono elements are reduced in volume you can end up literally losing parts when a mix that sounds great in stereo is summed to mono. To maintain the integrity of a mix, stereo enhancers – if employed at all – are best used on parts that are musically less important, like pads and percussive elements.

TIP Try placing a width enhancer after a stereo reverb effect on a bus. It can generate extra space without diffusing the dry original and can sound good on both vocal and melodic verbs.

STEREO SPREAD

The stereo spreader takes a different approach to the width enhancer, dividing the frequency spectrum into a number of bands and then panning each band in an opposite direction.

The degree of panning can be slight to give subtle stereo ehancement or extreme for a more obvious effect. Because spreaders don't use phase inversion techniques, the resulting sound doesn't cancel itself out when summed to mono. Additionally, because the frequency bands treated are usually in the higher reaches of the spectrum, the mono fidelity of the bass end is left intact.

Controls include:

Order/bands: Number of divisions to be panned. Lower values make the effect sound obvious. Higher ones give a more blended and natural result.

Range: Sets the high and low limits in the frequency range of the stereo spread. In dance productions bass frequencies are best left alone.

Intensity: Width of pan effect – increase to make it more audible.

AUTO-PANNER

Auto-panners move the sound between the speakers automatically, creating a sense of movement.

Although panning effects are easy enough to program using pan automation, auto-panners save time. Some also include hard-to-program functions, like changeable LFOs.

Auto-panners can be used on mono and stereo signals to add excitement and space to a mix. As with stereo delays and width enhancers, avoid (over)using if your tracks are going to be played in mono.

Distortion and overdrive effects

There are dozens of distortion effects, running the gamut between the mild warming tones of gentle overdrive to screaming distortion.

Borrowed largely from the world of guitar effects, distortion and its siblings can be used as creative tone manglers – turning a bland bassline into a roughed-up low-end blitzer, for example – and essential mixing tools, injecting warmth into cool-sounding digital signals, supplying girth to sounds and otherwise shaping a signal's frequency characteristics.

Different intensities of distortion include:

▸▸ **Overdrive:** The 'gentlest' kind of tone, intended to simulate the sound of a guitar amp driven to mild distortion. Useful for mellowing an over-bright signal or for adding bulk to almost any kind of sound, from snare drum to vocal.

▸▸ **Distortion:** Has a more rocky, intense flavour but still sounds vaguely organic. Use for tougher lead and bass sounds to ensure front-slamming presence in a mix.

▸▸ **Fuzz:** Anything from lightly driven grit to deliberate clipping of the waveform to produce something close to a square wave to deliver meat, girth and sustain. The use of corrective EQ to control the final tone is pretty much essential.

Each of these effects adds its own unique series of overtones to a sound while at the same time reducing the dynamic range of a signal in a similar way to a compressor. The result is a louder, richer and denser tone.

NOTE Because distortion effects reduce dynamic range and make signals denser, it is easy to fill up space in a mix, making for an overbearing, tiring result. To avoid this, distortion effects are best used on a limited number of parts and/or used in parallel (*right*) to control their power.

TIP The mechanics of distortion mean that the sum and difference frequencies generated become more complex with every additional notes played. Used on monophonic parts – like lead synth lines – the effect, even at high levels, can be focussed and distinct. On chordal parts, where two or more notes play at once, the effect gets steadily more blurred and confused as more notes are added. The secret to 'clean' distortion in such cases (if such a thing can sensibly be said to exist) is to use different monophonic instances of the sound generator and distortion effect on different tracks, each playing a different MIDI line, so that the end result is a cleaner chord stack comprised of multiple distorted monophonic synth lines.

CONTROLS

Drive: Increases the intensity of the effect, boosting the volume of the signal before clipping it, introducing distortion and additional harmonic overtones. Small amounts add warmth, larger amounts make a signal ever more aggressive. Acts as a natural compressor.

Tone: The classic tone control uses a simple high cut filter to back off frequencies that can swifty become harsh and tinny. Some units also offer a low cut filter to help shape the signal futher.

Mix/level: Allows you to blend the effect or simply control the output volume after the distortion effect has increased the level of a signal.

Distortion as a mix tool

Although rarely considered as important as EQ and compression as a mix tool, distortion can play a pivotal role during mixdown, performing a number of essential tasks:

1. 'Thickening' parts. Probably the most common use of distortion effects is to bulk up sounds. Used subtly – often with parallel processing – any part, from drums to vocal lines can be given extra weight.

2. Adding frequencies to extend a part 'upwards' in a mix. This is particularly useful on subby basslines that sound great low down but don't deliver the all-important 'radio bang' in the lower mids (*page 119*). Here, distortion is used to generate musically-pleasing overtones from a signal that lacks them.

3. Because distortion reduces a signal's dynamic range, it can also be used as a form of **compression**.

Tape emulation

With the increased level of interest in vintage sound and old-school production techniques, the market for tape saturation effects has grown rapidly over the past decade.

Tape saturation models the sound you get when recording to half-inch multitrack tape. In the plugin market products offer anything from simple two- or three-control interfaces to more complex models of classic kit like the Ampex ATR102 and Studer A800, where everything from tape speeds and saturation to wow and flutter is modelled to get ever closer to the 'real thing'.

Saturation generates much kinder results than distortion – think 'warm' and 'rich' rather than 'loud' and 'dirty'.

In the studio, tape saturation can be used to give a little analogue mojo to cool digital signals and can sound pleasing on pretty much any sound – from synth and keys parts to drums, vocals, percussion and group buses.

If you're looking to make specifically vintage mixes then you might even try a tape plugin set to around 10 per cent wet on the master bus itself – although regularly A/B the mix to ensure you're not losing high end definition.

PRO TIPS

THE POWER OF PARALLEL

Although commonly used as insert effects (*page 208*), unless you're after an obviously trashed sound overdrive, distortion, bit-crushing and saturation are often better used on a parallel aux channel to give more controllable bulk to signals that require it.

Amp and speaker simulators

Primarily designed for guitarists, amp and speaker simulators model the sound of re-amping a signal though a variety of pre-amps and speaker cabinets, many of them classic, rare or collectable.

These effects are used in a similar way to other distortion effects, to add bulk, body and character to a sound. Their more forensic EQ sections offer increased tonal control over a sound, making them ideal for augmenting and shaping various signals, from synths to individual drum hits that need more clout. Dedicated bass amp simulators are used to sweeten and sculpt bass sounds.

CONTROLS

Amp: Typically has controls for drive, volume and a three band EQ. Use the drive to increase distortion and compensate for the difference between pre- and post-processed signal levels.

Cabinet: There are usually a choice of mic types and placement positions. Brighter tones are acheived by using condenser mics 'front on' to the speaker grill. For warmer tones, move the mic away from/sideways to/behind the amp. Ribbon mics roll away high frequencies so deliver warmer tones.

Bit-crushers

The most extreme distortion effect is the bit-crusher, which doesn't aim to model the harmonic characteristics of analogue overdrive but instead performs its mayhem in the digital domain, distorting a signal by reducing its sample rate and bit-depth.

On subtle settings a bit-crusher delivers the kind of mid-range chunk exhibited by classic drum machines like the Linn Drum and Akai MPC60, both of which used digital chipsets featuring lower sample rates (the MPC60 is a 12-bit machine). At extreme settings bit-crushers totally destroy the signal fed into them, turning simple sine waves into fractured robotic wails. Automate the sample rate for all kinds of 'robotic' vowel effects (*page 111*).

CONTROLS

Bit-depth: Reduces the digital bit-depth from the rate you're working in to values down to 1-bit. Settings below 8-bit add background noise. As you hit 2-bit, the sound breaks up and splinters – ideal for tight, glitchy percussion.

Downsampling/frequency: Reduces the sample frequency below the normal 44.1 or 48kHz.

Waveform shape: The shape in which the bits get decimated.

Lo-fi and found sound production

In stark contrast to the full-frequency sounds of mainstream dance, many underground electronic genres embrace sonic imperfection by incorporating noise, dirt, grit and otherwise undesirable analogue and digital artefacts. This lo-fi aesthetic is particularly prominent in harder techno, lo-fi and glitch, where unusual found sounds, sonic degradation and distortion assume important rhythmic and melodic roles.

DIY DIRT

Bit-crushing and sample rate reduction: Synonymous with early digital hardware and primitive computer music, the gnarly fuzz of bit-crushing is prominently employed in lo-fi sound design. Reduce the bit-rate and/or sample rate to heavily degrade and virtually 'age' pristine audio.

Extreme distortion: Forget subtle warmth – lo-fi production is about extremes. Smash signals using overt distortion stages. Kicks, toms, basses and mid-range synths respond particularly well to forceful drive, creating rumbling beasts with grunt and personality.

Cheap sounds: Eschew the usual advice to use the best plugins you own and turn instead to the cheapest: freeware distortion plugs and antiquated spring (the poor man's plate) and metallic reverbs.

Contrast: A track featuring a contrasting array of timbres will exhibit more personality than one made exclusively from lo-fi sounds. Use a gritty bed of distorted rumble to provide the backdrop to a shiny synth line or paint a landscape of lo-fi sounds amidst a handful of pristine perc hits – *like in the walkthrough, right.*

Out and in: The quickest way to rough up flawless audio is to run the signal out of your audio interface, into a cheap piece of equipment, then back into your DAW. Second-hand mixers, budget signal processors and cheap rack effects can be bought for less than the price of a plugin.

Pedal power: If you're not a guitarist you probably know someone who is. Borrow a few cheap guitar effects – distortion, overdrive and fuzz pedals are ideal – then feed your pristine signals through them. Treat in parallel for more control.

Tape: Old cassette decks or cheap multitrack tape recorders are perfect for adding lo-fi grunge to sounds. Simply print your signal to cassette – being sure to overdrive the input – then record the tape deck's output back into your DAW.

Unwanted artefacts: The sound of malfunctioning or noisy gear can be incorporated into a track. Record the buzz of a faulty cable, resample the audio, then program it into a glitched bass or percussion part. In the digital domain exploit flaws and errors like digital pops or 'create errors' from scratch using hasty audio chops and/or stepping filters.

FOUND SOUNDS

Armed with a basic field recorder or even the mic on a smartphone, it's easy to capture all manner of sounds from the real world that can be incorporated into productions, and while it's generally better to record using the best quality mic you can, rough and ready recordings can add lo-fi charm – and unique personalisation – to a track.

Long, steady beds of ambience such as street noise and rainfall can be used to underpin beats or chords. Timestretch and pitchshift to warp them further and bring them into 'tune' with the track. Mix them beneath other elements, get them breathing with sidechain compression, and use filtering and delays to build creeping, vibe-laden sweeps. Volume-automate to weave them in and out of focus.

TIP Field recordings offer characterful layering tools. Back up a drum machine clap sample with a recording of a door knock for a Burial-style snare. Record 'air' to add organic layers to full beats.

IN THE BOX LO-FI

» Use extreme timestretching and/or pitchshifting artefacts to your advantage by pushing stretch and pitch algorithms too far.

» Many plugins distort when misused or clipped. Try heavily compressing a sound while keeping attack and release times unnaturally fast. The result? Overbaked pumping and distortion as the compressor struggles to keep up.

» Pushing digital faders into the red creates unpleasant distortion – which might be just the sound you're after.

» Dedicated glitch plugins such as Sonic Charge Permut8, Audio Damage Bitcom and MeldaProduction's MMultiBandBitFun use various types of digital distortion and/or sequencing to create crunchy rhythms and textures.

// WALKTHROUGHS

Techno beat using field recordings

1 We've started with a recording of a cheap microphone being knocked over. After loading the audio file into a sampler and pitching it down two octaves, we've created a 16th note pattern around a thumping 4/4 kick. Saturation, overdrive and EQ bloat and transform the bass rumble.

2 We ventured outside for this sound: a high-pitched 'clack' of a tree being struck which we're using in place of a hi-hat. Next, a two-beat loop of rustling leaves is heavily sidechained and bit-crushed in parallel. Together the parts supply a bed of ambience with rhythmic movement.

3 Another looped bed of real-world noise – this time rainfall – is pitched up two octaves and sidechained against the kick to reinforce the pumping off-beat hi-hat. The timestretch algorithm adds stutters and glitches to the signal. Treble-focussed distortion and heavy filtering thins the sound.

4 We've placed two different recordings of a door being slammed at strategic points in the groove. Short ping-pong delay with high feedback gives one of the sounds a metallic, ringing effect, while the other is aggressively saturated to near-breaking point.

5 A second tree strike sample is used as the groove's snare element on beats 2 and 4 of each bar. Exaggerated saturation transforms the puny signal – triggered across the stereo spectrum – into a thunderous whack. We've applied ringy, unpleasant reverb to cheapen the snare even further.

6 Bus processing is used to glue the disparate layers together. Obvious, analogue-style parallel compression, applied over the whole drum group, adds harmonic cohesion, then a bit-crusher emulates the degradation of a hardware sampler, mixing in a restrained amount of digital dirt.

Other effects

RING MODULATION AND FREQUENCY SHIFTERS

These two related effects modulate the pitch of audio to produce a range of tones from subtle wobbling to discordant clangs. Firm favourites of SFX designers, their sounds can be heard in a host of cult sci-fi big- and small-screen outings, supplying robotic voices in, among others, *Dr Who* and *The Clangers*.

The classic Bode **frequency shifter** takes the incoming signal and shifts it up or down by a fixed number of Hz. Small shifts give pads and soundscapes a spacey, phaser-like shimmer.

A **ring modulator** (or ring mod) is more complex, multiplying two signals, one the input signal and the second a synthesised tone — typically a sine wave or other simple waveform. The output signal is the sum and difference of the frequencies present in each waveform.

Ring mods excel at creating atonal and metallic effects. They can be used as simple insert effects to transform synth lines, to turn simple percussive lines into complex, tinny workouts or on a send before reverb to add wandering complexity to an ambient tail. Its ability to shift the pitch gives it utility when creating leftfield vocal harmonies. But most often, ring mods and frequency shifters are used in SFX creation, adding spacey vibes to risers, falls, sweeps and bombs. Controls include:

Speed/frequency: Tune the LFO to the key of the track or a harmony note to produce tonally useful melodic overtones. Higher frequencies produce more metallic timbres while slower speeds yield a more 'chime'-like quality.

Mix: Although traditionally used as an insert effect, where available a mix control allows you to tweak the wet/dry balance.

VOCODER

Originally designed to encode speech, the vocoder has become synonymous with synthetic robot voices and post-Daft Punk vocal production.

A vocoder takes two input signals, the carrier — which supplies the pitch — and the modulator — which supplies the tonal characteristics. The modulator signal is fed through a series of band-pass filters so that only the transients remain. These 'formant bands' are then modulated onto the carrier bands to form the 'spoken'/'sung' hybrid output signal.

In dance music production, the modulator is invariably a human voice and the carrier either a synth or a pad. Some vocoders, like Logic's EVO20, feature a built-in carrier oscillator or even a fully-formed synth unit. Controls include:

Filter bank: Use the individual bands to cut and boost frequencies to alter the spectral balance. Playing with these can help make the speech clearer and more defined.

Bands: Number of bands in use, typically between eight and 32 — although some, like Reason's BV512, offer more. Lower numbers deliver clearer robotic tones. Higher values give more complex results and are often better suited to non-vocal material.

Carrier envelope: Attack and decay parameters are used to make the speech transients tighter or more relaxed.

Input mode: Determines which signals are used as carrier and modulator. Most plugins require the modulator to be fed via a sidechain. If there's no on-board oscillator you'll need to select a carrier signal too.

TIP Although the modulator is typically a human voice, any kind of sound can be vocoded. Rhythmic loops can sound good, especially percussion. It's also worth experimenting with melodic elements, using the vocoder to force them into a new key.

TIP While tempting not to stray from a single (monophonic) MIDI sequence to control the vocoder's pitch *Around the World*-style, chordal parts work well too.

// WALKTHROUGHS

EQ – 'Search and destroy'

1 Solo the track you want to EQ - like this live Rhodes line. Open an EQ with forensic sound shaping capabilities. Most DAW EQs are up to the job. Now increase the Q value of an EQ band to maximum to hone in on a tiny bandwidth of frequencies and increase its level by 20dB+.

2 Slowly cycle the EQ band's central frequency through the spectrum until you hear any obviously overloaded frequencies. These tend to sound honky or unpleasantly abrasive – like this overload at 375Hz. An EQ's anaylser waveform can also help reveal congested areas.

3 Now cut the overloaded area. Cuts should be narrow – though you may want to widen the Q a little – and not too extensive; we've dialled in a cut of 4.5dB, which rounds off the sound nicely. This cut is supplemented by another forensic cut at 1.7kHz and low end bracketing.

'Mirror' EQ separation

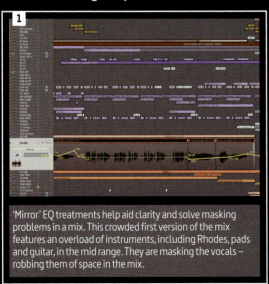

1 'Mirror' EQ treatments help aid clarity and solve masking problems in a mix. This crowded first version of the mix features an overload of instruments, including Rhodes, pads and guitar, in the mid range. They are masking the vocals – robbing them of space in the mix.

2 A wide EQ band (identified using above's 'search and destroy' technique, but this time employed to identify pleasing areas of the spectrum) is gently boosted (no more 3dB) to bring out the best of the vocal content.

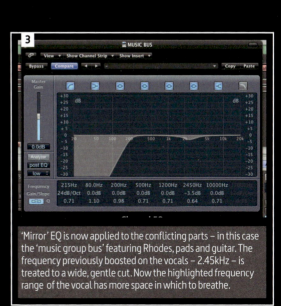

3 'Mirror' EQ is now applied to the conflicting parts – in this case the 'music group bus' featuring Rhodes, pads and guitar. The frequency previously boosted on the vocals – 2.45kHz – is treated to a wide, gentle cut. Now the highlighted frequency range of the vocal has more space in which to breathe.

Chapter eight
Mixing and mastering

Chapter eight
Mixing and mastering

Defining a great mixdown is almost impossible because there is no single set of factors that divide greatness from mediocrity.

To illustrate the point, take an hour out and listen to records from a range of genres that you think are mixed brilliantly. If you're out of ideas, a good starting point is our list opposite. Listen carefully to what's happening in the productions. Chances are you'll find different approaches to compression, EQ, effects, arrangement and structure in each mix – with different producers giving their personal stamp to the craft of each.

Every mixdown's unique greatness is down to a myriad number of artistic choices that culminate in the finished master. Any attempt at definition must start from a recognition that **all mixes are context specific**. It is the first rule of mixing. It may be an obvious point to make, but a classic vocal house track will be mixed in a different way to a mainroom banger. The vocal house producer will focus on the pivotal vocal/s and supporting instrumentation while the electro producer will invest their energy in ensuring the stacked synths punch in all the right places, pumping with the kick and bass to bump the groove along.

The **medium** is equally critical; the vocal house producer may be mixing for the terrace bar and home listener, giving more attention to the radio-critical and iPod-necessary mid range while the electro producer will have big club and festival rigs – and their big low end responses – in mind.

The desired **audience response** is important too. While the vocal house producer's aim will be a mix in which the lyrics are intelligible and the vocal cuts through loud and proud, the club banger's goal is to get pulses rising, feet moving, bass bins straining and hands in the air.

This means that before embarking on a mix the producer needs to know exactly what they are setting out to achieve. Is it going to be a dirty D&B slammer to get the crowd jumping? Or an intricate deep house number to soundtrack early evening bar sets? **What do I need my mix to do?**, is the question every producer should ask before they bring up a single fader. Which yields the first definition of the mix engineer's craft: **a great mix is one which does what it sets out to do – and then some**.

So if the electro producer's vision is a raucous party-starter of an anthem that has every pair of hands in the air then their mix has to do exactly that.

This definition might appear circular, but it's not. There are thousands of mixes that set out to do something and fail; mainroom bangers that don't bang, techno workouts that don't groove.

Those producers who have a sonic picture in their head before mixing and then replicate that in their DAWs are few and far between. The rest of us are forced to get somewhere close to our initial vision. But this doesn't lessen the importance of that vision. Rudderless mixing is the bain of the producer's life – it leads to wasted hours and sessions characterised by endless tweaking. To get somewhere you need a place to aim for.

If the overriding definition of a great mix is subjective there are sub-definitions that are more objective.

BOK BOK

Knowing where your music is going to be played will influence every mix decision, from the ground up.

Night Slugs co-founder Bok Bok notes: "This is club music first and foremost, so I need everything we put out to be engineered right ready for big systems."

Chapter eight
Mixing and mastering

When analysing timeless dance productions, four characteristics emerge time and again:

#1. A great mix fills the frequency spectrum – with clarity.

#2. A great mix is dynamic. It has shape, contrast and energy.

#3. A great mix has width and depth. It is three dimensional – but works equally well in two and one dimensions.

#4. A great mix is a living, evolving thing. It has sustained interest that engages the listener from start to finish.

These are the four cornerstones of high calibre mixing that the best producers know and practise instinctively.

They are genre-independent and hold true whether you're making house or dubstep, trance or techno.

And while there are examples that don't adhere to all four cornerstones, they are few and far between – the exceptions that prove the rules.

They're the **golden rules of mixing** that we detail in depth before moving onto the practicalities of mixing later in the chapter.

OUR PICK OF THE BEST...
Mixes

Daft Punk - 'Get Lucky'
Inescapable during the summer of 2013, 'Get Lucky' avoids the rough and ready sound of *Homework* and the more polished vibe of *Discovery* and *Human After All* in favour of a distinctly retro sound. Daft Punk recorded every instrument and vocal both to tape and Pro Tools then chose which version of each track to keep during mixdown. Engineer Mick Guzauski mixed the album on a Neve 88R desk, using almost entirely outboard processing rather than plugins.
The gear list for the album reads like a lottery winner's gear wish list: LA-2As, 1176s, API 2500s, Neve 33609s, EMT reverbs, Lexicon and Eventide delays, Avalon EQs... Thanks to Guzauski's deployment of those tools, the result is a mix which applies the sonic perfectionism of '70s disco and rock to DP's contemporary pop-dance formula.

Perc - 'My Head Is Slowly Exploding'
Ali Wells is a master of employing distortion and reverb to build dense industrial techno soundscapes. 'My Head Is Slowly Exploding' isn't minimal as such, but there's an efficiency at play that demonstrates how to produce sonically dense and rough music without creating a muddy mix. The percussive parts are the main focus of the track, consisting of cold metallic sounds rather than conventional drums. The sound design is part of the mix, and vice versa. Wells understands how and when to break rules. So, for instance, when the huge reverb in the opening of the track is applied to low-frequency sounds, space is left for the cavernous echoes which follow. As the track builds, the minimal synth parts are pushed back in the mix to allow the drums to take centre stage. This is visceral and intense stuff crafted with surgical accuracy.

Todd Terje - 'Inspector Norse'
A great example of how retro sounds can be brought up-to-date with modern production values. All the synth elements on Terje's *It's The Arps* EP come from the ARP 2600 analogue synth, but in spite of the vintage sound source this is most definitely nu disco rather than something more retrogressive. It's worth noting that the 2600, first manufactured in 1971, is a monophonic synth. Terje recorded multiple takes of the synth in order to build up a multi-track arrangement and it's the interaction of these simple parts that sets the tone of the arrangement.

Inner City - 'Good Life'
This huge crossover hit from 1988 is the vintage vocal house mix *par excellence*. The Detroit staples of TR-909 drums and DX100 bass underpin the track, topped with layers of synth stabs, strings and FX. Paris Grey's vocal sits high in the mix, acting as the focal point throughout. Producer Kevin Saunderson employs tricks more commonly found in pop than the average house or techno track: lots of reverb, delay and filter effects on the vocals during the chorus, heavy panning effects on the synths. It's a dynamic mix with near-constant movement.

Skrillex - 'Scary Monsters And Nice Sprites'
Love him or loathe him, this is a masterclass in loud mixing from Skrillex, who at the time was working exclusively with samples and soft synths in Ableton. The track's structure is split into two parts: the softer mid-range sections with their reversed vocals and the uber-fat drop with Skrillex's trademark synth work. The net result is a contrast between the two sections which serves to emphasise the loudness of the drops. Note how the vocal sample ("Yes! Oh my God!") separates the two sections before the drop, giving it even more space to breathe and increasing its impact. It's a classic trick for making the most of dynamics.

Storm Queen - 'Look Right Through' (MK Remix)
The Mark Kinchen remix is a good example of the more commercial side of modern house music. This is an undeniably poppy take on the retro house sound, but the mix is bang up to date. Compare and contrast with MK's remix of the Nightcrawlers' 'Push The Feeling On' from the early '90s. Similar elements are present – prominent vocals, simple 909-based drums and MK's trademark organ bass – but 'Look Right Through' is bigger, louder and cleaner, with modern EQ and compression techniques imprinted over the classic formula.

Rule 1: A great mix fills the frequency spectrum – with clarity

Every sound – that of a guitar string vibrating, a snare drum being hit, a synth oscillator generating a waveform – inhabits a frequency range that is defined by a unique pattern of a **fundamental frequency** and **overtones**. The frequency range of a tuned instrument depends largely on the note played. A sine wave tuned to middle C generates a pure **fundamental frequency** at 261.6Hz (see *Note to frequency chart, Appendix 2*).

But that's not the whole picture. Treat that same sine wave C with overdrive and the distortion process creates additional **harmonics** (*page 72*) that extend the frequency range upwards. Add in saw wave oscillators at upper and lower octaves and the narrow sine wave signal takes up an increasing amount of frequency bandwidth.

Each part in a mix occupies its own range of frequencies. A TR-808 kick drum generates signal across the 20Hz–4kHz range, a clap 450Hz–14kHz, a typical techno bass 40–500Hz and the human voice 80Hz–20kHz. Although these are rough figures (exact ones depend on the note/s played, the nature of the sound source and the processing applied), having a working knowledge of what plays where (easily honed by adding a frequency analyser to a channel) is a surefire way of improving both your ears and mixes.

There is an established school of thought in mixing circles which says that **a solid mix is one that features content across the frequency spectrum** or, in layman's terms, that there's stuff going on all the way from the low end of the mix (30–40Hz) to the airy 18–20+kHz highs. This means ensuring that the different elements used in a mix collectively fill out the spectrum – and, importantly, **without too much overlap**.

In this respect The Beatles got it right six decades ago: bass, guitar, kick, snare, hats and vocals. Job done. The whole frequency spectrum is filled with activity, and though George Martin and his engineers' mixdowns sound vintage by today's standards, they are full and round, and stand up well alongside today's brighter productions.

Why do mixes that fill the frequency spectrum sound better than those which don't? Suffice to say that while academics argue over the psycho-acoustic reasons, for our purposes it's enough to say that a rounded mix that balances energy and interest across the spectrum is more pleasing to our ears than one that is not. Finally, note the 'with clarity' caveat to Rule 1. It is supremely important. It's easy to pile instruments into a mix and end up with a busy, confusing, gloopy mess. But **a strong mix is one in which each part is clearly defined**, in which the kick, bass, synths and percussion are all afforded defined space in which to punch and shine. Of which more later...

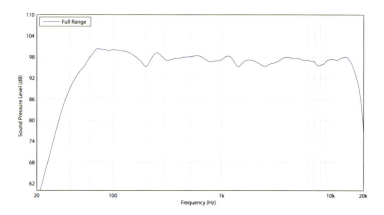

BELIEVE THE HYPE

🎧 Big club systems – powered by names like Martin Audio and Turbosound – deliberately hype the low end to give punters the bass they crave. EQ curves for the main models are freely available online on manufacturers' websites. The one above shows the curve for the Turbosound iQ15 2,500 watt speaker. Note the 'hype' EQ bump at 80Hz and the swift falloff from 40–50Hz down.

THE LOW END

Everything written so far on this page is good practice for mixing *any* kind of music. Dance mixdowns have additional demands.

Remember the overarching rule of production: that **mixes are context specific**. This has implications on the frequency spread because while a radio mix will have a more even spread of frequencies and more activity in the upper mids, the part of the frequency spectrum of most relevance to dance producers is the all-important low end. By and large we're mixing for club rigs, which bump the low end to get clubbers moving (*Believe the hype, left*).

Chapter eight
Mixing and mastering

A useful exercise for comparing the frequency 'shapes' of different types of mixes is to employ a frequency analyser. As a general rule, comparing a dance mix with a pop mix shows more low end activity and less happening in the mids – (*Mixes – and how they look, below*). In short, **energy is concentrated in the part of the mix that matters most to the audience**.

Got it, says the rookie producer, but why can't *every* part of the frequency spectrum have equal energy? *Why can't everything be loud?*

The answer is there's only so much sonic space (or '**headroom**' – *page 257*) available. A new mix starts with silence. As parts are added across the frequency spectrum the volume of the track builds towards the upper ceiling – which in the case of digital is 0dBFS (*page 256*). When 0dBFS is reached there's nowhere else to go. Adding level results in digital clipping.

The fixed limit imposed by digital (and to a lesser extent analogue) means the producer has to choose which parts to prioritise in volume terms – if you push the sub bass up to -2dBFS there's little space left in the mix for anything else.

By reducing the amount of mid and high end content, the producer frees space for a big low end. Conversely, when working on a radio mix, by reducing energy in the bottom, the mid range can punch through.

Thus say the rules. But the rules are there to be broken, and while mixes that fill the frequency spectrum are pleasing to the ear, there's no artistic reason why you can't try ignoring the guidance.

Mixes – and how they look

Daft Punk: 'Get Lucky' 🎧
A rounded – and controlled – low end, an obvious 'scoop' in the mid range and a general levelling of the highs make Mick Guzauski's production a celebration of vintage mix aesthetics with a modern twist. Note the relatively quiet volume of the master compared to the Skrillex mix.

Skrillex: 'Scary Monsters And Nice Sprites' 🎧
A huge low end, a marked dip around 450Hz and a bulk of activity between 800Hz–3kHz deliver both low end punch and trademark screaming mids. The high end sees a near diagonal drop-off in energy. It's worth noting the 450–500Hz dip in both this track and 'Get Lucky'.

The Beatles: 'Hard Days Night' 🎧
An interesting comparitor to show how mixes – and listeners' tastes – have changed over the years: quieter, with significantly less activity in the sub bass and bass regions, almost no very high end and a relatively gentle falloff between 200Hz and 7.5kHz with no obvious dips.

Note: Frequency graphs generated using RMS analysis for the complete chorus/drop of each track.

Chapter eight
Mixing and mastering

Rule 2: A great mix is dynamic. It has shape, contrast and energy.

The contrast between light and darkness is the enduring concern of art, from photography to fiction.

The music producer's version says **there can be no loud without soft**. Impacts punch hardest following periods of calm; the mightiest drops are preceded by carefully controlled builds. The inherent dynamism in dance music – which is fundamental to its DNA – is born of the contrast between lows and highs. Many of the structural devices used to shape dance tracks – builds, breakdowns, drops – exploit these contrasts.

It can be useful to picture the 'shape' – the ebb and flow – of a track's internal energy over time in graphical terms. The page opposite shows two different recordings with perceived energy levels overlaid. It's an artificial construct reflecting not just the energy in the track but also expectations of the response on the dancefloor, with peaks showing full-on hands-in-the-air moments.

Daft Punk's 'One More Time' (*Fig 1*) is a case study in brash, no-nonsense energy shaping, with the concentration of momentum changing throughout the track as verses flow into choruses and drum and melodic parts come and go from the mix. Their DJ backgrounds give Daft Punk a critical insight into how to shape dancefloor energy and 'One More Time' exploits those insights to the full.

But not all dance tracks have such obvious energy contrasts. Rolling techno grooves and downtempo productions typically shape energy in more subtle ways – instruments gradually enter and leave the mix, a kick drum is muted for a few bars, a bassline introduces a new motif... The André track 'New For U' (*Fig 2*) showcases this less dynamic kind of mix. The highs and lows are less obvious, but the track's energy is still constantly on the move.

Talking about a track's energy level in theoretical terms may feel arbitrary, but it has its roots in the very essence of music. Sound in its purest form *is* energy: a wave travelling through space. Sound waves hit our eardrums and provoke a response that is a mix of **emotion** (happy, sad, euphoric) and **movement** (sway, boogie, clap). Some tracks pack a more obviously emotional punch – the gut-wrenching lament of Coldcut's take on 'Autumn Leaves', for example, while others – a Skrillex mainroom workout – are energy distilled.

DJ TOOLS – WHEN 'STRAIGHT' RULES

There is a rare exception to Rule #2: DJ Tools.

The traditional approach to DJing is to shape energy over the course of an entire set, not just every three or four minutes.

As a consequence there's a need – and market – for tracks that in dynamic terms are fairly flat; tracks that, to put it bluntly, don't do all that much, but which in the context of a DJ set work perfectly, ensuring a seamless transition between more obviously dynamic tracks with big highs and lows.

These tools – which are often little more than extended beat workouts – serve an invaluable function even if they're no more than filler between the big bangs.

This heady mix of emotion and energy touches something deep in the listener – something tribal and universal that moves hearts, souls and – crucially for us as dance producers – feet.

It's *this* energy – the energy in the response – that dance producers (and DJs) craft, shape and refine through the use of light and dark, soft and loud, builds and drops. Failing to do so – by making a track that is all bang and no build, or that is all climax and no sonic foreplay – is just... *boring*. It won't ignite the dancefloor, it'll rarely interest a DJ and the home listener is likely to skip to the next track. In short, ignore energy and the emotional shape of a track at your peril. (Although there *are* exceptions – see DJ Tools, left).

ENERGY AT THE MICRO LEVEL

The manifestation of energy and its shape over time doesn't just exist at arrangement level. It's there in individual sounds and in the interaction between sounds too.

At this 'micro' level the difference between silence and signal is defined by the **transient of the waveform**. Shaping it is crucial to effective drum programming. Putting more energy into the opening transient makes for a tighter, tougher sound, while shifting that energy backwards gives a sound more body and weight (*page 10*). Even minute adjustments to the attack and

Chapter eight
Mixing and mastering

decay of a sound can radically change its energy and contribution to the groove.

Zoom out to beat level. Here dynamics are shaped by the rhythm, with bursts of loudness as drums hit, followed by dips to quiet in the gaps between. The result is an ever-changing flow of energy that is unique for each groove. And as any seasoned drummer will tell you, silence is as important as the hits themselves.

Which is all to say that the ebb and flow of sonic energy is ingrained at *every level of a production*, from zoomed-in sample level to the zoomed-out track structure.

As a signoff, it's worth noting what happens when you reduce dynamics to make everything loud.

One of the great production debates of recent times has been over the so-called **loudness wars** (*page 259*), which have resulted in ever-louder masters demanded by producers who want their track to outdo others over the club PA.

Critics of ever-louder masters argue that if you push a mix too far you do two things. Firstly, the mix becomes increasingly fatiguing to listen to. Secondly, and critically, you lose many of the transients (particularly in drums) which make a mix punchy. Says artist Kevin McHugh (aka Ambivalent): "Nothing

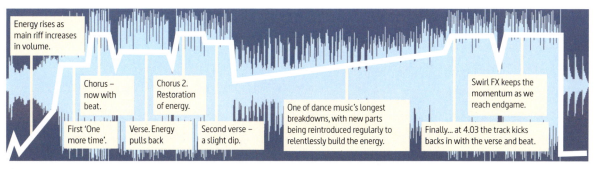

Fig 1: Daft Punk's 'One More Time' with perceived energy levels/dancefloor momentum overlaid in orange. Daft Punk are masters at shaping dancefloor energy, their talents reaching a zenith in the two-minute long breakdown, during which parts are reintroduced and volumes automated until the final drop at 4.03. The brief dips in energy throughout the track are drum fills in which all musical elements drop away.

Fig. 2: Andrés' 'New For U'. Note how much more uniform the waveform – and energy overlay – is, with only two major dips in momentum. The track has a different mission to 'One More Time'. This is not about big troughs and peaks of energy so much as a rolling late-night groove with regular changes of instrumentation to keep the listener's interest piqued and the blissed-out energy flowing.

is less exciting or danceable than a beat that's been crushed to the point of a flat-lined airhorn.

"This is particularly bad in dance music where a listener might hear hours upon hours of music this way."

Increasing a track's loudness to the point of flatline has precisely the opposite effect that one might expect: a mix that is louder, yes, but which also has less energy and subsequently delivers less clout on the dancefloor. Which is all to say that dynamics – at all levels – matter massively.

the secrets of dance music production /

Chapter eight
Mixing and mastering

Rule 3: A great mix has width and depth. It is three dimensional – but works equally well in two *and one* dimensions.

When visualising a mix we typically 'see' it in two dimensions, with the stereo field on the X axis and the frequency domain on the Y. In this construct the kick drum and bass sit low and central with lead synths higher and assorted musical elements – pads, keys, percussion– in varying positions to the left and right (*Fig 3, right*).

Both the **stereo field** and **frequency domain** offer different spaces in which to give musical parts their own identities, not only 'vertically' (in the frequency domain) but also 'horizontally' (in the stereo field).

But there's a critical **third dimension** – often underused – which allows producers to move parts back or forwards in a mix and which offers an additional means of aiding separation (*page 277*) while also adding **space** and **depth** to a mix.

First some theory. Sounds that appear up-front in a mix are generally **loud**, **transient-rich** and **bright**. This means that to push a sound backwards you can reduce its volume, reduce the impact of its attack transient or roll away its high frequencies. Do all three to push a sound a long way back.

Ambience offers a fourth means of controlling the immediacy of a sound. Increasing the amount of ambience on a signal ups the illusion of space around it and shifts it back in the mix. The larger the space around it, the further away the signal sounds. The tools of choice for adding ambience are **reverb** and **delay** (*page 286*).

In traditional rock mixes panning and reverb were used together to recreate the setup of a live gig.

The band was typically panned as it appeared on stage – guitarist stage left, organist stage right, drums and vocals in the centre with the bass a little to one side. Reverb was used not only to settle the vocal in the mix but also to aid separation between the instruments (bass mixed dry with the guitars pushed back in space with a liberal wash of reverb).

Although this classic mix paradigm may seem archaic now the fundamental principles for creating space, width and depth are as relevant as ever.

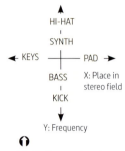

Fig 3: How a simple mix might 'look', with kick and bass low and central, lead synth higher and central, and keys and pads panned left and right.

WHY MONO MATTERS

Wide stereo mixes are fine if you're mixing for an audience that will be listening in stereo. But context – as our golden mix rule demands – is everything, and while radio and compilation mixes are likely to be played on stereo headphones or car stereos, the majority of dance tracks must translate to club rigs.

Although many rigs are now set up in stereo (and festival setups are always stereo), you can't assume that the listener is going to be located perfectly between the two speakers. Indeed you should assume the worst case scenario; that the hypothetical listener will be far closer to one speaker – meaning they will lose a significant portion of the stereo signal.

The practical outcome of this is that **any dance mix which is expected to be played in clubs must translate to mono**. Pivotal parts should never be pushed too far from the centre. And when mixing, you need to regularly switch to mono to check the mix stacks up.

The need for mono fidelity means that when mixing for clubs the stereo field cannot be relied upon to aid separation. Instead the producer must rely more heavily on solving overlaps in the frequency domain and moving sounds in the third dimension as well.

Rule 4: A great mix is a living, evolving thing. It has sustained interest that engages the listener from start to finish.

Rule #4 and rule #2 (**A great mix is dynamic. It has shape, contrast and energy**) overlap to a large extent, because a truly dynamic mix *is* one that engages the listener from start to finish.

But rule #4 goes even further, demanding not just *shifts in energy and focus* during a track but *perpetual momentum*.

What does that mean? It means, in a nutshell, that the listener never gets bored – that there's always something going on in the mix; a groove changes; a new synth part fills the mid tones; an FX swirl tickles the high end; a filter widens as a build develops momentum. Maintaining attention is achieved by using a range of tools and techniques, including:

▸▸ **Structural devices:** Breakdowns, builds and drops are the most obvious means of engagement; you simply *can't* get bored as a track builds towards payoff.

▸▸ **Arrangement:** Parts enter the mix then drop out, the bassline pauses for a few bars, a new synth layer adds a higher octave fizz, the rhythm section strips back to kick and snare... Every change in orchestration keeps the mix fresh.

▸▸ **Automation:** Less obvious than muting parts altogether, automation allows you to give a part movement over time. Sounds can be increased or decreased in volume, envelopes can be tweaked, distortion levels raised, filters opened... With an almost limitless number of parameters that can be automated, the sky's the limit.

▸▸ **Ear candy:** Spot FX, spins, drum fills, glitches and resampling tricks allow the producer to inject bursts of sonic colour into the arrangement to ensure there's never a dull moment.

There are three important caveats to Rule #4. First and foremost, **change doesn't have to be in-your-face obvious**. A track may demand big changes – massive builds and supersized drops.

But there's room too for subtler shifts in texture and tonality. Go back and listen to Daft Punk's 'One More Time' and check

PRO TIPS
LEE CABRERA

"Because I'm a touring DJ I get the luxury of test driving my music on the road and then making changes when I'm back in the studio. Most of the time those changes are around the arrangement.

"How long should the breakdown be? Did I lose the momentum of the crowd with it being too long? Could I have held it longer and created more drama? Was the impact of the drop as effective as it could have been? What FX could I use to make the build even more effective?

"These are all questions I'm asking myself when arranging a record. After some years in the studio and touring, the process becomes second nature."

out its energy profile (*page 239*). Yes, there are defining shifts in momentum. But there are gradual changes in the track too: volumes change; filters opening. These are cumulatively just as important to the track's engagement as the structural big guns.

Secondly, **perpetual change is considerably less important on the dancefloor**, where the audience (who may have imbued any number of substances) will have a much longer attention span than your average Radio 1 listener. This means if a track is destined for the club environment you can afford less change. But only *slightly* less: expecting an audience to stay engaged with a track that doesn't develop at all across a 64 bar section is demanding a lot.

Finally, a word of warning: **a mix can have too much change**. With multiple levels of automation available on every track it can be tempting to fiddle *ad infinitim* in the misplaced belief that complexity equals quality. *This is resolutely not the case.*

The best mixes are often deceptively simple, weaving their magic confidently with **no more than two or three parts changing at any one time**. The ear (and brain) can only process so much sonic information at once. The listener can shift their attention to a funky drum fill, a keyboard flourish or a new bassline – but not all three at once.

Chapter eight
Mixing and mastering

Arrangement, and why it matters

Not so long ago, the musical arranger played a pivotal role in the production process. In the swing and big band age, where orchestras featuring 50 or more musicians would play behind the likes of Frank Sinatra and Bing Crosby, the arranger – a musical all-star with knowledge and experience of a wide range of instruments – would decide which parts played where and with what voicing. The arranger's job was to write or rewrite parts so that they worked together, ensuring that the strings, for example, didn't play in the same frequency range as the brass and the backing singers' lines didn't interfere with the all-important lead vocal. So well thought out were these arrangements that when it came to mixing a track the engineer had very little to do but add a little delay here, a touch of EQ there.

Over time the role of traditional arranger all but disappeared. Big bands went out of fashion, rock and roll changed the landscape of popular music forever, orchestration (now pretty much reduced to drums, bass, vocals and a couple of guitars) was simplified and studios became better equipped, allowing engineers to solve some of the problems that the arranger had previously made redundant.

But the need for solid arrangement has gone nowhere. It remains as critical to a track's success now as it was in the heyday of the big band era, and though very few books or forum posts talk about its importance, the simple fact is that **a good arrangement is a precondition to an effective mix**. The mix is built on the arrangement's foundation and if that isn't solid then the mix isn't likely to be either.

At its crudest, **arrangement is the business of making sure the different elements of a composition – both melodic and rhythmic – work together**. If that sounds like it should be the definition of mixing then that's because the lines dividing composition, arrangement, sound design and mixing are so blurry they continually overlap.

EVERY DECISION IS AN ARRANGEMENT DECISION

As a dance music producer, we are usually songwriter, sound designer, arranger and mix engineer all in one. And because synths, samplers and the many plugins at our disposal allow us to 'sound design' mixes, practically every decision made as we build a track is an arrangement decision. So choosing a patch for the lead synth, picking a keyboard sound which fits best with the vocal, rewriting an arpeggio so that it grooves more intuitively with the beat or

DEFINING TERMS

Ask ten different producers how they define arrangement and structure and you'll get ten different answers.

For the purposes of this book we're keeping things relatively old school, with **arrangement** describing the relationship of different parts with each other and **structure** the time-based framework underpinning a track.

When making – and mixing – music the two are intrinsically linked and changes to one inevitably impact on the other.

transposing a pad down an octave to free mix space for other musical elements are all arrangement decisions that make for a stronger mix.

To illustrate the extent to which sound design impacts on a mix think about the process of creating a synth patch. You start out with a single sine wave, then add sawtooth harmonics using a second oscillator to give the sound more definition. By doing so you're expanding the sound's frequency demands in the mix upwards so that it potentially begins masking other melodic elements. Then you add a third oscillator an octave below to give the sound more body. But this strays into the lower regions, generating masking conflicts with the bassline and kick drum. Next you want to give the synth patch some bite, so you add a touch of distortion. Because distortion generates additional harmonics and volume you've done two things: added more girth to the sound, potentially creating more frequency conflicts, while also reducing the amount of headroom available for other parts…

In this example, every tweak to the original sound was made with a goal in mind – a big, stacked sound that would cut through a busy mix. But with each change, conflicts arose between other musical elements and before long our hypothetical mix was weighed down with problems.

Mixes built on poor arrangements are often muddy, confused, overbearing and not much fun to listen to. They're invariably the mixes that cause us as producers the biggest headaches too; we struggle to separate parts, levels keep changing, critical elements get lost... and on and on...

Fortunately, there are various arrangement approaches that can help establish a firmer foundation on which to construct a more solid mix.

TWEAKING ARRANGEMENTS TO SOLVE MIX PROBLEMS

To see how even minor tweaks to an arrangement can solve mix problems, consider the following three examples:

Example 1: Mix is over-busy with too much going on.

Arrangement solution: Try muting less important melodic and rhythmic tracks to see if any can be dropped. In the era of the near-unlimited track count it's easy to add parts without considering what they add to the cumulative picture. Do you really need a shaker as well as a hi-hat and tambourine? Is that fourth synth layer really adding anything? Remember each new part consumes frequency real estate and headroom – both of which are in limited supply. Often in mixing, **less is more**, so if a part's not doing a clear and defined job, cut it. Sometimes losing a few spurious elements is all that's needed to strengthen what remains.

Example 2: Two important synth parts are clashing with each other.

Arrangement solution: Firstly, identify which part is more important – which synth line you want as the focus of the track. When you've done that you need to find ways of helping the less important synth to complement the lead rather than fighting with it. You might try transposing it up or down an octave so that it inhabits a different part of the frequency spectrum. Or try changing its sound so that it tonally contrasts with the lead synth. Finally, try reprogramming/revoicing the melody and/or rhythm of the second synth part to give the lead more space to perform its more important role, muting some notes, pitch-shifting others, until the two parts have a clearer, more defined and complementary relationship.

Example 3: The verses in a vocal house track feel a bit 'samey'

Arrangement solution: It's easy when using layers of loops to hope that an overlaid vocal can be relied upon to keep things fresh. But that's asking a lot of the vocal. How about refreshing some of the backing instrumentation during the verses, changing the voicing of the rhythm guitar or adding a new keyboard element to keep things interesting? Or how about overlaying a simple percussive part on the second verse to supply groove variance?

In each of these examples, **common mix problems are solved not by mixing, but by reconsidering the parts themselves and making amendments to the arrangement**.

When asked how he made space for vocals in a busy mix, the great mix engineer George Massenburg (Earth, Wind & Fire, James Taylor, Billy Joel) said: "You have to arrange the music to leave space for them."

"I used to cram things into an arrangement," reflects Huxley (*left*). "Now I have a lot less and try and make it all work together." Aeroplane (*left*), agrees: "Keep the arrangement *absolutely essential*."

The arrangement forms the collective body of sounds that are then mixed. Keeping the arrangement intelligent and simple – stripped back to the essentials – makes for strong, defined mixes. Don't blindly cram new parts in as Huxley did in his early days. Ask what the arrangement needs. Consider carefully and consciously what is missing and what is overdone, then arrange to compensate.

Great producers are great arrangers. If you can improve your arrangement chops your whole sound will benefit.

PRO TIPS

HUXLEY

"I used to cram things into an arrangement. I was adding a lot of pointless stuff to try and fill the frequencies and make it sound big, but now I have a lot less and try to make it all work together."

AEROPLANE

"Keep the arrangement absolutely essential. Go crazy with the writing, find interesting chords and crazy hooks, but then the arrangement needs to be spot on."

Structure

In the world of rock and pop, structure is typically governed by a traditional verse/chorus paradigm. Dance structures tend to be more fluid but are still almost always based around eight or 16 bar sections.

LOOP FIRST, SONG SECOND

The tried and tested way of building a track is by perfecting a killer four or eight bar loop consisting of the track's major beat and signature musical elements – including drums, bass, synths and keys – and then building from there.

It's while programming this initial looped section that the early – and often most important – creative work happens, with decisions made on everything from the track's tempo and key to groove settings and instrumentation.

Use as many layers as you like when building this looped section. Although you don't need everything in yet – beds, FX and textures are often best left until later – anything that shapes the overall vibe should be in. Specifically, the groove should be established, underpinned by the bassline, and important melodic lines should be well developed. If a layer isn't adding to the sound, groove and/or tone, lose it and keep the arrangement simple.

EIGHT IS THE MAGIC NUMBER

When you've established a promising four or eight bar loop, it's time to expand it into a full length track. How you do so will depend on your intention for the track. If your audience is the dancefloor then structure, regardless of genre, is shaped by two things: **what the DJ *needs*** and **what the dancefloor *wants***.

The **DJ**'s demands are fairly simple. Other than a killer record all they need is eight, 16 or occasionally 32 bars worth of stripped beats at the start and end of a track (see *Intros and outros, right*). As for the **dancefloor**, unless you're prepared to go out on a limb, your track should mainly be defined by eight, 16 or very occasionally 32 bar sections (or **turnarounds**) – which is to say changes mainly happen in the arrangement every eight, 16 or 32 bars.

Deviating too far from these natural divisions may feel novel, but dancefloors are conservative in their expectations and adding a turnaround after two-and-a-half bars will likely throw clubbers and break dancefloor momentum.

Radio mixes have different demands. A typical radio mix should be shorter (no more than four minutes), does not need DJ playins or outs, and change should happen in faster succession – at least every eight bars

INTROS AND OUTROS

When DJs mixed exclusively on vinyl a 16 or 32 bar stripped lead-in and playout were pretty much essential to give them time to cue up and mix in the new record.

Nowadays this is less of an issue, although DJs still appreciate at least eight bars worth of lead-in.

This lead-in beat should be simple – a kick, hi-hat and single percussive element is usually enough – to make it easy to hear the beat in a loud club through headphones.

Ideally there will also be some kind of identifiable sound or fill that announces the start of the track proper. This helps the DJ know when to mix out the previous tune. Rising sounds, reverse swells and uplifters all do the job nicely.

A good example of a no frills dancefloor-friendly structure governed by clear turnarounds is Tiga's 2014 hit 'Bugatti'. Here arrangement changes are clearly defined against an eight bar grid that isn't deviated from throughout. Mix elements are added or dropped every eight bars with little in the way of automation to smooth transitions.

Note above that we say 'changes *mainly happen* in the arrangement every eight, 16 or 32 bars'. That 'mainly' is important. As long as *most* turnarounds occur at eight, 16 or 32 bar divisions, switching things up occasionally by extending fills/breakdowns or inserting transitions at unexpected positions (after, say, 12 bars, rather than 16) can give a track more flexibility while retaining a consistent structural backbone.

Swedish House Mafia's 'One' (*deconstructed overleaf*), is structured around eight and 16 bar turnarounds but with a few tricks up its sleeve. For the most part new elements enter on eight bar divisions with all the subtlety of a sledgehammer. But there are also frequent four bar switches. Blawan's 'Why They Hide Their Bodies Under My Garage' (*page 248*) features a less rigid structure, with new sections starting at eight, 12 and sometimes 16 bar intervals.

There are two other techniques that give 'Why They Hide Their Bodies...' a more fluid shape: firstly, extensive use of automation (of volume, pitch, FX) to keep the

Chapter eight
Mixing and mastering

arrangement shifting; secondly, turnarounds that cross the grid, like the ride part (bars 65–105) that enters and leaves the mix at apparently random points unrelated to the turnaround grid. *For more on smoothing transitions, see page 252.*

Some tracks reject grid authority completely. Nightmares on Wax's 'Les Nuits' (*deconstructed, page 250*) is a classic example of a track with a freeform structure. Here parts are faded in and out using volume automation so that they don't have definite start and end points. Nor do parts adhere to regular eight or 16 bar divisions. Although this fluid approach is a dancefloor no-go, it is commonplace in ambient and chillout arrangements, with their subtler, smoother shaping of energy.

TIP When working in the studio it's easy to worry that structural change isn't happening fast enough. *Remember your audience at all times*; while a radio mix demands change every few bars, clubbers expect longer mixes. Sometimes a mix won't change across a 32 bar section.

TIP Structuring a killer eight bar loop into a full track is something even pros struggle with. One technique is to analyse a track you know works on the dancefloor and replicate its structure. Do so by importing the guide track into your DAW as a Wav or mp3 and park it on a spare channel to be used as a structural guide.

THE BREAKDOWN

The breakdown has become a feature of almost all dancefloor genres in the past decade – reaching occasionally overindulgent proportions with the EDM explosion – whipping the crowd into an ever-wilder frenzy as a track approaches the drop. Although there are countless approaches to the breakdown, in almost all cases it features the withdrawal of rhythmic elements and/or the bassline.

TIP Where you want to maintain the rhythmic backbone supplied by the kick but still want to ease off the energy, use a low cut filter to temporarily remove bass clout from the kick, keeping the 'click' to supply momentum.

Breakdowns tend to have a feeling of direction and propulsion, beginning quietly – sometimes in silence – before slowly building, ever more layers being fed into the mix until it reaches epic proportions. Not only does the breakdown become more arrangemetically complex as it approaches the drop, it expands outwards and backwards in sonic space, with filters opening and reverb and delays building.

TIP To make the contrast between breakdown, build and drop greater, automate the master fader to dip the level of the track during the breakdown before bringing it back up for the drop (*page 301*).

TERMS OF THE TRADE

Breakdown: Section where the kick (and often bass) drops out and the track breaks down to its simplest elements. In some genres this is where the lead hook is introduced. Rarely lasts longer than two minutes.

Drop: Moment when the track 'drops' back in – either after the breakdown or an extended fill – and the track reaches full energy.

Build: A build in energy and momentum, typically at the end of the breakdown, where risers, reverse crashes, filters and new elements fill the mix, upping the tension before the drop.

Playout: Outro. Elements stripped back to beats and some FX.

Fill: Anything from a traditional drum break to a crazy noise sequence to round off a bar before a new section begins.

TIP Automation is your friend during breakdowns. Note the three rules for building momentum: *filters should open; pitches should rise; ambient space should increase*. Then when the drop comes, the three rules are reversed: filters close down, pitch returns to where it was and reverbs and delays get cut.

FINALLY… SHAPING ENERGY

It's not enough to simply move loop blocks around the arrange page and hope for the best. There has to be a *why* that governs the *when* – a reason for the structural shape of a track.

Read back over our golden mix rules. Most important when structuring a track are Rules #2 and #4 – that is to say, **energy** and **sustained interest**. Look again at how arrangement is used to shape energy in the graphs on *page 239*.

Consider how you want energy to build and drop during a track. Do you want it to be subtle and smooth like 'Les Nuits'? Or blazenly obvious, like 'Bugatti'? Shaping is often genre-dependent. Minimal, techno and ambient tracks tend to build and drop subtly and smoothly, with new elements easing into the mix. By contrast, electro, commercial dubstep, prog and D&B workouts are more obvious in their shaping of energy, with arrangements given a more defined 'cut and paste' structure.

Chapter eight
Mixing and mastering

Swedish House Mafia – 'One'

1 A DJ play-in featuring a heavily resonated clap opens the track. It is joined by a volume-rising 808 kick from bar 5.

2 The 9–26 section forms an extended setup leading to the exposition of the main synth motif. It starts with the clap receding into a wash of delays as the kick picks up the pace into a retriggered windup that morphs into a sustained buzzy synth note – the starting note of the 'buzz' lead.

3 Note the automation on the synth note – a mix of reverb and chorus to keep the sound evolving.

4 The first outing of the descending lead line. First time around it plays alone; second time it closes with two overlaid bit-crushed notes. Immediately before bar 30 a second recurring motif is introduced: the clap double-smack.

5 Enter the kick – a composite layer of subby 808 and mid-heavy slam. It drops away for the final two beats of the last bar to make way for the debut 'Slingshot' reversed clap FX.

6 A new synth layer is added, a digital organ that adds harmonic complexity to the buzz lead. The pace picks up into bar 42, where the on-beat clap returns.

7 All drums are cut as the lead melody is played on the organ alone. High-filtered noise burbles in the background.

8 *Epic starts here*. A bomb FX slam signals intent as chordal saw wave strings and a bass that traces the root expand the frequency bandwidth in both directions. A new high-octave synth layer adds high end energy.

9 The kick returns – though just the 808 for now – to underpin the entry of a new heavily effected trance-style synth.

10 In an arrangement characterised by eight bar turnarounds, the track's first big build transitions to 12 bars. It's a trademark EDM build: the synths break from the established melody into eighth note stabs. They're underpinned by a pitch riser and a snare, its volume and reverb send increasing as it rolls.

11 No headroom is spared as the track semi drops, launching a new pitch-rising acid synth line. The groove and pressure shifts up a gear at bar 94, where a rough 'Break Kick/Hat' combo adds breakbeat propulsion to proceedings.

12 The kick is reduced to a click as attention shifts to the acid synth.

ARRANGEMENT AT A GLANCE

Stacked synths: In all there are five layers making up the 'lead', adding different tonalities and harmonies to the combined composite rhythm.

Big builds and drops: With bomb FX, reverbed slingshots, risers and big crashes, not to mention pitch rise and filter cutoff automation, the arrangement is going to win no awards for subtlety. But that's the point: big, bold and brazen transitions to rock the dancefloor.

Near-endless build: 'One' offers a masterclass in building (and building) energy. Just when you think the track has peaked, it manages to weave in a new layer, adding momentum with each turnaround.

13 The main drop. Present are almost all defining elements.

14 The buzz lead melody is picked up by a new instrumental part: a house piano. The two play starkly above a full rhythm section, which includes a new sparsely programmed ride that provides sustained high-end continuity.

15 A short break opens with a bomb, focusses on the digital organ, then is joined by a meandering riser and a recurrence of the snare build.

16 A slingshot and double clap leads into the second big drop, a 12 bar replay of bars 110–118, this time with higher-level fizzing noise.

17 The kicks are silenced as the synths reach up to a new single-note peak.

18 It's back to basics with just kicks, bass, slingshot and lead synth – more distorted this time around. The sparse mix offers a chance to hear the bubbling, and surprisingly busy, sub bass.

19 The drum break is reintroduced for one last flex of rhythmic muscle.

20 Both sub bass and synth quit the mix to leave nothing but beat elements and a last double clap to round off the arrangement.

//ARRANGEMENT BREAKDOWN

DURATION: **5.50** RELEASED: **2010** LABEL: **SIZE REC** BPM: **125**

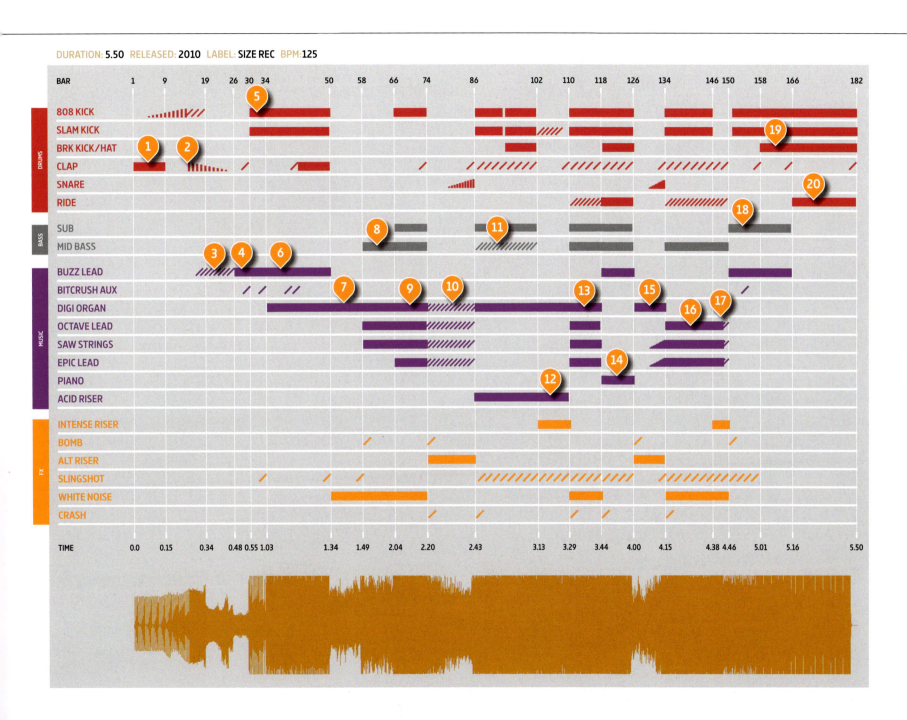

the secrets of dance music production /

Chapter eight
Mixing and mastering

Blawan – 'Why They Hide Their Bodies Under My Garage'

1 The track opens with its lead motif – a bubbling, filtered and tape-delayed synth playing eighths that gently drifts in pitch across an eight bar loop – against a raw off-beat hi-hat. An overlay of distorted noise adds a lo-fi atmospheric wash.

2 Enter the kick and bassline. The bass sound is simple enough – a waspish synth line that follows, for now, the same slow pitch-drift profile as the bubble lead. Its genius lies in automation: the filter opening slowly at bars 17 and 25 to give it an ever-shifting momentum.

3 A double hi-hat hit pre-empts a one bar break in which kick, hat, bass and bubble make way for a sparse resampled underlay of bubble delays and noise.

4 The beat fills out as a raw low-level percussive part debuts alongside a barking snare-style hit – 'dog' – that plays around the kick and hats. But it's the vocals that dominate. "Why they hide their bodies under my garage?," asks the monotone vocal lead, sampled from the Fugees' 'How Many Mics', while a pitched down and re-sampled (*page 128*) counterpoint repeats "under my garage". Tape delays abound, with automation picking out words and spinning them with different EQ and panning treatments.

5 All elements are cut bar the hi-hat, ahead of an isolated FX scream. In a track that eschews big dynamic flourishes, these short one and two bar breaks offer rare let ups in momentum.

6 The perc and dog drop away leaving a skeletal beat to support the vocals. Note the fluidity of the structure: some sections last eight bars, some 12, some 16. Trying to second guess turnaround points is impossible; this mix is about keeping the listener moving – and guessing…

7 Time for the full beat as the dog snare and perc return, joined by a ride playing the first two of each four bar section. With the vocals taking a break, mid and low end interest is supplied by the bassline, increasing in volume to fill out the mix as its filter opens and delays increase.

8 The arrangement is toyed with over this 24 bar development section. The ride pattern that was laid out from bar 65 is chopped and changed while the filters on the bass continue shifting, the pitch rise and fall drifting out of sync with the bubble lead.

ARRANGEMENT AT A GLANCE

Simplicity: There are only twelve elements in this track – just two of which are melodic. In the right hands, simplicity can be brutally elegant

Endless change: Beat aside, the parts are in constant flux, with filters, volumes and delays being tweaked throughout.

Relentless: Techno rarely embraces the kind of big-energy breakdowns and drops typical of Euro and trance. The breaks, when they happen, are short – brief halts in momentum before the relentless order of the beat returns.

9 The scream transitions into a one-off impact stab – with a suitably B-movie aesthetic – and the first breakdown worthy of the description. Note the regular stop-starting of the noise, now cut loose from its sidechain trigger, and the envelope tweaks to the hi-hat.

10 It's all change as the breakdown continues. The hi-hat plays a few regular hits before receding from the mix as the bassline rises in volume and the chewy bubble diminishes.

11 Momentum returns with the kick and hat, joined by the dog and perc. Another instance of the high scream and stab keep the ear candy coming.

12 With beat elements in and vocals out, the bass takes centre stage for a final twisted display of automation.

13 The kick is low-pass filtered, with nothing but a flabby sub left. It's not the only part trimmed down – the bubbles have also lost their high end, skittering around the lower mids as the vocals coda.

14 The last of the playout sees all beat elements muted, with low-volume and increasingly shady versions of the bubbles and bassline emerging from the ever-more dominant background noise soup as the vocals end with a final high scream and movie stab.

//ARRANGEMENT BREAKDOWN

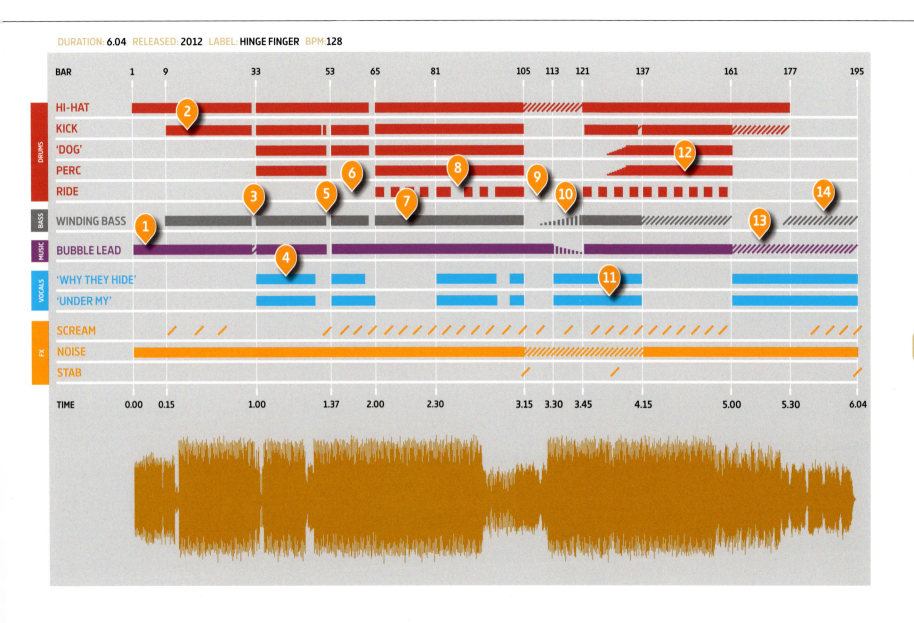

Nightmares on Wax – 'Les Nuits'

1 The track opens with a short found sound sample before a lush synth pad establishes the chord progression and a deep drone, volume rising and falling over time, fills out the low end.

2 The defining melody in 'Les Nuits' is a chordal string part that occupies the bulk of the upper mix. It rises in volume to break free from the pad and settle into the foreground. The slow, subtle addition – and retreat – of new parts is a characteristic feature of the Nightmares on Wax arrangement approach, see *Arrangement at a glance, right*.

3 Next in is the bassline, playing a simple falling ostinato (*page 160*). It enters the mix like the strings, with a volume rise over several bars.

4 The hi-hats follow, picking up the rhythm established by the bass and pinning it down with cleverly programmed 'live' eighth note hits (*page 21*).

5 The kick is next to fade in, playing alone for a few beats before a rim shot and subtle open hi-hat augment the groove. Note the simplicity of the part. There are no beat-building muscles flexing here; the groove bows to the music.

6 As the rhythm section fills out, a reversed synth fed through a 16th note tremolo and delay edges up in volume. It provides sporadic tempo-linked washes: atmospheric ear candy to maintain attention as the track builds.

7 The full beat is in, with the pad/string progression holding the melody. The lower drone part is now superfluous to requirements, its low end duties taken over by the combined weight of kick and bass.

8 Guitar stabs, treated to wah and multiple delays, are used as spot effects, adding rippling washes of interest as the exposition unfolds.

9 A chordal keys part adds lower-mid bulk. As with almost every other mix element, its entry is gradual, nothing more than hinted details at first before it establishes itself. This is joined by a second, single chord line (Rhodes topline), mixed lower, that offers a sparse response to the keys' call.

10 The rhythm section is expanded again: this time with a gentle ride flurry that adds another layer to the otherwise unchanging programmed groove. The open hat is now gone – in hindsight it was no more than an introductory rhythmic motif whose role has been adopted by the ride.

ARRANGEMENT AT A GLANCE

Fluid movement: Parts enter and leave the mix almost unnoticed as a result of volume automation across multiple tracks giving an organic, breathing feel to the arrangement.

No obvious turnarounds: While most dance genres are governed by clear eight or 16 bar demarcations, chillout is not one of them. Here what matters is the big picture – which pays no heed to the usual dancefloor norms.

Rhythmic backbone: Once established, the beat and bassline are only dropped once, for a few seconds, giving the track a near omni-present structural backbone on which the instrumental parts are hung.

11 As the keys parts announce a new section of the track, the strings fade in volume, followed by the pad.

12 At around 3.20 the strings leave the arrangement, making way for a leaner 'solo' section. Against the beat/bass backing, a Rhodes keyboard plays a jazzy improvisation joined a few bars later by a Leslie organ. A one-and-a-half bar drum and bass break offers the only respite to the rhythmic backbone in the entire six minute arrangement.

13 A new percussive part enters the mix: a swingy shaker playing 16ths.

14 Another new element is introduced: an ethereal female vocal loop that foreshadows the start of the build.

15 The reversed synth and chord pad return, levels low at first as tension is built throughout the mix, organ solo fading away as the strings make a low-level reappearance.

16 Everything is back in now – strings soaring, pad washing and beat grooving for one final epic flourish before the rhythm section and vocals begin a slow fade, leaving the strings and pads to carry the playout alone. The low level drone from earlier is resurrected in the closing bars to fill out the bass frequencies as all fade to silence.

//ARRANGEMENT BREAKDOWN

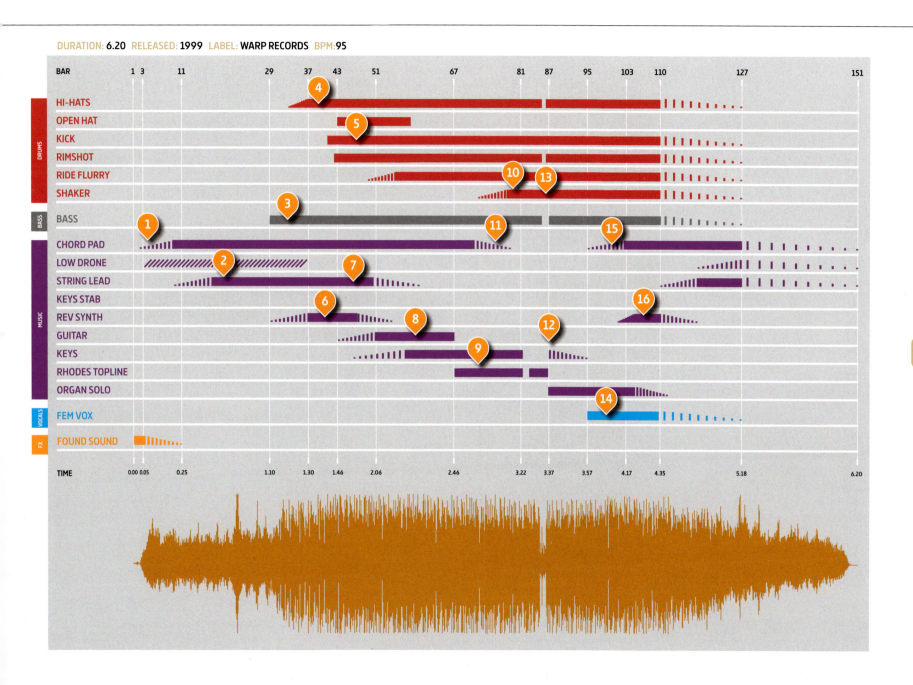

Transitions and FX

Transitions and effects (FX) serve multiple purposes, from creating bridges between turnarounds to highlighting and accentuating pivotal moments in a song's structure with unique fills and effects.

FILLS

Fills are used to add interest and sonic lifts at the end of eight or 16 bar cycles, or to lead into major transitions like the chorus or the introduction of a new motif.

Traditionally, fills were made using drum breaks or ever-denser snare rolls, old-school style. These days the raw material for fills is equally likely to be sourced from synths, percussive sounds or heavily effected/filtered versions of the backing track. Common tricks include reverse sections, filter swells or using glitch effects plugins like Ableton's Beat Repeat, Sugar Bytes' Effectrix or dBlue's Glitch to create glitched versions of the beat or even the whole track (*Full mix FX, page 254*).

SMOOTH TRANSITIONS

While no-nonsense cut and paste-style transitions a la SHM 'One' (*page 246*) have their place in certain genres, make them too abrupt and it can damage the flow of a track and lead to a falter of energy on the dancefloor. Placing big reverberated FX hits, dubby delays or white noise/traditional cymbals at the start of sections takes the edge off transitions. These spot FX do two things: firstly, they announce the start of a new section; secondly they help smooth changes, shaping the energy in a more fluid way. You can further blur boundaries by using build-specific effects – whooshes, reversed cymbals, windups – before a turnaround to ratchet up the tension before the on-the-bar transition effect.

TRANSITION IDEAS

▸▸ **Ambient bus build:** Here a part is fed to a reverb (sometimes delay) bus at an increasing level as the track reaches a turnaround. The effect is to build tension, muddy the production and push the part further back in the mix before the ambient effect reverts to its original level for maximum impact as the new section begins (*see Walkthrough, opposite*).

▸▸ **Ambient bus build – multiple parts:** Here not just one, but multiple parts are given the ambient build treatment to create more tension. Take the effect to the next level by automating the reverb size and tone, or delay feedback/filter settings.

▸▸ **Vocal riser:** Find a small section of a vocal where a note is held. Then begin trimming a loop cycle of that held note, extend the held note and create a pitch automation curve to slowly increase the pitch. Add automated bus send effects to ramp up delay and reverb times as the pitch builds (*Vocal riser walkthrough, page 255*).

▸▸ **Extra bar break:** An additional, and unexpected, single bar fill (occasionally silence) is inserted between build and drop.

▸▸ **Pitch and LFO risers:** To ramp up tension into a new section, use automation and/or modulation to rise the pitch of an existing part or increase the rate of LFO modulation. The technique works best on synth parts but can also be employed on anything from vocals to drums. When working with loops try simultaneously automating timestretch down and pitch shift up (and vice versa).

TIP Vary transitions, just like you do other mix elements, to keep things interesting. Even the same reverse cymbal transition may benefit from a different cymbal sample.

TIP Don't underestimate the impact of silence. It's tempting to think that adding FX layers will create more tension. But sometimes taking things away – either whole parts or frequencies using filters – can generate heightened drama.

TIP For next-level transitions switch bpm-synced LFOs to freeform/random waveforms, allowing a track to break apart rhythmically before it snaps back together at the turnaround/drop.

PRO TIPS

PETAR DUNDOV

"For FX sweeps [on 'Before it all ends' from his *At The Turn Of Equilibrium* album] I used a System 100 oscillator in combination with noise generator, and just recorded a bunch of takes while tweaking pitch frequency and filter."

SEE ALSO

- PAGE 95 WHITE NOISE FALL
- PAGE 96 WHITE NOISE WIND-UP
- PAGE 96 PITCH RISER
- PAGE 97 DUB SIREN
- PAGE 195 VOCAL TRANSITION RISER
- PAGE 254 THE BOMB
- PAGE 301 EDITS TO THE MASTER

Transition FX: Effect send automation – ambient bus build 🎧

1 Listen to the 'before' example, featuring two sections in the track. We want to drop the bass at bar 9 where the pad is introduced, but the transition currently sounds abrupt. Spot FX – like a cymbal – would remedy this, but the transition can also be smoothed using automation of the existing sounds.

2 The first thing to do is set up a couple of effect sends from the bass. Different DAWs offer different workflows for this. In Logic, click/hold on the Send box on the channel strip, then choose Bus > Bus 1. When that's set up, do the same in the slot below to set up Bus 2.

3 Bus 1 will provide the reverb. Valhalla's VintageVerb is added, set at 100% wet since we're using an effect send and the dry signal is already on the original channel. The reverb has a decay of 1.78 seconds, pre-delay of 20ms and a low cut filter at 440Hz to reduce mud.

4 Bus 2 houses a tape delay, again with a 100% wet mix. Feedback is set to 50%, Groove to eighth notes and the filters are positioned to bracket away lows and highs to tighten the signal in the mix (lows cut at 430Hz and highs at 6.6kHz respectively).

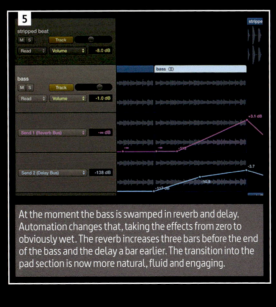

5 At the moment the bass is swamped in reverb and delay. Automation changes that, taking the effects from zero to obviously wet. The reverb increases three bars before the end of the bass and the delay a bar earlier. The transition into the pad section is now more natural, fluid and engaging.

6 Finally, place a chorus effect after both the reverb and delay. This adds depth and sparkle to the ambience. The effect also slightly diffuses and widens the signal, helping to settle the FX into the mix and reducing conflicts between the original sound and the effected versions.

Transition FX: The bomb 🎧

1 A kick drum sample, some reverb and an EQ plugin are all you need to create a huge bomb-style effect. Start by selecting a kick drum sample and dragging the audio into your arrangement or loading it in as a sample. We've chosen an 808-style kick with a long decay tail.

2 Pretty much any reverb will work as long as it's capable of producing a long, smooth decay tail. Valhalla's Vintage Verb, inserted onto the kick channel, is loaded in Concert Hall mode with a decay of 10 seconds and pre-delay of 6ms. A low end cut at 410Hz reduces the 'soggy bottom'.

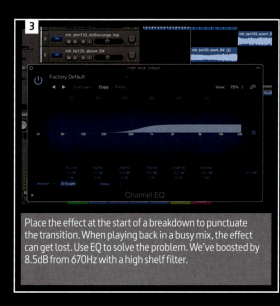

3 Place the effect at the start of a breakdown to punctuate the transition. When playing back in a busy mix, the effect can get lost. Use EQ to solve the problem. We've boosted by 8.5dB from 670Hz with a high shelf filter.

Transition FX: Full mix FX 🎧

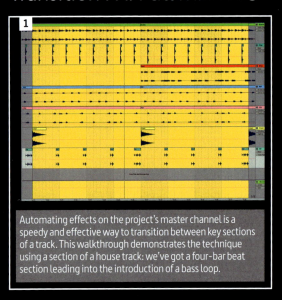

1 Automating effects on the project's master channel is a speedy and effective way to transition between key sections of a track. This walkthrough demonstrates the technique using a section of a house track: we've got a four-bar beat section leading into the introduction of a bass loop.

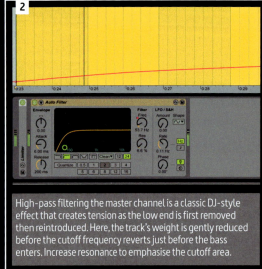

2 High-pass filtering the master channel is a classic DJ-style effect that creates tension as the low end is first removed then reintroduced. Here, the track's weight is gently reduced before the cutoff frequency reverts just before the bass enters. Increase resonance to emphasise the cutoff area.

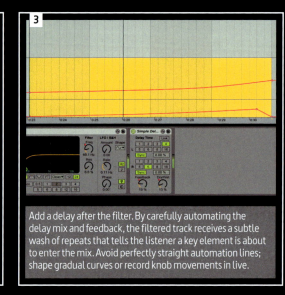

3 Add a delay after the filter. By carefully automating the delay mix and feedback, the filtered track receives a subtle wash of repeats that tells the listener a key element is about to enter the mix. Avoid perfectly straight automation lines; shape gradual curves or record knob movements in live.

Transition FX: Vocal riser

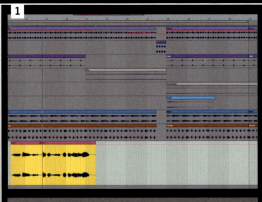

1 This walkthrough transforms a straightforward vocal into an epic riser. To set up the transition, arrange the track so that the vocal leads to a breakdown. At the point where the track reaches the break, bounce down a small vowel section of the vocal and load it into a sampler on a new MIDI track.

2 Create a MIDI region on this new track and draw a C3 note for the duration of the breakdown. Use the sampler's looping function to loop a sustained section of the vowel snippet. Experiment with the sampler's loop length and crossfade features to smooth clicks at the loop edges.

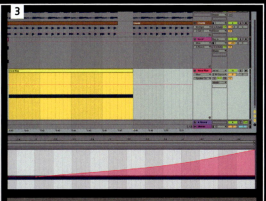

3 Draw or record pitch bend automation to cuase the sustained vocal phrase to rise in pitch. Drastic changes work best, so set the sampler's pitch bend range to +12 or even +24 octaves. Try introducing the pitch bend after a few seconds, extracting even more from the unexpected rise.

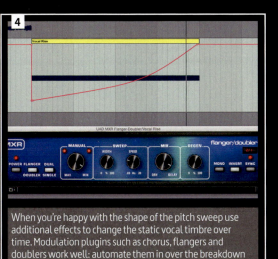

4 When you're happy with the shape of the pitch sweep use additional effects to change the static vocal timbre over time. Modulation plugins such as chorus, flangers and doublers work well: automate them in over the breakdown for a trippy 'swimming' effect.

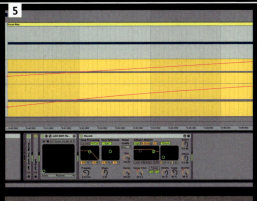

5 Next, add reverb and automate the Mix and Time values across the course of the breakdown, causing the reverb to swell towards the drop. Tweak the automation curves to squeeze every last bit of tension from the expanding effect. This is an example of the 'Ambient bus build' on *page 253*.

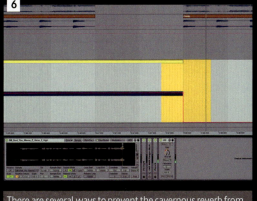

6 There are several ways to prevent the cavernous reverb from swamping the drop. Either revert the effect's level to 0dB just before the track kicks back in or render the vocal build channel (with FX tail) to audio and chop off the tail of the new audio region.

Chapter eight
Mixing and mastering

THE ESSENTIAL GUIDE TO...
Loudness and levels

Most artists want their tracks to sound loud. In a club environment, a track needs to stack up against others played in a DJ set. Even when mixing for headphones, you don't want your track to sound quiet in comparison with others on a playlist – which explains the genesis of the so-called 'loudness wars', explained overleaf.

But what do we mean, exactly, by 'loud'? How loud is too loud? And where should you set faders to get a healthy level of signal without pushing it too far? These questions, it turns out, are not easy ones to answer, and asking them opens more than a few cans of worms. Let's start at the top...

THE DECIBEL

Throughout this book you'll find numerous references to decibels (dB). The **decibel** (one tenth of one bel, named after telephone inventor Alexander Graham Bell) is a term used in sound engineering as a way of representing **the ratio of one signal's level to another**. Or to say that another way, decibels measure **changes in sound levels**. So when you push a tracks' fader up by 10dB, the signal increases in power ten times. The fact that dB measure change, rather than absolute values, explains why 0dB (or **unity gain**) doesn't mean *no sound*; it means *no change*. It also explains why it is meaningless to say a sound 'has a level of 100dB'. It begs the question '*100dB compared to what?*'

For those working in DAWs, there is a scale of measurement that brings a degree of objectivity. **dBFS – or decibels measured relative to full scale**. Here 'full scale' (0dBFS) is the maximum level the digital system can cope with before **clipping** (defined below) begins. Values below 0dBFS are measured in relation to full scale. So -12dBFS means a level that is 12dB lower than clipping level.

If that's not confusing enough, dBFS is just one of many sound measurement terms. You may also come across references to **dB SPLs** – for measuring sound pressure levels (SPL), **dBVs** – voltage measured relative to 1 volt and **dBus (sometimes labelled as dBVU)** – voltage measured relative to 0.775 volts. Unless you take an interest in the physics of sound or spend a lot of studio time in the analogue domain, understanding the nuances of these different terms is not necessary.

OPERATING LEVELS

Mixers and other devices are designed to work within a specific range of signal levels. The smallest signal they can accommodate

BIT DEPTH

Most smartphones include a digital camera with resolution measured in megapixels. The greater the number of megapixels, the more accurate a representation of the original image the digital photo is.

When recording digital audio an analogue-to-digital converter captures a rapid series of short 'snapshots'. Bit depth describes the number of bits of information in each snapshot; the higher the number – as with megapixels – the more accurate the representation of the original sound.

With 16-bit audio, there are 65,536 possible audio levels in each snapshot. At 24-bit there are 16,777,216 – more than enough to leave a healthy level of headroom when recording and mixing.

is determined by the background electrical **noise** of the system. The highest is determined by the level at which the analogue (or digital system) starts to **clip** the waveform – *see Fig 4*.

Clipping is a squaring of the tops and bottoms of a waveform caused when the circuitry can't deliver any more level, regardless of how much the gain control is turned up.

Analogue equipment typically handles signals that exceed the nominal operating level set by the manufacturer by 15dB or more before clipping occurs. Even when a signal enters the red, circuitry introduces a progressive increase in distortion above its nominal operating level and prior to clipping. This distortion may be used to deliberately 'warm' a signal.

A **digital** meter allows and shows **no safety margin above 0dBFS**. Unlike analogue mixers, there is no nice warming when a signal is pushed into the red; the system simply – and unpleasantly – **clips**.

In both analogue and digital systems, a signal's **optimum performance** is delivered when the signal level is as high as possible above the noise floor but still with enough safety margin (or **headroom**) left over to handle unexpected signal peaks (like transients in drums) without clipping. Doing so maximizes signal-to-

/ the secrets of dance music production

Chapter eight
Mixing and mastering

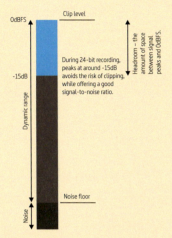

In a digital system there is no safety margin above 0dBFS full scale, so the nominal recording and mixing level of a track might be set at -15dB or thereabouts. Mix levels can normally be higher. If the red clip section lights, the signal is being clipped.

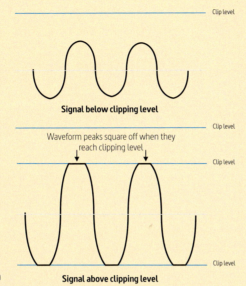

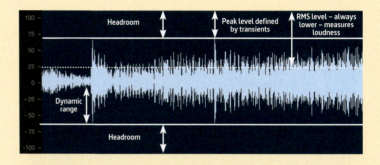

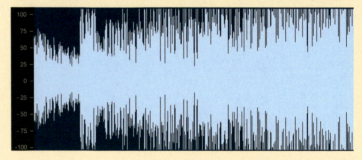

🎧 Fig 4: A before and after image of a badly processed mix. The top waveform shows an RMS value of around -15dB (-5dB on peaks) – plenty of room for the transients to punch and for a mastering engineer to work with. The second shows a louder, brutally slammed mix (-7dB RMS), with transients smashed, regular clipping and the transient energy lost in the flat wall.

noise ratio. In practice this means **keeping individual digital channels at between around -15dBFS and -18dBFS**.

Maintaining this optimum level – where each piece of equipment or circuitry in the signal chain is working in its 'happy range' – is referred to as optimising the **gain structure** and applies equally to analogue and digital systems.

TIP Gain structure matters when using plugins – particularly those that model analogue circuitry and which may therefore add saturation to signals that 'push the red'. Although a hotly debated subject, good practice is to settle a channel fader at around -15dBFS then feed signal into plugins at unity gain. If you're confident about a plugin's gain structure, experiment with increasing the input level to take advantage of any warming – but A/B the treated and bypassed signal to ensure you're not introducing clipping. If in doubt, **a foolproof rule of thumb when mixing in a DAW is not to let the input or output of any channel, insert, effects bus, group channel or main output go over 0dBFS**.

DYNAMIC RANGE AND HEADROOM

Dynamic range refers to the difference (in dB) between the quietest and loudest possible signals that can be accommodated by a piece of audio equipment. It also describes t**he difference between the quietest and loudest parts of an audio signal** (Fig 4, right).

Pinpointing the exact 'quietest' and 'loudest' parts of a signal is notoriously difficult as you have to look at things like noise and signal saturation, where the effects can be blurred. For example, audio CDs (encoded at 16-bit) have a theoretical dynamic range of about 96dB, but this can be perceived as up to 120dB with dithering. The smart use of 24-bit audio, meanwhile, offers the potential to capture a range of more than 140dB – greater than the range of human hearing.

Chapter eight
Mixing and mastering

The related concept of **headroom** can be defined broadly as the **available, or unused, dynamic range above the peak recording level** – in effect, space left 'just in case'. If you record or mix with little available headroom, you risk saturation and/or clipping.

Given that most of us record at 24-bit – a bit rate offering definition with even low-level signals – there is no need to push peaks to the 0dBFS mark when mixing, especially when going over, or even just under, this point can ruin recordings.

Instead best practice says leave around 12–15dB of headroom on peaks – enough space for a signal to punch and pump without compromising audio quality or risking excessive noise.

Overall it's better to go for a great sounding, well-balanced mix that sounds a little quiet compared to other tracks than one that is pushed too far. Remember that mastering will make your track louder – and DJs can always increase its volume if they wish.

MEASURING AUDIO

It's important not to confuse the **loudness** of musical material with its **peak level**.

A normalised drum loop usually has a few peaks at the maximum possible level of 0dBFS. But does that make it loud?

Not necessarily, because the peak level is only a part of the story. A signal with a higher *average level, less dynamic range* and *more content spread across the full frequency range* will invariably sound louder.

Because of the way our ears work, perceived loudness also depends on the duration, frequency content and density of a signal, as well as other factors. As such, determining the perceived loudness of a signal can be very hard.

A DAW's peak level meters aren't much help either, as they're designed for monitoring general signal level and to help highlight clipping. Instead, to measure loudness you need a specific kind of meter like the TT Dynamic Range Meter, which displays some form of **averaged level**, with the **RMS** (root mean square) method the most common.

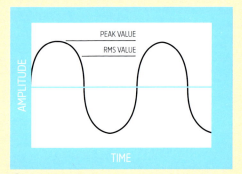

Fig 5: Peak value does not measure loudness. A more meaningful starting point is its RMS, or LUFS, value.

DITHER

A mathematical process known as dither is employed by algorithm designers to reduce low level distortion in digital systems at the expense of adding a little noise. The added noise is so trivially small as to be negligible.

With a correctly dithered signal, low level digital audio can be heard below the level of the noise – much as it can on analogue tape.

Without dither the signal simply disappears when its level falls below that required to activate the least significant single digital bit.

Dithering is also used as the final process in mastering when a 24-bit signal is reduced to 16-bit for CD replication.

Going into the physics of RMS calculations is to enter a rabbit hole. For our purposes it's enough to know that RMS measurements provide a useful average that fairly accurately represents how our ears perceive the volume of sound. The relative level of each is shown in *Fig 5, below*.

TIP In Cubase the Statistics window can be used to find the peak amplitude (the level of the loudest peak) as well as the averaged RMS power. Logic's native Channel EQ has an RMS Analyzer mode found in the expandable drop-down.

NOTE An alternative method for measuring loudness that you may come across is the Loudness Unit (LUFS). Although more relevant in broadcast where LUFS is used to ensure a consistent level of loudness, particularly during adverts, some plugins feature an LU scale. In most scenarios the **LUFS value is very similar to RMS**, and if you reduce your track volume be 1dB the LUFS value will reduce by close to 1dB.

NOTE If you run a complete track through a loudness meter it will only give part of the picture as it doesn't indicate how the power is distributed throughout the audio spectrum – or between the various contributory musical elements. For this, a **spectrum analyser** or similar multi-frequency level meter should be used alongside a loudness meter to show what's going on throughout the frequency range.

Chapter eight
Mixing and mastering

3D waterfall analysis tools plot frequency and level over time, although keeping tabs on what's going on when can be an issue. **Spectrograms** – 2D versions of waterfall plots – are suitable for more specialist applications such as audio restoration and correction, as they allow you to find audio anomalies relatively quickly.

NOTE The damping of meters is also important to consider. A meter which tracks every change in level instantaneously is almost impossible to read. Intentionally making the meter slower to respond to increases or decreases in signal level might seem to offer a less accurate approach, but the result is a more readable – and therefore more useful – meter.

INCREASING LOUDNESS

There are a range of practical techniques employed to increase the loudness of individual signals as well as full mixes:

▶▶ The most obvious is to use **compression** (*page 277*) and **limiting**. Both tools reduce the dynamic range of a signal.

▶▶ **Multiple levels of compression** are often better than high-ratio, big-pump compression that has the effect of nullifying transients and reducing punch.

▶▶ **Saturation plugins** such as PSP's Vintage Warmer round off transients while

CLIPPING

A surefire way of generating extra level is to deliberately clip the signal. It's a trick sometimes employed by less-than-scrupulous mastering engineers who are willing to forsake audio quality for extra volume. Although in the analogue realm a certain amount of red-lining is acceptable, in digital systems it's a no; digital distortion sounds bad. Period.

adding favourable harmonics to help increase perceived loudness by raising the gain of low level elements.

▶▶ One of the most effective ways of increasing loudness is, perhaps counter-intuitively, to **control the low end.** Use bracket filtering (*page 211*) on all tracks that don't need low end and trim sub fat at the 20-40Hz point from both the kick drum and bassline. Dance mixing is frequently about balancing the needs of the all-important – but headroom-hungry – bass frequencies and the energy of other parts higher up the spectrum.

▶▶ **Balance the mix.** A good mix should be balanced across the frequency spectrum, says Mix Rule #1. Concentrated frequency buildups sound bad and reduce headroom.

▶▶ **Automate levels across a track.** There's no point the drop maxxing out the meters while the rest of the track is quiet. Use level automation across mix buses to control levels over time and keep things loud for the duration of the mix.

TIP To avoid running out of headroom, **mix backwards from the loudest section** – usually the drop. Instead of starting at the start, loop and mix the drop first.

Loudness, transients and the 'loudness wars'

When making a signal louder there is a constant tension between retaining transient energy and the level of a signal.

Increasing loudness too far has the effect of rounding off transients – the front end of a kick, the crack of a snare. As a signal is pushed louder, with compressor/s and limiter/s handling ever more signal, transients are knocked into submission until a signal is effectively flatlined. At this point a signal or mix may be *loud* – but it will have been robbed of the energy and dynamic punch that transients bestow. Often an over-baked mix sounds plain nasty, with ambient tails getting overemphasised

and minor parts and detail all but lost in the mix.

The fine line that divides a 'good' loud mix from an overbaked one is the genesis of the so-called **loudness wars**. The term refers to the escalation in loudness of mixes over the past two decades or more in a never-ending 'race to the top', with each mix trying to outdo the last in the loudness stakes to sound 'better' in the club or on the radio.

The inevitable fallout of the worst excesses are mixes that sound aggressive, fatiguing and dynamically dead. As a consequence many mastering

engineers have bucked the trend, crafting masters that are less loud but which sound better and bring more momentum to the dancefloor. Their fight has been bolstered by tech giants like YouTube and iTunes engaging algorithms that aim for consistent playback volume, regardless of loudness when uploaded (do an online search for Ian Shepherd to learn much more).

The dance music producer's goal is to maximise loudness while retaining enough transients to ensure punch and energy. Knowing where that line lies is a matter of judgement, sensitivity and – above all – experience.

Chapter eight
Mixing and mastering

FIRST STEPS TO A BETTER MIX:
Monitoring, music and knowing your room

These two pages come with a large **READ THIS FIRST** label. They are the two most important pages in the mixing chapter – maybe even the entire book. Because you can dedicate your life to learning everything there is to know about compression ratios, bit depths and EQ curves, but if you can't hear what's going on in your mixes, that knowledge is pretty much redundant.

Before bringing up a single fader note that **your mixes will only ever be as good as the sound you hear from your speakers/ headphones**. You don't find Hollywood editors cutting their epics using black and white TVs. Nor should you expect to make informed decisions over how much bite a snare needs, where in the stereo field a delay should sit or how deep a bassline should reach if your monitoring isn't up to scratch. Return to *Chapter seven, pages 200–205* to remind yourself of the importance of monitoring and the studio environment. Because in many cases, **the factor that will improve your mixes most is the environment they're made in.**

This is not to say you need to spend a fortune on installing acres of acoustic treatment. Far from it. Every day, some of the world's best production talent is making great sounding tracks in studios that would make professional acousticians recoil in horror. They're able to do this because **they know their room inside out**. They know there's a honky frequency at 150Hz so they mix to compensate – refusing to correct what might sound dreadful in the studio because they know that when the track is played in Berghain their 150Hz honk will disappear on the club rig.

Until you're mega rich your goal shouldn't be a perfectly treated room or a flat response. It should be a mixing environment that reveals the frequencies most important to the music you make and which, most importantly, you understand inside out – sonic warts and all.

That kind of knowledge – a confidence in the sound of your space – comes with time and experience. You can build that confidence by listening to commercial mixes in your studio, analysing how they sound and then making your own tracks *sound like they sound*.

Monitoring is **context specific** too. We've not recommended the ubiquitous (in pro studios) Yamaha NS-10s as secondary speakers in the dance producer's studio (*page 204)* because their strength lies in exposing the mid and upper-mid

PRO TIPS

JAMES RUSKIN

"Let's be honest: there are techno records you don't listen to at home, so their translation in those environments is irrelevant.

"If I'm making something that's purely for a club, I want it to work on a system. The actual frequencies that you need to get across in a club are of no consequence when you're at home. I think it's what you're trying to put across and trying to achieve with that particular piece of music dictates how you mix it.

"What is it you want from this and what do you want people to take from it?"

frequencies which are most important in pop mixes. If you're mixing for radio or the CD market then speakers that are more revealing of mid tones are invaluable. But as James Ruskin notes, *left*, dance producers are most often mixing for clubs, where the requirements are different.

Club mixes are all about the extreme low (and often high) end – the start and end of the classic EQ 'smile'. Which means we need speakers that reveal the lows (and highs). It also explains why subwoofers are not uncommon in dance producers' studios. And while our line is that you don't need a subwoofer (*page 204*), used sparingly (switched on intermittently to check lower frequencies), a subwoofer can help fill in a picture of how a mix will translate in a club environment.

Also remember that for most dance music **the measure of success is impact on the dancefloor**. So as often as you can, check how a mix goes down while you or a friend DJs, then tweak it until your mix stacks up with the best of them.

MIXING ON HEADPHONES

It's one of the top questions on production forums: Can you mix using headphones? And with more people making tracks on the move – on flights,

in the living room – it has become more pertinent than ever.

A decent pair of headphones may not change your life, but they're an essential studio accessory for most producers. Even if you have a decent monitoring setup, headphones can still play a part in your workflow.

In a home studio setup the most obvious benefit may be allowing you to work into the small hours without disturbing the neighbours/family. But a good pair of monitor headphones also provides a useful secondary listening source. They are particularly strong on detail.

Being clamped so tightly to your ears, they also avoid problematic room acoustic issues – although they have their own deficiencies when it comes to low-end extension and smoothness.

For all-round studio use, **closed-back headphones** are the typical choice as they avoid spill into mics and can't be heard by other people. However, **open-back designs**, with their better low-frequency extension, are usually more accurate for mixing.

Headphone mixing comes with three caveats. Firstly, because of the exaggerated stereo field, double-check any panning decisions using speakers. Secondly, there's a temptation to pull back on reverb, making mixes drier than they should be. Finally, consumer-oriented headphones hype the bass end, which makes well balanced mixing hard to achieve.

Headphones, like monitors, are a personal choice. Avoid buying online if possible. Trying them out in person is the best way of ensuring you get a set which suits your personal taste.

ALL ABOUT THE MUSIC

Listening to tracks by artists and producers you admire is one of the easiest ways to improve your productions. And that means *really listening* – not just sticking on a mix podcast, cracking open a beer and dancing round the studio.

Critical listening sessions help in two important ways. Firstly – as outlined above – they enable you to tune your hearing to the sound of your speakers and room. This is important for delivering a final mix that

Magic AB v2. An indespensible referencing plugin. For effective referencing, use tracks that have the sound you're aiming to achieve. Some producers A/B using a range of tracks to refine different parts of a mix. They may like the bass response of one and the vocal production in another.

stacks up with the best in a club situation, particularly in terms of frequency balance. Indeed, it's often a good idea in the middle of a long session to take a break and refresh your ears with another track – partly to keep you sane and partly to remind yourself what you're aiming for.

But having third party tracks at hand opens up a second powerful technique for improving your mixes: comparing your own mix to that of a pro mix you admire. This process, known as **referencing** or **A/Bing**, is one that can dramatically improve your mixes, as well as teach you more about your room.

Referencing is straightforward. Simply import a selection of well mixed and relevant tracks into your DAW for direct comparison, then switch between them and your own mix at regular intervals during mixdown to check you're on the right track. An easy way of doing this is to cough up the £45 or so for Sample Magic's Magic AB.

You can get even more from reference tracks by coupling A/B comparisons with analysis tools like spectrum analysers and Goniometers. Like the sound of a Benga & Skream track? Then see what it looks like in a spectrum analyser then try to get your own mix 'looking' the same. Although using your eyes to make audio decisions is less reliable than using ears, visual feedback offers an important second opinion.

Chapter eight
Mixing and mastering

Mixdown

If you've read the preceding pages you're in good stead now it comes to mixing a track. You understand the importance of structure and arrangement. You know the difference between peak and RMS levels. And you've learned the golden rules of mixing. Now it's time to put them into action...

APPROACHES TO MIXING

Outside the world of dance music production the 'mixdown' is the last stage in a record's journey before it is handed to the mastering engineer. The track will have been written, arranged and heavily rehearsed, often during gigs. Then the band will enter the studio for the recording itself. With the various mics set up, the recording engineer captures the best possible performance of the track, overdubbing where necessary. When that's done, the best takes are auditioned, edited and comped together before – finally – the project is handed to the producer or mix engineer to weave their magic, setting levels and adding processing and effects during mixdown.

The typical dance music production rarely follows this journey. Although every producer works in their own way, the majority begin by crafting a groove or layering up a few loops to kick-start creative ideas. Onto this rough foundation more parts are added – a melodic element here, a percussion line there – in patchwork fashion until the mix begins to take shape. This **mix as you go** approach is more popular than ever, with producers using laptops on the move to tweak sounds and arrangements as a track journeys from conception to completion.

Mixing as you go means making mix decisions from the moment you start a track. Because even tweaking a synth patch has mix implications (*page 242*), it's impossible to separate mixdown from the composition and arrangement process – unlike with pop or rock recordings, in dance music the mix frequently *is* the track.

That's not to say there is no **final mixdown**. When the writing and arranging process is complete it can be helpful to draw a line in the sand before finalising the mix with fresh ears. And for producers who sketch ideas on the road before mixing down in the studio, the usual workflow is to get a track to an advanced stage before mixdown proper in the studio. The same is true if you use outboard during the final mix.

ESSENTIAL PREP

Whatever your workflow, you can make things easier on yourself – and save valuable studio time – by running a tight workflow ship (*see Smarter working, right*).

A well organised Logic arrange window, with tracks grouped by colour and clear track labelling. Anal? Maybe, but it'll improve your workflow.

THE ARRANGE PAGE

First up, spend a little time optimising your arrange page:

▸▸ **Arrange tracks in a logical order** so that similar parts sit together. Grouping them close to each other saves you from scrolling around windows.

▸▸ **Use colour to further differentiate similar objects.** You might colour all drum tracks red and all synth parts purple. Because humans identify colours faster than words, this saves time.

Chapter eight
Mixing and mastering

▸▸ **Label tracks clearly.** Trying to locate 'missing' parts is a pain. Clearly label all tracks and use pictorial icons to make life even easier if your DAW supports them.

▸▸ **Delete unused tracks.** If you're certain you don't need a track then save a backup copy of the project then delete all unused tracks. You can revert to the backup if you need to recall a track.

GROUP TRACKS

The next step is to assign sets of sounds that belong together to different mix **groups**. To do so, simply select the parts you want to group (common choices include drums, percussive elements, melodic elements, backing vocals) and route each to a different stereo group bus (*see walkthroughs, overleaf*).

Grouping in this way, also sometimes referred to as creating **subgroups**, not only aids workflow (balancing a mix is easier if you have only one fader to adjust for the whole drum section rather than a dozen), it also allows the whole group to be processed using a single set of plugins. Glue compression and EQ are the usual choices, helping to gel groups of sounds together and shape them tonally (*page 242*).

With a bit of care, you can set up a mix so that only a handful of faders are required to balance all constituent parts.

TIP Sample producer and mix engineer Hy2rogen groups his mixes with just a handful of channels, specifically: kick drum/s; rest of drums; bassline/s; all musical elements; FX and, if applicable, vocals (lead and backing vocals split).

NOTE When using processing on a group bus, note that *changing the track level of any constituent part will make a difference to the combined sound*. In the case of a drum group running through a compressor, for example, even slightly reducing the incoming level of the kick drum can radically change how the compressor behaves, potentially changing the drum group's cohesion, tone and even its rhythmic interplay. It is important therefore to listen closely to the impact on a group when changing the volume, EQ or any other aspect of a constituent track.

Although bussing tracks is both a time saver and a powerful means of generating more cohesive mixes, there is one drawback: when you reduce the group fader volume, any send effects on the individual tracks won't change unless the corresponding effects are also sent to the group bus.

An alternative which solves this problem is to use fader grouping, where all faders that control a group are assigned the same **fader group**. Moving any fader in the group changes the volume of the full group, as well as the relative level of post-fade effects.

QUICK GUIDE
Smarter working

We all want to waste less time in the studio and spend more time being productive, right? Although the concept of smarter working may feel a little clichéd, a smart approach can impact on many day-to-day production tasks. It's all about taking a step back and considering whether you're doing things in the most logical way or just making life hard for yourself by following the same inefficient process each time.

The most obvious way to speed up the creation of new tracks is to save **DAW templates** for common production scenarios. This can be as simple as configuring a few tracks with a selection of instrument, effect and master output settings, or as involved as taking an existing track, removing all the MIDI and audio then saving the project ready to be populated with new ideas at a later date.

If that sounds a bit like cheating, the fact is that being able to work quickly on the compositional side – without worrying too much about EQ, compression and other processing – can be extremely liberating.

You can go further, creating a **bespoke collection of channel strip** and **device rack presets** to call from when inspiration strikes.

If you work with samples, **organise your sample collection** by types of sound: a folder of kick drums, for example, split into sub folders of acoustic sounds, subby hits, processed sounds, and so on according to your personal preferences. Most importantly, **throw out all the excess**. Do you really need a library of 13,497 snare drums? Whittle your collection down to the hits you know sound great in your tracks.

Backing up your work may be the most boring thing you can do in the studio, but it's critically important. Online backups using utilities like DropBox make sense since cloud storage and specialist backup provision are easily available and cheap. But don't ignore old-school hard drives; backing up to both is the ultimate fail-safe.

If you keep your projects well organised, saving different versions as you go, you'll not only ensure that you never lose a project to a corrupt hard disk again, you'll also find it easy to go back to older projects if you need to remix, rework or plunder elements for a new track.

Grouping in Ableton

Grouping tracks allows you to process multiple tracks together as well as making mix balancing easier.

In Live, select all tracks you want to include in a new group by holding down Shift and clicking on the track title. Right/ctrl-click on the selection and Select Group Tracks. Right/ctrl-click and select Rename to give the new Group an appropriate name.

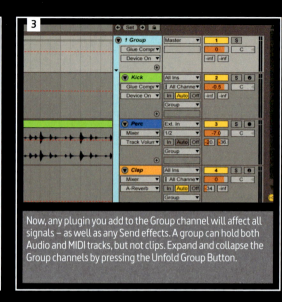

Now, any plugin you add to the Group channel will affect all signals – as well as any Send effects. A group can hold both Audio and MIDI tracks, but not clips. Expand and collapse the Group channels by pressing the Unfold Group Button.

Fader and bus groups in Logic

In Logic there are three ways to group tracks: auxiliary routing, grouping and VCA faders. To control volume and process audio together, select all tracks, click and hold on their outputs and select 'Bus 1' from the menu. This sends all channels to the same group bus for treatment.

To group controls like volume, pan, sends and more, select the channels you want to group then click on the empty Group slot on the channel. Select Group 1 from the menu then click on the yellow '1' and select Open Group Settings to change what parameters the group controls.

VCA groups control the volume of multiple channels regardless of where their outputs are routed. It can be superior to using auxes as it respects the volume of a channel *and* its sends. Select the channels to be grouped, click/hold the empty VCA slot and select Create New VCA channel.

EQ treatment: hi-hats – EQ bracketing demonstrated 🎧

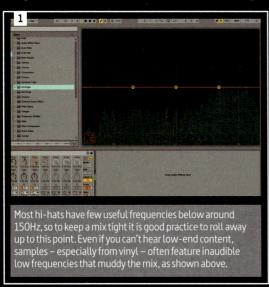

1 Most hi-hats have few useful frequencies below around 150Hz, so to keep a mix tight it is good practice to roll away up to this point. Even if you can't hear low-end content, samples – especially from vinyl – often feature inaudible low frequencies that muddy the mix, as shown above.

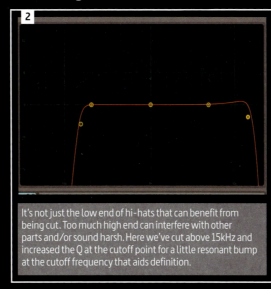

2 It's not just the low end of hi-hats that can benefit from being cut. Too much high end can interfere with other parts and/or sound harsh. Here we've cut above 15kHz and increased the Q at the cutoff point for a little resonant bump at the cutoff frequency that aids definition.

3 If you've got a pre-mixed drum loop with a harsh cymbal and you don't want to reduce the brightness of the snare, use dynamic EQ to trigger a dip in specific frequencies when the threshold is crossed. Here bx_dynamic is set to trigger at 6.5kHz, reducing the harshness of the ride cymbal.

EQ treatment: bass 🎧

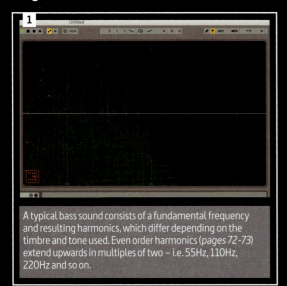

1 A typical bass sound consists of a fundamental frequency and resulting harmonics, which differ depending on the timbre and tone used. Even order harmonics (*pages 72-73*) extend upwards in multiples of two – i.e. 55Hz, 110Hz, 220Hz and so on.

2 This bassline is slightly muddy. We don't want to reduce its sub power, but we do want to ease back on mud so perform a low cut at 30Hz. A spectrum analyser reveals that the fundamental lies around 50Hz, so a precision cut is made at the second harmonic – 100Hz – of 7.5dB with a tight Q.

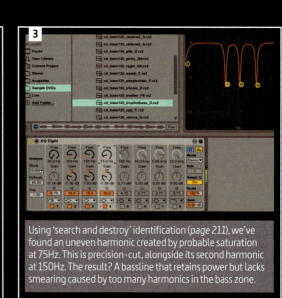

3 Using 'search and destroy' identification (*page 211*), we've found an uneven harmonic created by probable saturation at 75Hz. This is precision-cut, alongside its second harmonic at 150Hz. The result? A bassline that retains power but lacks smearing caused by too many harmonics in the bass zone.

Creating an initial balance

Every mix has to start somewhere, and the usual place is the most powerful tool at the producer's disposal: the humble volume fader.

The constituent parts in a mix are governed by a hierarchy of importance that should be roughly mirrored by their relative volumes.

When establishing an early balance select the elements you want to dominate the mix, pull up their faders, then build the rest of the mix at lower levels around them. If you're making D&B the big hitters are likely to be the kick drum and bass. With techno the key rhythmic drivers of the groove are usually loudest. For vocal-led songs the vocal will sit loud and proud at the front of the mix.

Over the coming pages, we investigate how tools like EQ and compression can be used to craft stronger mixes. But by far the most effective mix shaping tool is the volume fader.

The relative volumes of different parts do more to shape the finished mix than any number of other processes. Want to give the kick drum more clout? Simple – just increase its volume.

The ease with which you can bring more power to a part by simply upping its fader can present the indisciplined producer with problems. Because once you've increased the volume of the kick drum, it's likely you'll need to raise the level of the bass so that it isn't lost in the mix. And once those parts are louder, you'll need to increase the volume of the snare, then toms, then synths… Before long you've got a race to the top across the mixing desk and you end up back where you were: with the same relative volumes across the mix but – crucially – less headroom.

HEADROOM

Flip back to *page 256* and re-read our *Essential guide to levels*. Note again the point about space in the mix – specifically that *there is only so much of it*. The blank canvas on which you have to work starts in silence and ends at 0dBFS. Overload the upper limit on a digital system and you run out of headroom and clip the mix.

To avoid headroom famine **don't push faders too high at this early stage**. Although you can't second guess where the mix will end up, a useful starting point is to set the kick drum volume so that it peaks at between -15 and -12dB. The master output should be set at 0dB(FS), or unity gain.

TIP Because low frequency signals (kick and bass) demand more headroom in a mix than higher frequency ones (synth

JORGE SAVORETTI

"Mixing down is always a pain in the ass for me because I like my mixdowns to be perfect, so I mix every track on my albums like ten times – for real.

"In my tracks I always make a rough mix in Live, which is the DAW where I record the tracks. Then I export four subgroups to Logic X – kick, bass, drums and others – and make a final mixdown in there. I fine tune everything with a little bit of compression, EQing and colouring with aural exciters."

leads, percussion etc), it is worth getting these into the mix early to establish a firm foundation and reduce the chance of headroom squeeze further down the line.

TIP Every producer runs out of headroom sometimes. When it happens the solution is superficially obvious: select all faders and drag them down to free up a few dB. There are two problems with doing so. Firstly, if you have volume automation programmed that too will need to be edited. Secondly, the amount of signal sent to bus effects is suddenly reduced across the board, fundamentally changing a mix's sound. Making even minor level changes across multiple channels can radically alter a well balanced mix and generate hours of rebalancing work. It's far better to pre-empt such problems by setting initial levels too low rather than too high. Remember **you can easily use bus compression make-up gain – or the master fader itself – to increase the volume of a quiet mix if you need to**.

INITIAL AUTOMATION

Although it is theoretically possible that your final mix will require no automation, it's unlikely. Because **most dance mixes are dynamic** (*page 238*) and **change over time is usually a precondition of a great mix** (*page 241*), at least some parts will likely require automation – a synth's volume over time, a filter opening out on a music loop or the level of an overly dynamic vocal line, for example. In some mixes automation is so integral to a track's character that it is programmed from the start – indeed some tracks are pretty much exercises in continual, meticulously tweaked automation (check the deconstruction of Blawan's 'Why They Hide Their Bodies Under My Garage', *page 248*).

Automation on parts that require it is best programmed now. If you fail to do so you can end up in the frustrating position of having a mix that is perfectly weighted 40 bars in but when a critical synth part rises in volume at bar 60 loses its balance, requiring you to make remedial level changes that in turn destabilise the mix back at bar 40.

This early stage of the mix is about crafting a solid foundation on which to perform effects and processing tweaks later. Having important parts in balance for the duration of a track secures a good base to work from.

EQ BRACKETING

One thing that can help free up a surprising amount of headroom, as well as making mixes more coherent, is to trim unnecessary frequencies from signals. This practice – aka **bracketing** or **top and tailing** (*see EQ treatments: hi-hats, page 265*) – involves using EQ (usually high and low cut filters) to roll away frequencies that don't contribute to a sound. Common cuts include:

▸ **Bass at around 25–30Hz** – Extreme low, subsonic frequencies in the bass consume significant amounts of headroom. Although it might feel counterintuitive, cutting or rolling away extreme low frequencies can end up making a bassline more punchy and controlled (as well as the overall mix louder). **Kick drums** with lots of low-end content (808 kicks in particular) may also benefit from being trimmed.

▸ **Highs in hi-hat and/or percussive parts** – At the other end of the spectrum, extreme high frequencies (15kHz and above) in hi-hats, shakers, tambourines and some synth parts can have an unpleasantly harsh character. The exacting nature of digital sound reproduction means that today's mixes are brighter than ever. This might be the sound you're after – EDM, commercial dubstep and some trance productions demand a razor-sharp top end. But if you want a mix to be less aggressive, use shelving high cut filters to control the highs. If you're aiming for an obviously vintage vibe, high end reduction is pretty much essential, mimicking the natural mellowing effect of tape.

▸ **Highs and lows from other parts** – If other melodic and rhythmic parts don't require frequencies above or below their main ranges then you can often afford to (gently) cut these too. Such EQ decisions should be made in the context of the wider mix. If you want the bass to dominate, for example, you can usually afford to cut quite high into melodic elements. Not only does this help with separation, it also frees up low end space for the bass to do its thing.

A good way of deciding where to cut a signal is to set up a filter with a medium slope – say 12 or 18dB/Oct – and then slowly dial up and down the spectrum until you hear an obvious change in the timbre of the sound. When you get there, pull back a little and park the filter there.

NOIR

"I spent a lot of time over-producing 'Black' [from Noir's self-titled debut album] to make it sound under-produced.

"I wanted it to sound gritty and old school, which can be hard with the 'clean' equipment producers have today, so I used EQ and saturation effects from Ableton, and on some of the synthesisers I added slight distortion.

"I also used a random audio loop to make background noise."

TIP It's not unusual to use low cut filters on every channel in a mix. If you do so, tread carefully: pushing too high across multiple channels can result in a lightweight, brittle mix

TIP When bracketing, the shape of the cutoff slope is paramount. Using too steep a slope can result in mixes that have frequency 'holes'. Often a shelving filter is more suitable.

TIP If your EQ supports it, switch on its real-time frequency display to help when making tweaks. It gives a visual perspective on the mix that can be particularly useful when monitoring is substandard. It's often surprising how much 'null' inaudible low and high end content there is in a signal.

NOTE It's not only EQ that can be used to change the tonal character of a signal. Top-heavy sounds are often more naturally

Chapter eight
Mixing and mastering

controlled using tape emulation or saturators (*page 226*) than filters.

NOTE Performing any kind of EQ change has an impact on the signal's level (by tweaking EQ you're changing the level of a particular part of the frequency spectrum). This means EQing should be followed by level adjustments (and automation tweaks, if necessary) to keep a mix in balance.

PANNING

Panning is the process of placing sounds across the stereo spectrum to achieve a pleasing balance between left and right channels.

Panning is one of several methods used to aid **separation**. If you have two synth parts that inhabit the same frequency zone, for example, panning one left and the other right helps give each its own space.

Note, however, that because a dance mix needs to translate to mono, using panning to solve masking overlaps should be a last resort, while wild panning effects should be used sparingly and with an understanding that **a mix must work in one dimension** (*page 240*).

The practical upshot of this is that **only in rare cases should the bassline and kick drum be panned away from centre**. Because low frequencies carry more energy than high frequencies, moving bass-heavy parts from the centre risks destabilising a mix, making it sound lopsided. Panning kick and/or bass off-centre also causes nightmares when pressing vinyl.

Other parts that have been selected to be the focus of a mix should also sit in or close to the centre, including critical synth lines and the lead vocal. The snare is likely to be kept central too unless it's part of a stacked snare/clap combo (*pages 52–53*) where constituent elements are panned across the spectrum. In general, **the less important a part is to a mix, the further it can be panned from centre**.

The exception is where near-identical lead parts are panned (often hard) left and right to create **'super mono' sounds** that are so close in tone and rhythm that they create the illusion of an extra wide mono sound that is present across the stereo field.

A technique also used to mix **double-tracks** (*page 173*), **mono supersizing** is typically used to create stacked lead lines in mainroom, Euro and EDM styles (*page 86*).

TIP When working with super mono parts, check that phase issues don't mean the sound loses fidelity and focus when summed to mono.

TIP Try panning ambient returns to the opposite side of the mix as the dry signal.

PRO TIPS

JAY SHEPHEARD

"The main synth line [in 'Spring Up'] carries the whole track, drops and breaks, alternating from straight legato to the broken chord progression.

"One feature I love about this sound is the fast pan in the modulation matrix, which adds a great dynamic. However, it was quite a balancing act to get right as too much of it can affect the club sound – when stereo isn't always perfect or if the club's running a mono system.

"I played a very early version in a booth with just one monitor and it sounded terrible so it took a few tweaks to get it just right."

WIDER SOUNDS

There are various techniques for giving sounds greater width in the stereo domain:

▸▸ **'Haas' delay** – The simplest way of widening a signal is to add delays of a few milliseconds to one or both sides of a stereo signal (*see Approach 1, opposite*). With mono signals, use a mono to stereo delay.

▸▸ **Double-track and hard pan** – Although double-tracking is most commonly used on vocals, other parts, particularly keys and synths, can benefit from the treatment. Pan one take left and the other right (*Approach 2*).

▸▸ **Layering sounds** – Similar to double-tracking, pan the original sound one way and a layer the other. Although it's tempting to pan the same sound, this affects phase (*page 50*), so either tweak the sound – its oscillators, envelope settings or filter – or use a different sound altogether.

▸▸ **Mid/side EQ** (*Approach 3*) – Most bundled EQs offer mid/side processing. The theory and practice of mid/side processing is easy enough to grasp. The mid signal contains everything that is identical in both channels – effectively the mono material – while the side signal contains everything that's different. To widen a signal, all you need to do is select the side only signal and change its EQ settings for instant width.

Widening a signal – five approaches

1: The Haas effect is a psychoacoustic phenomenon where tiny differences in the time it takes a sound to reach our left and right ears are used to detect the direction a sound is coming from. You can use the effect to increase the width of a sound by delaying one channel by a few milliseconds.

In Logic add the Sample Delay utility to the track you want to widen. Ensure 'Link' is unchecked to control the left and right channels independently. Increase the delay on one channel by up to 300 samples to make the sound wider. Check the sound in mono to avoid phase issues.

2: You can use Logic's comping tools to create wide 'double-tracks' (*page 173*). Set a loop to record two takes of the same part. Logic creates a new take for each cycle. Once you're done, click on the take number, select 'Unpack to New Tracks' and hard pan each track L and R alternately.

3: Logic Pro X has an M/S mode on its Channel EQ, allowing you to EQ the mid (everything that's identical in both channels) and the side (everything that's different) separately. On the processing menu select 'Side Only', roll off below 100Hz, then increase Gain by 5dB to hear the effect.

4: Create two Aux tracks with a Pitch Shifter on each, then hard pan them Left and Right. On the left Pitch Shifter set Semitones to 0 and Cents to 10; on the right, set Semitones to 0 and Cents to -10. Mix should be 100% on both. Send 0dB to Bus 1 and Bus 2 by alt-clicking on each Send.

5: Create an Aux track and load Logic's Stereo Delay. Set the Mix on both L and R to 100% and Delay Time to quavers. Reduce the feedback on both to zero and set High Cut to 3.9kHz and Low Cut to 190Hz. Set one channel's groove to 51% and the other to 50% to subtly widen the signal.

▸▸ **Pitch shifted panning** – Pan an identical or similar copy of a sound hard left and right then use slightly different pitch shift treatments on both (*Approach 4*).

▸▸ **Delayed panning** – As with pitch shifted panning, but using different delay or groove times (*Approach 5*).

Stereo-specific plugins use a range of the above techniques to do their jobs, including:

▸▸ **Chorus-style effects** – Effects like Logic's Ensemble work by mixing identical copies of the same signal together and delaying the copy/copies (*page 220*). Because chorus effects diffuse sounds, they are a good choice for pads and keys, but should be avoided on elements that require up-front impact.

▸▸ **Width enhancers** – Dedicated stereo width enhancers use mid/side processing to give the illusion of width by reducing the volume of the mid/central channel so that the left and right channels have more presence. Their obvious drawback is the impact on the all-important centre of the mix, which is lowered in volume. This makes width enhancers unsuitable for important mix elements. Used carelessly width enhancers result in a 'missing' middle – a disaster for the typical dance mix.

▸▸ **Stereo spreaders** – divide the frequency spectrum into a number of bands and pan each band in an opposite direction (*page 225*). Stereo spreaders are often better choices than width enhancers because they don't rely on phase inversion techniques – and therefore don't cancel out when summed to mono. In addition, because spreaders can be tweaked to perform their work on higher frequencies only, the bass end is still able to punch through in mono.

WIDER SOUNDS – PRACTICAL APPLICATIONS

Although widening a sound often makes it sound momentarily more impressive, in the context of a mix the effect of widening is often less impact, not more – particularly when used on multiple parts.

▸▸ **Drums** – It is highly unlikely you would ever widen a kick drum or snare – the resulting lack of focus robs the beat of clout. In the case of a layered **clap/snare combo** widening a clap can help separate it from the snare, particularly if the clap hits a little earlier or later than the snare (*Walkthroughs, page 52–53*).

▸▸ **Percussion** – The diffusion introduced by widening can be helpful when applied to percussive parts, including loops, to aid separation. For example, if you have busy **shaker** and **hi-hat** lines, try widening the shaker to shift its focus away from the more defined (mono) hi-hat. Petar Dundov, *Pro Tip, right*, outlines his reasoning behind

PRO TIPS

PETAR DUNDOV

"In 'The Lattice' [from his *At The Turn Of Equilibrium* album] I went for simple 909 and CR-78 drums with a dominating phased shaker cutting out of the mix.

"I deliberately panned percussion sounds hard left and right and out of the middle as much as possible to leave more space for sounds – especially the Juno-106 string section that appears in the last third of the track."

hard-panning percussion in his track 'The Lattice': to keep the middle of the stereo soundstage free for other parts – particularly a Juno-106 string section – to shine in the mix.

▸▸ **Bass** – Because you generally want a defined bassline, stereo widening across the whole spectrum is a no go. For Reese-style basslines with movement and width, widening is fundamental to the sound – but, critically, only on higher frequencies. To do this, split the signal and widen the upper band (*Walkthroughs, page 118*).

▸▸ **Pads** – Many pads and soundscapes benefit from liberal widening. Because pads tend to be buried in the mix, sitting clear of lead melodic elements, widening can often be fairly extreme.

▸▸ **Backing vocals** – As with pads, widening harmonies and BVs can give them character while also separating them from a dominant lead vocal.

▸▸ **Rhodes and other keys** – In classic and vintage deep house, keys are frequently widened – especially if they serve a purpose akin to a pad.

▸▸ **Lead synths** – If they play an important role in a track, layering 'super-mono' style is almost always the best way of adding stereo impact to lead synth elements.

Chapter eight
Mixing and mastering

Compression in the mix

After EQ, compression is the most used processor in the dance producer's arsenal. This is partly explained by the number of tasks it can perform. As outlined in *Chapter seven*, not only can it be used for **levelling** – smoothing the volume of a dynamic part – it can also **shape transients**, particularly of percussive elements, **change the tone of a sound** and **treat groups,** adding glue, density and punch.

Although it's unlikely you'd place a compressor on every channel (doing so risks rendering a mix sterile), most sounds in a typical dance mix pass through a compressor at some point on their journey from channel to master bus.

COMPRESSOR AS VOLUME LEVELLER

The most obvious use for a compressor is to **reduce the dynamic range of a signal**. Where audio has volume spikes and troughs, a compressor can be used to shave level from the peaks so that the overall dynamic range is smaller, helping it settle more comfortably into the mix.

Vocals (*page 179*) and complex sweep/dive FX are prime candidates for levelling, but any signal you consider to be overly dynamic may benefit from subtle (or not so subtle) squashing. As a general rule live recordings are more dynamic than loops (which are frequently compressed already) and soft synths (whose volume is controlled to a large extent by the settings on the synth itself).

When setting up a compressor to perform levelling, start with a ratio of around 1.5–3:1 trimming up to 3dB of signal from peaks, then increase the make-up gain until the bypassed signal is as close in volume to the processed one as possible. For more assertive results, increase either the ratio, the amount of gain reduction, or both.

Although compressing a signal can help it sit in a mix, there is one drawback: *the more you compress, the less dynamic energy there is in a signal*. This becomes obvious when compressing the human voice; flatten it too much and it becomes lifeless – a flatlined version devoid of highs and lows.

The same is true for any kind of over-compressed material – including full mixes. This may, of course, be the effect you're after, but if you want to retain energy in a part, it can be better to use **level automation instead** – potentially alongside a compressor on a less aggressive setting. Remember that too much compression risks breaking mix Rule #2: that **great mixes are dynamic** (*page 238*).

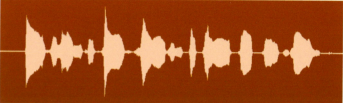

🎧 **Before and after using compression to level a vocal part.** Note the lower and more consistent overall (RMS) volume of the processed signal (*bottom*), even with 2dB of make-up gain applied. Also note the emphasised attack transients – achieved using a 10ms attack time (ratio 4:1).

NOTE Compressors don't just change the dynamics of a signal – they also alter a signal's **tone**, with different models altering the sound in different ways (*page 214*). Also remember that compression increases the volume of low-level noise and can make a signal feel denser and slightly 'darker' too.

TIP There *is* a way of bringing movement to over-compressed parts or mixes, which is to push the compressor to audibly pump, either using a sympathetic release setting alongside a heavy ratio or by triggering the compressor using the external sidechain linked to a kick drum. Of which more soon...

COMPRESSOR AS ENVELOPE SHAPER

Chapter one: Drums and beats, describes in detail at how to use a compressor to shape the transients of a drum sound (page 10). Although any signal that passes through a compressor has its transients shaped to some extent, it is most obvious when a sound is short and percussive. This gives the compressor a supremely important role in dance music production – allowing the producer to shape every hit in a beat and subsequently its rhythmic interaction with other beat elements.

It's not only drums that benefit from transient shaping; any sound that plays a rhythmic or percussive role including arpeggios and stabs are ripe for treatment.

Although alternatives to compressors are available – including envelope shaping and dedicated transient designers – often a compressor, with its bulking and tone shaping characteristics, is the best choice.

BUS COMPRESSION – GLUE, PUMP AND SLAM

Compression happens not only at track level, but also at bus level. Here compression, applied to a **group** (page 263), is frequently used to **glue** different signals together to make a more coherent and unified sound.

The most obvious practical application for bus compression is to gel the different drum elements in a beat. In this instance, all composite drum tracks – kick, snare, hi-hat, percussion, underlay loops etc – are fed to the same group (page 218). A compressor is then placed on the bus to process the combined drum group. Other common groups include: all music elements, bass, FX, synths and backing vox.

The choice of compressor is important when bus compressing. Common choices are variants of the infamous SSL Bus Compressor (Ableton's Glue is based on it), the Neve 33609 (for a warmer sound) and the Fatso from Empirical Labs (modelled by Universal Audio). DAW compressors are also up to the job – but pick one that can handle speedy transients (think VCA models over their more characterful optical cousins).

TIP When applying bus compression to a drum group, bear in mind that the kick drum – invariably the loudest signal – will disproportionately effect the compressor's behaviour, potentially masking sounds that hit at the same time. If this causes problems, try removing the kick from the group, or only sending a portion of the kick signal via an aux send to the drum group.

When setting up a bus compressor, particularly on a drum bus, you invariably want to preserve transients, so a **slowish attack** time is important. **Auto release**, if available, is usually the best bet for complex combined signals arriving on the bus. Although ratio and gain reduction settings will depend on how assertive you want the

OVERDRIVE TO COMPRESS

It is not just compressors that compress. Overdrive and distortion effects clip the signal, adding sustain and compressing the sound. Saturation and tape modelling plugins do a similar thing in less brutal ways.

So if you just want to subtly bulk up a live keyboard part without impinging too much on its natural dynamics, audition a saturation or overdrive plugin before reaching for a compressor. For more control, add overdrive effects in parallel.

combined effect to be, for more transparent settings, start at around 1.5:1 shaving off 2dB or so from peaks, while for obvious glue go up to 5:1 reducing 5–8dB of gain.

Used gently, bus compression is highly effective at gelling a mix, helping to pull different elements together into a unified sound.

But it doesn't need to be subtle, and many mixes go straight for the jugular in their use of compression to make a mix pump.

The heavily **slammed** sound, once popular among electro and EDM producers, is achieved by upping both ratio and gain reduction until the compression is obvious. The slammed sound generally uses ratios of 8:1 and beyond, delivering up to 10–15dB of gain reduction on peaks. The key settings here – which define the timing of the pump – are the compressor's attack and **release** times, release being most important. To get the timing right, play with the values until the material breathes or pumps in time with the beat (walkthrough, page 219).

More obvious **pumping** is generated using **sidechain compression** (walkthroughs, page 274). Here the compressor's sidechain is fed by an external signal, typically a kick drum. When the kick drum hits, the compressor is triggered, pulling back the gain. Once again, the attack and release times are critical – you need the pump to breathe in tandem with the groove. When a high ratio is twinned with a low threshold the pump gives the kind of sound heard in the anthem 'So Much Love To Give' by Together (Thomas Bangalter and DJ Falcon).

TIP Slammed and pumping compression can be used anywhere in a mix. Sidechain compression can, for example, keep the bass and kick drum from stepping on each other's toes (*page 283*). It can also be used as an effect. But more often this major-league compression is used either on group buses or the master bus itself (*Processing the master bus, right*).

TIP Although it's common for a track's kick drum to trigger the sidechain, it is not always the right choice. Where a kick drum has a sustained release transient, for example, the compressor may not be able to release fast enough to allow a timely pump. For 100% control over the sidechain trigger use a muted **trigger track** on which a trigger kick drum (or indeed any other drum), unheard in the mix, can be forensically crafted using ADSR envelopes or audio edits to make it the perfect shape to pull the trigger.

TIP Using a muted drum to trigger the compressor gives the producer more freedom when arranging. Instead of a bus only pumping when the kick plays, it can also pump during breakdowns when the track's audible kick isn't present.

BUS FLAVOURS

Ever wonder why successful engineers regularly use more than one type of compressor, or why certain models of compressor are favoured for particular tasks – even in the software realm? Classic hardware including the SSL G Series master compressor, Neve 33609 and API 2500 (and emulations of these and similar models) remain popular choices for mix compression despite apparently being limited in scope compared to newer alternatives.

Much of the characteristic sound of these models is down to the different method and components used to sense the input level and then instigate gain reduction.

Even compressors bundled with DAWs – such as Logic's Platinum Compressor – allow the user to dial in a range of alternative flavours based on various traditional hardware designs. (Logic's compressor features opto, VCA and 'platinum' modes, all inspired by different historic models and compression methods.)

What does this mean in practice? That it's worth auditioning a range of compressors for each job. Over time you'll develop an innate understanding of what type/model tackles a task best and form a shortlist of favourites that suit your sound – but even then, a leftfield choice may surprise you.

Processing the master bus

While few producers are likely to argue about the merits of compression at track or bus level, processing the master bus raises heckles and arguments.

Those that argue for extreme processing on the master bus often have a heavily compressed trademark sound. Because that sound is an aesthetic choice, it's something they want full control over – it's not something they'd leave to a mastering engineer.

Purists who rail against master bus processing argue that if you can't pull together a mix without heavy bus processing there's something wrong with the mix. They also argue that if you slam a mix too hard on the output then: a) there's virtually no space left for even the world's finest mastering engineer to improve your mix; and b) the mix loses dynamics and energy.

The truth lies somewhere in the middle. Many dance producers use at least one processor on the output bus. A common trinity is a glue-style compressor, a high quality tone-shaping EQ (like a Pultec) and a last-in-line limiter. Used sparingly, this kind of master bus treatment adds a final glue and sheen to the combined mix. It can also give a good insight into how the final mastered mix will sound. The processing can be removed prior to mastering.

If you're not planning on third party mastering and are 'mastering as you go', then there's nothing stopping you racking up the master processing – although we'd always recommend bouncing down the master and treating it as a new mastering project even if you take the DIY route.

MULTIPLE LEVELS OF COMPRESSION – A WARNING

Dance mixes frequently feature multiple levels of compression. Which is to say that a kick drum might be compressed at track level (for transient emphasis), at bus level (on the drum group), in parallel (a drum smash group) and then again on the master output.

This can be beneficial, resulting in a cohesive and solid mix. But beware the cumulative effects of too much compression. While reducing 3dB of gain from a signal is unlikely to trash it, when multiplied upwards you can end up shaving more than 10dB from a sound – resulting in flat, lifeless and bloated sounds.

// WALKTHROUGHS

Sidechain compression: Logic

1 Create a new audio track and name it 'Sidechain Trigger'. Click the output of the channel and select 'No output'. Place a kick on each beat of the bar. Select them, click on Functions > Folder > Pack Folder. This makes the trigger easier to loop.

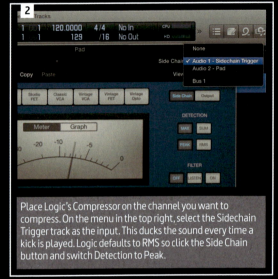

2 Place Logic's Compressor on the channel you want to compress. On the menu in the top right, select the Sidechain Trigger track as the input. This ducks the sound every time a kick is played. Logic defaults to RMS so click the Side Chain button and switch Detection to Peak.

3 For classic pump, sync release time to the bpm. On the left, click on the Region arrow to see the track Delay options. Here Logic details the millisecond setting needed to sync the release. This track is 120bpm so dial in 125ms for a 1/16th rhythm. You might also experiment with 1/32.

Sidechain compression: Ableton

1 Create a sidechain trigger track. Load an Impulse – a kick drum with a sharp transient from the library – and write a 4/4 MIDI pattern. It's good practice to create a separate (muted) sidechain trigger to a track's main kick to give you more control over transient shape and levels (*page 273*).

2 Load Live's Compressor on the channel you want to compress. Expand the plugin to access sidechain settings. Turn on the Sidechain button and select the Trigger track from the Audio From pull-down. Now lower the threshold until you hear the channel ducking with each trigger.

3 Attack and release settings are critical. Use a delay-to-ms calculator – *see Appendix 1* – to sync the release time with the bpm of your track. With a track at 120bpm, for example, a 16th note is 125ms. Set attack and release using this information and fine-tune the values to taste.

Chapter eight
Mixing and mastering

PARALLEL COMPRESSION

Over the previous pages we've been talking about compression applied 'in-line' – compression that treats 100 per cent of the signal on a track's insert point.

This kind of compression is sometimes known as '**downwards compression**' as the resulting signal is pushed down in level, making the louder elements quieter, whilst leaving the quieter parts untouched. But that's not the only way you can compress a signal. You can also compress **upwards**, where the opposite happens – the quieter parts are brought up in level whilst the louder elements remain untouched.

While the term upwards compression sounds counter-intuitive, it is easy to achieve; simply blend a heavily compressed signal with an uncompressed version of itself. Do this by taking an aux feed from a track/bus or duplicating the track featuring the signal you want to compress then leaving one of the tracks/buses uncompressed while heavily compressing the second (*walkthrough, page 276*).

Parallel compression (sometimes called **New York compression** due to its adoption among early New York mix engineers), is a great way of achieving a subtle bulking lift and can be far less noticeable in action when compared to its 'downwards' cousin. At the same time, if the compressed signal is slammed, it can give a dynamic signal serious 'bottom-up' balls and weight.

When setting up parallel compression, start with as fast attack time as possible, twinned with a medium release (about 300 ms). Ratios of around 2.5:1 tend to work well, but push in each direction for a more or less dramatic effect. For a transparent result, dial in a low threshold to give almost continuous gain reduction. For obvious bulk reduce even more gain. Finally, set the compressed signal's fader at anywhere between 5–50% of the dry original (the higher the volume of the compressed track, the more weighty the combined signal).

Drum groups and basslines are popular choices for parallel compression, but other sound sources, from synths to vocals – even entire mixes – can benefit from extra 'ground up' body.

TIP Some compressors include a wet/dry mix control to allow parallel processing on an insert effect.

TIP In the walkthrough overleaf we use the same parallel bus to treat drums, bass and a keyboard part. While using a single parallel bus can help unify a mix, there's no reason why you can't use multiple parallel treatments – one for the drum group, one for the lead vocal, one for synths etc. In some mixes there may be more parallel auxes than original instrumental tracks!

Multi-band compression on the bus – and why you don't need it

Although marketing videos might suggest that powerful multi-band processing tools are the tool of choice for anything from crafting bulkier beats to shaping gargantuan mixes on the master bus, in 90 per cent of cases a single band compressor is usually a better choice for bus compression.

Aside from unnecessarily complicating the compression process, the purpose of compression on a bus (group or master) is usually to add glue and cohesion to a mix. But by dividing up the frequencies and treating each differently, multi-band compression does the opposite. Used badly, multi-band compression can end up splitting a snare – or entire mix – in half.

A better option if you need a frequency/compression double-whammy is to use high quality EQ alongside a bus compressor to tweak both the tonality and unity of the mix – if there are mix problems that you think would benefit from a multi-band compressor, take the time to solve the problems in the mix.

That said, there are occasions when the only tool for a job is a multi-band processor.

A multi-band compressor can be used to tame **sibilant signals**, where a middle band is set up to target the rogue sibilance, then reduce it in volume, leaving the rest of the sound intact – though a dedicated de-esser is usually faster to set up.

Where a multi-band really comes into its own is when **tonally shaping sampled material**. In the case of a sampled loop in which you want to isolate the bassline, a multi-band compressor can be used to reduce the volume of the whole signal except the bass.

To do so, use a compressor with at least three bands. Set the low band at around 0–40Hz to catch sub bass. Then set up the top band to capture all signal above, say, 200Hz. On each of these bands, use a high ratio to reduce up to 15+dB of gain. Then on the middle 'target' band, carefully set up the attack and release time to pump with your mix, start with a ratio of around 3:1 and reduce its gain by no more than 2-3dB. The result? A pronounced bassline that is clearly separated from its wider mix.

Fine-tune the mix by balancing the volume of each band and adjusting the crossover frequencies to taste.

Parallel compression: Drum bus

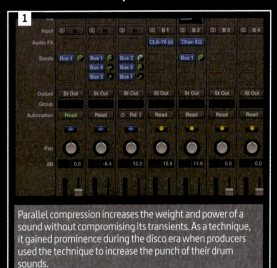

1 Parallel compression increases the weight and power of a sound without compromising its transients. As a technique, it gained prominence during the disco era when producers used the technique to increase the punch of their drum sounds.

2 When you're happy with the mix of a drum section, create a new auxiliary track and load a compressor. Although the technique works with any compressor, better results are typically achieved using a character compressor with a snappy attack like the classic UA 1176.

3 Getting the right attack and release settings is crucial for a tight, unified response. To start with, we've set the Attack time to 2 and Release to full. Next, switch Ratio to 'All' and increase the Input level to 24 and Output to 18.

4 Reduce the fader of the parallel aux channel and, on the original channel, increase the send amount to 0dB. Now slowly increase the level of the parallel aux. The drums become punchier and thicker as more of the compressed signal is blended in.

5 Once you've got a good balance of bulk and dynamism for the drums, try sending other mix elements to the parallel bus too. Sending a few dB of bassline, for example, helps solidify the low end and gel the rhythm section, ensuring a stable foundation on which other mix elements can rest.

6 Parallel processing isn't just for compression. Create a new aux with an EQ curve featuring a broad 10dB boost around 5kHz and a cut either side. Send 0dB from the keys to the parallel aux. Finally, route the EQ aux back to the parallel drum bus. The keys are now brighter and tighter.

Chapter eight
Mixing and mastering

EQ: before you start

One of the hardest things to get right when mixing is giving each part its own confident identity. Although later in this chapter we dedicate four pages to solving kick and bass conflicts, frequency overlaps occur everywhere in a mix. The more elements a mix has, the more overlaps there are likely to be.

Keyboard parts, for example, typically overlap with synths, drums, percussion, guitars, FX and vocals in the mid tones, meaning that when some – or all – are present in a mix, frequency overlaps, and subsequent conflicts, become inevitable.

The industry term for these overlaps is '**masking**'. One part may be said to mask another when it shares the same frequency space and subsequently diminishes – or obliterates – its contribution to the mix.

The result at track level is that some sounds become hidden or 'choked' – unable to find their own space or identity in which to breathe and thrive. Clarity and detail become lost in the resulting sonic soup.

Masking also impacts on the loudness of a mix. Where too many parts dominate the same core frequencies, frequency buildups

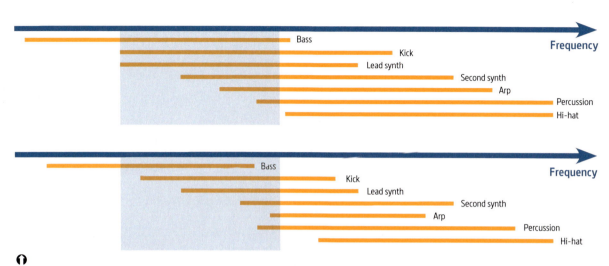

Fig 6: Before and after illustration of how a very basic mix might 'look' in the frequency domain after bracketing and tonal shaping to improve separation in the clogged lower mid range (shaded in blue). The low end is improved by cutting the extreme lows of the kick and then re-balancing the kick/bass so that the bass dominates the subs while the kick hits slightly above. All other musical elements are cut higher up to improve clarity, while at the top end the percussion is rolled away in the highs so that the hi-hat has less work to do to cut through the mix. Finally, the two synth and arp parts are allowed to shine at different – and distinct – areas – to reduce masking. The cumulative effect is a clearer, louder and more confident mix.

are inevitable: energy spikes that not only sound unpleasant, but also squander headroom – as seen on *page 231*.

SOLVING MASKING PROBLEMS

The best mixes feature effective **separation** between parts, with **every part in its place**.

A range of separation techniques have already been touched on. From an arrangement point of view, the producer might choose to change instrumentation, transpose parts or remove conflicting tracks to clarify focus. Mix options abound too: panning may be used to shift conflicting signals away from each other while ambient and chorus effects can shift sounds backwards and forwards in the mix.

But by far the most common tool used to reduce overlaps and masking is EQ. **Filters** are employed to narrow and define a part's frequency footprint and **tonal EQ** can be used to resolve masking clashes. By intelligently altering the frequency make-up of parts, it is possible to move from the muddy 'before' mix in *Fig 6*, to the clearer, louder, more confident mix below.

Chapter eight
Mixing and mastering

EQ in the mix

As noted in **Chapter seven,** EQ is typically used in one of three ways while mixing:

▶▶ **1. Corrective** – to remove unwanted frequencies from a signal.

▶▶ **2. Tone shaping** – to sculpt the frequency footprint of a signal.

▶▶ **3.** As a **special effect** – in the case of, for example, 'telephone EQ' (*page 194*).

Given its forensic ability to dramatically alter the frequency make-up of a signal, EQ is the primary tool for helping fulfil mix Rule #1 – **a great mix fills the frequency spectrum**. By shaping the make-up of individual signals different parts can be given greater identity and separation.

CORRECTIVE EQ

Corrective EQ is used for two related jobs, both of which have the same result: **the reduction in level of frequencies the producer wants to hear less of in the mix**.

The first job, covered extensively on *page 267*, is **bracketing** – using filters or shelving EQ to remove unwanted low and high end frequencies from a signal. Bracketing tightens the focus of a sound and can be used to reduce frequency overlaps when different parts – a clap and snare for example – share a similar place in the mix. Turn back a page to see how bracketing can be used to shift the bandwidths of different frequencies to deliver a fuller mix (*Fig 6*).

In addition, bracketing, particularly at the low end of a mix, thins out unwanted bass and sub bass frequencies, maximising headroom and thus increasing the overall volume of a mix.

The second use of corrective EQ is to **forensically remove unwanted, usually harsh frequencies**, in a signal. These frequency buildups – identified using the 'seek and destroy method' (*page 211, 231*) – can be caused by dozens of factors including a sound's original recording environment, interactions between filters and resonance, and the specific tonality of an instrument. Cutting these peaks, invariably using high Q forensic cuts (as in the *EQ treatments: Bass walkthrough* on *page 265*), results in a more rounded mix.

In both cases, the EQ used needs to be up to the job. Forensic cuts demand forensic tools – so leave smooth Pultec curves out of it. Instead you need the ability to reduce bandwidth (Q) to minute values (some EQ plugins offer bands as narrow as a single note). Although models like the Cambridge, SSL EQ and FabFilter are widely regarded, any DAW's native EQ is up to the job.

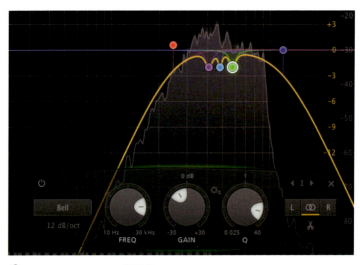

🎧 Step 6 from the 'Tuning and EQ tweaks for better drums' walkthrough, *page 13*, showing both bracketing and forensic cuts in action. The effect is to make the percussive cabasa part warmer while stopping it from interfering with the hi-hats.

TIP A useful starting point when tightening a muddy signal is to identify its fundamental frequency (use a tuner if you need to – *page 12*), then make forensic cuts to its **even order harmonics** (*page 265*).

By the time you've bracketed key sounds and weeded out resonant frequencies your mix should be sounding clearer. But there's more work to be done to improve clarity...

TONE SHAPING

If correction is about getting rid of the unwanted and bad bits, tone shaping is about making more of 'the good stuff', while at the same time aiding **separation**.

Pleasing tones can be augmented using gentle filter curves (wide Qs). So if a vocal sounds sweet around 4kHz, or you want to make more of its airy 12kHz highs, wide parametric or subtle shelving boosts can be used to enhance the sound in a natural way.

Equally, a signal may be cut to sound better, or to fit the mix more naturally. Our imaginary vocalist might have a slightly nasal tone at around 1kHz, for example, which could benefit from a targeted 1–2dB cut.

Using tone shaping to tackle **masking clashes** is common throughout the mix, but is indispensable for solving kick/bass conflicts. On *page 286, the Side-by-side kick and bass walkthrough* demonstrates a typical treatment, where a notch cut is made into the bassline at the fundamental frequency of the kick drum (61Hz). This allows the kick to 'poke through' the dominant bassline. A subtle resonant lift at either end of the cut frequencies ensures the bassline doesn't lose noticeable power.

This approach can be taken further using a 'mirror EQ treatment', in which the cut frequencies in the kick are matched by a boost at the same frequencies in the bass. The result? A tighter, more unified low end with less clutter and more headroom.

NOTE When tonal rebalancing, use the highest quality EQ you can. If you have access to them, plugins modelled on hardware units famed for their musical curves, like Pultecs and Neves, are good choices. For shaping, forensic capabilities matter far less than the sound of the curves.

RECAP The EQ rule that says **cut narrow, boost wide** applies to both forensic cuts and tone shaping. It can be expanded by saying **cuts can be more aggressive than boosts**.

REBALANCING AT BUS LEVEL

It's not just individual sounds that benefit from tone shaping; group buses – and occasionally the master bus – also benefit from EQ shaping.

Turn to the 'Tuning and EQ tweaks for better drums' walkthrough on *page 13*. Step 6 shows last-in-line EQ tweaks made to the drum bus, both to shape the beat's tone in relation to the wider mix and to cut two resonant builds that only become apparent when all beat elements are playing together.

EQing groups allows you to make quick changes to multiple signals, saving time and allowing you to balance frequencies across a busy mix using no more than a handful of faders.

TIP Any EQ tweak has the effect of changing a part's relative volume in the mix, so usually requires a subsequent fader change. Sometimes EQ cuts are more appropriate than lowering a part's volume.

QUICK GUIDE
What goes where

KICK: Lows at 20–60Hz. Weight at 60–80Hz. Knock/thump at 120–600Hz. Click/bite at 1–4kHz. Crack at 3–8kHz. TR-808 peaks at 40–60Hz, 909 at 90–100Hz.

SNARE: Balls at 120–250Hz. Body at 200–400Hz. Crack around 1kHz. Snap at 6–8kHz. If kick hits high, roll away snare lows to avoid masking.

HI-HATS: Body at 1–3kHz. Sparkle at 8–11kHz. Sibilance at 5–8kHz. EQ hats to fit wider rhythm. With synthetic hats, roll away lows from 300Hz down.

PERCUSSION: Can sit anywhere depending on sound and purpose. Congas have body at 150–200Hz and slap at 5kHz. Tambourines sparkle above 5kHz.

BASS: Critical power at 50–120Hz. Small changes here have a major impact and can cause a bass to sound fat or thin. Additional harmonics up to 8kHz.

SUB BASS: 16–60Hz. Bear in mind domestic systems rarely reach lower than 40Hz while club rigs fall off around 30Hz. Sub frequencies are greedy for headroom.

BASS GUITAR: Bottom at 50–80Hz. Fat and chunky around 250Hz. Growl at 600–700Hz. Finger noise 700Hz–1.2kHz. Snap at 2.5kHz.

LEAD SYNTH: Can be hot anywhere from 60Hz (in 'bass as lead' mixes) to 8kHz. Must work alongside bass so check for overlap – if bass must dominate, cut lows; in bass as lead scenarios, don't forget sub frequencies – you may need to extend low end reach.

PADS: Body and warmth at 200–400Hz. Presence from 1.2kHz. If pad is playing a supportive role, mix low and vigorously top and tail to preserve headroom.

KEYS: Fullness as far down as 80Hz. Presence at 2.4–4kHz. Roll away lows.

ELECTRIC GUITAR: Body at 250–450Hz. Presence at 1.3–2.8kHz. Clarity at 3kHz. Muddy below 80Hz. Beware spiky frequencies.

VOCAL: Body at 200–700Hz. Nasal at 1kHz. Presence at 4–6kHz. Male vocal range from 100Hz–8kHz, female from 250Hz–9kHz; overtones above. Air at 11–12kHz+. Roll away below 80Hz. Boosting 5–10kHz risks adding sibilance.

GENERATING NEW FREQUENCIES

So far we've mainly spoken about how to remove unwanted frequencies from a signal. But what happens when you want to add frequencies *that aren't there*? What do you do if you need a bassline to extend down into subsonic territory, or if a euphoric trance lead is unable to slice through a busy top end?

The first tool the rookie producer reaches for when confronted with the problem is EQ. *But EQ is only able to boost frequencies already present in a sound.* When the frequencies you want to boost don't exist in the first place an alternative is needed.

If the sound in question is generated by a synth there's an easy solution: add another oscillator at a different pitch or layer in a new patch (*page 119*).

But where the signal is a sample or real instrument you'll need to use an alternative method. The easiest is to use one of two dedicated tools to generate the missing frequencies.

At the **low end of the mix**, sub-bass generators (*page 212*) introduce new frequencies below a pre-existing bassline (or other instrument). Although different tools use various methods, the usual approach is for an in-built synth to generate a new waveform, typically a sine wave, an octave below the existing signal. Only small amounts (5-10% wet signal) are needed to add the missing low-end beef.

Exciters (*page 212*) do a similar job at the opposite end of the frequency spectrum, taking a signal and using a mix of dynamic EQ, harmonic generation and/or phase shifting to give the signal more zing.

Used carefully, both tools can yield powerful results. But they have drawbacks.

Sub bass generators might generate the wrong kind of sound for the mood of a track; on complex material they can track the wrong pitches; and – most of all – it can be difficult to hear how much impact they're having on the extreme low end of a mix, particularly if your listening space isn't ideal. If pushed too far, exciters, meanwhile, can add abrasive high end with the subtlety of a razor blade attacking a blackboard. *Which is to say, use these tools with care, regularly bypassing them to ensure you're not making a signal worse.*

Often more pleasing results are achieved by generating 'missing' frequencies using other tools.

Although **overdrive** is usually thought of as a brash sound mangling effect, at low levels it is a fantastically flexible tone shaper. Because overdrive (and **distortion**,

THE ORDER OF PROCESS

EQ before compression or vice versa is a topic of perennial and hot discussion with no definitive answer.

Although common sense would suggest that EQing first makes more sense as you're then only compressing the sound you want to hear, practical comparisons of both arrangements don't always bear that out.

In the end it's largely academic. Given that it takes all of five seconds to flip the order, try both and go with what sounds best. You may find that different tracks and applications change your view on the 'right order'.

or any of its other variants – *see page 226*) clips a signal and introduces new overtones – including odd and even harmonics – it can be used at low levels to extend a subby bassline into the radio-friendly mid range (*see Step 3, Using distortion to generate new frequencies, opposite*), to give more bulk to a synth or more presence to a percussive line.

Indeed, any signal that needs a little more body, life and confidence may benefit from a gentle dose of distortion. The tone control on most distortion units allows you to shape how warm or cool you want the distorted sound to be, and by applying the effected signal in parallel – as in the walkthrough opposite – you can balance the original signal with the bulkier, bigger distorted sound to taste.

TIP The specific nature of introduced harmonics depends on the effect used. Vacuum overdrive, with its 'warm' soft clipping, typically generates additional odd and even harmonics, while solid state distortion, hard clipped, adds high-amplitude odd harmonics yielding a colder, more brutal sound.

Tape emulation and **saturators** offer subtler means of adding harmonics to sounds. Models of tape decks generate a more controlled top end than overdrive effects, coupled with smoother, warmer mid tones.

Using distortion to generate new frequencies 🎧

1 Distortion adds new frequencies by generating harmonics based on the signal fed into the effect. Load an Overdrive plugin onto the channel you want to stand out. Increase Tone to 20kHz, Drive to 1dB and Output to -1dB. Already the sound – like this bassline – is fuller and thicker.

2 For more control, go parallel (*page 118*). Create an aux, load an instance of Distortion and set Drive to 10dB and Output to -10dB. Use EQ to roll away below 100Hz. Now send any track/s in the mix that you want bulking to the parallel distortion channel and bring up its fader to taste.

3 Parallel re-amping can bring a bassline out on smaller speakers. Create an aux and load Logic's Channel EQ rolled off at 200Hz followed by Amp Designer. Set amp to Studio Amp and cab to British 2x12. Turn Gain to 10 and slowly mix it back into the track to hear the extra frequencies cut in.

Building a tape-style saturator 🎧

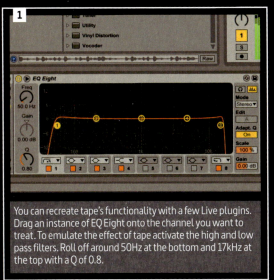

1 You can recreate tape's functionality with a few Live plugins. Drag an instance of EQ Eight onto the channel you want to treat. To emulate the effect of tape activate the high and low pass filters. Roll off around 50Hz at the bottom and 17kHz at the top with a Q of 0.8.

2 Next, add the Saturator plugin and set Drive to 1.5dB and Curve Type to Soft Sine. Ensure the Color button is switched off. Set Output to -1dB and check Soft Clip is switched on. Finally load Ableton's Glue Compressor.

3 On the Glue Compressor, set Attack to 1ms, Release to .8ms, Radio to 10:1 and turn on Soft Clip. The high ratio means that once a sound passes the threshold it is dramatically decreased in level. Adjust the threshold to reduce 1-2dB of gain. Add the 'tape rack' in parallel for more control.

Mixing kick and bass

In almost every dance genre the relationship between kick drum and bassline is the most important in the mix. The interplay between the two parts anchors the groove and lays the foundation upon which the rest of a production is built. Get it right and you're 80 per cent of the way to a solid mix. Get it wrong and all that follows is built on shaky ground. Often it's the hardest relationship of all to get right.

Why do producers struggle when mixing kick and bass? Primarily because **the two parts share the same core frequency space** and are therefore often forced into conflict. With other parts in a mix it is easy enough to solve frequency clashes using separation techniques like panning, reverb, EQ and chorus effects. But because low frequency parts – with their significant headroom demands – are best served dry, central and focussed these are off-limits. Nor is it usually desirable to relegate either the kick or bass to play a secondary role; in almost every genre **both the kick and bass play equally important roles**. In addition, there's the pragmatic fact that kick and bass inhabit the area of the mix that project studios struggle most to translate. **Accurate bass reproduction** is a luxury that most of us mixing in home studios (or worse, on headphones) simply don't have. The result of these combined challenges? Mixes that are lopsided, muddy and confusing, where the low end is either overbearingly loud or doesn't pack enough punch.

Fortunately, there are a few tried and tested techniques that give both the kick drum and bassline clarity and power – while also aiding separation.

COMPLEMENTARY SOUNDS

Before looking at production problem solvers, it's important to note that getting a solid low end is far easier if you **program the bassline so it doesn't overlap with the kick** or **pick sounds that don't compete with each other** for headroom territory in the first place.

So if you have an 808 kick drum that peaks at 60Hz, don't pick a bass sound that also peaks at 60Hz. Pick a bass patch that peaks instead at 80Hz – problem solved. Choosing complementary sounds isn't just a frequency concern. Consider the envelopes of each sound, too, and twin short clicky kicks (909-style) with more sustained Juno-style basslines – or vice versa.

With so many kick and bass sounds available it is perverse to the point of masochism twinning sounds that share the *same frequency and transient profiles*. The point may be obvious, but it's surprising how

HOW HIGH TO CUT

One of the best ways of controlling a flappy or over-weighty low end is to roll away the extreme low frequencies on both the kick drum and bassline. The question is how far up is to safe to cut?

Conventional mixing wisdom says you can cut up to around 30Hz, and if you're mixing for radio or home listeners then that's good advice (remember Rule #1, Context is everything).

But club rigs reach as low down as 20–30Hz. And even though clubbers may not *hear* these frequencies (the average human's hearing stops at around 30Hz), lower frequencies can certainly be *felt* in a club environment.

Which is to say be wary of cutting too high and too steep, while also understanding that too much information this low is unlikely ever to make for a stronger mix.

many producers overlook it, making their lives immeasurably harder by doing so.

THE THREE MODELS

Assuming you've paired a kick and bass that aren't fighting from the off, there are three approaches that further aid separation:

▸▸ **Low bass, upper kick**
▸▸ **Low kick, upper bass**
▸▸ **Side-by-side kick and bass**

Each approach recognises that mixes generally feature a hierarchy of importance but make a merit of that rather than a drawback. Here's how they work:

LOW BASS, UPPER KICK

In this approach, commonly used in D&B, an all-consuming bass fills the subsonic low end while a tight kick drum packs its punch higher up the spectrum. If the bassline requires power higher up the frequency spectrum, additional synth layers can be stacked into upper octaves, but these are arranged and EQd so that they expand *above* the kick (*walkthrough, page 284*).

LOW KICK, UPPER BASS

The opposite approach, in which the kick dominates the low end (often an 808 kick or a sample that features a layered 808) while a bassline peaks at around 75–125Hz.

Chapter eight
Mixing and mastering

Basslines that have short attack and decay times work well in this model, allowing the boomy kick to fill the lows as the bass skips between notes (*walkthrough, page 284*).

SIDE-BY-SIDE KICK AND BASS

Some producers want to have their low-end cake and eat it. For these fearless souls, a mix of notch EQ and sidechain compression can help deliver the best of both worlds.

'Side-by-side kick and bass' starts with a **'mirror' EQ** treatment (*page 231*), in which the kick drum's defining frequencies are slightly boosted (with a mid Q), while the same frequencies are *dipped* in the bassline (*walkthough, page 285*).

Next, the bassline's defining frequencies are gently notch boosted, while the same frequencies are *dipped* in the kick drum. The effect of this EQ mirroring is to create small 'pockets' in the kick and bass that its counterpart pokes through, giving each extra clarity while reducing masking.

When this is done, place a **compressor** with sidechain capabilities or a **ducker** on the bass channel. Set up the routing so that the bass dips in level when the kick hits (*page 115*). Tweak the attack and release times to ensure the volume and rhythmic interplay fits seamlessly with the groove. If the mirror EQ treatment has worked, you should only need to pull back between 1–2dB of gain to give each part greater definition. For heavily pumping mixes up the ratio and the amount of gain reduction on the sidechain compressor.

ARRANGEMENT AS PROBLEM SOLVER

There's a final solution to the kick/bass problem, hinted at above, which is the most effective of all: simply write a bassline that works seamlessly with the kick rather than one that is forced to wrestle with it. Kick and bass interaction is only an issue if the two overlap in terms of timing and frequency simultaneously.

The most obvious archetype here is the off-beat bass (*page 104*), in which the potential conflict between kick and bass is resolved by ensuring they never play at the same time. In its elegant way, it's a perfect solution to the problem, keeping the energy, weight and momentum in the

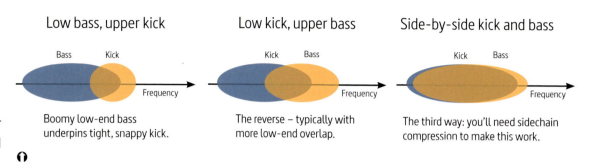

Fig 7: The three approaches to bass/kick mixing, with the coloured blobs showing where the bulk of energy resides for each part. In the third scenario, sidechain compression effectively changes the timing so that both parts dominate at different times.

PRO TIPS
TREVINO

When you're working through a mix, never lose sight of the feeling – or vibe – behind the track. "There's a lot of producers out there who are great engineers but they're not making great music. They make everything sound fucking brilliant… but the vibe's always the first thing. It has to be about the vibe and then you work around it."

bottom end constant and allowing each part to shine.

Disco basslines take a similar approach, with many of the fingerpicked notes falling between kick drum hits. And because notes are kept short, even when a kick and bass note strike together, the effect is rarely overbearing.

TIP If you're mostly happy with a bassline but there's the occasional kick clash, try revoicing (*page 154*) offending notes in the bassline so that their frequencies are shifted away from the kick drum hotspot.

TIP Tuning clashes are sometimes to blame for muddy low ends. If you've tried one, or all, of the above approaches and the kick and bass still don't fit together, try retuning the kick drum (*walkthrough, page 12*). A few notches change on the fine tune dial is sometimes enough to turn discord to unity.

// WALKTHROUGHS

Low bass, upper kick 🎧

1 In this example the starting kick and bassline combination needs work. The bouncy bassline, a simple Massive patch, overlaps with the big kick, and with no control at the low end of the spectrum, headroom is being squandered.

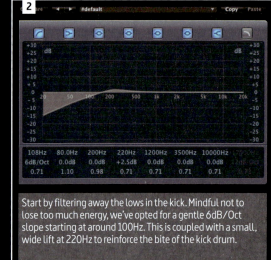

2 Start by filtering away the lows in the kick. Mindful not to lose too much energy, we've opted for a gentle 6dB/Oct slope starting at around 100Hz. This is coupled with a small, wide lift at 220Hz to reinforce the bite of the kick drum.

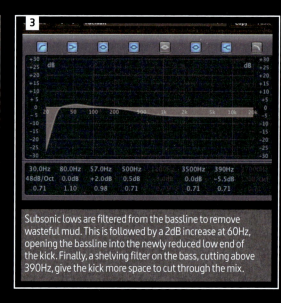

3 Subsonic lows are filtered from the bassline to remove wasteful mud. This is followed by a 2dB increase at 60Hz, opening the bassline into the newly reduced low end of the kick. Finally, a shelving filter on the bass, cutting above 390Hz, give the kick more space to cut through the mix.

Low kick, upper bass 🎧

1 There can be times when you want the kick to dominate the sub frequencies – a classic example being a booming 808. In such cases, like in this nu disco workout, the bassline's sub frequencies need to be controlled so they don't clash with the kick.

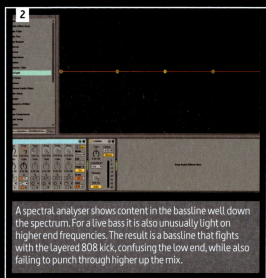

2 A spectral analyser shows content in the bassline well down the spectrum. For a live bass it is also unusually light on higher end frequencies. The result is a bassline that fights with the layered 808 kick, confusing the low end, while also failing to punch through higher up the mix.

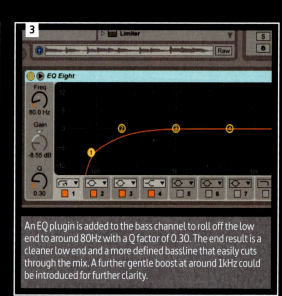

3 An EQ plugin is added to the bass channel to roll off the low end to around 80Hz with a Q factor of 0.30. The end result is a cleaner low end and a more defined bassline that easily cuts through the mix. A further gentle boost at around 1kHz could be introduced for further clarity.

Side-by-side kick and bass

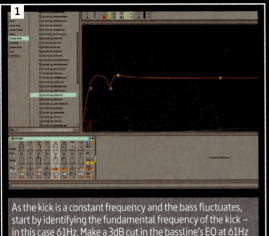

1 As the kick is a constant frequency and the bass fluctuates, start by identifying the fundamental frequency of the kick – in this case 61Hz. Make a 3dB cut in the bassline's EQ at 61Hz so that the kick 'pokes through'. Gently boost frequencies around the cut point so the bassline doesn't lose weight.

2 Add a compressor plugin to the bassline track. Click the arrow to activate the sidechain. Choose the kick track from the drop-down and set Ratio to 2:1, Attack to 1ms and a Release time that's in sync with the bpm – in this case 125ms. Trim around 2–3dB of gain to make the kick cut through.

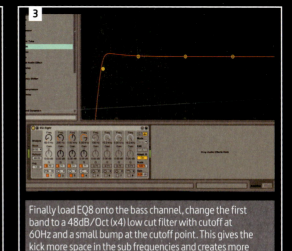

3 Finally load EQ8 onto the bass channel, change the first band to a 48dB/Oct (x4) low cut filter with cutoff at 60Hz and a small bump at the cutoff point. This gives the kick more space in the sub frequencies and creates more definition for both parts in the mix.

Arrangement to solve the problem

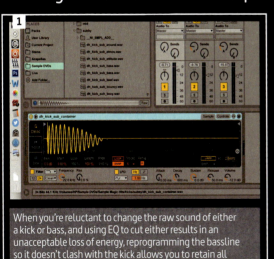

1 When you're reluctant to change the raw sound of either a kick or bass, and using EQ to cut either results in an unacceptable loss of energy, reprogramming the bassline so it doesn't clash with the kick allows you to retain all frequencies of both sounds.

2 In our 'before' example, some of the bass notes hit at the same time as the kick, causing obvious problems. Edit the MIDI so that no bass note falls on the first or third (kick) measures of the bar. Play with the MIDI placements until you get a groove you're happy with.

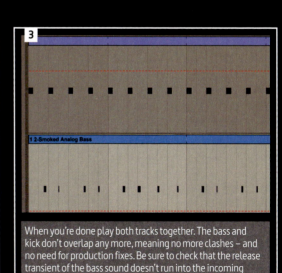

3 When you're done play both tracks together. The bass and kick don't overlap any more, meaning no more clashes – and no need for production fixes. Be sure to check that the release transient of the bass sound doesn't run into the incoming kick; shorten it if needs be.

Ambient effects in the mix

After EQ and compression, reverb and delay are the third essential tools used to craft a solid mix. Ambient effects perform a variety of tasks. They:

▸▸ **help mix coherence** – by blending different signals into a single acoustic space,
▸▸ **help shape sounds** – their tone and length,
▸▸ **add depth and space** – moving sounds in the 'third dimension', and
▸▸ **create special effects**.

MIX COHERENCE

A typical dance mix uses sounds from dozens, maybe even hundreds, of different sources – a sample here, a soft synth there. The resulting production is a patchwork of sounds with few common origins. In that respect it is fundamentally different to a rock or indie mix, in which most sounds are captured in the same acoustic space – a studio's live room.

Although sourcing, shaping and sequencing these different sounds is the pleasure and genius of dance music production, it is critical to the coherency of the mix that these myriad disparate sounds are woven into a unified whole.

Ambient effects play a pivotal role here, allowing the producer to feed multiple signals to the same reverb so that they are all given a subtle – or not so subtle – wash of the same ambient effect.

A decade or so back the way to do this was to set up a reverb or two on aux buses then feed the different tracks to these in varying degrees, allowing even the driest sounding band to be placed into a pleasingly ambient acoustic space.

Although this approach might feel old-school and restricting for dance mixes, the principal remains solid. It's perfectly possible to create a good mix with a couple of reverb processors set up on buses – one short reverb and one long. This is a good approach for reducing processor use while creating a cohesive mix. Where a part requires either an 'effect' reverb – see below – or a unique ambient treatment (in the case of the lead vocals, for example), additional insert reverbs can also be employed.

When adding ambient effects, the law of diminishing returns soon kicks in. Adding more than three or four reverbs and/or delays makes for complex and confused mixes smeared with disparate ambient tails. To keep a mix focussed, use no more than a handful of ambient effects, choose pre-delay and tail times carefully and bracket-EQ effects returns to keep them lean.

TAMING RETURNS

It's easy to 'choke' a mix with too much ambience. Given that at any one time dozens of signals may be treated with one or more ambient effects, the amount of reverb and/or delay/s in the mix can soon spiral out of control.

Cumulative ambience requires mix space in the same way as musical elements and too often in poor mixes it is left to either fight with more important sounds or serve as an ill-defined soundbed that smears the lower end of a mix.

One way of controlling ambience is to use EQ bracketing (*page 211*) to roll away unwanted lows and highs on bus returns. Take particular care to control the low end, where ambience is unlikely to be necessary and where the kick and bass need space to work without having to trudge through reverb swamps.

SCULPTING TONE AND SHAPE

One of the most powerful but least obvious uses for reverb is to sculpt both the tone and shape of a sound.

Because reverbs have their own sonic character that they imprint onto a signal (making it sound like it is in a hall or studio for example), they can be used to change the **tonality** of a sound. At higher settings (50 per cent of signal treated plus), you get more of the room sound than the dry original. The nature of the reverb setting is critical here. Reflections are equalised by the type of surface and its physical properties. So a marble surface, for example, reflects both high and low frequencies equally while a wood panelled room reflects the low end more efficiently than the high end. This means if you want to impart a mellower tone on a sound, choose one that models a wooden room or similar.

You can get even more creative by using convolution reverb to imprint leftfield and other-worldly impulses onto source material. You might imprint the ambient sound of a gunshot in a car park onto a humble clap to give it a unique transient flavour. By tweaking the reverb's filters you can further control the tonality of the tail to help it fit the mix.

It's not just the tone of a sound that can be altered though. Because ambient effects add waveforms at the end of a signal, reverb can also be used to lengthen sounds and **control sustain and release envelopes**. Where you have a sampled snare that ends a little too early, for example, adding a controlled burst of non-linear reverb – like gated reverb – can be all you need to give it the required tail.

ADDING DEPTH AND SPACE

Mix Rule #4 says: **A great mix has width and depth. It is three dimensional – but works equally well in two and one dimensions.** Width we've covered on *pages 268–270*. Depth is largely controlled by the use of ambient effects (though not entirely – *see page 240*).

Because reverb gives the impression of space to a sound, it can be used to 'move' sounds from the front of a mix to the back. So if a D&B mix demands that the kick, bass and lead go up front, leave them mostly dry (or heavy on ERs) while giving supportive synth and percussive parts more ambience.

Our impression of how far away a sound source resides from us is governed by a complex array of interactions, including:

▶▶ **Pre-delay** – The time before the onset of the reverb (*page 223*) can be lengthened to increase the apparent distance of a sound from the listener. As the pre-delay time increases the delayed portion of the sound becomes more prominent.

NOTE Setting the pre-delay time to match the tempo of the track becomes more important if you opt for longer pre-delays. If it doesn't match, the reverb can feel out of sync with the track.

▶▶ **Early reflections (ERs)** – ERs sound stronger the closer you are to a sound source. So if you want a signal to have a halo of ambience without being pushed too far back, change the ER/tail ratio so that the bulk of the reverberation is provided by ERs.

TIP Using ERs without a tail avoids cluttering space in a mix.

▶▶ **Reverb/tail time** – The longer a reverb tail, the further away a sound will appear. *This is usually the most important control in setting the appearance of depth.*

TIP For more movement in a reverb tail, add a chorus effect after the reverb. Some plugins offer 'wander' options as standard.

▶▶ **High frequency roll off** – Increasing the high frequency roll-off makes for a duller ambience, which helps push the sound further back in the mix. In the real world, high frequencies fall away the further they have to travel through a space (high frequencies are more easily absorbed and diffused than low frequencies).

JULIEN BRACHT

"The Eventide Space Reverb Unit is one of the favourite effects units in my studio. It's a reverb for electric guitars, but it's also perfect for any other kinds of instruments or sounds. I use it both in the studio and when playing live."

REBOOT

"The main theme [in 'Timelive'] is the dubby synth line, which was sculpted with the Elektron Analog 4 synth. After recording, I sent it through the Roland Space Echo and the Strymon Big Sky Reverb to add more modulation and make it sound more alive."

EFFECTS

Reverb is not just a mix tool; it's a creative tool inextricably linked to sound design. There are plenty of opportunities to get creative with unique sounds:

▶▶ **Reverb builds** – in which the amount of wet signal is increased over an element or whole track during a fill or build to diffuse and distance the sound before the wet signal is switched off and the track punches back in 100 per cent dry (*walkthrough, page 253*).

▶▶ **Reverb and delay spot spins** – A regular trick in techno and minimal productions. Highlight occasional drum or percussion hits by automating the reverb send (*walkthrough, page 187*).

▶▶ **Reverse reverb** – A classic trick for washy, sucking loveliness, particularly on vocal parts (*walkthrough, page 194*).

▶▶ **Lo-fi verb** – It's easy to overlook more basic (and freeware) reverbs but if you want to give a part a more lo-fi vibe, experiment with outdated models. Even better, buy a cheap-as-chips hardware effects processor.

TIP In an overly ambient mix, try substituting reverb for delay. Because delay tails are dry between repeats, they are less muddy. Tuck tails in by mixing returns low. Control them using EQ bracketing.

Chapter eight
Mixing and mastering

Ear candy, automation and endgame

With a refined arrangement, a good balance and the cumulative improvements offered by tweaking EQ, compression and ambience, your mix should be getting close to completion. Fundamentals in place, it's time to enter the endgame, adding any last ear candy to the mix, finalising automation and working at bar level to tweak details before exporting the master. When making these last-in-line tweaks, let Rule #4 guide you: **a great mix is a living, evolving thing. It has sustained interest that engages the listener from start to finish**.

EAR CANDY

Ear candy – sonic 'treats' and flourishes that delight the ear, supply sonic interest and help shape the arrangement – range from crashes to complex glitched fills. They are covered in detail on *pages 94 and 252*. As part of the mix endgame, listen to the full track several times and see if additional candy would help its flow and engagement.

AUTOMATION

Track-critical automation – of levels, synth parameters, FX sends – should be in place already (*page 266*). Now is the time to fine-tune that existing automation as well as using subtle level and EQ changes to maintain listener engagement over time.

If a mix features 16 or 32 bar turnarounds in which little changes, automation can keep things fresh. A piano part might be increased in volume to give it more prominence; a synth's cutoff filter may be closed to ease it back in the mix; a lead line's attack envelope can be increased towards a build. Even barely perceptible changes – a 1dB volume rise over the course of a section – contribute to the perception of mix in constant flux.

DETAIL

The mix close to completion, it's time to get up close and personal in the arrange page. Set up loop points across two or four bar sections then cycle through the arrangement to perform forensic tweaks.

Forget the big picture for an hour or so and ensure that at bar-level all is working: groove, balance, programming, automation.

Intensive micro listening, through monitors and headphones, allows you to fix problems you may previously have missed. Work in short bursts, putting each section through a final quality control. Don't be afraid to edit MIDI data, tweak synth settings, fine-tune

KEEP A/BING

If you took our advice from *page 261*, you will have been regularly A/Bing your emerging mix against a selection of your favourite masters.

As you approach endgame the need to assess your mix independently becomes ever more important. It's easy, now you've spent so long in its presence, to lose focus on the sound you're after and impartiality over the flaws and strengths of your mix.

So keep referring back to your references, noting the use of transients, the overall tonality of the mix and treatment of specific sounds. Pay particular attention to the bass end.

automation, adjust EQ settings... Anything to add a last-in-line five per cent polish to your work.

WHEN TO STOP

Art is never finished, only abandoned. So said Leonardo da Vinci way back in the 15th century. The idea you'll ever make the perfect mix needs to be disavowed right now: that way only madness – and many wasted hours – lie.

In the world of commercial mixing the popular maxim says: **a mix is complete when no amount of extra tweaks will change the number of record sales**. Another way of saying the same thing is **a good time to close a mix is when you're 98 per cent happy with it** – when you know it will translate to its target environment and when you're proud enough for others to hear it.

Music production is replete with stories of perfectionists who dedicate months to a single track – and who are still dissatisfied with it at the end. *Don't become one of them!* Generally speaking, if a mixdown is taking you longer than a day or so there's probably something wrong with the track – the structure, the choice of sounds, the groove, the vibe or the melodies.

It's also important to be realistic. *Some mixes just don't work out*. They may start well, but they falter along the way. Part of being an artist is understanding that some tracks aren't meant to be – and that abandoning a project isn't a sign of failure. Either start a new project or return to the troubled mix a few weeks or even years later, when you can approach it with fresh ears and enthusiasm (plus more experience).

LOUDNESS

As you make these final tweaks to your track it's worth bouncing a few 'trial masters' and viewing them graphically. Do any transients stick out of the mix? Spiky transients reduce overall loudness, meaning a quieter track. Manually automating the volume of transient hotspots down by a dB or two can free up headroom. At the same time, return to the tips for increasing loudness on *page 259*.

EXPORTING THE MASTER

When you've given your mix a few last listens on as many systems as you can (*Checking the mix, right*), it's time to export the master, either to pass on to a **mastering** engineer or for your own self-mastering (*page 296*). When exporting the master:

▶▶ **Export at the sample rate and bit depth your session was – which to preserve as much information as possible should be at least 24-bit, 44.1kHz.** Wav or AIFF files are both acceptable. *Do not bounce the master as an mp3.* If you're using a mastering house, they will confirm what format they prefer.

▶▶ **Leave at least 6dB of headroom** to give enough space to apply further processing during mastering. When mixing in 24-bit, there is more than enough signal-to-noise ratio to allow even more headroom if you want to play it ultra safe. *Although the odd peak breaching -6dB is fine, ensure there is no clipping* (*page 256*).

▶▶ **Leave a bar or so of silence** at the start and end of the mix.

▶▶ **Consider whether you want to retain or bypass master bus processing.** Although if characterful pumping is a key part of the production (*page 219*) you may want to retain it on the master output, the usual advice is to bypass master bus processing, including compression, limiting and exciter plugins like Sonnox Inflator. If in doubt and you're using third party mastering, send one master with processing and one without.

TIP Triple check the final bounced mix before signing it off. Check for clicks, pops and digital clipping – particularly if you've bypassed master bus processing that reduced the mix's dynamic range. Zoom in on the audio file to check no transient hits 0dBFS. Finally, live with the mix for a few days and test it on as many systems as possible (*Checking the mix, right*).

Checking the mix

Mix sounding great in your studio? Excellent. But that's only part of the picture. You also need to ensure the mix translates to its expected listening environment/s too. So if your target listener is an iPod user then you need to listen to the mix not only on open back studio cans but also earbuds and/or Beats headphones. If – most likely – you want your track rocking the clubs, beg, borrow or steal some time to audition the mix on a club rig. Other tricks for testing a mix include:

CAR STEREO
Having any kind of third party sound system on which to test a mix can give useful feedback on final tweaks. The humble car stereo is great, not only because many consumers listen to music in their car, but car systems typically hype the low end club-style. Practically, the car is a space we often spend time in outside of the studio, and you can also force others travelling with you to give their feedback. Don't take the hyped frequency bumps as gospel – but for spotting programming flaws and arrangement issues, the car is a surprisingly helpful mix improvement ally.

OUTSIDE THE STUDIO
As counter-intuitive as it sounds, standing outside the studio with the door closed can give you insights you don't get inside the studio itself. It's particularly useful for giving a second view on whether a part is mixed too high or low in a mix.

MIX LOUD, MIX SOFT
In general you make better mix decisions when music is played back at a comfortable and relatively low volume. But if you're mixing for clubs it's essential to ramp up the volume now and then. Do so in short, concentrated bursts. *Mixing loud permanently doesn't deliver stronger mixes and risks long-term hearing damage.*

IPOD/PHONE
If you expect any kind of radio support, you need your mix to translate onto earbuds. Many producers working on crossover tracks have a pair plugged into their headphone out socket to check compatibility as the mix progresses. It may be painful to hear your wonderfully nuanced full-frequency mix butchered by a £5 pair of buds, but as producers our role is to make music for its intended medium – which is rarely fantasy hi-fi.

Common mix problems and how to fix them

It's frustrating to reach the endgame of a mix to discover it isn't working out. Occasionally this requires a back-to-basics rebuild of the track. More often than not, if the track has a sound arrangement and the mix foundations are solid, a few judicious tweaks may be all you need. To round off the mixing pages of this chapter, here are a range of common mix problems – and suggested solutions:

TOO MUCH AMBIENCE

With so much processing power at our fingertips it's easy to pile ambient and delay effects onto multiple channels without thinking of the cumulative effects across the mix – background mud and 'smear' that reduces clarity and definition.

Solutions include:

▶▶ **Muting ambience** – Do you need every ambient effect? Try bypassing each in turn. If muting an effect makes no difference in the context of the mix, lose it for good.

▶▶ **Dial back** – Move along the reverb and delay return tracks and reduce each in volume by half. Listen to the difference. Do you miss the ambience? If not, keep the return at its new lower level. Even reducing a small amount of ambience makes for a less muddy mix. Remember that compression during mastering will increase the presence of ambience in the mix.

▶▶ **Fine-tune tails** – Do reverb times (including pre-delay, ER entries and the tail itself) fit the groove of the track? Ambient effects weave their magic through time; ensure that tails don't conflict with the track's natural rhythm. Use an ms-to-delay calculator to double check times.

▶▶ **Bracket returns** – There are almost no cases when it is desirable for ambience to bleed into the bass and ultra high frequency zones of a mix. Use EQ or the reverb/delay plugin's filters to clamp down on return bandwidths to keep them focussed.

TONALLY UNBALANCED

Sometimes you end up with a mix that sounds well balanced in its own right but which sounds bass heavy or bass light when compared with other tracks. In these cases the track is internally coherent but tonally unbalanced.

Solutions include:

▶▶ **Macro rebalance** – Use high quality tone-shaping EQs (Pultec, Neve-style) on group buses (or individual tracks) and carefully rebalance the track using wide curves and gentle boosts/cuts using commercial masters as references.

OVER-COMPLEX MIX

Too much going on in an ambitious mix? We've all been there. It's a problem frequently born of the mistaken belief that more is better, when in reality the best mixes are often fairly simple in structural and arrangement terms.

Solutions include:

▶▶ **Simplify** – Go through the mix, mute minor parts and see if they're missed. If not, lose them. This is particularly pertinent with layered sounds; you're often better off with one well programmed sound than multiple versions with slight differences. When using layers, ensure every sound complements the others and adds something unique.

▶▶ **Make fewer parts work harder** – If you've been able to lose a few tracks, try tweaking envelope, EQ and compression settings on the remaining sounds to give them more space and profile in the mix. Sometimes easing back on compression by a dB or two is enough to let a pinned sound expand and breathe.

▶▶ **Go easy on changes** – Yes, detail and change in a mix is a good thing. But

PRO TIPS

PHILIPP GORBACHEV

Sometimes an overly complex mix can only be rescued by going back to basics...

"Originally on 'Lazer' (from the *Unlock The Box* album), there were dreamy vocals about a red laser, lonely dancefloor stars and an emo choir in the background. They were all cut out. Radical surgery. Just the basic elements left."

constant change can be confusing and tiring. Remember that at most the ear and brain can only process two or three changes in a track at any one time.

HARSH MIX

A mix can sound abrasive, over-strident and fatiguing when there's too much energy in the perennially busy 2–5kHz zone. When played on club rigs the vocals sound peaky and synths honky. This is an area even the best mix engineers struggle with as it's where the majority of instruments contain important frequency content, which in turn leads to bandwidth overload.

Solutions include:

▸▸ **EQ trims** – Investigate which instruments are most active in the region then use EQ bracketing (*page 267*) to remove unnecessary content from parts that don't need space in the area. Next, turn your attention to the remaining content and use tone shaping EQ (*page 278*) to reduce obvious frequency buildups.

▸▸ **Consolidate / re-arrange parts** – EQ alone won't solve frequency buildups. Solo individual elements in the problem frequency zone and ask how changes to synth settings and/or the arrangement might help reduce activity in the problem zone. Can you dial back a synth's cutoff frequency? Could you shorten a percussion part's sustain and release envelopes to diminish its energy? Try muting parts to see if they are missed. With layered sounds, audition new patches and/or reprogram them into lower or higher octaves to spread the bandwidth load. Look at the track's structure too; does the vocal have to be present at the same time as the lead synth? If so can a gentler synth peaking at a different frequency be twinned with the vocal? Think creatively; look at where every sound peaks and do what you can to avoid more than a couple of sounds peaking in the same spot.

▸▸ **Music bus EQ** – Finally, employ a wide 1–2dB frequency dip in the 3–5kHz area.

LOW END PROBLEMS

An all-too-familiar scenario in smaller studios, where budget speakers don't faithfully reproduce the bass end, in which the low end is either overbearing and flabby – a muddy mess when the PA's limiter kicks in – or, just as bad, underwhelming and flat. Although bass problems can be caused by various factors, the critical ones are the sounds used for the kick drum and bassline and their overlap/extension in the mix.

Solutions include:

▸▸ **Start with the facts** – If your ears aren't giving you the information you need, open

Eight tips for better mixes

1. REST YOUR EARS DURING LONG MIX SESSIONS
When you listen to music at even relatively loud volumes for long periods, your sensitivity to high frequency sounds drops off – which is a recipe for disaster. Take a 15 minute break every couple of hours to rest/reset your ears.

2. LEARN FROM THE MASTERS
Admire both the structure and sound of a particular track? There's no shame at all in copying it onto a track in your mixer and using it as a structural guide and an A/B reference. *Even the stars A/B.*

3. GIVE YOURSELF A DEADLINE
The endless deadline is the bane of the unfinished mix. Give yourself deadlines for specific tasks – and stick to them. Having a list of what you want to achieve in a session (mixing the drums, finalising the arrangement etc) gives structure and a sense of achievement to your time. Breaking a mix down into easily achievable bite-size tasks can make a daunting challenge seem less so.

4. DO SOMETHING DIFFERENT
If you usually make deep house try mixing a chillout track (yours or someone else's). Flexing your mix muscles into areas you're not familiar with is a way of expanding your experience and developing new creative skills.

5. RESTRICT YOURSELF
Too much choice is a burden. As an experiment, limit yourself to 24 tracks and three plugins per track. You may be surprised by how quickly a track comes together and how much better it sounds.

6. MOOD MATTERS
We all have creative off-days. Don't think of them as a problem. Instead get on with other tasks that don't call for creative energy. Back files up. Weed samples. Have a studio spring-clean. There are ways to be productive in the studio that don't involve making music.

7. BUY SAMPLES
Probably the cheapest way of giving your sounds a creativity injection is to splash out on a new sample pack. For less than the price of a pizza you can buy hundreds of new sounds and potential song-starters.

8. SHARE YOUR MUSIC
Developing a network of supportive producers who critique your work is one of the best ways of getting feedback on your sound. Form relationships on any number of genre-specific production forums.

a spectrum analyser and see what's going on. If you've got significant energy punching below 20Hz, rein it in. You can usually afford to roll away lows up to around 30–40Hz.

▸▸ **A/B for confidence** – Import a commercial reference track and observe it using the same spectrum analyser. What's going on in the bass frequencies of the reference track? How low does the bass extend and where are the bulk of the frequencies? With that knowledge in mind, start rebalancing your kick and bass.

▸▸ **Tune the kick** – One of the main causes of low end grief is a kick drum whose fundamental frequency clashes with the bassline. The solution? Either trial a new kick drum, or transpose it until the pitching of both fits like a glove (page 12).

▸▸ **Sidechain compression** – One of the most effective headroom-saving techniques in the book, apply sidechain compression to the bass, triggered by the kick. Even a small amount of compression can give the kick definition and open up enough space for it to pump through the mix.

▸▸ **High or low?** – Revisit the kick and bass relationship and check that they stack up together using a low/higher/side-by-side mix approach (pages 282).

▸▸ **Try new sounds** – It's never too late to try new sounds for the critical low end.

BASS DOESN'T PUNCH

The flip side of the same coin, in which the bass end of a mix doesn't deliver.

Solutions include:

▸▸ **Start with the facts** – Check frequencies visually and A/B with confident references.

▸▸ **Don't cut too high** – Low end cuts control the bass and free up headroom. Go too high and you lose warmth and power.

▸▸ **Sweeter lows** – Use an EQ known for low-end flattery – think Pultec and Neve – to gently inflate the 50–70Hz region.

▸▸ **Embrace the subs** – Though we recommend CAUTION, specific low-end enhancers used sparingly will extend the reach of timid basslines and kicks.

FLAT MIX

Mixes that are tonally balanced and structurally sound but seem 'flat' and devoid of emotional highs and lows are often symptomatic of too much compression coupled with an arrangement that doesn't deliver an energy narrative.

Solutions include:

▸▸ **Re-evaluate the processing** – A surefire way of robbing a mix of energy is to nullify

ALAN BRAXE

Never underestimate the contribution of luck to the creative process. Here's hyper-humble French house hero Alan Braxe on the subject:

"The writing process is a mixture of capturing stuff which arrives by accident and a more formal way of writing; a mix of formality and luck. It's about having a studio which allows you to have access to luck. That's very important in music, I think. Once luck happens it just turns to a more formal process.

"Some people are really strong because they can control the luck factor but I can't so I'm just waiting for luck to fall on me. Most of the tracks I've released, I decided to release them because I felt luck happened."

transients through over-compression and limiting (page 259). Return to compressors on tracks, buses and the master output. Try muting them or reducing their ratios and/or gain reduction levels. Consider their impact both alone and combined. On a single compressor 5dB of gain reduction is a lot unless you're after an obvious effect. With multiple stages of compression 8dB or more is enough to dissolve punch and momentum. Bear in mind, too, that a compressor should generally be returning to 0dB of gain reduction a few times every bar. *Always compressing* is a legitimate aesthetic choice, but one that's hard to get right; if you need more compression, it's usually better to either up the ratio and/or add a second compressor in series.

▸▸ **Energy flow: what's the story?** – If highs and lows are important to the track, have you shaped its energy to allow it to ebb and flow? Is there a strong energy 'story' – a narrative of clear builds and drops? If not get busy on the arrangement page and with automation to take control of that energy (page 238).

▸▸ **Ear candy** – Although never a solve-all, interesting and unusual fills, edits and spot FX all help lift a mix.

HIGH TEMPO MASKING

High tempo genres like D&B pose the risk of 'high tempo masking', where sounds arrive at the playhead fast and furious; a hi-hat immediately follows the kick, which is instantly followed by an arp hit. In tracks at lower bpms, mix elements are given space to breathe. But where the constraints of speed remove that space, sounds can be robbed of definition and vitality. In extreme cases, sounds – particularly percussive ones – mask and trip over others, with dynamics reduced as a constant barrage of hits arrive in quick succession.

Solutions include:

▸ **Cut tails** – Long decay tails on reverb and delay effects risk overlapping foreground elements and congesting the mix background. Keep things tidy by reducing the length of tails, using bracket filters on returns and using an ms-to-delay calculator to refine effects times. Where big verb treatments are important – on snares for example – ensure there is space in the mix for them to ring out unimpeded by busy percussive workouts. Return to mix Rule #2 and remember that dynamic flow demands space between hits.

▸ **Tidy transients** – As with effects tails, long transients in high bpm tracks risk clogging the mix. Use transient designers and/or sampler ADSR settings to tighten up both the front and tail ends of all percussive sounds. Note that this doesn't just mean drums; delve into synth parameters on leads, FX, bass sounds and arps as well.

HIGH END OVERLOAD

It's easy, especially during long mix sessions, to unintentionally over-bake the high end. Although they may sound exciting at the time, strident upper frequencies in hi-hats, synths, vocals and percussive elements sound irritatingly aggressive when reproduced on a loud club system.

Solutions include:

▸ **De-ess** – Although de-essers are mainly used to tackle harsh sibilant frequencies in vocals, this dynamic compressor can be great for taking out harsh spikes on closed and open hi-hats, percussion loops or on filtered, resonant noise sweeps.

▸ **Go vintage** – Tape emulators and saturator plugins are both capable of reining in spitty highs and giving a warmer, less aggressive top end to signals. Sometimes they offer a more organic solution than simple EQ reduction.

SAMPLE-BASED GENRES

Working with pre-mixed material and loops offers fast inspiration and unique creativity, but trying to get samples to gel with your own ideas can be a challenge.

Solutions include:

▸ **'Match EQ'** – Employ one of the many 'match' EQ plugins to imprint the general sound of your emerging mix onto an imported loop. Although match EQs are often a little trial-and-error, when they get it right they can help give even the most wayward loop a more fitting timbral character.

▸ **Gates and/or transient shapers** – For control over the transient make-up of a loop, gates and/or transient shapers can be used: to reduce the volume of unwanted detail; to emphasise specific hits in a loop; and to bring the transient construct of a loop into line with the existing dynamic feel of a track – so if your track has a loose, lazy disco feel, reduce the attack transient of the imported loop so it has a similar feel.

▸ **Multi-band compression** – Because multi-band compressors shape both the dynamic and tonal make-up of mixed stereo material, they are ideal for changing the flavour of both in a pre-mixed loop. Start with a simple preset and tweak until the loop/s fits your mix.

AWFUL MIX

We've all been there… Every single recording artist has spent days on a bum mix. Rest easy in the knowledge that it's the real stinkers – and the recognition that we can do better – that improve our game. As Daft Punk sing in 'Technologic': *"Trash it, change it – upgrade it"*.

PRO TIPS

OSKAR OFFERMANN

Coming back to 'rested' tracks when you have the skills to do them justice is something even the pros do. Here's Berlin-based Oskar Offermann taking about completing his track 'Find yourself':

"I had this one lying around for a long, long time – around two years in total – having this writer's block to get it all finished.

"I clearly remember listening to it on a train ride through France and thinking to myself: 'Gosh, I really like this. Why the hell am I not able to finish it?' And at some point I just had to let it go, so I started working on other stuff. Then the album sort of happened by itself. Once I let go of the basic idea to produce a meditation album, I could finish it."

Mastering: an introduction

Mastering is the process of taking the final mix and treating it in a number of ways to prepare it for release and distribution. The result is a single 'master' track from which all subsequent copies are derived. Although even mastering engineers themselves often disagree over what is and should be involved in the process, a typical mastering job:

▸▸ **Makes the track louder** – No-one wants their track to sound weak in comparison to the competition. Compression and limiting is employed to ensure when a track comes on the DJ playlist it doesn't pale into insignificance alongside its neighbours.

▸▸ **Refines the frequency balance** – Because professional mastering rooms are equipped with sophisticated speaker systems and are acoustically treated to very high standards, the mastering engineer will be able to identify – and cut – any problem frequencies. Many mixes are also given a 'gloss' of high-end tonal EQ to subtly flatter the low and high end. This final sonic polish is designed to make the master sound as commercially attractive as possible.

▸▸ **Brings a fresh set of impartial ears to the project** – One of the constant frustrations of the solo dance producer is that they have no third party to 'test' their mix on. The mastering engineer can be that person. When they receive your mix, their experienced ears will be able to identify problem areas and minor distortions that may not have been evident when the material was mixed.

▸▸ **Ensures consistency** – On EP and album projects the mastering engineer will ensure a consistent tonal balance and volume between different tracks.

Mastering has a reputation as a dark art among producers. In theory it's a fairly straightforward process. The skill lies in listening deeply to a mix and knowing intuitively what is required to turn that mix into a master – a skillset which can take a lifetime to learn.

NO FIXED PROCESS

If you were to believe the marketing hype of the typical 'mastering' plugin you'd be forgiven for thinking mastering was a fixed process that involved some compression, an EQ lift at the top and bottom of a mix and some last-in-line limiting.

Dispel that thinking now. *There is no such thing as a 'typical' master chain and 'finalising' presets are best avoided.* Instead every mastering job is unique to the **genre** (a chillwave master is going to sound very different to a trance banger), the intended **medium** (mastering for vinyl requires a different approach to mastering for mp3) and its intended **context** (a club mix will emphasise a different set of frequencies to a radio mix).

In addition, some mixes require significant hands-on work and dozens of tweaks while others need no more than a little high end EQ boost to add sparkle.

MASTERING: THE PRO ROUTE

If you've got the money to spend then you will almost always get a better job if you leave mastering to the pros.

These are engineers who dedicate careers to their craft. They have listened to hundreds of thousands of hours of music, have immaculate-sounding rooms and have 'golden ears' which are able to pick up a track's tiniest flaws on first listen. They are also likely to have some serious kit on hand.

The good news is that many of these pros are not prohibitively expensive. As online mastering takes off, you can barter even a top engineer down to less than £50–100 a track, and as little as £250–500 for a full album.

If you go down the pro route, there are a few things that will help ensure you get the most for your investment:

PRO TIPS

MATT COLTON

"Working with clients present gets the best results in my opinion – the communication is instant and it's easier for me to get a handle on how they want things to sound. It also means we can discuss and deal with any problems or issues that arise there and then.

"Plus it's always more fun hanging out and having a laugh with people. Music should be fun and although we are getting a job done, I like my sessions to be chilled and relaxed – which makes for a more creative atmosphere."

Chapter eight
Mixing and mastering

▸▸ **Pick the right engineer** – It may sound obvious but pick a mastering engineer that you know has pedigree in the genre you make. If you produce banging hardcore, don't pick someone famed for their folk mastering skills. Most often recommendations come by word of mouth, but you can also find out who mastered a track from sleeve/online credits. If you're releasing through a label they will often have a go-to engineer.

▸▸ **Give a clear brief** – Tell the engineer what kind of sound you're after ('Loud, Open, Warm, Banging…') and where you expect the track to be played. As with mixing, context is everything, and the engineer will approach the mastering differently depending on whether the track is destined for the dancefloor or the iTunes charts. A commercial reference or two will help the engineer understand the sound you're after.

▸▸ **Leave them something to do** – There's no point in sending a mastering house a hyped-to-the-max mix with no headroom; they'll have no space in which to work. Most mastering houses ask for a mix to peak at no more than -3 to -6dB. Where heavy bus mastering is an essential part of your style, speak to the mastering engineer before submitting a mix; it may be they have better soft or hardware for making a mix pump in which case your own mix processing may be redundant. Equally, they may ask you to tone it down so that they still have some space to up the volume. If in doubt, supply two versions of the mix, one with your own master bus processing and one without – that way the mastering engineer can make an informed choice over which is best for their purposes.

▸▸ **Attend the session** – As Matt Colton notes (*left*), the best results are almost always achieved with the client present. It takes guesswork out of the equation and can be both instructive and fun.

▸▸ **And finally… Don't expect a miracle** – It can be disheartening to get a mastered track back to find it doesn't sound like it's destined for the top of the Beatport charts. Get real; *mastering never transforms tracks*. There is only so much fixing a mastering house can do so ensure your expectations are realistic and ensure your mix is the best it can be before it is passed to the engineer.

PRO TIPS

AMBIVALENT

"Nothing is less exciting or danceable than a beat that's been crushed to the point of a flat-lined airhorn.

"This is particularly bad in dance music where a listener might hear hours upon hours of music this way."

TIP A good mastering engineer should be prepared to ask for a track to be resubmitted – no professional wants to do shoddy work, after all. In the case of a mix that mastering will not improve, it is in the interests of the track for the producer to fix problems before resubmitting the track for mastering. In these rare instances the mastering engineer's feedback can be invaluable.

TIP Cheap mastering jobs using race-to-the-bottom 'gig' websites, as well automated online mastering services, should be used with caution. By all means give them a go, but scrimping on this last crucial stage is a false economy.

Mastering for vinyl – leave it to the pros…

Aside from the usual considerations, additional care is needed at the extreme ends of the frequency spectrum when mastering (and mixing) for vinyl.

Too much information, and any stereo signal, in the **low end** can make pressing difficult and risks various playback nightmares – including the needle jumping from the groove.

If there is too much stereo processing, it may need to be reduced (or removed) at source. Alternatively, the engineer may choose to sum the low end to mono and add a low cut filter at around 20–30Hz to regulate the signal.

There are potential issues with the **high end** too. Vinyl cannot handle high frequency information in the same way as digital playback systems. Hi-hats, cymbals, tambourines, FX sounds and sibilant vocals can all contribute to high-end overload, leading to distortion.

This is dealt with using a high-cut or shelving filter set around 16kHz to reduce the amount of problem signal reaching the cutting lathe.

The issues at play here are complex and involve knowledge not only of mixing and mastering but also of the mechanics of cutting and working lathes. Because mastering is an intrinsic part of the cutting process, **if you're considering a run of vinyl, leave mastering to the pros**. With the pressing costs involved, there's no point risking errors across a whole run for the sake of £50 or so spent on professional mastering.

Mastering: the process

Whether you decide to take the pro mastering route or perform the job yourself, the set of tools used to master a track are the same. And while every track requires its own individual approach, the workflow follows a similar pattern.

EQ

Problem frequencies are identified using your ears and 'search and destroy' (*page 211*) and/or a spectrum analyser. When harsh frequencies are identified, **precision EQ cuts** (small Q) are used to slice out overly resonant frequencies. Cuts should be kept small – 2-3dB at most – to avoid compromising the tonal balance of a mix.

A **low-cut filter** is often employed to roll away the lowest bass frequencies (20Hz and down). This maximises headroom, giving the engineer more space in which to notch up loudness. A similar approach is used to thin out brittle highs at the extreme upper end of the spectrum. Optimising the high end can also make a track sound warmer.

Elsewhere in the spectrum, **shelving or parametric EQ with wide curves** (high Q) may be employed to boost or cut the main bass region followed by wide parametric bands to either sweeten or subtly reduce mid and high frequencies.

Specific areas of attention include:

▸▸ **150–400Hz** – Muddiness can easily build up in the lower mids. Identify areas that are particularly crowded and apply a gentle rounded cut (mid Q, typically no more than 3dB of reduction).

▸▸ **2–5kHz** – The ear is highly sensitive to signal in the so-called 'presence' region (which is where many critical melodic synth, arp and keyboard parts in a dance track peak). A gentle, wide dip can be applied to tone down stridency.

▸▸ **8–12kHz** – A wide and gently-shelving boost in this area can add airiness and transparency. Pushing too far can make a mix sound brittle.

This macro EQ work is about bringing the overall tonality, which is shaped by the producer's studio setup and ears, into line with commercial masters. As such, comparing the spectrogram of the track to that of a reference track can be informative – although don't get too hung up on the specifics, which will always be determined by a track's unique mix of instrumentation and the key it is in. Instead look at the overall 'shape' of each mix (*page 237*) to check that you're in the right ball park.

STARTS AND ENDS

Pay special attention to the start and end of a track when mastering.

Trim track starts – or automate the master volume – so that nothing is heard before the first sound enters the mix.

At the end of the track, add a tapered fade to ensure a seamless transition to total silence.

Take care not to interfere with the natural fade of any instruments or FX tails.

TIP Use the best EQ you have for both forensic cuts and tonal shaping. The pros opt for passive designs for shaping alongside a good parametric for precision cuts. Manley's Massive Passive is often used for the job as even small boosts can lift a sound without compromising clarity or focus – something that can be a problem with low-grade equalisers.

COMPRESSION

Compression is used to enhance the loudness and density of a track, and to glue constituent elements together.

Typical compression for mastering employs a very low **ratio** – often as low as 1.5:1 (up to around 3:1 in rare circumstances). A medium **attack** time of around 20-40ms allows transients – like the front end of the kick and snare – through before gain reduction kicks in. This retains clarity and detail. The **release** time should be short enough for the compressor to return gain to 0dB before being retriggered. For dynamic mixes, **gain reduction** of more than 5dB would be unusual. Listen to the point at which depth and space lose out to dominant sounds at the front of the mix. The **type of compressor** used during mastering will depend on the kind of sound you're after. For smooth sounding gloss, audition an SSL-style bus compressor. For more obvious colour try a model based on a tube or optical gain control circuit (*page 214*).

Chapter eight
Mixing and mastering

TIP If you're faced with a mix that hasn't got enough bulk and 'weight', parallel compression (*page 275*) may be used to introduce a smashed version of the signal at a low level to increase density.

TIP When you want audible pumping, ensure the attack and release times breathe in time with the track. For smashed masters, up to -12dB of gain reduction may be appropriate – though this kind of extreme mastering job will almost certainly compromise dynamic energy (*page 256*).

LIMITING

Last in line is usually a limiter, used to eke a final dB or so of loudness from a mix and control any remaining transient peaks.

Although tempting to set the **output ceiling** to 0dBFS for the maximum possible peak output level, it is good practice to reduce it to around -0.5dB to avoid overloading at the digital to audio stage or when converting to lossy formats such as mp3. 2–4dB of peak reduction should be enough to tighten most mixes.

TIP Worried you've overdone the processing? A good test to see if you've gone too far is to play back the mastered mix louder than you normally would. If the tonality makes you want to turn it down, the mix has been overbaked. Return to it and ease off on the bus processing.

MONO BASS AND M/S

As noted in *Mastering for vinyl, page 295*, when cutting to vinyl you need to ensure that there are no radically out of phase sounds in the bass end of the spectrum.

There are various plugins like Brainworx' Bx_control that allow you to narrow the stereo image of a signal (or even sum it to mono) below a chosen frequency.

Another option is to use mid/side processing to adjust the balance between centre panned sounds and those at the side above a certain frequency – typically anywhere from around 40Hz to the 100Hz, as detailed in the walkthrough, *overleaf*.

OTHER TOOLS

In rare circumstances the mastering engineer may call on other tools:

▸▸ **Multi-band compression** allows different areas of the frequency spectrum to be treated to different levels of compression (*page 236*). Where you want a highly compressed low end alongside transient highs, multi-band compression offers a potential solution. In reality you're usually better off fixing the mix at source then running it through a single band compressor. Multi-band compression is easy to get wrong, risking a master where different frequency areas operate independently with no backbone holding them together – polar opposite of the unified sound required from a master.

▸▸ **Maximisers** offer a simplified approach to mastering. Most are based around a look-ahead brickwall limiter. The ability to look ahead is facilitated by a small audio delay buffer, which helps the plugin minimise the distortion added as a by-product of fast and extreme gain changes. The appeal of the maximiser's user-friendly approach is obvious, but such tools rarely offer as much control or flexibility as traditional limiters. It's also easy to overdo automatic loudness processing, so comparison with reference mixes is essential. *In general, a manual approach to mastering is recommended.*

▸▸ **Tape emulation or distortion** – used subtly – can add warmth, glue and flattering roundness to a master. It can also replicate the kinds of mastering procedures used back in the day. If you make music that embraces a vintage aesthetic by all means give it a go – although bear in mind tape saturation sacrifices both high-end and transient detail.

▸▸ **Stereo width expanders** can be a tempting mastering proposition – who doesn't want a wide-sounding mix? Remember even careful use of width plugins risks robbing energy from the crucial mix centre and/or introducing phase. *Use sparingly and keep the low end in mono.*

CHECKLIST

A/B CONSTANTLY. Regular referencing against commercial tracks is a must during mastering. Remember the goal is for your track to stand up against others – so use them as benchmarks.

NEVER RUSH THE MASTER. Toiling on a mix for a week and hoping to finish the master in ten minutes is plain silly.

BEWARE MASTERING WITH TIRED EARS. Although it can be tempting to complete a master on the same day as a mix, it's better to do the job with fresh ears. Otherwise the temptation is to keep upping loudness at the expense of fidelity and transient detail.

USE HEADPHONES FOR A LAST CHECK. Clicks, hums and tiny distortions are often more easily identified on headphones.

IT'S NEVER TOO LATE TO FIX THE MIX. Don't let pride, frustration or laziness get in the way of returning to a mix.

Mastering: A starters' approach in 12 steps

1 Before you begin mastering any track it's important to note that the process will not fix problems in a mix. So ensure you are happy with both the tonal and level balance of a track before proceeding. Note also that the following steps are unique to this track – *every mastering job is different.*

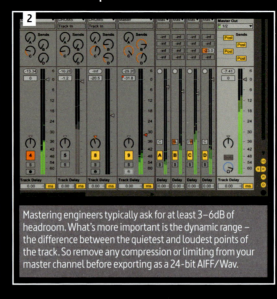

2 Mastering engineers typically ask for at least 3–6dB of headroom. What's more important is the dynamic range – the difference between the quietest and loudest points of the track. So remove any compression or limiting from your master channel before exporting as a 24-bit AIFF/Wav.

3 Load your track into a new project with a spectrum analyser on the master output and listen to the track. If you're mastering in the same room you mixed in, look out for any resonant peaks or problem frequencies that may be cancelled or emphasised by the room.

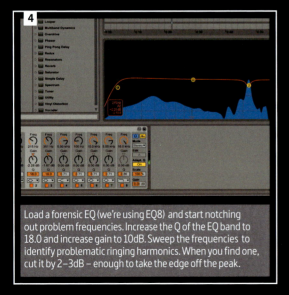

4 Load a forensic EQ (we're using EQ8) and start notching out problem frequencies. Increase the Q of the EQ band to 18.0 and increase gain to 10dB. Sweep the frequencies to identify problematic ringing harmonics. When you find one, cut it by 2–3dB – enough to take the edge off the peak.

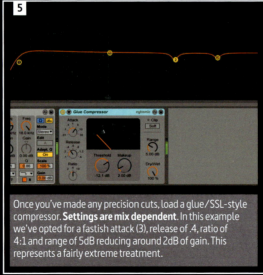

5 Once you've made any precision cuts, load a glue/SSL-style compressor. **Settings are mix dependent**. In this example we've opted for a fastish attack (3), release of .4, ratio of 4:1 and range of 5dB reducing around 2dB of gain. This represents a fairly extreme treatment.

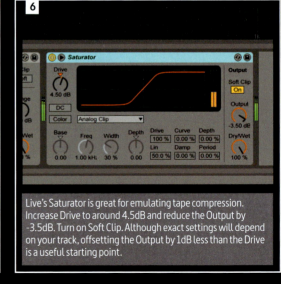

6 Live's Saturator is great for emulating tape compression. Increase Drive to around 4.5dB and reduce the Output by -3.5dB. Turn on Soft Clip. Although exact settings will depend on your track, offsetting the Output by 1dB less than the Drive is a useful starting point.

7

A second round of EQ is sweetens the mix. The golden EQ rule – cut narrow and boost wide (and gentle) – matters more than ever in mastering. We've increased 5.5kHz by 1dB with a Q of 2.00 to bring out some crunch. Low end warmth is boosted by 1.4dB at 40Hz.

8

Using two compressors in series to increase loudness can be more effective than upping the ratio/reducing the threshold of one. Here Glue is set with an attack of .3, release of .8, range of 70dB and ratio of 4:1. The slower attack catches remaining peaks and the longer release keeps the compression smooth.

9

Bx_control from Brainworx is a great plugin for changing the stereo contribution of different frequencies. Here we've set the 'Mono maker' at 100Hz to ensure the bass is kept in powerful mono while the Stereo Width (the volume of the 'sides') above 100Hz has been boosted by 25 per cent.

10

Last in line is a limiter, which adds level and stops any remaining peaks from crossing a set ceiling. Keep returning to the second compressor – to reduce peaks – and the initial EQ – to reduce problem frequencies – to eke a little more loudness from the mix.

11

Live's Limiter loads with Ceiling set at -0.3dB – enough headroom to allow for any potential clipping when converting to the end medium. Increase the Gain until you're achieving around 2–3dB of gain reduction. Leave Release on Auto for complex full mix material.

12

When checking levels during mastering use a dedicated metering plugin. There are two types of readings for levels – Peak and RMS. There is no perfect level, but -10RMS is a good guide. Here 4dB of gain on the Limiter allows us to reach -10dB RMS comfortably.

Mastering: final duties and edits

When you're happy with the master it's time to perform the final export.

The main master should be a 24-bit 44.1kHz Wav file (or higher quality). This is the file you will use to generate any other formats you need. These may include:

▸▸ For **CD** you'll need to dither to 16-bit.

▸▸ **mp3s** should be encoded to at least 224Kbps, although many music retailers including Beatport have standardised 320Kbps. For upload purposes, many online sites and stores, including SoundCloud and Beatport, accept Wavs which they dither using their own algorithms.

▸▸ Beatport also offer **AIFF** downloads.

CD and mp3 masters should be embedded with the relevant PQ codes (CD) and meta data (mp3 and AIFF).

Don't forget to listen to all final versions of the master/s to ensure any dithering/encoding hasn't introduced undesirable artefacts.

TIP When mastering is complete, back up all files associated with the mix and master.

EDITS TO THE MASTER

At this stage, most masters would be considered complete. With some dance mixes, however, further tweaks may be required. Common examples include:

▸▸ **The pre-drop fade.** Because the mastering process makes everything louder, a breakdown can get hyped in volume so that the drop doesn't have the impact it needs when it kicks back in. To reintroduce the energy differential automate the volume of the track so that it decreases during the breakdown before returning to full volume at the drop (*walkthrough, right*).

▸▸ **Ear candy edits.** Some ear candy can only be generated after a track is mastered. For reversed, retriggered and warped fills that involve slicing and dicing 'full track' edits, cut and re-arrange the master track as you see fit (*walkthrough, right*).

STEM MIXING AND MASTERING

An increasing number of engineers offer stem mixing and mastering, where they take mix stems as stereo Wavs or AIFFs, then use their own effects and processing to complete the mix and/or master.

The benefit of using stem mastering is that the engineer has more control. They can perform final tonal balancing and bus

AMBIVALENT

"Many years ago some engineers were daring to push their tracks to -13dB RMS of headroom in order to get a loud, impressive sound.

"Now, it is common to find mastered files for sale on digital sites with a staggeringly small -6dB RMS of headroom.

"To many seasoned producers and engineers this is profoundly saddening.

"My label actively resists the pressure for louder files and Manmade [mastering house] has always done respectful and good work, shooting for an average of -10 to -9dB RMS headroom."

processing with the benefits of better kit, a better listening environment and years of experience. Engineer requirements will differ depending on the job and their personal workflow. You will typically be asked to provide:

▸▸ Bounced stereo stems (24-bit Wav or AIFF) for every track in the mix **or** for all sub mixes (drums, synths, vocals etc). All bounced stems should start from the same point, preferably a bar or so before the first track enters to preserve opening transients.

▸▸ Dry tracks, with some or all effects/processing bypassed. It is usually best for mix-critical effects to be retained or dry and treated options of tracks with critical effects/processing to be supplied.

▸▸ Automation of important elements to be printed. Mix bus processing is usually best removed.

▸▸ Clearly labelled tracks, with notes where applicable ("Track 03 Synth, Supplied wet and dry") alongside a handful of commercial references.

TIP Quality control exported files by loading them into your DAW. Check for clipping and that all files are present and play from the correct point.

TIP Most DAWs have 'Export all tracks' facilities, with options to bypass effects.

// WALKTHROUGHS

Edits to the master

1 Reverse a section by moving the playhead to the start of the reverse effect, expanding the toolbar and selecting Split by Playhead. Move the playhead to the end of the desired reverse effect and click again. Now double-click, select File > Functions and select Reverse from the menu.

2 Create a tape-style pitch stop effect using Logic's Fade. Double-click the file you want to affect and expand the Region section on the left. Expand More to access Fade In and Fade Out. Click on these and change to Speed Up and Speed Slow Down. Enter '500' in each box.

3 When cutting the master, be careful not to introduce clicks. If you do, open Logic's Prefs > General and Editing and ensure Fade Tool Click Zones is ticked. Now when you click and drag on the top corner of a region Logic will automatically create a fade or crossfade between clips.

Pre-drop fade

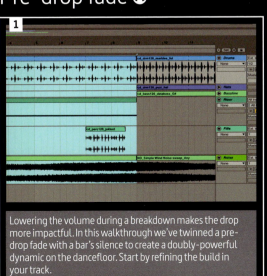

1 Lowering the volume during a breakdown makes the drop more impactful. In this walkthrough we've twinned a pre-drop fade with a bar's silence to create a doubly-powerful dynamic on the dancefloor. Start by refining the build in your track.

2 Gradually increase the volume during the breakdown by choosing Mixer and Track Volume from the Automation menu. Click at the start of the breakdown to create a node, and do the same at the end. Drag the first node down until there's a 20dB ramp up for the duration of the breakdown.

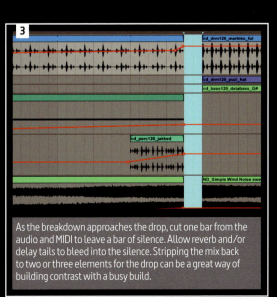

3 As the breakdown approaches the drop, cut one bar from the audio and MIDI to leave a bar of silence. Allow reverb and/or delay tails to bleed into the silence. Stripping the mix back to two or three elements for the drop can be a great way of building contrast with a busy build.

Appendix 1

Bpm to tempo (ms) chart

BPM	1/4 NOTE	1/4 NOTE TRIPLET	1/8 NOTE	1/8 NOTE TRIPLE (1/12 NOTE)	1/16 NOTE	16 NOTE TRIPLET (/124TH NOTE)	1/32 NOTE
60	1000.00 ms	666.667	500.00	333.33	250.00	166.667	125.00
65	923.08	615.385	461.54	307.69	230.77	153.846	115.38
70	857.14	571.429	428.57	285.71	214.29	142.857	107.14
75	800.00	533.333	400.00	266.67	200.00	133.333	100.00
80	750.00	500.000	375.00	250.00	187.50	125.000	93.75
85	705.88	470.588	352.94	235.29	176.47	117.647	88.24
90	666.67	444.444	333.33	222.22	166.67	111.111	83.33
95	631.58	421.053	315.79	210.53	157.89	105.263	78.95
100	600.00	400.000	300.00	200.00	150.00	100.000	75.00
102	588.24	392.157	294.12	196.08	147.06	98.039	73.53
104	576.92	384.615	288.46	192.31	144.23	96.154	72.12
106	566.04	377.358	283.02	188.68	141.51	94.340	70.75
108	555.56	370.370	277.78	185.19	138.89	92.593	69.44
110	545.45	363.636	272.73	181.82	136.36	90.909	68.18
112	535.71	357.143	267.86	178.57	133.93	89.286	66.96
114	526.32	350.877	263.16	175.44	131.58	87.719	65.79
116	517.24	344.828	258.62	172.41	129.31	86.207	64.66
118	508.47	338.983	254.24	169.49	127.12	84.746	63.56
120	500.00	333.333	250.00	166.67	125.00	83.333	62.50
122	491.80	327.869	245.90	163.93	122.95	81.967	61.48
124	483.87	322.581	241.94	161.29	120.97	80.645	60.48
125	480.00	320.000	240.00	160.00	120.00	80.000	60.00
126	476.19	317.460	238.10	158.73	119.05	79.365	59.52
128	468.75	312.500	234.38	156.25	117.19	78.125	58.59
130	461.54	307.692	230.77	153.85	115.38	76.923	57.69
132	454.55	303.030	227.27	151.52	113.64	75.758	56.82
134	447.76	298.507	223.88	149.25	111.94	74.627	55.97
136	441.18	294.118	220.59	147.06	110.29	73.529	55.15
138	434.78	289.855	217.39	144.93	108.70	72.464	54.35
140	428.57	285.714	214.29	142.86	107.14	71.429	53.57
142	422.54	281.690	211.27	140.85	105.63	70.423	52.82
144	416.67	277.778	208.33	138.89	104.17	69.444	52.08
146	410.96	273.973	205.48	136.99	102.74	68.493	51.37
148	405.41	270.270	202.70	135.14	101.35	67.568	50.68
150	400.00	266.667	200.00	133.33	100.00	66.667	50.00
152	394.74	263.158	197.37	131.58	98.68	65.789	49.34
154	389.61	259.740	194.81	129.87	97.40	64.935	48.70
156	384.62	256.410	192.31	128.21	96.15	64.103	48.08
158	379.75	253.165	189.87	126.58	94.94	63.291	47.47
160	375.00	250.000	187.50	125.00	93.75	62.500	46.88
162	370.37	246.914	185.19	123.46	92.59	61.728	46.30
164	365.85	243.902	182.93	121.95	91.46	60.976	45.73
166	361.45	240.964	180.72	120.48	90.36	60.241	45.18
168	357.14	238.095	178.57	119.05	89.29	59.524	44.64
170	352.94	235.294	176.47	117.65	88.24	58.824	44.12
172	348.84	232.558	174.42	116.28	87.21	58.140	43.60
174	344.83	229.885	172.41	114.94	86.21	57.471	43.10
176	340.91	227.273	170.45	113.64	85.23	56.818	42.61
178	337.08	224.719	168.54	112.36	84.27	56.180	42.13
180	333.33	222.222	166.67	111.11	83.33	55.556	41.67

Appendix 2

Note to frequency guide – What goes where in the frequency spectrum *

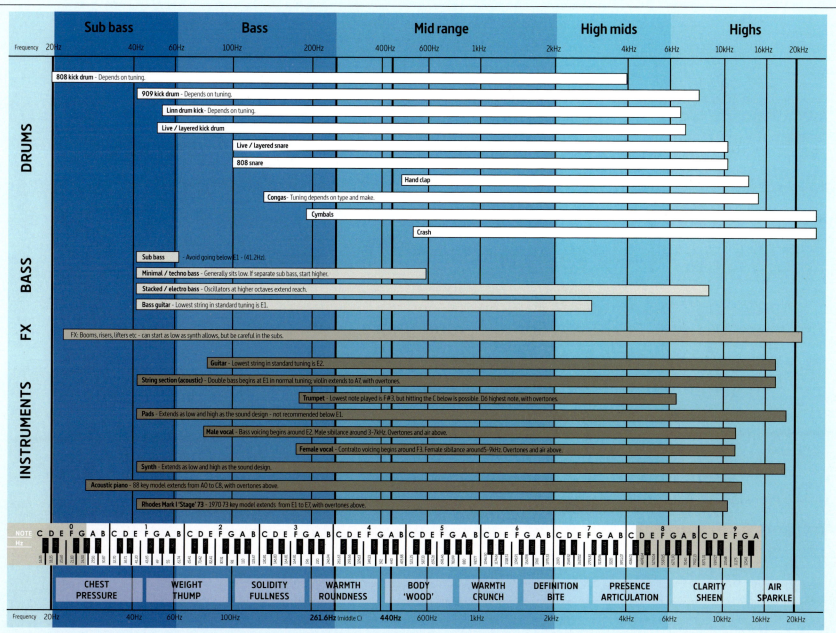

* This Note to frequency chart is a rough guide to the frequencies different parts may cover in a dance mix. Note that each bar represents the extended frequency range of a part, including its fundamental frequencies and overtones extending upwards. For example, the fundamental frequencies of a typical bass vocal are from around E2 (164.81Hz) to E4 (329.63Hz), but with harmonics extending upwards to around 12kHz. Use this guide as a starting point only. For a more accurate picture of a specific sound's frequency make-up in your own mix, open a frequency analyser. The blocks at the bottom ('Warmth, roundness') indicate the kind of sonic qualities exhibited in that frequency area. For more 'crunch' in a snare drum, for example, you may choose to add signal in the 800Hz–1.6kHz area.

the secrets of dance music production /

Index

1970s (influences) 66, 89, 122
1980s (influences) 66, 98, 99, 122, 222
2-step - **58-59,** 68
3rd (chord) - see either major or minor third
7th (chord) - see either major or minor seventh
9th (chord) - see either major or minor ninth
11th (chord) - see eleventh (chord)
13th (chord) - see thirteenth (chord)

a cappella 139, 170
A/Bing 261, 288, 292, 297
absorber 202-203
accent 158, 164
acoustics (studio) 200-205
added tone chords (music theory) 154-155
additive synthesis 83
ADSR (envelope) 76
AKAI MPC60 - see MPC60
AKAI S950 - see S950 (AKAI)
AKAI S1000 - see S1000 (AKAI)
ambience/ambient effects - see either **reverb** or **delay**
amp simulation **227,** 281
amplitude envelope - see envelopes
anacrusis (music theory) 157, 162
analogue kick drum - see kick drum (synthesis)
analogue snare drum - see snare drum (synthesis)
anticipation (music composition) 149
arp (short sound) synthesis 76, 84, 85, 89
arpeggiator (note generator) 79, 85, 89, **158-159**

arpeggio (music theory) **158-159,** 162
arrangement 182, 238, 241, **242-243,** 246-251, 283, 285, 291 - see also structure
attack (envelope) - see envelope
automation (during synthesis) 83, 88, 92, 93, 94, 96, 97, 99, 106
automation (while mixing) 177, 179, 241, 253, 255, 259, 266, 267, 271, 288
auto panner (effect) **225**
Auto-Tune (effect) 192, 193
aux (bus) 208 - see also groups/grouping

backing vocals - see VOCALS
bandwidth splitting - see dual band processing
bar (or measure) 26
BASS AND BASSLINES - Chapter three, 102-119
- compression 115, 215
- conflict with kick - see kick and bass (relationship and mixing)
- distortion 117, 119
- dual band processing **116-119**, 270
- EQ 117-119, 265, 267, 279, 291, 292
- layering 117, 119
- live bass - see slap bass
- mixing 14, 116-119, 279, **282-285,** 291, 292
- mono fidelity 116, 118
- programming 107, 152, 161, 283, 285
- radio-friendly bass 117, 119 - see also radio mix
- 'Reese' bass 106, 108, 110, **130-131,** 270
- reverb 110, 116

- sampled 139
- slap bass 106, 112
- splitting **116-119,** 270
- sub bass 73, 108, 110, **114-115,** 279
- sub bass enhancer 114, **212,** 279
- synthesis 73, 76, **108-115**
- types of bassline **104-107,** 161
- wide basslines 117, 118, 270
bass and kick (relationship and mixing) - see kick and bass (relationship and mixing)
bass drum - see kick drum
bass trap 202
beat - see DRUMS
beat grid - see drum grid
beats per minute (bpm) 26, 54, 302
bit-crushing (effect) 19, 98, 111, 117, 119, 126, 127, 183, **227,** 228-229
bit depth 126, 127, 227, 256
body (transient section) 10, 14
bongo 9, **22,** 23, 25 - see also percussion
bracketing EQ 24, 51, 98, 114, 119, 138, 139, 211, **265,** 267, 278, 290, 291
brass synthesis - see SYNTHESIS
breakbeat 68, 122, 123, 130, **134-137**
breakdown (structural device) 241, **245,** 300, 301 - see also structure
breaks (genre) 122, 130, **134-137**
build (structural device) 241, 245, 246, 247 - see also structure
bus 208-209, 286
- bus FX 252-253
- compression 188, 191, 215, 218, 219, 229, 272, 276, 298
- drum bus 13, 51, 68, 69, 215, 218, 219, 229, 272-276
- master bus 215, 219, 273, 289

Index

casaba - see shaker
Chicago house - see house
chillout 15, 23, 26, **62-63**, 250-251
chillwave 62, 184, 186
choke group - see mute group
chord inversion - see inversion
chord progressions 148-155, 159
chords (music theory) 100-101, **144-155**
chorus (effect) 90, 91, 94, 98, 117, 183, **220**, 270
circle (or cycle) of fifths (music theory) 148-149
clap 9, 13, 16, 17, 52, 53, 59, 64, 268, 270
clave 9, 22
clipping 256, 257, 259, 289
closed hi-hat - see hi-hats
club mixing 114, 234, 236, 237, 240, 260, 282
club rig/speaker setup 114
compression 11, **213-216**, 259, **271-276**, 292
- bass 115, 215
- controls 213-214
- drum bus/group 62, 66, 136, 215, 218, 219, 272, 276
- glue 188, 191, 215, 218, 219, 229, 272, 276, 298
- hi-hat 18
- kick drum 14, 215
- limiting - see limiting
- master/output bus 215, 219, 273, 289
- mastering 296-299
- multi-band 98, 216, 275, 293, 297
- optical model 214
- parallel 180, 215, 216, 219, 229, **274-276**
- ratio 213
- sidechain 224, 64, 65, 69, 87, 94, 100, 101, 112, 114, 115, 184, **214**, 218, 219, 229, 272, 274, 283, 285, 292
- snare drum 16, 215
- threshold 213
- valve model 214
- VCA model 214
- vocals 179-181, 184, 185, 188, 191, 215
conga 9, 11, **22-23** - see also percussion
contrary motion (music theory) 156, 162
control voltage (CV) 80
convolution reverb - see reverb
corrective EQ - see EQ - corrective
cosmic disco - see nu disco
cowbell 9, 22 - see also percussion
crash cymbal - 9, **24**
cross modulation 74
crotchet (1 beat note) 26
cutoff frequency 74
cymbal - see hi-hats, ride cymbal and crash cymbal

D&B (drum and bass) 15, 23, 26, **68**, 105, 106, 123, 130, 134, 137, 220, 266, 287, 292, 293
decay (envelope) - see envelope
decibel/dB 75, 256-259
de-esser 18, 181, 188, **217**, 293
deep house 31, 49, 56, 57, 98-99, 109, 113, 146
delay (effect) 69, **224**
- FX 94, 95, 97
- hi-hat 19
- keys 98, 113
- pads 90, 93
- ping pong 224
- snare drum 17
- stereo 224
- synth 84, 89
- tape delay/echo 183, 224
- vocals 182, 183
diffuser 202-203
digital clipping - see clipping
diminished chords 145
disco - **23**, 41, 55, **66-67**, 105, 107, 122, 134, 146, 152, 184, 186, 283
dither 258
distortion (effect) 110, 117, **226-229**, 280, 281, 297 - see also overdrive, saturation, clipping and bit-crushing
DJ tools 238
DMX (Oberheim) 40, 62, 66, 126
double-tracks 44, 173, **185**, 188, 268, 269
down-beat 27, 135, 164
downsampling 126, 227
drones 92
drop (structural device) 241, 245, 246, 247, 300 - see also structure
DRUMS - Chapter one, 6-69
- bus/group processing 13, 51, 68, 69, 215, 218, 219, 229, 272-276
- clap - see clap
- compression 66, 215, 218, 272-276
- crash - see crash cymbal
- cymbals - see hi-hats, ride cymbal and crash cymbal
- distortion 228-229
- drums 8, 9, 16, **52-53**, 67, 268

Index

- ghost hits 32, 55, 60
- grids 13, 21, **54-69**, 135
- hi-hats - see hi-hats
- kick drum - see kick drum
- programming - 21, **30-33, 35-44, 54-69,** 134-137, 164, 229
- reverb 33, 56, 63
- ride - see ride cymbal
- slicing 128
- tone/timbre 10-11
- transients 10-11
- tuning 10-11, 12, 13, 25, 35, 52, 65, 283, 292
- saturation 68, 228-229
- snare drum - see snare drum
- synthesis - see synthesised drums

drum grid - 13, 21, **54-69**, 135
drum group - 13, 51, 68, 69, 215, 218, 219, 229, 272-276
dual band processing 115, 116, 117, 118, 138, 270
ducking - see sidechain compression
dub 19, 27, 69, 97
dubstep 23, 28, **69**, 105, 106, 117, 267, 292, 293
DX7 (Yamaha) 81, 82, 92
dynamic range 213, 226, **257-258**, 271 - see also dynamics and loudness
dynamics 25, 213, **238**

'ear candy' 189, 241, 252-255, 288, 292, 300, 301
echo - see delay
EDM 53, 64-65, 84, 86-87, 100-101, 105, 106, 108, 117, 123, 246, 247, 267, 268, 272
effects (sound manipulation tools) 208-231
effects (special effects - sounds) - see FX
electro 15, 23, 106, 117, 272
eleventh (chord) 154-155
E-MU SP-12 - see SP-12
ensemble (effect) 90, 98, 117, 220, 270
envelope 11, 18, 46, 271, 272
- ADSR envelope 76
- ADSHR envelope 76
- attack 76
- decay 76
- generator 76
- in drum programming 21, 31, 33, 36, 37, 46, 47, 49, 58, 64
- in synthesis (voltage controlled amplifiers - VCAs) **76-77**, 84, 90, 94, 108
- release 76
- sustain 76
EQ **210-211, 277-280**
- bandwidth ('Q') 210
- bass 117-119, 265, 267, 279, 291, 292
- bracketing 24, 51, 98, 114, 119, 138, 139, 211, **265**, 267, 278, 290, 291
- corrective 211, 278
- filters 51, 210
- hi-hat 18, 19, 21, 265, 267
- kick drum 15, 51, 64, 265, 267, 279
- mastering 296, 298, 299
- mid/side processing 268
- 'mirror' treatment 283, 285
- parametric EQ 210
- percussion 24, 267
- rules 210, 236-237, 279
- samples 127, 139
- 'search and destroy' technique 15, 211, 231, 265, 278
- separation 16, 17, 268, **277-279**
- snare drum 16, 17, 48
- 'telephone' EQ 189, 194, 211
- vocals **177-179**, 184, 185, 188, 191
ergonomics 205
exciter 212, 279
expander 217
exporting the master 289, 300
extracting a groove 44-45
extract to MIDI 99, 136

fader groups - see groups/grouping
Fender Rhodes - see Rhodes (Fender)
fill (structural device) - see structure
filter (VCF) **64**, 76, 108, 267, 277
- band pass 74
- band reject/band stop 74
- dual 75
- high pass (low cut) 74, 139, 254, 296
- low pass (high cut) 74, 133, 139
- notch 74
- overdrive 108
- slope/roll-off 75, 267
- vowel 74
fine tuning (synthesis) - see tuning
flange (effect) 90, 117, **220**
flutter echo 201
found sound production 23, 92, **228-229**
frequency modulation (FM) synthesis 46, 78, 82, 83, 92
frequency shifter (effect) 230
fundamental frequency 12, **72-73**, 83, 235
full mix FX 254

Index

fuzz - see distortion
FX (sound effects) 94-97, 130, 189-197, **252-255**

gain structure 257
garage 58-59 - see also **2-step**
gate - see noise gate
ghost snares (rhythm element) 32, 55, 60
glide - see portamento
glitch effects 106, 192, 228
glue compression - see compression (glue)
granular synthesis 83, 128
grime 28 - see also **dubstep**
groove - see swing
groove extraction - see extracting a groove
groove markers 44
groups/grouping 209, **263-264**, 266, 279 - see also bus
- drum group 13, 51, 68, 69, 209, 215, 218, 219, 229, 272-276
guitar (rhythm) - see rhythm guitar

'Haas' delay 268, 269
hand clap - see clap
hardcore 26, 28
hard house 108
hardstyle 65
harmonics 46, **72**, 73, 76, 83, 236, 278, 280
harmonies (vocal recording and production) 173
headphones 203, 204, 260-261, 297
headroom 116, 172, 173, 237, **257-258**, 266,

289, 297, 299, 300 - see also loudness and dynamic range
hi-hats 9, 13, **18-21**, 57, 63, 68, 293
- compression 18
- de-essing 18, 19, 293
- EQ 18, 19, 21, 265, 267
- 'live' hi-hats 21, 62
- programming 21, 62
- reverb 21
- stereo treatment 58, 270
- synthesis 46, 49
- transient design 18, 57
high pass (low cut) filter 74, 139, 254, 296
'hoover' (sound) 108
house 15, 22, 23, 31, 46, 49, 56, 57, 99, 109, 113, 122, 146
humanisation 41

indie dance 55, **64-65**, 112
insert (effects) 208-209 - see also bus
interval 145, 147
intro 244
inversion (music theory) 150, **151-153**, 158
isolating samples 138-138, 170

jack - see swing
jungle 106, 117, 130, 134, 292, 293 - see also **D&B**
Juno 106 (Roland) 81, 97, 106

key (music theory) 144
key-tracking 75
keys (sound type) 98-99, 270, 279
kick drum 8, **14-15**, 51, 58, 107, 273
- compression 14, 215
- EQ 15, 51, 64, 265, 267, 279
- mixing **282-285**
- synthesis 46, **47**
- transient shaping 15
kick and bass (relationship and mixing) 14, 116, 279, **282-285**, 291, 292
Korg MS-10 - see MS-10
Korg MS-20 - see MS-20

layering
- clap/snare 9,16, **52, 53**, 268
- drums 8, 9, **50-53**, 67
- synths 92, 100-101, 268
lead synth **84-88**, 100-101 270, 279
legato - see portamento
levels **256-259**
limiting 180, **216**, 259, 297, 299
linear drumming 29
Linn, Roger 38, 39, 40
LinnDrum 9, 11, 14, 15, 22, 38, 62, 126, 227
listening 200, 261
lo-fi production techniques 63, **228-229**, 287
loop/s 244, 293
- drum loops 13, 29, 30, 33, 34, 67, 68
loudness **256-259**, 288
loudness wars 239, 259

Index

low frequency oscillator (LFO) 75, **77**, 108
low pass (high cut) filter 74, 133, 139
lyrics 168, 171

macros (synthesis) 83
major (chord) 145, 148
major (scale) 107, 144, 148
major ninth 146
major seventh 146, 158
major third 107, 145
maraca - see shaker
'masking' (frequency overlap) - see separation
master (mix) 289
master bus processing 215, 219, 273, 289
MASTERING - Chapter eight, **294-301**
measure - see bar
melodies - see toplines
mid/side processing 268
Minimoog - see Moog
minim (2 beat note) 26
minor (chord) 145, 148
minor (scale) 107, 144, 148
minor ninth 146
minor seventh 146
minor third 107, 145
minor 7 (chord) 98
minor 9 (chord) 98
MIDI
 - clock 77
 - gate 80
 - programming 32, 44, 53, **54-69**, 99, 112, 135
'mirror' EQ - see EQ

MIXING Chapter eight, **232-301**
 - A/Bing 261, 288, 292, 297
 - automation - see automation
 - balancing 266-268, 279
 - bass 116-119, 279, 291, 292, 293
 - bass and kick relationship - see kick and bass relationship
 - clarity - see separation
 - club mixing 114, 234, 236, 237, 240, 260, 282
 - compression (use of during mixdown) 271-276, 292
 - depth 240, 286
 - distortion (use of during mixdown) **226-229**, 280, 281, 297
 - EQ (use of during mixdown) 265, 267
 - great mixes 234-241
 - kick and bass relationship 279, **282-285**, 291, 292, 293
 - loudness **256-259**, 288
 - medium 234, 236, 260, 294
 - mono fidelity 240, 268, 297
 - panning **268**
 - philosophy of 234-241, 262, 277
 - preparation 262-265
 - problems (and how to fix them) 243, 277, 282, **290-293**
 - radio 237, 260
 - reverb (use of during mixdown) 240, **286-287**, 290
 - samples 138-139
 - separation 16, 17, 268, 268-270, **277-279**, 282
 - sub bass 114-118, 279
 - vocals **177-193**, 243, 279
 - when to stop 288-289

 - width 240, 268-270
modular synthesis - see SYNTHESIS
modulation (synthesis) **74-78**, 90, 94-97, 106, 108, 111, 117
mode (music theory) 145
monitor setup - see speaker setup
monitoring **260-261**
mono fidelity 240, 268, 297
monophony - 19, **78**, 108
Moog (synthesiser) 72, 74, 81, 89, 108
Moog basslines 108, 109, 115
MPC60 (Akai drum machine) 30, 43, 122, 125, 126, 227
Mr G 46
MS-10 74
MS-20 74, 81, 82
multi-band compression 98, 216, 275, 293, 297
multisampling 44, 124, **132-133**
music theory - see THEORY
mute group 9, **19, 20**, 21, 67

negative polarity - see phase
'New York' compression - see parallel compression
ninth (9th) chord (music theory) 146
nu disco 15, 23, 55, **66-67**, 112
noise - see white noise
noise gate 217, 293
noise generator 73
note-on triggering 77

Index

O

Oberheim DMX - see DMX (Oberheim)
off-beat 9, **27**, 104, 164, 283
old-school production - see vintage production techniques
open hi-hat - see hi-hat
optical compressor - see compression
organ - see SYNTHESIS
oscillator (synthesis) **72-73**, 84-101
- low frequency oscillator - LFO 75, **77**
- master 74
- sawtooth (saw) wave 73, 108, 109
- slave 73, 74
- sine wave 46, 73
- square wave 73
- sub oscillator 72, 108, 110, 114
- supersaw wave 73, 84, 100-101
- sync 73
- triangle wave 73, 115
- white noise 46, 48, 49, 53, 64, 73, 87, 90, 92, 94-96, 113

ostinato (music theory) 106, 158, **160**, 162
outro 244
overdrive 98, 117, 126, 183, **226-229**, 280, 281 - see also distortion
overtone - see harmonics

P

pads 76, **90-93**, 270, 279
panning **268**
- synth sounds 89
- vocals 185, 188
parallel processing **208-209**, 219, **275-276**, 279
- basslines 117, 118
- compression 180, 215, 216, 219, 229, **274-276**
- distortion and saturation 101, 209, 226, 280, 281
- EQ 276
parametric EQ - see EQ
paraphony 79
passing note (music theory) 107
peak level 258, 299, 300 - see also loudness
pedal (hi-hat) - se hi-hat
percussion 9, **22-25**, 223, 267, 270
- programming 23-25, 44, 60
piano roll - see MIDI programming
pitch bend 195, 255
pitch riser (FX) 96, 195, 255
pitchshifting - 127, **128-131**, 132, 137, **221**, 228, 269
pitching (drums) - see tuning (drums)
phase 50, 78, 138, 139
phase cancellation - see phase
phasing (effect) 19, 87, 90, 221
phrasing (rhythm) 27
polarity/polarity inversion 50
polyphony 19, **78**
polyrhythm 28, 159
portamento (glide) 78, 84, 98, 108
presets 77
production - see MIXING
programming grid - see drum grid
programming
- bass 107, 152, 161, 283, 285
- bongos 25
- drums 21, **30-33, 35-44, 54-69**, 134-137, 164, 229
- hi-hats 21, 62

- percussion 23-25, 44, 60
- shaker 25
- sub bass 114
progression - see chord progressions
prog (or progressive) 15, 53, **64-65**, 184, 220
pulse wave 73
pulse-width modulation (PWM) 73, 84, 90, 91

Q

'Q' (EQ bandwidth) 210
quaver (eighth note) 26
quantisation **38-39**, 45

R

radio mix 237, 241, 244, 245, 260, 282
ratio (compressor control) - see compressor
rave 107, 134
recording vocals - see VOCALS
'Reese' bass 106, 108, 110, **130-131**, 270
reference tracks - see A/Bing
reggae 27
release (envelope) - see envelope
repitching - see pitchshifting
resampling - see sampling
resolution (music composition) 105, 149
resonance (synthesis) 74, 108
reverb **222-223**, 240, **286-287**, 286
- bass 110, 116
- convolution 222-223, 286
- drums 33, 56, 63
- early reflections 223, 286
- FX 94, 189, 194, 195, 253, 254, 255, 286-

Index

287
- keys 98
- kick - 223
- percussion 24, 223
- pads 90, 92, 223
- pre-delay 17, 182, 223, 287
- reverse 193, 194, 287
- snare 17, 52, 53, 223
- synth lead 101
- vocals 182, 184, 191, 223
reverse crash FX 24
reverse reverb 193, 194, 287
Rhodes (Fender) 98, 99, 270
rhythm theory **26-29, 35-43**
rhythm guitar 44
ride cymbal 9, **24**
ring modulation 183, **230**
rim shot 22
RMS (root mean square) 258, 299, 300
Roland Juno 106 - see Juno 106
Roland RE-201 Space Echo - see Space Echo
Roland TB-303 - see TB-303
Roland TR-707 - see TR-707
Roland TR-808 - see TR-808
Roland TR-909 - see TR-909
room modes 201
room setup - 203-205
root (music theory) 98, 104, 107, 144
routing 208-209

S

S950 (AKAI) 51, 128
S1000 125
SAMPLES and SAMPLING **120-141**

- bit depth 126, 127
- chords 146-147, 162
- copyright 140-141
- downsampling 126, 227
- editing 34, 44, 52
- effects 130
- fades 138
- history of 122, 123, 125
- isolation 34, 138-138
- layering 50, 132
- law 122, 140-141
- micro-sampling 122
- mixing 138-139
- multisampling 124, **132-133**
- preparation 138
- resampling 126, **130-131**, 191
- sample rate 126, 127
- sampler 124, 125
- start/end points 33, 52, 133
- velocity layers 124
sample rate - see samples and sampling
saturation 13, 56, 59, 68, 90, 98, 101, 117, 126, 131, 183, 192, **227**, 229, 259, 268, 279, 293, 298 - see also distortion
sawtooth (saw) wave 73, 108, 109
scale (music theory) 144
'search and destroy' (EQ technique) - see EQ
semibreve (four beat note) 26
semitone 145
semiquaver (16th beat note) 26
send (effects) 208-209
separation 16, 17, 268, 268-270, **277-279**, 282 - see also MIXING
series processing **208-209**
seventh (7th) chord (music theory) - see wither major or minor seventh

shaker 9, 19, **22, 25**, 270 - see also percussion
shuffle - see swing
sibilance 181, 188, 189, 217 - see also de-esser
sidechain 214
sidechain compression (and 'pumping') 24, 64, 65, 69, 87, 94, 100, 101, 112, 114, 115, 184, **214**, 218, 219, 229, 272, 274, 283, 285, 292
signal flow 208-209
sine wave 46, 73
slap bass 106, 112
slope (filter) - see filter
sound design - see also synthesis, layering
soundscape (sound design) - 92
soulful house - see house
SP-12 (E-MU) 30, 38, 122, 125
Space Echo (effect) 17, 97
speaker setup 201-203, 260-261
speaker simulation **227**
spectrum analyser 258
split band processing - see dual band processing
spoken word vocals - see VOCALS
square wave 73
snare drum 9, **16-17**, 34, 37, 270
- compression 16, 215
- delays 17
- EQ 16, 279
- ghosts (rhythm element) 32, 55
- layering 16, **52-53**, 268, 270
- reverb 17, 52, 53, 223
- synthesis 46, **48**
standing waves 201
stem mixing 300

Index

step sequencer 30, 31, 79
stereo enhancement 58, 59, 64, 110, 117, 118, 183, **225, 268-270**, 297, 298
stereo spreader (effect) 17, 24, 64, 183, **225**, 270
stretching - see timestretching
strings synthesis - see SYNTHESIS
structure 239, 241, 242, **244-245**, 246-251, 252-255, 300, 301 - see also arrangement
- breakdown 241, **245**, 300, 301
- build 241, 245-247
- drop 241, 245-247, 300
STUDIO - Chapter seven, 198-231
- absorber 202-203
- acoustics 114, 116, **200-205**
- bass trap 202
- diffuser 202-203
- ergonomics 295
- flutter echo 201
- room setup 203-205
- routing / signal flow 208-209
- speaker setup 201-203
- standing waves 201
sub bass 73, 108, 110, **114-115**, 279
sub bass enhancer 114, **212**, 279
subgroups - see grouping
sub oscillator - see oscillator
subsonic frequencies 117
subtractive synthesis 46, **72-81**, 98, 108
subwoofer 294
'super mono' sounds 268, 270
supersaw wave 73, 84, 100-101
suspended chords 154-155
sustain (envelope) - see envelope
swing 35, **38-45**, 55, 59, 60, 61, 158, 164

syncopation 27, 100, **164-165**
SYNTHESIS - Chapter two, 70-101
- additive synthesis 83
- arps **84-85**, 89
- bass 73, 76, **108-115**
- brass 88
- cross modulation 74
- drums 9, **46-50**
- frequency modulation (FM) synthesis 46, 78, 82, 83, 92
- FX (sound effects) 94-97
- granular synthesis 83, 128
- keys 98-99
- layering 92, 100-101, 268
- leads - **84-88**, 100-101 270, 279
- low frequency oscillator (LFO) 75, **77**, 108
- modular synthesis 82
- modulation **74-78**, 90, 94-97, 106, 108, 111, 117
- organ 113
- oscillator - see oscillator
- pads 76, **90-93**
- percussion 23
- pulse-width modulation (PWM) 73, 84, 90, 91
- soundscapes 92-92
- stacking/layering 84, 86, 87
- strings 76, 91
- subtractive synthesis 72-81
- unison mode 90, 117
- wavetable synthesis 72, 80, 83, 95, 110

talk box 190
tambourine 9, 13, 19 - see also percussion

tape delay/echo 17, 97, 183, 224
tape emulation 136, **227**, 228, 268, 280, 293, 297
TB-303 74, 78, 81, 83, 105, 108
techno 15, 22, 23, **60-61**, 122, 146, 248, 249, 266
'telephone EQ' - see EQ
tempo 26
THEORY - Chapter five **142-165**
third (chord) - see either major or minor third
thirteenth (chord) 154-155
threshold (control) - see either compressor or gate
time signature **26-27**
timestretching **128-130**, 132, 137, 193, 228
tom-tom (or tom) 9, 22, 24, 46, 49, 64
tonal enhancers - see either sub bass enhancer or exciter
tone/timbre (drums) 10-11, 16
tonic - see root
toplines 156-163
TR-707 15, 57, 58, 60, 62, 66
TR-808 9, 10, 11, 14, 15, 16, 22, 51, 58, 60, 107, 267, 282
TR-909 9, 10, 11, 13, 14, 15, 16, 22, 27, 30, 41, 57, 61, 64, 164, 282
triad (music theory) 145, 146, 148
triangle wave 73, 115
triplet (timing) 19, 29, 100
trance 15, 23, 26, 46, **64-65**, 104, 160, 184, 220, 267, 283
transient (warp) markers 128, 135, 137
transient designer/shaper 11,
- kick drum 8, 10, 14
- hi-hat 18

Index

- snare drum 15
transients 10-11, 17, 35, 36, 44, 50, 52, 58, 213, 238, 239, 259, 271, 293
transitions (and transition FX) 195, **252-255**
tuner (plugin) 12
tuning (drums) 10-11, 12, 13, 25, 35, 52, 65, 283, 292
tuning (synthesis) 73
turnaround - see structure

unison mode (synthesis) 90, 117
up-beat 27

valve (compressor model) - see compression
VCA - see envelopes
VCA (compressor model) - see compression
VCA groups - see grouping
VCF - see filters
velocity
- mapping 80, 124
- of drum hits 35, 36
vibrato 88, 128, **220**
vintage production techniques - 56, 78, 79, 85, **126-127**, 136-137, 147, 227, 228-229, 267, 293, 297
vinyl mastering - see mastering
vinyl processing 136-137
VOCALS - Chapter six - 92, 93, 128, **166-197**, 248
- ad-lbs 174, 189
- automation 177, 179, 184
- Auto-Tune (effect) 192, 193

- backing vocals 185, 270
- chorus block 181, 191
- comping (compiling) 174, 175
- compression 179-181, 184, 185, 188, 191, 215
- 'cut-up vocals' 130, 189, 196
- de-esser 181, 188 - see also sibilance
- delays/echo 189, 191
- double tracks 173, 185, 188
- editing 174, 176
- effects 129, **189-197**, 252
- EQ **177-179**, 184, 185, 188, 191
- harmonies 173
- isolating (an a cappella) 139, 170
- lyrics 168, 171
- microphone choice 171, 173
- microphone setup 175
- production **177-193**
- recording 171-177
- reverb 182, 184, 191, 223
- sampled 139
- saturation 184, 192
- sibilance 181, 188, 189, 217
- spoken word 178, 189
- types of 168-169
vocoder 190, 197, **230**
voice groups - see mute groups
voicing (music theory) 92, **151-153**, 283

waltz time 26, 29
warp (transient) markers 128, 135
waveform - see oscillator
wavetable (synthesis) 72, 80, 83, 95, 110
widening **225, 268-270**

- snares/claps 17
- synths 101, 101
width enhancer **225**, 270, 297
white noise 46, 48, 49, 53, 64, 73, 87, 90, 92, 94-96, 113
Wurlitzer 98

X-mod - see cross modulation

Yamaha DX7 - See DX7

zero crossing (or origin) point (audio editing) 34, 44, 134